Greeks and Barbarians

This book is an ambitious synthesis of the social, economic, political and cultural interactions between Greeks and non-Greeks in the Mediterranean world during the archaic, classical and Hellenistic periods. Instead of traditional and static distinctions between Greeks and Others, Kostas Vlassopoulos explores the diversity of interactions between Greeks and non-Greeks in four parallel but interconnected worlds: the world of networks; the world of *apoikiai* ('colonies'); the Panhellenic world; and the world of empires. These diverse interactions set in motion processes of globalisation; but the emergence of a shared material and cultural *koine* across the Mediterranean was accompanied by the diverse ways in which Greek and non-Greek cultures adopted and adapted elements of this global *koine*. The book explores the paradoxical role of Greek culture in the processes of ancient globalisation, as well as the peculiar way in which Greek culture was shaped by its interaction with non-Greek cultures.

KOSTAS VLASSOPOULOS is Associate Professor in Greek History at the University of Nottingham. His earlier publications include *Unthinking the Greek Polis* (Cambridge, 2007) and *Politics: Antiquity and its Legacy* (2010); he is currently co-editing the *Oxford Handbook of Greek and Roman Slaveries* (forthcoming). He is a member of the Institute for the Study of Slavery, the Legacy of Greek Political Thought Network and the Centre for Spartan and Peloponnesian Studies.

Greeks and Barbarians

KOSTAS VLASSOPOULOS

CAMBRIDGE
UNIVERSITY PRESS

CAMBRIDGE
UNIVERSITY PRESS

University Printing House, Cambridge CB2 8BS, United Kingdom

Cambridge University Press is part of the University of Cambridge.

It furthers the University's mission by disseminating knowledge in the pursuit of
education, learning and research at the highest international levels of excellence.

www.cambridge.org
Information on this title: www.cambridge.org/9780521148023

First published 2013

A catalogue record for this publication is available from the British Library

Library of Congress Cataloguing in Publication data
Vlassopoulos, Kostas, 1977–
Greeks and barbarians / Kostas Vlassopoulos.
    pages   cm
Includes bibliographical references and index.
ISBN 978-0-521-76468-1 (Hardback) – ISBN 978-0-521-14802-3 (Paperback)
1. Greece – Civilization – To 146 B.C.   2. Mediterranean Region – Civilization – Greek
influences.   3. Mediterranean Region – History – To 476.   4. Hellenism – History.
5. Greece – Relations – Mediterranean Region.   6. Mediterranean Region – Relations – Greece.
I. Title.
DF78.V63   2013
938–dc23
                                                                    2012044105

ISBN 978-0-521-14802-3 Paperback

Additional resources for this publication at www.cambridge.org/9780521764681

To the memory of *Anna Missiou (1943–2011)*

Contents

Maps and figures

Maps

Figures

Acknowledgements

When Michael Sharp and Paul Cartledge invited me to contribute a volume on the relationship between Greece and the Near East back in 2008, my initial impression was to doubt whether I had developed the tools that might allow me to say anything interesting on such a vast subject. But it occurred to me that broadening the topic into a consideration of the relationship between Greeks and Barbarians could provide a better framework within which to examine the interaction between Greece and the Near East. I doubt that I would have undertaken this exploration without Michael's and Paul's invitation; I am grateful for their support of this project from inception to completion, and I hope that the result will fulfil some of their expectations.

I owe a great debt to those colleagues who were kind enough to devote their time and energy into reading the full manuscript in its various forms: Erich Gruen, Johannes Haubold, Aleka Lianeri, John Ma, Robin Osborne and Christopher Tuplin. Their comments have saved me from numerous mistakes and have helped me to improve substantially the argument and its presentation. This should obviously not be taken to imply that they agree with much that is argued in this book, and responsibility for the views presented here lies solely with the author.

Writing this book would have been impossible without the space and time provided by the institution of research leave. I am deeply grateful to the Department of Classics at the University of Nottingham for granting me a semester of research leave in spring 2011, and to the Arts and Humanities Research Council for an Early Career Research Fellowship between August 2011 and May 2012. For permissions to reproduce images from their collections and publications, I would like to express my gratitude to the Alpha Bank Numismatic Collection, Athens; the Antikensammlung of the Archäologisches Institut of the Goethe Universität, Frankfurt am Main; the British Museum, London; the Hermitage, St Petersburg; the Librairie Droz, Geneva; the Museum für Kunst und Gewerbe, Hamburg; the Österreiches Archäologisches Institut, Vienna; the Rijksmuseum van Oudheden, Leiden; the National Archaeological Museum, Sofia; and the Swedish Labraunda Expedition.

The list of thanks includes the audiences at Cambridge, Cardiff, Durham, Istanbul, Kent and Melbourne, who have listened to papers on various aspects related to this book project, and whose comments, reactions and disagreements have helped me immensely to clarify my thinking. I would finally like to express my gratitude to various friends and colleagues who have kindly helped me in this project in a number of ways, which are far too diverse to list: Zosia Archibald, Yorgos Avgoustis, Elton Barker, Euphrosyne Boutsikas, Anastasia Christophilopoulou, Denise Demetriou, Patrick Finglass, Michael Flower, Alexey Gotzev, Tom Harrison, Stephen Hodkinson, Michalis Iliakis, Kyriaki Konstantinidou, Koray Konuk, Sokratis Koursoumis, George Kyriakou, Doug Lee, Irad Malkin, Evi Margaritis, Judith Mossman, Ioanna Moutafi, Ian Moyer, Katerina Panagopoulou, Robert Parker, Spyros Rangos, Martin Seyer, Joe Skinner, Dorothy Thompson, Isabelle Torrance, Maro Triantafyllou, Dimitra Tsangari, Gotcha Tsetskhladze, Rebecca Usherwood and Luydmil Vagalinski.

My thinking on the subjects covered in this book goes back to a seminar on the Persian Empire organised by Anna Missiou at the University of Crete in Rethimno, which I attended as a young graduate student back in 1999. Anna was a great teacher and always insisted that historians should constantly ask themselves 'what is the historical question?' before writing their works; I would like to hope that this has been a lesson I have learnt and applied. One of our tasks for that seminar consisted in writing reviews for a set number of books and articles, and I still remember how impressed I was after reading Momigliano's *Alien Wisdom* as a set text. It was with a mixture of shock and pleasure that I discovered that the nucleus of my argument on the Barbarian repertoire in Greek culture was already contained in the review of Momigliano's book I wrote for Anna's seminar. The shock was due to the fact that I had completely forgotten for almost a decade the conclusions I had reached then and was under the impression that I had made an original discovery in the process of writing this book; it is a painful lesson for anyone interested in the history of historiography to see how difficult it is to reconstruct the development of one's own thinking, let alone that of others. The pleasure resided in realising how much we owe to our teachers, and how rarely we recognise our debts. Anna died unexpectedly in May 2011, only a few months after her retirement. Her sudden death has deeply saddened all those who knew her, and it is to her memory that this book is dedicated.

Note to the reader

This book has tried to combine three different aims, which are not easily compatible. The first aim is that of providing a text that could be used as a textbook for undergraduate teaching and would also appeal to a wider non-scholarly readership; accordingly, I have tried as much as possible to assume zero prior knowledge on behalf of the reader and to provide sufficient contextualisation for the evidence used and the phenomena examined. The second is that of providing a synthesis of the political, economic, social and cultural interactions between Greeks and non-Greeks across the archaic, classical and Hellenistic periods of the first millennium BCE, taking into account the full range of literary, epigraphic, archaeological and numismatic sources. No such synthesis exists in any language and, as a result, the study of the interactions between Greeks and Barbarians has been characterised by deep fragmentation: scholars working, for example, on the Black Sea are often not familiar with the scholarship on Egypt or the western Mediterranean; scholars working on, for example, archaic Greek 'colonies' do not often converse with scholars working on Hellenistic Jews; literary scholars working on, for example, the depiction of Barbarians in Greek tragedy are often unaware of the specialist scholarship on archaeology or numismatics; finally, scholarly approaches in different academic traditions can often talk past each other. I hope this book will provide some bridges across disciplinary divisions and stimulate further interaction and dialogue. The third aim is that of approaching the interaction between Greeks and non-Greeks from a novel methodological and theoretical approach that will link ancient history with current debates in other fields of history, in anthropology and in post-colonial studies. I propose to re-examine the interactions between Greeks and non-Greeks within processes of globalisation and glocalisation in the Mediterranean and Near Eastern world of the first millennium BCE. I hope that this approach will prove to be beneficial and stimulating to scholars working on intercultural interaction in the ancient world, as well as initiate a dialogue with scholars working on global history and globalisation in other periods and cultures.

The enormity of the subject has necessitated some very difficult choices about what issues and areas to discuss, in how much detail, and in what manner and context. I have tried to be as inclusive as possible under the circumstances; but the need to combine didactic purposes with synthesis and a novel approach means that the same area or different aspects of the same phenomenon might be discussed in different chapters or sections. I have tried to ameliorate any problems created in this way by creating smooth transitions from one section to the other and by providing extensive cross-references to different sections and chapters. Unavoidably, there have been restrictions and omissions. I regret that I could not devote more space than I do to the Greek communities of Asia Minor and their interactions with various non-Greek communities and cultures, as well as to the Greek communities in the far west of southern France and Spain. But the most serious omission is that of Cyprus, which provides a most fascinating test case of the hybrid interaction between Greek and non-Greek cultures in the archaic and classical Mediterranean. I have consciously avoided almost any reference, in the hope that the enormity of the gap will stimulate other scholars with better acquaintance with the evidence to do it justice elsewhere. I explain the structure of the book in more detail in section 1.6 of the Introduction.

The range of subjects covered in this book has produced an enormous scholarly literature. To keep the bibliography of a massive topic within bounds, as well as to allow the reader without foreign languages to pursue further study, I tend to give references, wherever possible, to recent works in English, which provide a synthesis of existing literature as well as full bibliographical references. At the same time, I have also tried to cater for the advanced reader and scholar who would like to explore further areas outside his or her expertise, or the work of different academic traditions. Accordingly, my references might often appear idiosyncratic: I might, for example, give a single reference to a synthetic English work on a large and complex topic, and two or three references to works in German or Italian for a rather secondary issue, on which no synthetic works exist. I hope different kinds of reader will find that in practice the system works rather well.

The book also quotes and cites a wide range of evidence from literary, epigraphic, papyrological, archaeological and numismatic sources. All texts quoted have been translated. Translations of literary sources are from the relevant volumes of the Loeb Classical Library, unless otherwise stated; translations of epigraphic and papyrological sources are by the author, unless otherwise stated. Non-specialist readers and those who cannot read ancient Greek tend to be least familiar with the epigraphic and papyrological evidence; for those who would like to read further, or employ the sources mentioned in their own research, I have tried to provide references to easily accessible translated sourcebooks, in tandem with references to the standard epigraphic and papyrological corpora for specialist readers. For readers unfamiliar with the languages and literatures of the ancient Near East, I have provided references to collections of translated texts, where passages can be easily consulted.

I have tried to provide illustrations for much of the archaeological and numismatic evidence mentioned in the book; given the practical limits to the number of illustrations that could be included, I have also given references to publications where readers can find images of those objects and monuments which have not been illustrated. This book mentions numerous places and regions, and it is often difficult even for the specialist reader to keep track of all of them, let alone the student or the wider audience. The book contains eight maps whose purpose is to enable readers to place the phenomena, events and processes discussed. To make consultation easier, the entries for places and regions in the Index include in square brackets the number of the map at which each place is depicted.

The transliteration of Greek names and places in English is a perennial problem. To achieve maximum consistency with minimum opaqueness, I have opted for Latinised versions of Greek names and places (Herodotus for Hêrodotos, Boeotia for Boiôtia), with the minor exception of those names and places whose English version has become so common, that it would be impractical to use the Latinised version of the Greek original (Aristotle instead of Aristoteles, Antioch instead of Antiocheia).

All dates are BCE unless otherwise stated.

Abbreviations

AchHist 2	H. Sancisi-Weerdenburg and A. Kuhrt (eds), *Achaemenid History, vol. 2: The Greek Sources*. Leiden, 1987.
AchHist 3	A. Kuhrt and H. Sancisi-Weerdenburg (eds), *Achaemenid History, vol. 3: Method and Theory*. Leiden, 1988.
AchHist 6	H. Sancisi-Weerdenburg and A. Kuhrt (eds), *Achaemenid History, vol. 6: Asia Minor and Egypt: Old Cultures in a New Empire*. Leiden, 1991.
AchHist 8	H. Sancisi-Weerdenburg and A. Kuhrt (eds), *Achaemenid History, vol. 8: Continuity and Change*. Leiden, 1994.
AchHist 11	M. Brosius and A. Kuhrt (eds), *Achaemenid History, vol. 11: Studies in Persian History: Essays in Memory of David M. Lewis*. Leiden, 1998.
ACSS	*Ancient Civilisations from Scythia to Siberia.*
AION (arch)	*Annali dell'Istituto universitario orientale di Napoli. Sezione di archeologia e storia antica.*
AJA	*American Journal of Archaeology.*
AJP	*American Journal of Philology.*
Arvanitopoulos	A. S. Arvanitopoulos, Θεσσαλικά μνημεία. Athens, 1909.
AS	*Anatolian Studies.*
Austin	M. Austin, *The Hellenistic World from Alexander to the Roman Conquest*, 2nd edn. Cambridge, 2006.
AWE	*Ancient West and East.*
B-D	R. S. Bagnal and P. Derow (eds), *The Hellenistic Period: Historical Sources in Translation*, new edn. Malden, MA and Oxford, 2004.
BASOR	*Bulletin of the American Schools of Oriental Research.*
BCH	*Bulletin de correspondance hellénique.*
BIFAO	*Bulletin de l'Institut français d'archéologie orientale.*
BNJ	I. Worthington (ed.), *Brill's New Jacoby*, available at: www.brillonline.nl/subscriber/entry?entry=bnj_title_bnj.
BSA	*Annual of the British School at Athens.*
CA	*Classical Antiquity.*
CAH	*Cambridge Ancient History.*
CC	W. Blümel, P. Frei and C. Marek (eds), 'Colloquium Caricum', special issue of *Kadmos*, 37, 1998.

CHI 2	I. Gershevitch (ed.), *The Cambridge History of Iran, vol. 2: The Median and Achaemenian Periods.* Cambridge, 1985.
CHJ 1	W. D. Davies and L. Finkelstein (eds), *The Cambridge History of Judaism, vol. 1: Introduction; The Persian Period.* Cambridge, 1984.
CHJ 2	W. D. Davies and L. Finkelstein (eds), *The Cambridge History of Judaism, vol. 2: The Hellenistic Age.* Cambridge, 1989.
CIRB	V. V. Struve *et al.* (eds), *Corpus Inscriptionum Regni Bosporani.* Moscow and Leningrad, 1965.
CJ	*Classical Journal.*
Confini e frontiera	*Confini e frontiera nella Grecità d'Occidente: atti del trentasettesimo convegno di studi sulla Magna Grecia.* Taranto, 1999.
COP	M. T. Lenger, *Corpus des ordonnances des Ptolémées,* 2nd edn. Brussels, 1980.
CQ	*Classical Quarterly.*
CRAI	*Comptes Rendus de l'Académie des inscriptions et belles-lettres.*
Curty	O. Curty, *Les parentes légendaires entre cités grecques.* Geneva, 1994.
D-K	H. Diels and F. Kranz, *Die Fragmente der Vorsokratiker,* vols I–III, 6th edn. Berlin, 1951–2.
DdA	*Dialoghi di Archeologia.*
DHA	*Dialogues d'histoire ancienne.*
EA	*Epigraphica Anatolica.*
EAD	*Exploration archéologique de Délos.*
EGF	M. Davies, *Epicorum Graecorum fragmenta.* Göttingen, 1988.
FD	*Fouilles de Delphes.*
FGrH	F. Jacoby, *Die Fragmente der Griechischen Historiker,* vols I–III. Leiden, 1923–58.
Fornara	C. W. Fornara, *Archaic Times to the End of the Peloponnesian War,* 2nd edn. Cambridge, 1983.
G&R	*Greece and Rome.*
Grandi santuari	*La Magna Grecia e i grandi santuari della madrepatria: atti del trentunesimo convegno di studi sulla Magna Grecia.* Taranto, 1992.

GRBS	*Greek, Roman and Byzantine Studies.*
Gusmani	R. Gusmani, *Lydisches Wörterbuch: mit grammatischer Skizze und Inschriftensammlung.* Heidelberg, 1964.
H-N	W. Horbury and D. Noy, *Jewish Inscriptions of Greco-Roman Egypt.* Cambridge, 1992.
IA	*Iranica Antiqua.*
ICS	O. Masson, *Les inscriptions chypriotes syllabiques,* 2nd edn. Paris, 1983.
IEOG	F. Canali de Rossi, *Iscrizioni dello Estremo Oriente Greco: un repertorio.* Bonn, 2004.
IG	*Inscriptiones Graecae.*
JEA	*Journal of Egyptian Archaeology.*
JHS	*Journal of Hellenic Studies.*
JMA	*Journal of Mediterranean Archaeology.*
JRS	*Journal of Roman Studies.*
K-A	R. Kassel and C. Austin, *Poetae Comici Graeci,* vols I–VIII. Berlin, 1983–2001.
L-P	E. Lobel and D. Page, *Poetarum Lesbiorum fragmenta.* Oxford, 1955.
Labraunda	J. Crampa, *Labraunda. Swedish Excavations and Researches, vol. III.2: The Greek Inscriptions.* Stockholm, 1972.
LdÄ	W. Helck and E. Otto (eds), *Lexikon der Ägyptologie,* vols I–VII. Wiesbaden, 1972–92.
LIMC	*Lexicon Iconographicum Mythologiae Classicae,* vols I–XVIII. Zurich, 1981–99.
L'Or perse	R. Descat (ed.), 'L'Or perse et l'histoire grecque', special issue of *REA*, 91, 1989.
M-S	R. Merkelbach and J. Stauber, *Steinepigramme aus dem griechischen Osten,* vols I–V. Munich, 1998–2004.
M-W	R. Merkelbach and M. L. West, *Fragmenta Hesiodea.* Oxford, 1967.
MAS	*Modern Asian Studies.*
MEFRA	*Mélanges de l'Ecole française de Rome. Antiquité.*
MHR	*Mediterranean Historical Review.*
Michel	C. Michel, *Recueil d'inscriptions grecques.* Brussels, 1900.
Modes	*Modes de contacts et processus de transformation dans les sociétés anciennes.* Rome, 1983.

Moretti	L. Moretti, *Iscrizioni agonistiche greche*. Rome, 1953.
NC	*Numismatic Chronicle.*
OGIS	W. Dittenberger, *Orientis graeci inscriptiones selectae*, vols I–II. Leipzig, 1903–5.
OJA	*Oxford Journal of Archaeology.*
OpAth	*Opuscula Atheniensia.*
P. Col. IV	W. L. Westermann, C. W. Keyes and H. Liebesny (eds), *Business Papers of the Third Century* BC *Dealing with Palestine and Egypt*, vol. II. New York, 1940.
P.Enteux.	O. Guéraud, *Enteuxeis: requêtes et plaintes adressées au roi d'Égypte au IIIe siècle avant J.-C.* Cairo, 1931.
P. Mil.	A. Calderini (ed.), *Papiri Milanesi*. Milan, 1928.
Page	D. L. Page, *Poetae melici Graeci*. Oxford, 1962.
PCPS	*Proceedings of the Cambridge Philological Society.*
PdP	*Parola del Passato.*
PP	W. Peremans and E. Van't Dack (eds), *Prosopographia Ptolemaica*, vols I–IX. Louvain, 1951–81.
QdS	*Quaderni di Storia.*
R-O	P. J. Rhodes and R. Osborne, *Greek Historical Inscriptions 404–323* BC. Oxford, 2003.
REA	*Revue des études anciennes.*
REG	*Revue des études grecques.*
RICIS	L. Bricault, *Recueil des inscriptions concernant les cultes isiaques*, vols I–III. Paris, 2005.
Rigsby	K. J. Rigsby, *Asylia: Territorial Inviolability in the Hellenistic World*. Berkeley, CA, 1996.
Rose	V. Rose, *Aristotelis qui ferebantur librorum fragmenta*. Leipzig, 1886.
Rowlandson	J. Rowlandson (ed.), *Women and Society in Greek and Roman Egypt: A Sourcebook*. Cambridge, 1998.
Sardis	W. H. Buckler and D. M. Robinson, *Sardis, vol. VII.1: Greek and Latin Inscriptions*. Leiden, 1932.
SB	F. Preisigke *et al.* (eds), *Sammelbuch griechischer Urkunden aus Ägypten*, vols I–XVIII. Strasbourg, 1915–93.
SEG	*Supplementum Epigraphicum Graecum.*
SGDI	H. Collitz and F. Bechtel (eds), *Sammlung der griechischen Dialekt-Inschriften*, vols I–IV. Göttingen, 1884–1915.

Sibari	*Sibari e la Sibaritide: atti del trentaduesimo convegno di studi sulla Magna Grecia.* Taranto, 1993.
*SIG*³	W. Dittenberger, *Sylloge Inscriptionum Graecarum*, 3rd edn. Leipzig, 1915–24.
Snell	B. Snell, *Pindari carmina cum fragmentis*, vols I–II, 6th edn. Leipzig, 1980.
TAPA	*Transactions of the American Philological Society.*
TL	E. Kalinka, *Tituli Lyciae linguis Graeca et Latina conscripti.* Vienna, 1920–44.
Tod	M. N. Tod, *Greek Historical Inscriptions*, vol. II. Oxford, 1948.
UPZ	U. Wilcken, *Urkunden der Ptolemäerzeit: ältere Funde*, vols I–II. Berlin, 1927–57.
Wehrli	F. Wehrli, *Die Schule des Aristoteles: Texte und Kommentar*, vols I–XII, 2nd edn. Basel, 1948–69.
West	M. L. West, *Iambi et elegi graeci ante Alexandrum cantati*, vols I–II, 2nd edn. Oxford, 1989–92.
YCS	*Yale Classical Studies.*
ZPE	*Zeitschrift für Papyrologie und Epigraphik.*

1 | Introduction

1.1 Historiographies

Few topics in ancient history attract such wide attention as the relationship between Greeks and Barbarians. To mention just two recent Hollywood movies should be enough: Oliver Stone's *Alexander*, on Alexander the Great's overthrow of the Persian Empire and the conquest of various peoples in the East; and Frank Miller's *300*, on the battle of Thermopylae between the Greeks and the Persian Empire, were great commercial successes and created considerable cultural and political debates.[1] But there are also few topics in ancient history that lead to such fundamental differences in scholarly approaches and views. On the one hand, there is a long-standing approach that focuses on polarity and conflict. The relationship between Greeks and Barbarians is seen as part of the wider distinction between West and East; the Greeks are the ancestors of the West, the people who invented democracy, freedom of thought, science, philosophy, drama and naturalistic art, and whose literary works stand as the foundation of Western literature; the world of the East, the world of the people whom the Greeks described as Barbarians, is a wholly different world, characterised by despotism and theocracy and the absence of all the Greek achievements.[2] The confrontation of the Greeks with the Persian Empire was the fight to preserve these achievements and values that we still cherish, and should be seen as part of a perennial confrontation between West and East; back in 1846, John Stuart Mill expressed this view in a famous adage:

Even as an event in English history, the battle of Marathon is more important than the battle of Hastings. Had the outcome of that day been different, the Britons and the Saxons might still be roaming the woods.[3]

But this is by no means an old-fashioned view:[4] for many people 9/11 is another act in a long play which started in the summer of 490 at the

---

[1] For scholarly responses on the former, see Cartledge and Greenland 2010.
[2] For example, Meier 2011.   [3] Mill [1846] 1978: 271.   [4] For example, Billows 2010.

battlefield of Marathon.[5] It is not for nothing that the UNESCO delegation of Iran officially complained about the depiction of ancient Iranians in the film *300*, in the context of a deepening confrontation between Iran and the West. But views do change; if scholars at the time of Mill instantly identified with the Greeks at Marathon, this is no longer automatically the case in the post-colonial and multicultural world that we inhabit. The post-colonial critique of Western imperialism has led many scholars to turn the tables and approach the relationship between Greeks and Barbarians in a wholly different manner. The publication in 1978 of Edward Said's famous *Orientalism* played a fundamental role in the changing of perspectives by providing a consistent critique of Western discourses about the Orient and showing how Western knowledge about the Orient had functioned as the handmaid of Western imperialism. Aeschylus' tragedy *The Persians*, enacted in 472, just eight years after the battle of Salamis, was the first portrait of the Oriental in Western literature and was seen by Said as the origin of Western Orientalism.[6]

Since then, many scholars have explored the sinister consequences of Greek ethnocentrism. François Hartog in an influential study explored how Herodotus' work and his descriptions of various Barbarian Others functioned as a mirror of the Greek Self: according to him, Herodotus' discourse, and Greek discourses in general, showed little genuine interest in understanding foreign cultures and more in using them as a mirror to reflect a number of stereotypes about non-Greeks which were essential for constructing Greek identity.[7] Edith Hall, in another ground-breaking work, took a similar approach and explored how Greek tragedy invented the Barbarian;[8] more recently, Benjamin Isaac has examined the origins of racism in classical antiquity and in Greek writings about the Barbarians.[9] The tables have truly turned: academics are as likely nowadays to focus on the ethnocentric, xenophobic and racist aspects of Greek views and Greek attitudes towards the Barbarians, as on exalting the Greek defence of democracy and free thinking against Oriental despotism. But no matter which perspective one might adopt, this is a discussion of the relationship between Greeks and Barbarians which focuses on conflict and unbridgeable polarities.

Be that as it may, there has also long existed an alternative approach with a very different focus. This approach has a long pedigree, but perhaps its most influential statement ever was by Johann Gustav Droysen, one of the most famous German historians of the nineteenth century.[10] In 1836,

---

[5] Pagden 2008.   [6] Said 1978: 56–7.   [7] Hartog 1988.
[8] Hall 1989; cf. Hall 2006: 184–224.   [9] Isaac 2004; cf. Tuplin 1999.   [10] Bravo 1968.

Droysen published the first edition of a monumental work titled *Geschichte des Hellenismus*.[11] Droysen created the concept of *Hellenismus* to describe the process of the fusion between Greek and Oriental culture that took place in the aftermath of Alexander the Great's conquest of the Persian Empire. According to him, the emergence and spread of Christianity, one of the foundational forces of the West, would have been impossible without the gradual fusion of Greek culture with the cultures of the Near East, which took place in the centuries after Alexander. Droysen's concept of *Hellenismus* and his view of the fusion of Greek and Oriental cultures have been deeply influential as well as widely criticised; we shall have the opportunity to discuss them more extensively in Chapter 7.[12]

What is of importance here is the very different approach to the relationship between Greeks and Barbarians. Instead of conflict and polarity, this approach stresses interaction and exchange. The discovery and decipherment of the cuneiform documents of the Near East in the decades since Droysen have shown the significant extent to which cultural interaction went both ways. The discovery of the Hittite poetic cycle of Kumarbi, to give merely one example, has shown that Hesiod's famous description of the succession of gods in the *Theogony* is clearly of Near Eastern origin (see p. 61).[13] Influential scholars, including Walter Burkert and Martin West, have explored in various works the ways in which the cultures of the Near East influenced Greek culture and society already from the archaic period;[14] others, such as Sarah Morris, have argued that the influence goes back all the way to the Bronze Age and is a constant aspect of Greek culture.[15] And in 1987 the publication of the first volume of Martin Bernal's *Black Athena* trilogy created shockwaves in the academic world and beyond.[16] Bernal argued that the ethnocentric and racist presuppositions of Western scholars since the nineteenth century had led to the disparagement of Eastern cultures and the minimisation of their deep influence on Greece. In fact, Bernal, using a variety of archaeological, linguistic and literary evidence, went on to claim that the emergence of Greek culture was the outcome of the migration of Egyptian and Phoenician populations to the Aegean during the Bronze Age and later periods, and that Greek culture was effectively an offshoot of the older cultures of the Near East.[17] As with Droysen, Bernal's views have been both inspiring and deeply contested.[18] Again, no matter what perspective one might adopt, and whether one

[11] Droysen 1887/8. [12] Canfora 1987; Moyer 2011a: 1–41. [13] Rutherford 2009.
[14] Burkert 1992, 2004; West 1971, 1997. [15] Morris 1992. [16] Bernal 1987.
[17] Bernal 1991, 2006.
[18] Lefkowitz 1996; Lefkowitz and Rogers 1996; Berlinerblau 1999; Vlassopoulos 2007.

stresses the impact of Greek culture on non-Greeks or the other way round, the important thing is that this approach puts its focus on cultural inter-action and exchange, and denies or minimises the deep polarities between East and West.

We are accordingly faced with two diametrically opposite approaches to the study of the relationship between Greeks and Barbarians: one stresses conflict and polarity; the other stresses interaction, exchange and mutual dependence. Which one should we prefer? Or should we try to reconcile them? And if so, how exactly? Given the extent to which the study of the relationship between Greeks and Barbarians is enmeshed with so many issues relating to modern debates and identities, it might be worth starting by examining whether these two different approaches can already be found in the ancient sources, or are a mirage of modern scholarship and modern preoccupations. I want to explore this question by means of a number of different stories relating to a paradigmatic figure: this figure is Thales, a citizen of Miletus on the west coast of Asia Minor, who lived in the first half of the sixth century, and to whom modern histories of philosophy accord the honour of being the first Western philosopher.

1.2 A test case: Thales the Milesian

There is an old Belfast joke about a stranger who goes to a pub. The regulars look at him apprehensively and one of them suddenly asks: 'Stranger, are you a Catholic or a Protestant?' 'Well,' says he, 'as a matter of fact, I am a Jew.' The long silence that ensues is finally interrupted by the only question that really matters: 'Well, fair enough; but are you a Catholic Jew or a Protestant one?' No matter what, at the end of the day there is a single, clear dividing line and one has to belong to one side or the other. Even more, this discourse of polarity is also an evaluative one: depending on one's point of view, it is a good thing to be a Catholic or a Protestant and a bad thing to be the opposite. Something in the spirit of the Belfast joke is clearly expressed in a Greek story about Thales:

Hermippus in his *Lives* refers to Thales the story which is told by some of Socrates, namely, that he used to say there were three blessings for which he was grateful to Fortune: 'first, that I was born a human being and not one of the wild animals; next, that I was born a man and not a woman; thirdly, a Greek and not a barbarian'.[19]

---

[19] Diogenes Laertius, *Lives of the Philosophers*, 1.33.

The mentality of the Belfast joke is clearly evident here: one is either human or beast; a man or a woman; a Greek or a Barbarian; and, in fact, it is preferable to be a human rather than a beast, a man than a woman, and a Greek than a Barbarian. This story therefore clearly confirms that polarity and conflict were essential aspects of how Greeks approached their relationship with the Barbarians. At the same time though there are a number of other stories relating to Thales which point in rather different directions. Let us start with a story reported by Socrates in one of the Platonic dialogues:

Why, take the case of Thales, Theodorus. While he was studying the stars and looking upwards, he fell into a pit, and a neat, witty Thracian servant girl jeered at him, they say, because he was so eager to know the things in the sky that he could not see what was there before him at his very feet. The same jest applies to all who pass their lives in philosophy.[20]

This is a nice anecdote: a Thracian Barbarian, who was also a woman and a slave, got the chance to jeer at the great philosopher Thales, who was so grateful to the gods for being a Greek and a man. The story is not exactly a reversal of Thales' prejudices; in fact, the ridiculing of philosophers is made even more poignant precisely because it is attributed to the lowest of the low: a Barbarian female slave. The story is illuminating about an important way in which Greeks came into contact with Barbarians. Slavery was an essential institution of Greek societies, and most slaves were Barbarians; it does not take much thinking to understand why the Greeks might have despised Barbarians and consider them slavish and inferior. But the fact that the stereotype of the Barbarian slave can be used to poke fun at a quintessentially Greek phenomenon like that of philosophy underlines the complexity and subtlety with which Barbarians can be portrayed in Greek sources: the moral of the story is put in the mouth of the witty Barbarian, not the super-wise Greek.

A third story presents a radical reversal:

The advice given before the destruction [of the Ionians] by Thales of Miletus, a Phoenician by descent, was good too; he advised that the Ionians should have one place of deliberation, and that it be in Teos (for that was the centre of Ionia), and that the other cities be considered no more than *demes* [villages].[21]

Thales might have praised the gods for being born Greek: but according to Herodotus, he was in fact Phoenician in origin. We do not know on what basis Herodotus claimed that Thales was Phoenician; according to later

---

[20] Plato, *Theaetetus*, 174a.   [21] Herodotus, 1.170.

sources, he was the descendant of the Phoenician Thelidae and became a citizen of Miletus when he was expelled from his Phoenician homeland;[22] what is interesting is that in no way is Thales' alleged foreign origin used against him, since Herodotus immediately commends his wise advice to the Ionians. But Herodotus also knew another story about Thales and Croesus, the famous king of Lydia, the most powerful king of Asia Minor in the first half of the sixth century, and the first Barbarian, according to Herodotus,[23] to subjugate Greek communities:

When [Croesus] came to the river Halys, he transported his army across it – by the bridges which were there then, as I maintain; but the general belief of the Greeks is that Thales of Miletus got the army across. The story is that, as Croesus did not know how his army could pass the river (as the aforesaid bridges did not yet exist then), Thales, who was in the encampment, made the river, which flowed on the left of the army, also flow on the right, in the following way.[24]

Thales might be happy he was not a Barbarian, but according to this story he could also be a loyal servant of a Barbarian king who had subjugated Greek communities. We saw above in the story with the Thracian slave how Greeks would come to know Barbarians from a position of superiority as masters towards slaves. But here we see how exactly the opposite could also be the case; Greeks could interact with Barbarians from a position of inferiority, as the employees and subjects of Barbarian kings. The model of interaction and exchange is not therefore inapplicable to Thales. Not only was he, according to some stories, a Barbarian who had migrated to a Greek city and become a citizen, but according to other stories he had worked in the entourage of a Barbarian king: what better context to imagine for interactions and exchanges? And in fact, according to a final story, the very wisdom of Thales was the result of such interactions with Barbarians:

Pamphila states that, having learnt geometry from the Egyptians, [Thales] was the first to inscribe a right-angled triangle in a circle, whereupon he sacrificed an ox.[25]

We have come full circle: if a Barbarian slave could successfully poke fun at Thales for his astronomical interests, we are now told that his very scientific achievements were the result of his education among the Egyptians, who were, according to Herodotus, the first people to discover geometry.[26] If Thales could boast about his Greek origins, other Greeks circulated stories about his Barbarian origins. If Thales had a Barbarian

---

[22] Diogenes Laertius, *Lives of the Eminent Philosophers*, 1.22.   [23] 1.6.   [24] 1.75.
[25] Diogenes Laertius, *Lives of the Eminent Philosophers*, 1.24.   [26] Herodotus, 2.109.

slave, he was also the employee of a Barbarian king. Is Thales the model of a proud/bigoted Greek who despises Barbarians, lords it over Barbarian slaves and instigates the Greek invention of philosophy? Or is he a model of a Barbarian who becomes a citizen of a Greek city, a Greek who works as an employee of a Barbarian king, a Greek who owes his wisdom to Barbarian teachers? We can consequently conclude that conflict and polarity, as well as interaction and exchange, are not mirages of modern preoccupations and debates. They can already be found in the different stories that circulated in antiquity about the same individual. We cannot choose one model and discard the other: but how are we to understand them and explain their coexistence?

1.3 Hellenicity and Hellenisation

The relationship between Greeks and Barbarians is often presented within a chronological trajectory which differentiates sharply between the archaic (*c.* 700–479), the classical (479–323) and the Hellenistic (323–31) periods, with the Persian Wars (490–79) and the conquests of Alexander the Great (334–23) serving not only as the major dividing lines between the archaic/ classical and classical/Hellenistic periods, but also as the major explanatory forces behind the presumed radical differences and changes between the three periods.[27] The key factor in this traditional account is Greek identity (Hellenicity): the narrative focuses on the formation and development of Hellenicity, and the role of non-Greeks and their cultures in its formation and development. According to this traditional account, the archaic period is characterised by the expansion and transformation of the Greek world out of the fragmented world of the Iron Age (1100–700). Around 700 the Greek world was emerging as a backward periphery, which was highly stimulated through contact with and influence from the older, richer, more developed and more powerful world of the Near East. In the same way that the adoption of the Phoenician alphabet enabled the Greeks to become literate, with significant effects for the transmission of their literature and for the transformation of their intellectual pursuits,[28] the stimulus of the artistic traditions of the Near East led to what has been variously described as the Orientalising period, the Orientalising phenomenon or the Orientalising revolution.[29] Greek artists and artisans adopted and adapted countless Near Eastern techniques, products, motifs and iconographies; they were thus able

---

[27] See already Jüthner 1923.   [28] Burkert 2004: 16–20.
[29] Burkert 1992; cf. Riva and Vella 2006.

to break through the long established traditions of Geometric art and begin the process of continuous artistic transformations that characterises the history of Greek art.[30] This transformation of Greek culture and society through the stimulus of the Near East was accompanied by the gradual process of the formation of Greek identity out of the multiple local and regional identities that characterised the Iron Age. There was not yet any clear distinction between Greeks and Barbarians, as is also evident by the (relative) lack of references to such distinctions in archaic Greek literature.[31]

The Persian Wars are traditionally seen as a radical juncture between the archaic and classical periods.[32] The military confrontation and the Greek victory created a new world, polarised between Greeks and Barbarians. The ensuing classical period was the time when the Greeks were 'inventing the barbarian' and investing heavily in this invention.[33] Greeks became highly aware of their common cultural and ethnic characteristics, while categorising all non-Greek people as Barbarians, who lacked Greek virtues and exhibited all non-Greek vices, such as luxury, effeminacy, despotism and lack of self-control.[34] If the archaic period was characterised by exchange and Near Eastern influence on Greek culture, the classical period is characterised by confrontation and polarity.

Alexander's conquest of the Persian Empire is then seen as a new radical change of the plot. In the aftermath of the dismemberment of Alexander's empire by his successors, Greco-Macedonian dynasties came to rule over non-Greeks from Asia Minor and Egypt all the way to modern-day Afghanistan and Pakistan. A major result of these new states was the adoption of Greek culture and identity by many individuals and communities across the eastern Mediterranean and the Near East. The creation of new settlements by the Hellenistic kings, which took the form of Greek poleis, was based on the migration of Greeks into Egypt and the Near East, and played an important role in the spread of Greek culture. The reformulation of Hellenicity as a cultural identity, which took place primarily in classical Athens,[35] made it relatively easy for non-Greeks to acquire a Greek education and to adopt Greek culture; many of the most important Greek intellectuals and artists of the Hellenistic period came from Syria, Phoenicia and Cilicia. Given the large numbers of non-Greeks who had adopted Greek culture, the old, polar distinction between Greeks and Barbarians progressively lost much of its importance in the course of the Hellenistic period.[36]

---

[30] Poulsen 1912; Akurgal 1968.   [31] Hall 2002: 90–171, 2004.   [32] Morris 1992: 362–86.
[33] Hall 1989.   [34] Cartledge 2002: 51–77.   [35] Hall 2002: 179–226.
[36] For example, Burstein 2008.

This account of the emergence and transformation of Hellenicity and its interaction with other cultures over the archaic, classical and Hellenistic periods coexists with another approach: that of Hellenisation. Scholars have rarely defined carefully and explicitly what they mean by Hellenisation, but in most cases it describes the process through which non-Greek communities adopted Greek material culture, language and literature, styles and iconography, cults and myths, cultural practices like athletics, and even Greek identity.[37] The focus of this approach is the process through which elements of Greek culture make their presence clearly felt among non-Greek societies across the Mediterranean and the Black Sea from the archaic period onwards.[38] While the Hellenicity approach presents a clear chronological narrative that distinguishes between the archaic, classical and Hellenistic periods, the Hellenisation approach is less interested in drawing chronological distinctions, and more willing to portray Hellenisation as a continuous process.

As regards the study of the archaic and classical periods, the Hellenicity and the Hellenisation approaches coexist implicitly, because they are applied to different problems and aspects.[39] The Hellenicity approach is applied to the study of the mainland Greek world and its interaction with the empires of the East, while the Hellenisation approach is primarily applied to the study of the wider world of *apoikiai* ('colonies'), the Greek settlements that spread from the eighth century onwards across the Mediterranean.[40] It is to the progressive adoption of elements of Greek culture by various non-Greek societies in the areas where Greek *apoikiai* emerged, from Italy, Sicily and southern France to Thrace and the Black Sea, that the Hellenisation approach is usually applied. It is only in the Hellenistic period that Hellenicity and Hellenisation finally mingle, with the creation of a cultural form of Hellenicity open to non-Greeks, the Greco-Macedonian rule over non-Greek societies in the Near East, and the progressive Hellenisation of non-Greek communities from Asia Minor to Syria and Egypt.[41]

While there are elements of truth in the traditional account presented above, it is also deeply misleading in many of its assumptions and conclusions. The traditional account presents a clear chronological division that is identical with the division between archaic, classical and Hellenistic periods, and posits two great political events as explanatory forces for

---

[37] See, e.g., Domínguez 1999: 324.   [38] See, e.g., the case of Greek art: Boardman 1994.
[39] See already Chapot *et al.* 1914.   [40] Blakeway 1935; Dunbabin 1948: 191–3; Benoit 1965.
[41] See already Jouguet 1928.

what are seen as major changes in the relationship between Greeks and Barbarians. This political explanation is deeply flawed, as we shall see. While both the Persian Wars and the conquests of Alexander were significant developments, they did not constitute radical breaks in the relationship between Greek and non-Greek cultures. To start with, this is because most of the changes attributed to these political events long predated them. We shall see in Chapters 2 and 5 that the Panhellenic community and the Barbarian repertoire in Greek culture predated the Persian Wars. While Droysen attributed the expansion of Greek culture in the Near East to Alexander's conquest, scholars have long discovered that many of the interactions that Droysen posited as being a result of the conquests of Alexander had in fact started long before that. Everybody knows that the Mausoleum of Halicarnassus was one of the seven wonders of the ancient world: this was the funerary monument of Mausolus, a native dynast of Caria in Asia Minor, who was also a satrap of the Persian Empire and who died in 353, three years after the birth of Alexander the Great and nineteen years before Alexander crossed to Asia Minor. Mausolus used Greek artistic models and the most famous Greek artists of the day; he was a Hellenistic ruler before the emergence of the Hellenistic world.[42]

Furthermore, the major flaw of the traditional approach is the assumption that each historical period is dominated by a single form of interaction between Greeks and non-Greeks. It is as if, in the various stories about Thales we have examined above, the stories about his learning of Egyptian wisdom or working for a Lydian king would represent the archaic period, while the story about his polarised pronouncements concerning Barbarians would represent the classical period. In fact, the various stories about Thales and the realities they reflected coexisted: Greeks went on working for foreign kings and presenting Greek thought as the beneficiary of alien wisdom, while also presenting polarised images of Barbarians, throughout the course of the classical period. The interactions and encounters between Greeks and non-Greeks exhibited a wide range of forms during the whole of the first millennium and in all three periods (archaic, classical and Hellenistic). We need a methodological framework that will allow us to examine the full range of Greek–Barbarian interactions over the long term. This is the framework of the four parallel worlds that we shall shortly explore in section 1.4.

Equally problematic are the assumptions of the Hellenisation approach.[43] The adoption of elements of Greek culture by non-Greek communities did

---

[42] Hornblower 1982: 352–3.
[43] Whitehouse and Wilkins 1989; Hodos 2006; Dietler 2010: 43–53.

not transform them into Greeks; Etruscan art and mythology borrowed heavily from Greek, but this did not make the Etruscans Greeks. Hellenisation, conceived as the process through which non-Greeks adopted Greek identity (Hellenicity) and became part of the Panhellenic community, is a very misleading approach to how the Etruscans and other non-Greeks interacted with Greek culture. This does not mean that there are no examples in which non-Greek communities and cultures adopted Hellenicity, in particular from the Hellenistic period onwards, as we shall see in Chapter 7 (pp. 298–301). But this is only one aspect of the much wider process of the interaction of non-Greeks with Greek culture, and we need a wider approach that will allow us to explore and analyse the complexity of this interaction.

At the same time, the adoption of foreign elements by non-Greek communities was not restricted to the adoption of Greek culture, but was a much more diverse phenomenon. During the archaic and classical periods various communities across the Mediterranean adopted and adapted goods, ideas, techniques and practices that originated from Greek, Phoenician, Egyptian, Aramaean, Assyrian, Persian and other cultures. As part of the same process of cultural interaction and exchange, Greek culture was also deeply affected by its interaction with non-Greek cultures. It is a great methodological flaw to separate the adoption of elements of Greek culture by non-Greek communities from the wider processes of cultural interaction and exchange. We need therefore a theoretical approach that will enable us to study these wider processes. This is furnished by the concepts of globalisation and glocalisation that we shall examine in section 1.5 of this chapter.

1.4 Four parallel worlds

In order to understand the complex relationships between Greeks and Barbarians we need to move beyond a simplistic distinction between two separate and self-enclosed entities. Greeks and non-Greeks encountered and interacted with each other in a variety of different ways and contexts; exploring these encounters and interactions requires situating them within four parallel, yet interconnected, worlds: the world of networks; the world of *apoikiai*; the Panhellenic world; and the world of empires. To a certain extent, these four worlds involved different geographical areas: while, for example, the world of empires comprised the eastern Mediterranean, the world of *apoikiai* largely focused on the western Mediterranean and the Black Sea. But more important is the fact that these four worlds involved different forms of interactions and encounters between Greeks and non-Greeks.

I use the term 'world' in a way similar to that used when we talk, for example, of the world of fashion. There is no doubt that the world of fashion has its own geography: its centres are Paris, Milan and New York, not Berlin, Moscow or Mexico City. Nevertheless, the geography of the world of fashion is created by the nexus of relationships that link it together, rather than being a separate geographic world: it coexists with other parallel, but interlinked, worlds, such as the world of finance, of media, of drugs, of human trafficking, of diplomacy, of sports. What differentiates these parallel, yet interlinked, worlds is, apart from their different geographic focus, the difference in activities, in flows and in the form of relationships that bind each world together. The interaction between a Brazilian photographer and an Italian model in the world of fashion can be very different from that of a Brazilian investor and an Italian stockbroker in the world of finance, of a Brazilian diplomat and an Italian journalist in the world of diplomacy, or of a Brazilian trafficked girl and an Italian policeman in the world of trafficking. Moreover, the concept of the 'world' allows us to avoid making misleading distinctions between supposedly separate sectors, such as the economy, culture, society or state. The world of fashion includes economic, social, cultural and even political aspects; but they are interlinked in a very different manner than the world of finance, or the world of diplomacy. The four parallel worlds examined below exemplify four different configurations of economic, social, cultural and political aspects, and represent four different contexts of interaction between Greeks and non-Greeks; the distinction between Greeks and non-Greeks was drawn in very different ways in these four parallel worlds, and the importance of this distinction could range from being highly significant to having no importance whatsoever.

The world of networks

This is the world of the networks that moved people, goods, ideas and technologies across the Mediterranean and beyond.[44] Countless people

---

[44] On Mediterranean networks, see Malkin *et al.* 2009. I am using the term here in a more restricted sense than Malkin 2011; but important elements of Malkin's approach are included in my analysis of the Panhellenic world. For a similar approach to my use of the world of networks, see Magee and Thompson 2010.

moved from one community to another as traders, sailors, artisans, mercenaries, artists, religious specialists, doctors, courtesans, pilgrims, exiles or simply as immigrants.[45] Linking the movement of people with the movement of goods was a special kind of commodity: slaves. Archaeological excavations have revealed the mobility of goods throughout the Mediterranean world and beyond. The exchanged goods included raw materials (metals, timber, grain), processed materials (oil, unguents, incenses and perfumes, wines, and other exotic delicacies) and, finally, manufactured goods (pottery, metal utensils, textiles, jewellery, seal-stones and amulets).

The mention of the last item brings us to the mobility of ideas and technologies. Some goods might not carry any other luggage with them: the exchange of timber or grain would not necessarily transfer any ideas or technologies between most Mediterranean and Near Eastern communities. But it was different with certain kinds of goods, which were linked with accompanying ideas and technologies. The importation of Greek wines in areas where no cultivation of the vine existed beforehand, like southern France or the Black Sea, could be connected with new forms of commensality, such as the symposion and its rituals, as well as accompanying goods, like Greek pottery sets, whose design was shaped in order to serve in symposia and whose decoration recalled, reflected and constructed the world of the symposion.[46] Accordingly, the mobility of a commodity like wine could also attract the mobility of other goods in its wake, as well as accompanying ideas and technologies.

As we shall see, the mobility and adoption of such goods by one society could lead to various outcomes: the adoption of the accompanying technologies, or their significant modification by the host societies, and even the travel back of the modified technology and its adoption by the original exporting society. Plenty of other ideas and technologies, including literacy, coinage, military technology and equipment, music and rituals, were created, transferred and transformed through the networks of mobility that linked together Greek and non-Greek communities in the Mediterranean, the Black Sea and the Near East. Finally, we should not forget communication: the networks of mobility were also communicative networks which circulated news, information, stories and tales across very extensive areas; the importance of intercultural communication will be the focus of Chapter 4.

---

[45] McKechnie 1989.   [46] Dietler 1999, 2010: 183–256.

The world of *apoikiai*

The networks of mobilising people, goods, ideas, technologies and information are not a unique aspect of Greek–Barbarian relationships. There are hardly any communities in world history that were not enmeshed in such networks to a greater or lesser extent.[47] People belonging to all kinds of Greek or non-Greek communities moved around as traders, mercenaries or even permanent immigrants. Many Greeks and non-Greeks created immigrant nuclei within host communities; in first-millennium Egypt we can find Greek, Carian, Assyrian, Babylonian, Aramaean, Jewish, Arab and Persian immigrants.[48] But a special aspect of the relationship between Greeks and Barbarians is the world created by Greek *apoikiai*. *Apoikia* literally means a settlement away from home; as we shall see in Chapter 3, from the eighth century onwards the Greeks started to plant *apoikiai* across the Mediterranean. By the end of the classical period Greek *apoikiai* extended from the far west of southern Spain and France to the Black Sea in the north and to Libya and Egypt in the south.[49]

The peculiar aspect of these *apoikiai* was that they were self-organised communities, which were often in a position to be politically independent. This special phenomenon was important for Greek–Barbarian relationships in a number of ways. To start with, a significant number of Greek–Barbarian interactions took place in the context created by Greek *apoikiai*. The Greek interaction with Scythians, for example, took place in the context of the creation of Greek *apoikiai* in the Black Sea and their relationship with their Scythian neighbours. But while the creation and maintenance of Greek *apoikiai* were predicated on the world of networks, the world of *apoikiai* had a character of its own.

This world was characterised by a perennial contradiction.[50] On the one hand, Greek *apoikoi* were living among a variety of non-Greek communities in situations that ranged from conflict and subjugation to cohabitation, intermarriage and collaboration. In order to deal with this complex world, historians and archaeologists have utilised the concept of frontier societies.[51] This does not mean societies that are separated by a frontier, but societies that emerge and develop in situations of constant osmosis and interaction between different groups. The social, economic, political and cultural history of Greek *apoikiai* has to be situated within the frontier interactions with various non-Greek communities. These local interactions

---

[47] See, e.g., Curtin 1984.   [48] Vittmann 2003; Winnicki 2009.   [49] Tsetskhladze 2006a, 2008.
[50] Dana 2011b: 381; see also the comments of Mairs 2008, 2011a.
[51] Lepore 1968; *Confini e frontiera*.

and encounters created local varieties of Greek culture and affected non-Greek communities in particular ways; in a few fascinating cases they even led to the creation of new, hybrid cultures, which mixed Greek and non-Greek elements in complex ways.

At the same time though, Greek *apoikiai* were highly conscious of being Greek communities and of being part of the Panhellenic world.[52] The long-term experience of creating self-sustaining and self-organised communities had a powerful effect on Greek culture. The experience of encounters with foreign cultures led the Greek *apoikoi*, who often descended from diverse Greek communities, to realise what they had in common. It is not for nothing that the earliest attestation of dedications to 'the gods of the Greeks' is found in the Greek *apoikia* of Naucratis in Egypt (pp. 99–100). The experience of living in Egypt goes a long way to explaining why the Greek *apoikoi* constructed a sanctuary called 'Hellenion' and made dedications to the 'gods of the Greeks'; despite their diverse origins, they all shared a number of common deities and a common form of cult.

But the experience of creating self-organised communities was also important for the extent to which Greek culture became highly canonical, an essential aspect of Greek–Barbarian interactions. People who were constantly in the habit of creating new, self-organised communities would become very self-reflexive about such communities, and would have to create a mental pattern, a canonical package, of what such communities should consist of. The implications of *apoikiai* for the creation of a highly canonical form of Greek culture, and the implications of this canonical form of Greek culture for the interaction between Greeks and Barbarians, will be explored in the course of this book.

The world of *apoikiai* presents therefore a fascinating spectrum of ways in which diverse communities across the Mediterranean and the Black Sea combined or opposed these two different tendencies: the tendency to create frontier societies through interaction with various non-Greeks; and the tendency to create communities that stressed their Greek identity and helped to create a canonical form of Greek culture.

The Panhellenic world

Greek history has a peculiarity which is rarely noticed: it is a history without a centre. Egyptian history is essentially the history of the pharaonic state.[53] Iranian history is in many ways the history of the successive Iranian

---

[52] Dana 2011a; Malkin 2011.   [53] Kemp 1989.

empires: the Achaemenid, the Parthian, the Sassanid, etc.[54] The history of Rome can be centred on the history of the city-state of Rome and its imperial expansion;[55] and Jewish history for long periods was a history centred on the Temple.[56] When we turn to Greek history there is simply nothing equivalent. The Greeks had no centre or institution around which their history could be organised. Greek-speaking communities were scattered all over the Mediterranean, and they never achieved political, economic or social unity; even their cultural unity was not centred on a dominant institution. Because they lacked a centre, Greek culture and Greek identity could exist and maintain their unity only because of a peculiar and complex set of factors.[57]

The unity of Greek culture was the result of networks of mobile artists, poets and intellectuals, which linked together the various Greek communities. Greek culture and Greek identity were also maintained by a peculiar form of literature which was primarily based on a peculiar form of mythology (pp. 164–8). Greek identity was based on common descent from mythical heroes; and Greek literature and the cultural identity based on that literature focused on the exploits of these heroes, whose most famous achievement was the joint expedition against Troy, immortalised in Homer's *Iliad*. It was the shared imaginary world of literature and myth which underlay Greek identity and linked Greeks to each other. A second level of the Panhellenic world was created by Panhellenic sanctuaries, primarily Olympia and Delphi, which provided an arena of display for the whole Greek world, and the Panhellenic festivals which brought together Greeks from all over the Mediterranean. A final level was the discourse of a Panhellenic community: the debates about who should belong to it and who should lead it, about its common interests and joint actions against common enemies, allowed another sense of Greek identity to be articulated.

The Panhellenic world affected the interaction between Greeks and Barbarians in two contrasting ways. On the one hand, the Panhellenic world was to an important extent the outcome of such interactions. The discourse of the Panhellenic community was effectively the result of the confrontation between the Greeks and the Persians during the Persian Wars, and it both fed on and was fed by such confrontations in subsequent centuries. Attempts at Panhellenic hegemony by Greek states, such as the Athenian fifth-century empire, were constructed in opposition to the

---

[54] Wiesehöfer 1996.   [55] Woolf 2012.   [56] *CHJ 1*; *CHJ 2*; Schürer 1973, 1979, 1986, 1987.
[57] Malkin 2011: 3–15.

Persian Empire, but were also shaped by constant interaction and borrowing from it; the conquest of the Persian Empire by Alexander on the basis of a Panhellenic ideology is another eloquent example. At the same time, Persia was able to play a fundamental role in Greek politics precisely because of the decentralised nature of the Panhellenic world and its inherent instabilities (pp. 65–72).

But perhaps more important is to look at this process from the opposite end. The peculiar way in which the unity and mutual comprehension of Greek culture was maintained had also a significant effect on the relationships between Greeks and non-Greeks. Greek temples looked practically the same all over the Greek world because of networks of mobile Greek artists who moved around and built them. But these networks did not stop at the limit of the Greek world: it was the same network of mobile artists that brought the most famous Greek artists of the time to Halicarnassus in Caria to build Mausolus' legendary funerary monument. Greek myth was essential in linking together Greek communities through their heroic ancestors; but at the same time, this peculiar mythology was also used to link together Greeks and Barbarians. Panhellenic sanctuaries were an arena of display for Greek communities and individuals; but they could also function as arenas of display for non-Greek rulers who wished to maintain relationships with Greek communities, as the examples of Croesus, Mausolus and the kings of Thrace will show. Participation in the Panhellenic Games was an essential way of affirming one's membership in the Greek community; it was such practices that allowed the Macedonian kings to be recognised as part of the Greek world and to use Panhellenism as a springboard for their campaigns against the Persians. Despite the fact that many Greeks considered the Macedonians to be non-Greeks, it was the decentralised nature of the Panhellenic world that had brought into existence institutions and practices that ultimately allowed the Macedonians to be counted as part of the Greek world. And it was participation in these Panhellenic practices that allowed Phoenicians, Lycians or Carians to be accepted as members of the Panhellenic community from the Hellenistic period onwards.

The world of empires

An essential aspect of the interaction between Greeks and Barbarians during the archaic and classical periods is the existence of powerful non-Greek empires in the eastern Mediterranean. From the second millennium onwards, an extensive area that stretched from the Zagros Mountains in modern Iran in the east to the Mediterranean coast in the west and from the

Black Sea in the north to Egypt in the south saw the rise of powerful empires that were linked together in a number of different ways. In certain periods, such as those between 1500–1200 and between 900–550, the links and interactions between these states and empires were strong enough to merit talking about an interconnected world-system; during the latter period Assyria, the Neo-Babylonian kingdom, Lydia and Egypt dominated the eastern Mediterranean and the Near East. Finally, in the second half of the sixth century, the Persian kings managed to conquer all the various states included within this large area and to create an empire that stretched from the Indus River in modern Pakistan to the Aegean Sea, and from the Black Sea to modern Sudan.

This imperial world had enormous consequences for the communities of the eastern Mediterranean and the Black Sea. Many Greek communities, in particular those in Asia Minor, were subject to these empires for the greater part of the archaic and classical periods. The military confrontations, the diplomatic negotiations and the political interventions between these empires and the Greeks shaped Greek history in important ways. But equally important were the enormous manpower needs of these empires: they required soldiers, administrators, scribes, artisans, advisers, entertainers, doctors and courtesans; they also employed many foreigners as vassals and dependent rulers of cities, fortresses and territories within their empires. Thousands of Greeks, alongside thousands of non-Greeks of course, entered the service of these empires in one capacity or another.

The stories of these people are fascinating in themselves, and we will have plenty of opportunities to discuss them; but they also had significant consequences for the interaction between Greeks and Barbarians. Imperial warfare and its consequences moved people around as exiles, deportees and slaves, and settled them in new and unfamiliar territories. Imperial peace brought the extension of travel and communication into the farthest reaches of the known world; Herodotus' description of Babylon, whatever its sources, would have been impossible without the possibilities of travel and communication created by the Persian Empire.[58] The various people employed by these empires moved and resided thousands of miles away from their homelands. Around 600, Greek mercenaries were leaving their graffiti in the deep south of Egypt; nearby, a military post of Jewish soldiers was also serving an empire far away from home. In the capitals of Persian satraps (governors) and kings, from Dascyleion and Sardis in Asia Minor to Memphis in Egypt and Persepolis in Persia, we are able to see Greeks living

---

[58] Kuhrt 2002; cf. Rollinger 1993.

alongside people of different cultures and to observe the fascinating interactions that were engendered in such multicultural centres. Residents of the
United Kingdom are familiar with the portrait of the Queen on the coins
they use; but the first human portrait on a coin in world history was that of a
Greek who ruled three cities of Asia Minor as a Persian vassal: none other
than the great Themistocles.[59]

The complexity and diversity of interactions between Greeks and
Barbarians in the four parallel worlds necessitate a different chronological
perspective. The traditional account posited radical differences between the
archaic, classical and Hellenistic periods. The argument of this book is that
this is deeply misleading, and that it distorts the diversity of interactions
which existed in every period of the first millennium BCE. By the later sixth
century, the main forms of interaction between Greeks and Barbarians in
the word of networks, the world of *apoikiai*, the Panhellenic world and the
world of empires were already in place, and would remain so for the rest of
the first millennium. Subsequent developments added further factors: the
Persian Wars created a third level of the Panhellenic world in the form of the
discourse of the Panhellenic community (pp. 60–1), while the conquests of
Alexander added the new element of a Greco-Macedonian ruling elite to the
world of empires (pp. 282–90). But the continuity of the major modes of
interaction and their constant plurality from the late archaic period
onwards is truly impressive and can hardly be overemphasised. The four
parallel worlds allow us to perceive the diversity and complexity of interactions between Greeks and non-Greeks in a long-term perspective.

1.5 Globalisation and glocalisation: two paradoxes

The processes set into motion by the four parallel worlds created the space
for globalisation.[60] By that I understand the intensification of economic,
social, political and cultural processes that tend to expand on the scale from
local to global. The outcome of these processes is the emergence of a *koine*,
in which individuals and communities come to participate in a world of
shared symbols and meanings, as expressed, for example, in literature,
intellectual exploration and religion; use shared forms of material culture;
employ shared means of communication; and even partake of shared forms

---

[59] Cahn and Gerin 1988; Cahn and Mannsperger 1991.
[60] For a comparative perspective on parallel but interconnected worlds and globalisation in the
modern Indian Ocean, see Bose 2006.

of identity. This cultural *koine* might result either through the adoption of a previously existing cultural system or by the creation of a novel cultural system through the process of the formation of a *koine*.

Strictly speaking, of course, globalisation, seen as a process that encompasses the whole globe, is inapplicable to the first millennium BCE, which is the focus of this study. While the processes we shall examine covered an immense area from modern-day Pakistan to Spain and from Ukraine to Sudan, the greatest part of Asia, temperate Europe and sub-Saharan Africa, as well as the continents of America and Australia, remained outside. The global reach of the world of the first millennium BCE pales into insignificance in comparison even to the later Middle Ages, when the whole of Eurasia became part of an interacting system, and an itinerant scholar like Ibn Battuta could travel from Morocco all the way to China.[61] The first truly global interactions emerged during the early modern period (1500–1800 CE) with the incorporation of the Americas and Australia within the systems of Eurasia and Africa,[62] and the modern period has witnessed a massive expansion of the processes of globalisation.[63]

But globalisation necessitates a long-term historical perspective, and the process by which interactions became truly global includes as one of its essential components what happened in the Mediterranean, the Black Sea and the Near East in the course of the first millennium BCE.[64] This should not mean that we should adopt a unilinear and teleological approach, in which a straight line leads from the small beginnings of the first millennium BCE in the Mediterranean and the Near East to the global interactions of modern times. The processes of globalisation were often reversible, and there have been far too many transformations, discontinuities and changes to render traditional accounts like that of the progressive 'rise of the West' and its transformation of the globe invalid. Modern historians have distinguished between different forms of globalisation (archaic, proto-globalisation, modern and post-colonial) which have emerged at different points, have had different features, but have also coexisted, transformed and built on each other in the last 500 years.[65] But if globalisation is a process through which interactions tend to expand on the scale from local to global, to intensify interconnections across cultures and borders, and to create extended material and cultural *koinai*, then the processes that we shall

---

[61] Abu-Lughod 1989; Bentley 1993.   [62] Parker 2010.   [63] Wolf 1982; Bayly 2004.
[64] For such a long-term historical perspective, see Christian 2004.
[65] For a historical perspective on globalisation, see Hopkins 2002.

examine in the Mediterranean, the Black Sea and the Near East of the first millennium BCE certainly deserve such an appellation.[66]

At the same time, scholars have emphasised that globalisation does not necessarily lead to the extinction of local cultural systems; the process of globalisation can also provide the means by which a local cultural system can be redefined, elaborated, codified or modified for new circumstances. Accordingly, globalisation is inherently linked to the concept of glocalisation.[67] The variety of ways in which local communities and cultures adopt and adapt the global *koine* is what I understand as glocalisation.[68] The process of globalisation can lead to the disappearance of a local cultural system through the adoption of the global *koine*; it can lead to the *koine*'s affecting certain areas of life, while the local cultural system remains valid for others; it can lead to an accommodating coexistence of the global *koine* with a glocalised system; or it can lead to conflict and confrontation between the *koine*, the glocalised system and the 'original' cultural system.

I should point out that I am using the concepts of globalisation and glocalisation as heuristic tools, rather than as theoretical models. I do not subscribe to the view that globalisation is a theoretical model that allows us to perceive the direction of developments, either in the present or in the past. Instead, my employment of these two concepts serves two heuristic purposes. On the one hand, it allows us to move beyond the problematic Hellenisation approach we have examined above and avoid a Hellenocentric perspective. The concept of globalisation allows us to situate the spread of elements of Greek culture across the Mediterranean and the Near East within a wider process which included elements and practices from many other cultures (Egyptian, Aramaic, Phoenician, Persian, etc.). The diverse elements of the process of globalisation were due to the diverse forms of interaction that we have tried to capture through the concept of the four parallel worlds. The world of networks globalised 'Orientalising' objects, Egyptian scarabs or Greek pottery from the Near East all the way to Spain; the world of *apoikiai* led to the adoption of the alphabet or Greek-style temples by various non-Greek communities in the western Mediterranean; the world of empires led to the spread of imperial languages like Aramaic. Globalisation is not an explanation of these processes; it is rather a heuristic tool that allows us to see the large picture, identify changes and describe them. The explanation of the variety of processes that constitute globalisation can only come through concrete historical analysis of

---

[66] For a study of globalisation before the first millennium BCE, see Jennings 2011.
[67] Robertson 1992; Appadurai 2001.　　[68] Cf. Bowersock 1990: 7–9.

Figure 1 Silver stater of Issos, fourth century BCE.

the different processes and the different contexts and places. This is why the distinction between the four parallel worlds is essential for understanding, explaining and analysing the diverse processes of globalisation.

The concept of glocalisation allows us to perceive the agency of individuals, communities and cultures in their interaction with the global *koine*. The processes of globalisation enabled the widespread circulation of goods, people, ideas and technologies of diverse origins; communities and cultures made different choices about which elements to adopt and in which ways; and their choices had a reciprocal effect on the process of globalisation, as glocal forms emerging in one particular area re-entered the global *koine* and became further globalised and glocalised. Glocalisation is not a theory that explains how different cultures adopt elements of the global *koine*; again, only concrete historical analysis can illustrate that and explain the choices made. This concrete historical analysis is what I attempt in Chapters 5 and 6.

An early fourth-century coin from Issos in Cilicia, in southeast Asia Minor, provides an excellent illustration of the processes of both globalisation and glocalisation (see Figure 1). Before the seventh century BCE, the exchange of goods and services across the globe took the form of barter, or used as media of exchange particular goods, which differed greatly from one community to the other. Around 600 in western Asia Minor there emerged the first forms of coinage: pieces of metal of the same weight, stamped with an image to guarantee their weight, purity and acceptance as money. Coinage was invented by the Lydian kingdom, but it was quickly adopted by Greek communities and spread widely across the Greek world. Gradually, within the world of networks, the world of *apoikiai* and the Panhellenic world there developed a standard form of Greek coin, with a legend defining the issuing community and images in Greek style and iconography expressing its identity.

It was this form of Greek coin that became part of a global numismatic *koine*, which gradually encompassed the whole Mediterranean. The reverse of our Cilician coin shows a statue of a male deity in Greek iconographical style; on the basis of iconographic parallels with other Cilician coins, it can be identified as Baal of Tarsus, the chief deity of the most important city of Cilicia and a popular one throughout Cilicia. It is accompanied by an inscription in Greek (Issikon), identifying the issuing community in the standard Greek form. But it has also an inscription in Aramaic, a Semitic language spoken over large areas of the Near East and commonly used by the Persian bureaucracy, giving the name of the Persian satrap Tiribazus. Although Aramaic was not the main spoken language in Cilicia, it had become the lingua franca of the area, and its use to identify the Persian satrap should not surprise. The obverse of the coin shows the chief Persian deity Ahura Mazda, depicted inside a winged disc in typical Persian icon-ography; but, in contrast to the standard depiction of Ahura Mazda in profile in Persian iconography, his body is here depicted frontally and with a developed torso, which is, of course, typical of Greek artistic style.[69]

This is a clear example of both globalisation and glocalisation. On the one hand, there is the use of the form of the Greek coin, the use of Greek artistic style and the inscription in Greek, alongside the use of Aramaic and the depiction of a Persian deity. All these are elements of globalising processes: the creation of a numismatic *koine*, an artistic *koine*, and two communica-tion *koinai* in Greek and Aramaic. But at the same time this is a coin of a Cilician community, which has glocalised these elements in order to portray its local identity. Greek language is employed in order to express the identity of the issuing authority; Greek iconographic style is employed in order to depict a local Cilician deity, Baal of Tarsus; the Persian deity Ahura Mazda is incorporated into the iconography of the Cilician coin, but Greek artistic style is employed for its Cilician depiction.

The concepts of globalisation and glocalisation serve a second heuristic purpose: to identify two important paradoxes with regard to the global-isation of Greek culture and the Greek glocalisation of other cultures. The phenomenon of one culture having a deep impact on other cultures is by no means rare in world history. It is a largely safe generalisation that whenever one culture is widely adopted by other societies, this is normally because the influential culture belongs to a society or state with political, social or

---

[69] Capecchi 1991.

economic power. The globalisation of French culture across Europe during the seventeenth and eighteenth centuries was in many ways the result of the fact that the France of the Sun King Louis XIV was the most powerful state in contemporary Europe; the global spread of American culture since the second half of the twentieth century is clearly related to the economic and political hegemony of the United States in the same period. In the ancient world, historians and archaeologists have long been familiar with the spread of various elements of Roman material culture (baths, villas, amphitheatres, basilicas, inscriptions) over wide areas of western and northern Europe in the first centuries CE. Although there is considerable debate on how to explain this complex phenomenon, there is no doubt that the conquest of those areas by the Roman Empire is an essential part of any possible explanation.[70]

When we come, though, to the relationship between Greeks and non-Greeks during the archaic and classical periods, we are immediately faced with a great paradox. The Greeks were a small and relatively impoverished periphery of a wider, older, richer and much more powerful world. Confronted with the antiquity of Egyptian civilisation and its enormous temples and statues, or with the rich and powerful Persian Empire which ruled over a considerable number of Greek communities, the Greeks could not help but feel awe and envy. Given that the Greeks were an unruly periphery of the immense Persian Empire, it is truly amazing to observe how already from the sixth century various non-Greek societies that were subjects to the Persians had started to adopt and adapt various elements of Greek culture. We have already mentioned the case of Mausolus in Caria, and we have seen the globalisation of Greek culture in the case of our Cilician coin; in Lycia, another area of southwest Asia Minor under Persian rule, local potentates started in the fifth century to adopt Greek architectural and sculptural models for their impressive funerary monuments (pp. 264–7). Phoenicia, another area under the Persians, had an old artistic tradition that was commonly influenced by the artistic models of nearby Egypt, which had ruled the Levantine coast for long stretches of time before also becoming subject to the Persians. But starting again in the fifth century BCE, Phoenician artists were creating magnificent stone sarcophagi on the basis of Greek artistic models (pp. 271–3).

Perhaps the most telling example of the globalisation of Greek culture is a famous trilingual inscription from Xanthos, the most important city of Lycia in southwest Asia Minor.[71] This inscribed stele dates to the second

---

[70] Hingley 2005; Wallace-Hadrill 2008.   [71] Translated in Kuhrt 2007: 859–63.

half of the fourth century. One of its faces bears an inscription in the Lycian language recording a decision of the community of Xanthos concerning local religious issues; another face contains a shorter inscription in Aramaic, containing a letter by the Persian-appointed satrap (governor) of Lycia confirming his approval of the decision of the Xanthians. So far, nothing would cause surprise; but the third face contains a text in Greek, which is effectively a translation of the decree in Lycian. Why on earth would a Lycian community under Persian suzerainty feel the need to record a decision of purely local importance in a Greek translation? The equivalent of all the above examples would be for the areas within the Roman Empire to adopt the culture of the Barbarian periphery, instead of the Barbarians adopting Roman culture: for example, the Iberian communities of the Roman Empire setting up inscriptions in, for example, German instead of Iberian, and German communities setting up inscriptions in Latin.

How should we explain this paradox? In the past, this paradox was obscured by a widely shared assumption. Greek culture was considered to be obviously superior to anything the Barbarians might have to offer; once the Barbarians could open their eyes and see, scholars thought, they would naturally adopt what was superior.[72] If they ever wanted to advance and become civilised, they would have to become Hellenised; this was also long the sort of explanation offered for the spread of Roman culture to western Europe.[73] It can conceivably be granted that communities in Iberia, Gaul or Britain, with no native traditions of monumental building or sculpture in stone, could not fail to adopt and adapt the technology and models offered by the stronger, wealthier and more technologically advanced Rome. But this would hardly work in the case of the Persian Empire: why should Phoenicians, with a long artistic tradition of their own, which influenced Greek art in its early stages, come to adopt the models of the Greek periphery? If we have stopped subscribing to the classification of cultures into inferior and superior and to the idea of the inherent superiority of Greek culture, then we are faced with a very important paradox. We need to try to explain, rather than take for granted, the fact that Greek culture played such an important role in the processes of globalisation and glocalisation in the archaic and classical Mediterranean.

My second paradox goes in the opposite direction; again, the example of Rome provides a helpful parallel. When Latin literature came to light in the course of the third century, it was directly modelled on and referred to Greek literature.[74] Some of the earliest works in the Latin language were

---

[72] For example, Boardman 1999: 190.   [73] Hingley 2005: 14–48.   [74] Gruen 1990: 79–123, 1992.

translations of famous Greek models, such as Livius Andronicus' translation of Homer's *Odyssey*; the genres of Latin literature were all based on the genres of Greek literature, satire being the only genre without a Greek equivalent; early Latin compositions, like the comedies of Plautus, were adaptations of Greek plays and presented the Greek world as the setting of their dramatic action. Finally, in certain genres Roman authors composed in the Greek language, rather than in their native Latin tongue: Fabius Pictor, the first Roman to write on Roman history, famously composed his Greek-style history in Greek. The same applies to Roman art: Roman art is directly based on Greek artistic models and uses various Greek artistic styles for different aims and effects. Similar points can be made about myth and religion: the Romans adopted Greek religious iconography as well as the names of Greek divinities. The acroteria of a sixth-century temple in the Forum Boarium in Rome depict Heracles and Athena in the style of Greek religious iconography (Figure 2); and a sixth-century dedication from nearby Lavinium is dedicated to the Greek deities Castor

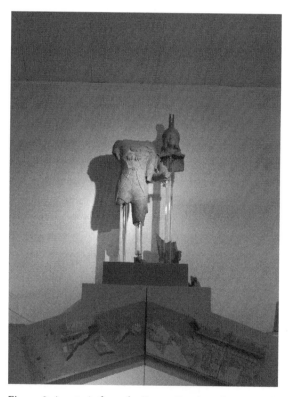

Figure 2 Acroteria from the Forum Boarium, Rome, sixth century BCE.

and Polydeuces.[75] While the Romans identified Athena with their own deity Minerva, but depicted her according to Greek iconography, they adopted the name of Heracles alongside the iconography and mythology.

What is truly impressive is that there is hardly anything equivalent in the interaction between Greeks and non-Greeks, as we shall fully explore in Chapter 5 (pp. 164–6). Greek literature borrowed a number of elements and themes from the literatures of the East, as we shall see. But the differences with the Roman glocalisation of Greek culture are telling: we hardly encounter any translations of non-Greek works; there is no intertextuality between Greek and Eastern literature during the archaic and classical periods, as we do not find a single Greek work which refers to Eastern works, as, for example, Virgil refers to Homer; and we do not find a single Greek who composed a work in a non-Greek language. The same applies also to art and religion. Barring a few exceptions (pp. 215–18), we will not find, for example, foreign deities represented in Greek religious iconography, in the way that Heracles and Athena were represented in Greek style in the Roman temple mentioned above. In other words, Greek literature, art and religion present themselves as closed systems, which exclude any conscious and explicit reference to foreign models and styles.

Perhaps this is not so surprising; perhaps it is the widespread Roman willingness to adopt and imitate which should be explained, rather than the Greek closed system. Is it not the case, at the end of the day, that all people have their own native culture and only subsequently, if ever, do they adopt elements from foreign cultures? A cursory examination of other ancient civilisations would immediately show that this is in fact not the case. We have already mentioned how Phoenician artistic tradition commonly adopted Egyptian artistic models and styles. The literature and mythology of Assyria, the most powerful state in the first half of the first millennium, were directly modelled on the art and literature of Babylonia, when they did not simply adopt and translate: Assyrian mythology is effectively Babylonian. Excavations in the Hittite Bronze Age capital of Hattusas in Anatolia have revealed texts in Akkadian and Hurrian, in addition to the native tongue; many works in the Hittite language are translations and adaptations of Mesopotamian models.[76]

How should we explain this Greek reaction towards other cultures? Many people would be tempted to interpret it as evidence of the superiority and inventiveness of the 'Greek miracle', following one of the scholarly approaches that we described above. And, in fact, we would again be able

---

[75] Wiseman 2004: 22–9.   [76] Beckman 2009.

to quote ancient support for this view; for did not Plato write that 'whatever the Greeks acquire from the Barbarians is finally turned by them into something nobler'?[77] Some scholars might react to this phenomenon by condemning Greek ethnocentrism and parochialism, or attributing the lack of translations of foreign works into Greek to the supposed Greek unwillingness to learn foreign languages.[78] Other scholars have in fact argued that after an initial phase of inspiration from the East (the Orientalising period), the Greeks were quickly able to move beyond imitation and to turn the various influences they received into something quintessentially Greek.[79]

What does it matter therefore that some influences in Greek culture might have come from the East? What really matters, some scholars would argue, is what the Greeks did with them, and what they did answered to Greek quests and needs, not to those of the societies from which the influences might have originated.[80] It might be the case that Hesiod's *Theogony* borrows from Hittite or Levantine works; but while we need to know Homer in order to understand Virgil, because there is intertextuality between the *Iliad* and the *Aeneid*, there is no intertextuality between Hesiod and the Hittite poems, and accordingly we should elucidate the Hesiodic *Theogony* with reference to other Greek literature, not to a Hittite poem. The Hittite loan has been transformed into something uniquely Greek, and its origins no longer help us to understand anything important about it (see pp. 165–6).

Recognising the peculiar closed nature of Greek culture is undoubtedly important, but it is also quite misleading if stated without an important qualification. There are few areas of Greek literature and art which were not affected by interaction with non-Greeks, but they are affected in a very peculiar way. In the fourth century the Athenian Xenophon wrote an innovative and deeply influential work on the relationship between education and the ideal ruler, called the *Cyropaedia*. And who plays the role of the ideal ruler in Xenophon's work? None other than Cyrus the Great, the creator of the Persian Empire. The fact that a deeply Greek-centred discussion of the relationship between education and power takes the form of a biography of a Persian king is an excellent illustration of the peculiar way in which Greek culture is deeply shaped by its relationship to the Barbarians. We have already seen how Greeks could attribute Thales' achievements to his education by the Egyptians; in fact, from early on

---

[77] Plato, *Epinomis*, 987d–e.   [78] Momigliano 1975: 8–11.   [79] Burkert 2004: 12–15.
[80] See, e.g., Osborne 1993; Whitley 2001: 102–33.

Greeks were particularly willing to attribute pretty much everything valuable in their culture to their Barbarian neighbours. Herodotus famously claimed that all of Greek religion came from Egypt;[81] the Greek alphabet was the gift of Cadmus the Phoenician, who was also considered the founder of the Greek city of Thebes, and whose sister Europa gave her name to the continent of Europe.[82] In other words: non-Greeks and their cultures were deeply incorporated in Greek culture in many ways; but they were present in a peculiar way, which is very different from the traditional model of imitation and influence that we are accustomed to expect. The Greek glocalisation of foreign cultures is a very peculiar form of glocalisation.

Greek culture lacked intertextuality with and translation of foreign texts, or the direct adoption and use of foreign styles and iconographies, which is so strikingly the case in the relationship between, for example, Roman and Greek culture; but in their place Greek culture developed a process of filtering the complex interactions with non-Greek cultures in the four parallel worlds and redeploying them within what we can call a Barbarian repertoire. By this I mean the development of a range of cultural practices in which foreigners and their cultures are employed in the most diverse ways and for the most diverse purposes. Two aspects of this phenomenon were particularly important: the peculiar nature of Greek myth and the Greek textualisation of the interactions with non-Greeks.

Greek myth spread quickly among non-Greek people in both West and East. We see depictions of Greek heroes and Greek myths in native artistic production already during the sixth century in both Etruria in the west[83] and Lycia in the east.[84] This testifies to the paradoxical influence of Greek culture on other societies that we have commented on above. At the same time, there is practically no movement in the opposite direction. Greek mythical narratives hardly incorporate foreign deities, nor do Greek depictions show foreign heroes and deities, in the manner of the Etruscans who mix Greek and Etruscan heroes and deities in their depictions (see Figure 31). A Greek who stood in front of a fourth-century funerary monument in Limyra in Lycia would be readily able to recognise the depiction of the Greek hero Bellerophon killing the monster Chimaera on the acroteria of the monument (see Figure 3);[85] there is simply nothing equivalent that a non-Greek could observe in the decoration of a Greek temple. But at the same time there is no other mythology in the ancient world where the foreigner has such a strong presence: Greek heroes move to foreign places

---

[81] 2.50. [82] Gruen 2011: 223–36. [83] De Grummond 2006. [84] Mellink 1998.
[85] Bruns-Özgan 1987: 81–91.

Figure 3 Heroon of Pericles, Limyra, fourth century BCE.

and give birth to Barbarian people; Barbarian heroes like Cadmus and
Danaus move to Greek lands and give birth to Greek people.[86] The
Barbarian is deeply present in Greek mythology, but in a paradoxical and
largely unfamiliar way. Barbarian heroes are not figures of non-Greek
mythologies: there was no Cadmus in Phoenician mythology, no Danaus
in Egyptian; but the fact that Greek mythology, literature and art accord
such an important place to Barbarian heroes had very important consequences for Greek culture as well as for the interaction between Greeks and
non-Greeks.[87]

Let us move to the second aspect of the Barbarian repertoire in Greek
culture. There should be no doubt that Persians, Egyptians or Carians
participated in intercultural communication in a primarily oral universe
in which countless stories, customs, information and ideas endlessly circulated. The Greek peculiarity was the textualisation of this oral universe
through the development of literary genres which were based on the

---

[86] Bickerman 1952; Lane Fox 2008; Gruen 2011: 223–52.   [87] Erskine 2005; Gehrke 2005.

encounters and interactions of the four parallel worlds and the processes of intercultural communication. Sailors from all societies developed stories and a stock of information which was crucial for navigating in foreign lands and waters; what was peculiar about the Greeks was the textualisation of this information and stories into a literary genre, the *Periploi*, descriptions of foreign lands from a coastal perspective, which further developed into the literary genre we would describe as anthropology. Stories and discussions about the great kings and their acts circulated among all Mediterranean societies; the Greeks used such stories to create new literary genres including political theory, moral philosophy or manuals for political and economic administration.

The result of these two peculiar aspects of Greek culture was the development of a Barbarian repertoire with an impressive range of uses. Non-Greeks and their cultures were not just strangers, enemies or Others, even though these images accounted for a significant part of the Barbarian repertoire (see pp. 189–90). Non-Greeks and their cultures could also be depicted as utopian societies; they could provide models for practical reforms in politics, law, economics, education or warfare, as well as means of debating morality and religion (pp. 196–206). Foreign cultures could be depicted as possessors of alien wisdom, the original source of Greek philosophical, religious and scientific ideas and discoveries (pp. 206–14). This Barbarian repertoire had a very important role in Greek culture; but it was also important for the role of Greek culture in the processes of globalisation and glocalisation in the ancient Mediterranean.

Globalisation and glocalisation are very useful heuristic tools in order to identify and analyse both significant developments across the ancient Mediterranean, as well as paradoxes such as the two we have examined above. But there is a final point worth making. We started this discussion by examining two different perspectives on the relationship between Greeks and non-Greeks: polarity and conflict, on the one hand, and interconnection and exchange, on the other. There is a grain of truth in both approaches; but as the four parallel worlds and the two abovementioned paradoxes show, neither perspective sufficiently captures the peculiar complexity of the interactions between Greeks and non-Greeks during the archaic and classical periods. It is a good thing that many of us no longer subscribe to the Eurocentric and Orientalist identification with the Greek freedom fighters against the despotic Orientals, as exemplified by thinkers like Mill; but it is equally misleading to just turn the tables and identify the Greeks and their attitudes towards the East with the experience of Western imperialism and colonialism in the last 200 years. The widespread glocalisation of Greek culture by various non-Greek societies shows eloquently that unbridgeable polarities are deeply misleading.

This globalisation of Greek culture was no Greek 'civilising mission' equivalent to the projects of modern Western imperialism and colonialism. On the contrary, it was a process in which Greek craftsmen, artists, poets, doctors, mercenaries and traders served a variety of non-Greek communities and rulers, who used Greek manpower and Greek practices in order to construct and redefine their own cultures, identities and power structures. Even in the case of Greek *apoikiai*, where similarities with modern colonialisms have been assumed implicitly or explicitly, it was far more common for Greek communities to come under the power of non-Greek communities than for them to rule over non-Greek 'natives'.[88] Assimilating the relationship between Greeks and the Near East during the archaic and classical periods to the relationship between the modern West and the Orient is deeply misleading as a historical analogy.[89] But it is equally misleading to try to understand this relationship through a simplistic model of influence and imitation, or by collapsing the distinction between Greek culture and other cultures. If Greek culture is the origin of Western civilisation, it was a culture deeply shaped by processes of globalisation and glocalisation in the four parallel worlds we shall examine; but the peculiar form of this culture, and the peculiar ways in which it interacted with other cultures, show the importance of recognising and exploring the paradoxes we have emphasised. Herodotus, the first historian to compose a work devoted to the interaction between Greeks and Barbarians, uses the verb 'to marvel' (*thaumazo*) constantly; there is no reason why we should do so any the less.

1.6 The structure of the book

This book tries to provide both chronological and thematic approaches. Accordingly, some chapters are arranged in a largely chronological order, while others follow a thematic one. The choice has in the main been determined by convenience and by the need to cater for readerships with different qualifications and background knowledge. Chapter 2 presents a narrative of the development of the Panhellenic world and its interaction with the world of empires, while Chapter 5 presents the development of the Barbarian repertoire in Greek literature and art in the course of the archaic

---

[88] Malkin 2004; Purcell 2005.   [89] Cf. Vasunia 2001; Moyer 2011a: 1–10.

and classical periods. Together, they provide the reader with a chronological framework within which the various phenomena and processes discussed can be located. Other chapters follow a largely thematic order: Chapter 3 presents a thematic discussion of the networks of mobility of goods, people and ideas, of the cosmopolitan hubs (*emporia*) that facilitated these networks, and of the frontier societies of Greek *apoikiai* across the Mediterranean and the Black Sea; Chapter 4 explores the various aspects and forms of intercultural communication; Chapter 6 examines the forms, patterns and currents of globalisation and glocalisation, and presents a geographical overview of these processes in various areas and cultures within the Persian Empire; finally, Chapter 7 presents a thematic discussion of the four parallel worlds and globalisation and glocalisation in the Hellenistic period in order to assess continuities and changes. Nevertheless, many chapters include thematic discussions in chapters arranged in a chronological order and vice versa; the thematic Chapter 3 is introduced by a chronological overview of the development of the world of *apoikiai* and the world of networks, while the chronologically arranged Chapter 2 freezes time to provide a thematic exploration of the structure of the world of empires.

In terms of the wider argument of this book, Chapters 2 and 3 largely aim to illustrate the diversity and complexity of the interactions between Greeks and non-Greeks in the four parallel worlds. The next three chapters build on this exploration of diversity and complexity in order to focus on their results and historical importance. Chapter 4 is transitional: it explores intercultural communication as the medium through which interactions and encounters were culturally processed, filtered and employed in the literature, art and other cultural practices of Greek and non-Greek communities. Chapters 5 and 6 explore the different ways in which Greek and non-Greek cultures employed the contents provided by intercultural communication. Chapter 5 is devoted to the exploration of one of the paradoxes I presented above; it explores the peculiar form of Greek culture and the peculiar forms in which Greek culture filtered interactions with other cultures and glocalised non-Greek cultures. Chapter 6 is devoted to the opposite paradox: it examines how non-Greek cultures were affected by the processes of globalisation, explores the diverse ways in which they glocalised Greek culture, and provides an explanation for the important role of the Greek current of globalisation in the archaic and classical Mediterranean. Finally, Chapter 7 assesses the continuities and changes that took place in the four parallel worlds and in the processes of globalisation and glocalisation during the Hellenistic period.

2 | The Panhellenic world and the world of empires

2.1 The Panhellenic world

Where should our account start? At which point in history does it become possible to talk of Greeks and Barbarians? Thucydides, a fifth-century Greek historian, thought he had an answer:

Before the Trojan war there is no indication of any common action in Hellas, nor indeed of the universal prevalence of the name; on the contrary, before the time of Hellen, son of Deucalion, no such appellation existed, but the country went by the names of the different tribes, in particular of the Pelasgian. It was not till Hellen and his sons grew strong in Phthiotis, and were invited as allies into the other cities, that one by one they gradually acquired from the connection the name of Hellenes; though a long time elapsed before that name could fasten itself upon all. The best proof of this is furnished by Homer. Born long after the Trojan War, he nowhere calls all of them by that name, nor indeed any of them except the followers of Achilles from Phthiotis, who were the original Hellenes: in his poems they are called Danaans, Argives, and Achaeans. He does not even use the term barbarian, probably because the Hellenes had not yet been marked off from the rest of the world by one distinctive appellation.[1]

According to Thucydides, there existed no Greeks or Barbarians in the age of Homer: the words Hellas (Greece) and Hellenes (Greeks) were not used by the poet to describe collectively the countless Greek communities, and he had no term to describe collectively the non-Greek communities (Map 1). Modern historians have sometimes taken this ancient argument at face value and reconstructed the history of Greek identity and Greek–Barbarian relations on the basis of it.[2] According to them, Greek identity was something that emerged gradually during the archaic period out of the multitude of diverse Greek communities. Some scholars tend to put the stress on the process of aggregation through which local and regional identities coalesced into the formation of a Greek identity: the role of genealogy, sanctuaries and festivals in creating this aggregation is seen as particularly important.[3] Others stress the role of opposition to non-Greeks

[1] 1.3. [2] For example, Hall 2002: 125–34. [3] For example, Hall 2002: 134–71.

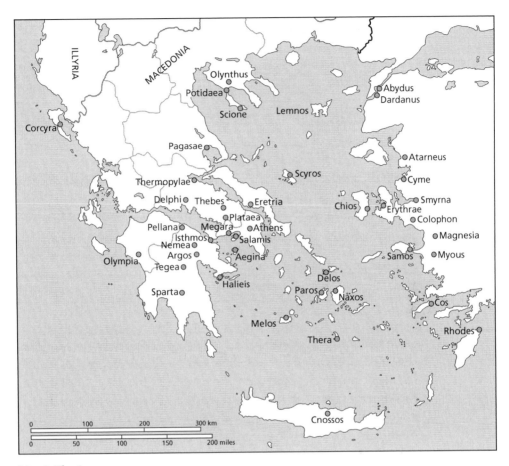

Map 1 The Aegean

and the formation of the concept of the Barbarian as an essential aspect of the emergence of Greek identity: the Persian Wars are seen by these scholars as a key point in the formation of Greek identity.[4]

Whatever the emphasis, many scholars agree that the distinction between Greeks and Barbarians had little importance during the archaic period; it was only in the early classical period that Greeks created a categorical distinction between themselves and the Barbarians, and constructed a discourse of identity that exalted Greek identity and Greek culture, and viewed Barbarians in a dismissive and pejorative manner that sometimes bordered on being racist.[5] After Alexander the Great's conquest of the Persian Empire and the emergence of the Hellenistic kingdoms, in which

---

[4] For example, Hall 1989.   [5] For example, Malkin 1998: 18; Burstein 2008: 60.

a Greek elite ruled over non-Greeks and Greek culture expanded from the
Balkans to Egypt and India, the relationship between Greeks and Barbarians
changed again: Greek identity was now identical with Greek culture, and it
was possible for non-Greeks to cross the Greek–Barbarian divide by acquiring Greek culture. From a world in which identities were inchoate and there
was little distinction between Greek and Barbarian in the archaic period
there emerged a highly polarised distinction during the classical period,
which was followed by a Hellenistic world in which it was now relatively
easy to cross the divide.

There is undoubtedly an element of truth in the above description, but it
is also deeply misleading.[6] This description presupposes that each period
had a single way of constructing Greek identity and its relationship to the
Barbarians. But this is hardly credible given the peculiar nature of the Greek
world. Greek history has a very peculiar subject compared with other
'national' histories. Roman history always centred on the city-state of
Rome and its imperial expansion; for most of antiquity Jewish history
largely centred on Jerusalem and its Temple; but there was never a single
political, economic, social or cultural centre which could give unity to the
Greek world and Greek identity. From the eighth century, as we shall also
explore in Chapter 3, Greek communities existed not only in the Aegean,
but also across the Mediterranean, from Egypt to the Black Sea and from
Thrace to southern France; by the classical period there were more than a
thousand Greek communities, mostly independent of each other.[7] Greek
communities were very diverse, not only geographically, but also socially,
politically, economically and culturally.[8]

Given the perennial lack of unity or of a centre, and the great diversity
among Greek communities, the existence of a Greek world was always
predicated on the emergence and maintenance of certain practices, media
and institutions, which functioned as a peculiar kind of unifying link. These
various practices, media and institutions were never integrated into a concerted whole; rather, they provided a spectrum of levels of Hellenicity,
which were partly overlapping and mutually reinforcing, and partly dis-
cordant and contradictory. This fact has important implications for relations between Greeks and Barbarians. Because there was never a single way
of being Greek, there never was a single way of defining non-Greeks, but
rather a range of contradictory approaches and attitudes. Even more, the
peculiar and contradictory way in which these media, practices and

[6] Sourvinou-Inwood 2005: 24–63; L. G. Mitchell 2007.   [7] Hansen and Nielsen 2004.
[8] Vlassopoulos 2007: 143–220.

institutions created Greek identity and the Panhellenic world also had important implications for the ways in which non-Greek communities interacted with the Greek world.[9]

Let us start with language, which played such an important role in definitions of Greeks and Barbarians. The earliest attestation of the word barbarian in Greek literature is in Homer's description of the Carians as 'barbarophônoi';[10] whether this should be interpreted as meaning 'of foreign speech', 'of cacophonous speech' or 'speaking Greek with a harsh accent' is debatable.[11] But by the archaic period there is no doubt that one of the major meanings of the word was linguistic: the Barbarians were those who did not speak Greek.[12] But did *anyone* speak Greek? In a certain way there never was such a thing as a spoken Greek language during the archaic and classical periods: there existed a variety of local and regional dialects, which were mutually comprehensible to a larger or smaller degree. Most Greeks spoke local versions of dialects employed over wide areas of the Greek world: the three most important were Doric, spoken widely in the Peloponnese and the south Aegean; Aeolic, spoken in Boeotia, Thessaly and the north Aegean; and Ionic, spoken in Euboea and the central Aegean and related to Attic, which was spoken in Attica.[13] Nevertheless, there was no common dialect spoken in addition to the local ones, in the way that in modern Italy local dialects, such as Sicilian and Venetian, coexist with the common Italian dialect taught at school and used in the media.[14]

But things were very different as regards Greek literature. Admittedly, during the archaic and classical periods there did not exist a single common dialect used for written communication by all Greeks, in the same way that the common Italian dialect is used in writing in modern Italy. But Greeks had early on decided that different genres would be composed in a single common literary dialect, irrespective of the native dialect of the author or composer. Epic was written in an artificial literary dialect heavily based on Ionic, choral poetry was written in literary Doric, while monodic lyric and scientific prose were usually written in Ionic. Accordingly, the Boeotian Hesiod must have used Aeolic as his native tongue, but, since he composed in the epic genre, all his poetry was in the literary Ionic dialect of epic; another Boeotian, Pindar, used literary Doric for his choral poems; in tragedy spoken parts were written in literary Attic, but choral parts in a form of literary Doric, even though the authors were Athenians. Accordingly, Greek literature was Panhellenic from its

---

[9] L. G. Mitchell 2007: xxi–xxii.   [10] *Iliad*, 2.867.   [11] Lévy 1984.   [12] Cf. Hall 2002: 111–17.
[13] Colvin 2010.   [14] Hall 1997: 143–81; Bakker 2010.

earliest attestations: no matter their origins, poets had to compose their works in literary dialects shared across the Greek world.[15]

From the very beginning, composing and consuming Greek literature meant participation in a world much bigger than the poet's own community; this also applies to the content of this literature.[16] Archaic Greek literature was dominated to an unusual extent by Greek myth: we shall have the opportunity to examine in detail this phenomenon and its implications in Chapter 5 (pp. 166–8). As with all societies, Greek communities had their local myths, as well as shared myths in an immense variety of local versions, which could diverge significantly from each other.[17] From our earliest attestation of Greek myth around 700, in the poetry of Homer and Hesiod and in the earliest depictions in Greek art, we can also see that there existed Panhellenic versions of these myths, shared across the Greek world. It is particularly telling that, when artists in various regions of the Greek world started to depict myths on vases or metal ware, they largely eschewed local myths or local versions of shared Greek myths, but depicted myths in their Panhellenic form. The same applies to literature: a huge part of archaic Greek poetry is based on myths concerning expeditions involving heroes from across the Greek world (the Trojan War, Seven against Thebes, the Argonautic expedition, the hunt of the Calydonian Boar).

To sum up: one level of the Panhellenic world is its literary culture, and in particular its literary dialects and myths. This way of constructing the Greek world was already present when we come across our earliest evidence around 700; we simply cannot tell how far back into the Dark Ages (1100–700), or even into the Mycenaean world of the Late Bronze Age (1500–1200), this goes.[18] But this was a way of being Greek which continued to exist in the classical, Hellenistic and later periods.

In the course of the archaic period another level was added to the Panhellenic world. Sanctuaries and festivals are essential elements of what constitutes communities: to worship and be under the protection of a deity, to own and take care of a sanctuary, and to join together in a festival always create strong bonds of affection and identity. In the Greek world participation in a cult was restricted to members of each community, and it was a privilege to grant to outsiders the right to take part.[19] While every Greek community always had its own sanctuaries and festivals, Panhellenic sanctuaries and festivals, in which Greeks from all over the Mediterranean could

---

[15] Morpurgo Davies 2002; Tribulato 2010.   [16] Nagy 1990.
[17] Wickersham 1991; Graf 2011.   [18] Cf. Hall 2002: 30–55; Finkelberg 2005.
[19] Sourvinou-Inwood 1990.

gather together, worship their gods, and compete with each other as well as create a sense of community, emerged gradually in the course of the archaic period.

Olympia was a cult centre of regional importance during the Dark Ages, when elites from the area, but also across the Peloponnese, gathered to worship and feast; by the seventh century its radius had expanded across the whole of the Greek world, as seen in the enormous range of objects dedicated in the sanctuary. Delphi as the site of a famous oracle of Apollo was already known to Homer, but it was only during the seventh century that Delphi started to acquire a truly Panhellenic appeal.[20] The traditional date for the establishment of the Olympic Games was 776, and participation expanded quickly across the Panhellenic world: 688 saw the first victor from Asia Minor, and the first victor from the *apoikiai* of southern Italy triumphed in 672.[21] Alongside Olympia the establishment of the re-organised and expanded Pythian Games at Delphi took place in 582. Both games were held every four years, and by the early sixth century two other festivals, held every two years, were added to the Panhellenic circuit of games: the Isthmian and Nemean games were established in 582 and 573, respectively.[22]

The importance of Delphi and Olympia for the Panhellenic world can be seen in two different ways. First, that they provided a Panhellenic arena of display. In most Greek sanctuaries it was primarily the local community and its members who took part in the festivals and made splendid dedications that advertised their piety and success. But in the Panhellenic sanctuaries the vast majority of participants were not locals, but came from across the whole Greek world; moreover, these participants could see dedications from individuals and communities from across the Greek world. Furthermore, these festivals came to include athletic and musical competitions in which Greeks from all over the Mediterranean took part and competed not for monetary prizes, as in most local games, but for simple crowns. By the early fifth century at the very latest we are told that participation at the Olympic Games was restricted to Greeks, while the judges in the Olympic Games were called Hellanodicae, judges of the Greeks.[23]

Panhellenic sanctuaries and festivals were of the utmost importance for the Greek communities that emerged from the eighth century onwards across the Mediterranean and the Black Sea, in particular for the Greek communities of southern Italy and Sicily. For these communities, situated

---

[20] On the emergence of Olympia and Delphi as Panhellenic centres, see Morgan 1990.
[21] L. G. Mitchell 2007: 43.   [22] Richardson 1992.   [23] Nielsen 2007: 20–1.

far away from mainland Greece among foreign people, dedications in Panhellenic sanctuaries and participation in Panhellenic Games were essential means of maintaining their Greek identity; it is not accidental that at Olympia most of the *thesauroi*, buildings constructed by communities to house dedications and advertise their piety and wealth, were created by Greek communities from the western Mediterranean.[24]

It is important to stress, though, that the Panhellenic sanctuaries were not just places which celebrated and materialised the existence of a Panhellenic community. Panhellenic sanctuaries also made visible the constant lack of unity within the Greek world.[25] The Olympian, Nemean and Isthmian sanctuaries and games were organised and controlled by individual Greek poleis: Elis at Olympia; Corinth at the Isthmus; and, ultimately, Argos at Nemea. It was only at Delphi that the organising body, the Delphic Amphictiony, consisted of representatives from most communities of central Greece.[26] It is equally important to remember that Panhellenic sanctuaries were also places where the perennial internal fights among Greek states were exhibited in a monumental form: there were countless dedications of spoils taken from Greek enemies and monuments commemorating victories against other Greeks.[27]

But equally important is the fact that Panhellenic sanctuaries also hosted dedications from non-Greek communities, rulers and individuals. We will have plenty of opportunities to come across the dedications from the empires and kings of the East, but let us focus here on the dedications from Italy and Sicily. On the one hand, one would encounter at Delphi the dedications of the Greek *apoikia* of Taras in southern Italy, which are possibly the most jingoistic Greek monuments ever made.[28] The first monument depicted horses and captive Messapian women, the result of a Tarantine victory against the non-Greek Messapians; the second, a tithe after a victory against the Peucetians, depicted Taras and Phalanthus, the founders of Taras, standing on the dead body of the Iapygian king Opis.[29] But at Delphi one could also encounter the treasuries erected by the Etruscan city of Caere and the Etruscan–Greek *emporion* of Spina, along with a monumental dedication to Apollo by the Etruscans (or to Etruscan Apollo); at Olympia one could encounter the text of the treaty between the Greek *apoikia* of Sybaris in southern Italy and the non-Greek community of

[24] *Grandi santuari*; Mastrocinque 1993.   [25] Scott 2010.   [26] Sánchez 2001.
[27] Nielsen 2007: 71–8.   [28] Beschi 1982; Pontrandolfo and Rouveret 1983.
[29] Pausanias, 10.10.6, 10.13.10.

the Serdaioi, alongside the throne of an Etruscan king, the first Barbarian ever to make a dedication at Olympia.[30]

Panhellenic sanctuaries and festivals supported a second level of the Panhellenic world, alongside language, literature and myth; but they also exhibited the inherent disunity of the Greek world and provided an arena of display that could also be exploited by non-Greeks. A third level of the Panhellenic world was the result of confrontations with the world of empires during the Persian Wars: before we examine these confrontations and their outcome, it is essential to take a closer look at the world of empires and the role of Greeks within this world.

2.2 The world of empires

During the Late Bronze Age (1500–1200) the eastern Mediterranean and the Near East were linked together in a world-system created by the interaction between rival empires that stretched from Iran to Asia Minor and the Sudan; the Aegean communities of the time were linked to this wider world-system.[31] The collapse of this world-system around 1200 meant that in the next few centuries different regions developed in largely local terms and without any strong interconnections with other areas; accordingly, the development of the Greek communities during the Dark Ages was relatively unaffected by the states and cultures of the eastern Mediterranean. It was only around 800 that the expansion of the Assyrian Empire created a novel interconnected world of empires (see Map 2).[32] From its heartland in northern Mesopotamia, the Assyrian Empire expanded to the south and east, and was linked in constant conflict and interaction with Babylonia and Elam; to the northwest, Assyrian armies reached Asia Minor, conquered Cilicia and became enmeshed with the kingdoms of Phrygia and Lydia; to the southwest the Assyrian armies conquered Syria before reaching the Mediterranean, subdued the whole Levantine coast and came into long-term conflict with Egypt, which they even briefly conquered around the middle of the seventh century. The novelty of this interconnected world created by Assyrian expansion is illustrated by the bewilderment of the Assyrian interpreters who were unable to understand the language spoken by the emissaries of the Lydian king Gyges, at the time when Lydia first established relationships with

---

[30] Colonna 1993.   [31] van de Mieroop 2007.   [32] Kuhrt 1995; Gunter 2009.

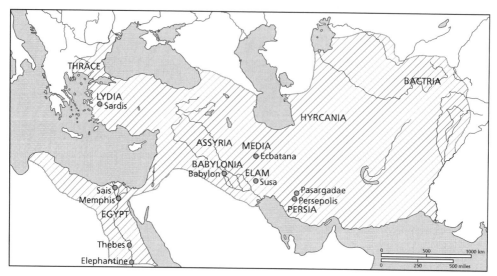

Map 2 The Persian Empire

Assyria.[33] After the destruction of the Assyrian Empire in 612, the new imperial world-system included Lydia, ruling a large part of Asia Minor, Egypt, whose rule extended to the Levant, Babylon, ruling most of Mesopotamia, and the Medes, controlling areas from the Zagros Mountains in Iran to Asia Minor.[34]

This novel world of interacting empires affected Greek communities in a variety of ways. On the one hand, there was imperial conquest; the Lydian kingdom was a powerful neighbour of the Greek communities on the coast of Asia Minor.[35] From the seventh century onwards, Lydian kings attacked, plundered and even destroyed Greek communities, until King Croesus finally succeeded in subjugating all Greek communities and forcing them to pay tribute. The Greek communities of Asia Minor experienced subjugation for the first time and would remain subject to various imperial powers, Barbarian and Greek, for the rest of their long history.[36] The Lydian kings did not install governors and garrisons in the Greek communities: their control depended on collaboration with the Greek ruling elites. Accordingly, Lydian kings developed a range of practices that would ensure the collaboration of those elites, alongside the ever-present threat of force. Intermarriage was a common practice: King Alyattes had two sons, Croesus by a Carian woman and Pantaleon by an Ionian one, while he gave one of his daughters to Melas, the tyrant of the Greek city of Ephesus.[37]

---

[33] Mellink 1991: 649.   [34] Boardman *et al.* 1991.
[35] Mellink 1991; Roosevelt 2009; Cahill 2010.   [36] Gabrielsen 2008.   [37] Georges 1994: 30–1.

The patronage of Greek sanctuaries was another particularly successful strategy.[38] Croesus sponsored the temple-building of communities under his control, such as the famous temple of Artemis at Ephesus, where some columns still bear the dedication by Croesus in Greek script,[39] and a moulding and inscription in Lydian.[40] But equally important was Lydian presence in Panhellenic sanctuaries such as Delphi. There were countless stories concerning Lydian consultations of Greek oracles and the fabulous gifts bestowed by Lydian kings,[41] but particularly interesting is the Delphian response to these gifts:

The Delphians, in return, gave Croesus and all Lydians the right of first consulting the oracle, exemption from all charges, the chief seats at festivals, and perpetual right of Delphian citizenship to whoever should wish it.[42]

This is another example of how complex Panhellenic shrines like Delphi were and the role they could play in Greek–Barbarian relationships.

Finally, imperial conquest was accompanied by cultural interaction that moved in both directions: as we shall see in more detail in later chapters, Lydian luxuries were particularly popular among Greek elites (pp. 177–8), while Greek artistic styles and iconographies were employed in the Lydian capital, Sardis (p. 252). While many of the above interactions involved collaboration and mutual exchange, we should not forget that the very same processes could produce the opposite results. Foreign conquest was always abhorrent to significant parts of the population of Greek cities; what to some Greeks were desirable Lydian luxuries, were evidence of corrupting foreign effeminacy to others.[43] It has been plausibly argued that the Greek concept of the Barbarian as the stereotypical anti-Greek was first formulated in sixth-century Asia Minor in the context of conquest and resistance.[44]

If subjection and tribute were one way in which Greek communities related to the world of empires, service and reward were another. We have already examined the story of how Thales the Milesian had served under Croesus in his confrontation with the Medes (p. 6), and the conflicts between these empires resulted in the large-scale employment of foreign soldiers. Our best evidence for Greek involvement comes from Egypt.[45] Herodotus narrates how pharaoh Psammetichus I was given an oracle to the effect that he would find support from men of bronze coming

---

[38] Buxton 2002.   [39] *SIG³*, 6; translated in *Fornara*, 28.   [40] Cahill 2010: 256.
[41] Herodotus, 1.46–55.   [42] Herodotus, 1.54.2.   [43] Kurke 1992.
[44] L. G. Mitchell 2007: 57–63; Kim 2009: 25–9.
[45] For the wider picture, see Haider 2004; Luraghi 2006.

from the sea; the oracle was fulfilled in the shape of Ionian and Carian raiders, sporting the characteristic hoplite bronze panoply, whom Psammetichus promptly employed as mercenaries, opening the way to the long-term presence of Greek and Carian mercenaries in Egypt.[46] The graffiti left by Greek mercenaries on the colossal statue of Ramses at Abu Simbel in Nubia, 700 miles away from the Mediterranean, constitutes impressive testimony for their employment:

When King Psammetichus went to Elephantine, this was written by those who, with Psammetichus son of Theocles, sailed and came above Cercis, as far as the river allowed. Potasimto led the foreign-speaking and Amasis the Egyptians. Archon son of Amoebichus and Peleqos son of Eudamus wrote us.[47]

The occasion commemorated was the campaign of Psammetichus II to Nubia in 591.[48] It is worth noting that the leader of the Greek mercenaries carries the name of an Egyptian pharaoh, obviously that of the earlier pharaoh Psammetichus I, who ruled between 664–610. It appears that Psammetichus' family had a long-term relationship with Egypt, if it had not actually migrated in the previous generation. But it was not just Greek mercenaries who left their graffiti at Abu Simbel on that occasion; other graffiti in Phoenician, Aramaic and Carian show the multiethnic composition of the Egyptian mercenary force.[49] One mercenary left a graffito in Phoenician and his name has the typical Phoenician composite form 'servant of deity x': but in this case it is 'Abd-Ptah, servant of the Egyptian god Ptah of Memphis.[50] So this Phoenician is likely to have been at least a second-generation immigrant, nicely paralleling the case of the Greek Psammetichus.

Some Greeks in Egypt managed to acquire prominent positions.[51] A demotic papyrus from Hermoupolis of the late sixth century records a petition by an Egyptian priest to a district official, requesting his help for the transportation of a dead sacred Ibis to the Fayum area for burial; the official's name is Ariston, a Greek in Egyptian service.[52] Some of these Greeks could be completely assimilated in the new Egyptian milieu. A typically Egyptian anthropoid sarcophagus with Egyptian iconography was created for a prominent individual called Wahibre-em-achet; we would never have guessed he was of Greek origin if it was not for the names of his parents, Alexicles and Zenodote (see Figure 4).[53] If Wahibre-em-achet was a Greek

[46] 2.152. See Pernigotti 1999; Vittmann 2003.
[47] *SEG* XVI, 863; translation from *Fornara*, 24.   [48] Bernard and Masson 1957.
[49] Kaplan 2003.   [50] Bernard and Masson 1957: 7.
[51] For Greeks in Egypt, see Austin 1970; Braun 1982b; Vittmann 2003: 194–235.
[52] Zaghloul 1985: 23–31; Burstein 2009: 137.   [53] Grallert 2001.

Figure 4 Sarcophagus of Wahibre-em-achet, sixth century BCE.

who had completely assimilated in his new country, other Greeks opted to return to their old homelands, bringing back the wealth and prestige they had acquired by serving abroad. Such was the sixth-century Greek who dedicated an Egyptian statue in Priene in Asia Minor with the following inscription: 'Pedon, the son of Amphinous, who brought me from Egypt, dedicated me, and Psammetichus, the Egyptian king, gave him as a reward a gold bracelet and a town for his valour.'[54]

Greek interaction with the world of empires was expanded and modified by the drastic changes that were the result of the coming to power of Cyrus, ruler of the region of Fars (Persia) in far-away Iran, in 559. Within a few years, Cyrus had subjugated the Medes, and by 546 he had defeated Croesus and conquered the Lydian kingdom; by 540 he had conquered the Neo-Babylonian Empire. It remained for Cambyses, Cyrus' son and successor after his death in 530, to conquer Egypt in 525: the system of interacting empires was now overtaken by a single Persian Empire that stretched from

[54] *SEG* XXXVII, 994; Masson and Yoyotte 1988.

central Asia all the way to the Aegean coast of Asia Minor and Egypt.[55] The Greek communities of Asia Minor which were under Lydian control were swiftly conquered by the Persians in 545 despite their resistance; because the Persians lacked a navy at the time, the Greek communities in the islands and mainland Greece escaped Persian rule for another half century, when a series of confrontations we call the Persian Wars changed for good the nature of interactions between the Greek world and the world of empires.[56]

We shall examine the Persian Wars in the next section; for the time being it is essential to explore the nature of the Persian Empire and its forms of interaction with the Greeks. The Persian Empire was a complex structure governed in a variety of different ways; to an important extent, it was based on a multitude of pre-existing states and communities. Old kingdoms, such as Egypt and Babylonia, were maintained, and the Persian kings ruled in Egypt as pharaohs and in Babylonia as the traditional rulers of the land. Many areas within the Persian Empire were not unified kingdoms before Persian conquest, but were divided between multiple small polities: in some of these areas the city-state was the preponderant state form, in others local dynasts exercised more personal forms of power. In such areas (e.g., Phoenicia, Cyprus, Lycia and Caria) communities continued to be governed in their traditional local form; the same also applied to the Greek communities of Asia Minor that came under Persian control.[57]

The extent to which the Persians intervened in the affairs of subject Greek communities could range widely. One option was to give Persian support to citizens who were trying to rule their communities as tyrants: in that case the Persians provided a court of appeal to decide the perennial internecine struggles within Greek communities.[58] In other cases the Persians would grant the revenues or even the rule over a Greek community to individuals they wanted to reward. The most famous example is that of Themistocles, the renegade Athenian leader who sought refuge at the Persian court and was granted the revenues of three Greek cities under Persian control: Magnesia on the Maeander for his bread; Myous for meat; and Lampsacus for wine.[59] The descendants of the exiled Spartan king Demaratus were still ruling Greek communities in Asia Minor in the fourth century,[60] while Xenophon describes how Mania, the widow of the Greek ruler of the city of Dardanus in the Troad, managed to convince the Persian satrap Tissaphernes to entrust her with ruling her husband's domains.[61] Under

---

[55] Briant 2002a: 31–61.   [56] Balcer 1995: 43–73.   [57] Briant 2002a: 472–511.
[58] Austin 1990.   [59] Plutarch, *Life of Themistocles*, 29.7.   [60] Hofstetter 1978: 45–6.
[61] *Hellenica*, 3.1.10–13.

certain conditions the Persians could also support broader constitutional forms in Greek communities: Herodotus presents the Persian general Mardonius suppressing tyrannies in the Greek poleis of Asia Minor and setting up democracies in their place.[62] Finally, the Persians could underwrite procedures for arbitration and the settlement of disputes among Greek communities: Herodotus reports that the Persian satrap Artaphernes forced the Ionians 'to bind themselves by oath to settle their differences by arbitration instead of raiding',[63] and a fourth-century Greek inscription records how the Persian satrap Strouthas delegated a dispute among Ionian communities to Ionian judges, who submitted their resolution to the satrap for the final decision.[64]

How did the Persian Empire manage to hold together this vast mosaic of states, communities and rulers? While the Persians usually maintained pre-existing structures, they superimposed on them a new administrative structure that was largely manned by the Persian dominant ethno-class, which owed full allegiance to the Persian king. In large kingdoms like Egypt and Babylonia native kings were suppressed and Persian power was represented by satraps, members of the Persian aristocracy entrusted with governing substantial areas in the name of the Persian king; in areas that were not unified as 'national' kingdoms before Persian annexation, the Persian king appointed satraps who coexisted with local rulers and self-governing communities. While the bulk of governmental functions was exercised by local structures manned by members of the local elites, Persian power in the provinces was maintained by the presence of satraps and their courts, as well as garrisons and guards at areas of strategic importance.[65] At the same time, it was essential to maintain communication between the local communities and rulers, on the one hand, and the satraps and the king, on the other, as well as between the imperial centre and the satraps. Because the Persian kings were itinerant, and constantly moved their court in the course of every year, they maintained palaces in Persepolis in Persia, Ecbatana in Media, Susa in Elam and Babylon in Mesopotamia. Constructing and maintaining these palaces and manning the courts, as well as the bureaucratic structures that kept the system running, necessitated enormous resources in wealth and manpower.

Communication, management of resources, security and reward of loyalty were the four main tasks of the imperial system. The Persian Empire was held together by the personal bonds that linked the Persian king with the Persian aristocracy, who served the king in positions in the army, in the

---

[62] 6.43.   [63] 6.42.1.   [64] *SIG*³, 134; translated in *R-O*, 16.   [65] Tuplin 1987.

court and in satrapal administration; similar personal bonds linked the king with the various native rulers within the Persian Empire. While the dominant ethno-class was overwhelmingly Persian, this does not mean that people of other origins did not gain entrance to the court, or gain power and prestige through the Persian king and his officers.

The Persian kings were famous for keeping a list of their benefactors and for generously rewarding them:[66] Histiaeus of Miletus was highly honoured at court for saving Dareius I in his disastrous expedition to Scythia;[67] Syloson of Samos became tyrant of his island as a reward for making a gift to Dareius when the latter was still a commoner;[68] while Xeinagoras of Halicarnassus was given the rule of Cilicia for saving the life of Xerxes' brother.[69] But the Persian king could also honour his valiant enemies: when Metiochus, the son of Miltiades, the Athenian general who defeated the Persians at Marathon, was captured by the Phoenicians and sent to Dareius, he was not punished, but given possessions and a Persian woman, and his children counted as Persians.[70] Prominent Greek exiles often found refuge at the court of the Persian king or of his satraps: the Athenian tyrant Hippias, the Spartan king Demaratus and the exiled Athenian politician Themistocles are among the most famous examples, who were often rewarded by becoming rulers of Greek communities under Persian control.

Let us continue with communication. Empires include a variety of different peoples speaking their own languages and thus necessitate communication intermediaries: taxation and conscription, the formulation and promulgation of inventories, treaties, edicts and correspondence would have been impossible without bilingual or multilingual individuals in imperial service.[71] We should distinguish between oral and written communication. Oral communication with Persian authorities necessitated learning Persian, or using interpreters who spoke Persian; Greeks who found themselves at imperial courts, such as the Milesian Histiaeus and the Athenians Themistocles and Alcibiades, managed to learn Persian, while Laomedon of Mytilene was put in charge of Barbarian prisoners by Alexander the Great due to his knowledge of Persian, acquired while Mytilene was in the Persian sphere of influence.[72]

Written communication was more complex. The Persian language was little used outside oral communication; Persian officials would give their instructions orally in Persian, but these would be transcribed into a variety

---

[66] Briant 2002a: 302–54.	[67] Herodotus, 5.11; Hofstetter 1978: 90–2.
[68] Herodotus, 3.139–41; Hofstetter 1978: 169.	[69] Herodotus, 9.107; Hofstetter 1978: 188.
[70] Herodotus, 6.41; Hofstetter 1978: 131.	[71] Briant 2002a: 472–511.	[72] Asheri 1983: 20–2.

of languages and scripts by the multilingual scribes who communicated them through written media. The Persians were happy to use a variety of languages and scripts for written communication, and accordingly a variety of scribes and administrators of different origins. The fifth-century archives of Persepolis, one of the Persian capitals, provide a snapshot of the multi-ethnic character of the imperial bureaucracy and its means of communication.[73] The Persepolis Fortification archive, dating between 509–494, concerns mostly the management of resources and personnel in the region of Fars, where Persepolis was located. The most prominent individuals in the bureaucracy are, of course, Persians, but one also encounters an Egyptian, a Scythian and an Indian in prominent positions, alongside an individual who is called Yauna (the Ionian) and is likely to have been a Greek.[74] The range of languages used in the archive is equally impressive.[75] Although most tablets are written in a cuneiform script in the language of Elam, an area close to Persepolis with a long scribal tradition, there are also cuneiform tablets written in Babylonian and a unique cuneiform tablet in Persian, as well as alphabetic Aramaic subscriptions on Elamite tablets and tablets written in Aramaic. More surprising is the presence of a tablet in Phrygian, alongside one in Greek, which records the distribution of wine: 'wine, two maris. Tebet'. The use of the Babylonian month-name Tebet by a Greek scribe operating in Persepolis illustrates the complexity of life within the imperial bureaucracy.[76]

Taxation and security were the two main preoccupations of satrapal authorities. These necessitated the presence of administrators, soldiers and other professionals; an imperial diaspora emerged out of thousands of people who migrated and often resettled from one corner of the empire to another in order to man these structures. The Persian kings used grants of land and other resources as a means of establishing a settled military and administrative force in faraway provinces. Thousands of Persians and other Iranians migrated and settled in Asia Minor, along with other ethnic groups.[77] A characteristic example of this imperial diaspora is the Persian noble Asidates, who had received a land grant in the valley of the River Caicus near Pergamon in Asia Minor. He lived in a residence fortified with towers, along with his family and hundreds of slaves, and controlled many dependent villages. In this area there also lived other Persians, alongside

---

[73] Briant 2002a: 422–71.   [74] Cf. Tavernier 2007: 365.
[75] Lewis 1994; Stolper and Tavernier 2007.   [76] Translation from Kuhrt 2007: 763–5.
[77] Sekunda 1988.

Syrian infantrymen and Hyrcanian cavalrymen, who were benefiting from land grants and were crucial for maintaining Persian control of the area.[78]

Apart from the great beneficiaries, therefore, we also have to take into account the thousands of soldiers and guards needed to maintain peace and security, and to man local operations. Part of these needs was covered by the settlement of soldiers and the allocation of small land grants for their maintenance; but the satraps also covered their needs by hiring mercenaries. We have already seen how thousands of Greek mercenaries were making a living by serving the Saite pharaohs in Egypt; the Persian Empire continued to provide steady employment for Greeks, as well as mercenaries from many other groups. Tens of thousands of Greek mercenaries were constantly in Persian service; by the time of Alexander's invasion of the Persian Empire, there were possibly more Greeks fighting in the Persian army than there were in Alexander's. We shall have plenty of opportunities to come across Greek mercenaries in Persian service.[79]

The Persian kings ruled over a multinational empire: they proudly declared in their inscriptions that 'the spear of a Persian man has gone forth far',[80] and the splendid reliefs from the Persepolis palace stairways depict processions of tribute-bearers from all the subject communities of the empire.[81] King Dareius I's description of the building of his palace at Susa parallels the illustrations at Persepolis by listing the far-flung origins of the materials used and of the craftsmen that fashioned them:

This palace, which I built at Susa, its materials were brought from far away . . . The cedarwood was brought from a mountain called Lebanon; the Assyrian people brought it as far as Babylon; from Babylon the Carians and Ionians brought it as far as Susa; the *yaka*-wood was brought from Gandhara and Carmania. The gold which was worked here was brought from Lydia and Bactria; the lapis lazuli and the carnelian which was worked here were brought from Sogdiana; the turquoise which was worked here was brought from Chorasmia. The silver and ebony were brought from Egypt; the decoration, with which the walls were ornamented, was brought from Ionia; the ivory which was worked here was brought from Nubia, India and Arachosia. The stone columns which were worked here were brought from a village called Abiradu in Elam; the masons who crafted the stone were Ionians and Lydians . . .[82]

This was no idle rhetoric: the use of Ionian Greek craftsmen at the imperial palaces of Pasargadae, Persepolis and Susa, hundreds of miles away from the Aegean, is documented in many different forms.[83] The

---

[78] Xenophon, *Anabasis*, 7.8.8–24.   [79] Seibt 1977.   [80] Translation from Kuhrt 2007: 503.
[81] Root 1979: 227–84.   [82] Translation from Kuhrt 2007: 492.   [83] Boardman 2000: 128–34.

employment of Ionian craftsmen at the palace of Pasargadae is attested by
the employment of carving tools that were used only in western Asia Minor
and not in Mesopotamia or Iran;[84] one artist working on the feet of a relief
of Dareius I left Greek-style doodles of human heads and animals;[85] amid
the limestone quarries of Persepolis, a cliff bears a Greek inscription with the
name of the Ionian contractor: 'I am [the property] of Pytharchus'.[86] Greek
artistic works could be seen in Persian palaces, and some interesting finds
were made in the Persepolis Treasury: if the statue of a female figure
identified as Penelope might be the result of looting a Greek sanctuary,[87] a
marble plaque depicting Heracles and Apollo was most probably made by a
Greek artist in Persepolis.[88] But the multicultural workforce did not include
only artists. The archives recording the distribution of foodstuffs to palace
workers and labourers working royal land make references to skilled artisans such as Lycian craftsmen and Lydian silversmiths, as well as workers of
various nationalities, including Egyptians, Cappadocians, Lycians, Carians,
Bactrians, Syrians and Ionians.[89]

These craftsmen and labourers were probably recruited through conscription and deportation, two age-old practices of the Assyrian and Neo-
Babylonian empires which were also adopted by the Persians.[90] Deportation
could be used both as a punitive measure against enemies and as protection
for friends, coupled with the productive exploitation of unused lands
through the deportees.[91] Herodotus reports the deportation of defeated
Milesians from Asia Minor,[92] Eretrians from mainland Greece,[93]
Paeonians from Thrace[94] and Barcaeans from Libya as a punishment.[95]
But the Branchidae from Miletus, who had betrayed the temple of Didyma
to the Persians, were resettled thousands of miles away in modern-day
Uzbekistan, as protection from reprisals in the aftermath of Persian defeat;
two centuries later Alexander the Great came across their descendants, who
had still kept some of their native customs, but had become bilingual.[96]

Things could be different with those who offered their personal services
to the Persian kings. Assyrian kings employed in their courts Egyptian
scribes and priests alongside Syrian and Anatolian augurs,[97] and the
Persian kings were equally happy to recruit and employ talent wherever
they could find it. Some of this talent was recruited as captives or purchased
as slaves; this was particularly the case with the courtesans who filled the

---

[84] Nylander 1971.   [85] Richter 1946: 28.   [86] *IEOG*, 228; translation from *Fornara*, 46.
[87] Olmstead 1950; Palagia 2008 argues that it was a gift by the polis of Thasos.
[88] Roaf and Boardman 1980.   [89] Kuhrt 2007: 793–801.   [90] Oded 1979.
[91] Briant 2002a: 433–4.   [92] 6.20.   [93] 6.119.   [94] 5.12–17.   [95] 4.200–4.
[96] Hammond 1998.   [97] Radner 2009.

harems of the Persian kings. The renegade Themistocles managed to avoid the checkpoints in order to reach the Persian court by concealing himself in a closed wagon and by having his attendants claim that they were carrying a woman of Greek origin, whom they were taking from Ionia to one of the Persian nobles at the palace.[98] There were plenty of stories about Greek concubines at the Persian court, but the most famous was by far Aspasia from Phocaea in Asia Minor, who rose to become a powerful concubine of Artaxerxes II.[99] Entertainers also included dancers, like Zenon the Cretan, who was the favourite dancer of Artaxerxes II.[100]

Persian kings were also very fond of foreign doctors: the fame of Egyptian doctors brought them to the Persian court, but we also know of Greek doctors like Democedes of Croton and Ctesias of Cnidos; interestingly, both doctors seemed to have initially entered the Persian court as captives, although they both subsequently rose very highly in prestige and managed to return to their homelands.[101] Other foreigners were recruited to the Persian court as a result of their fame and without coercion: Dareius II, learning of the great exploits of the Thessalian athlete Polydamas, invited him to the court at Susa, where he showed his prowess by fighting three of the Immortals (royal guards) and killing all three of them. Polydamas dedicated a statue at Olympia, on the base of which the athlete is depicted defeating the Immortals in front of the king.[102]

The above examples make clear the multiple ways in which Greeks related to the world of empires as subjects, mercenaries, vassals, beneficiaries, professionals, artisans or entertainers. There was a constant Greek presence in satrapal and royal courts even as far away as Persepolis; and that presence could work in a variety of different ways. This is illustrated nicely through the example of Conon, an Athenian general who had become admiral of the Persian navy a few years after 400; when sending a letter to the Persian king, he asked the carrier to deliver it through the intermediary of Greeks present at the court: the dancer Zenon and the doctor Polycritus, or, in their absence, Ctesias the doctor.[103] In the end, it was Ctesias the doctor who acted as diplomatic envoy of the Persian king to Greek commanders in Persian service like Conon, or to Greek states at war with Persia, like Sparta.[104] We shall return time and again to the importance of these Greeks in imperial service (see pp. 153–4, 218–22).

---

[98] Plutarch, *Life of Themistocles*, 26.5.   [99] Stevenson 1997: 45–56; Kuhrt 2007: 593–4.
[100] Plutarch, *Life of Artaxerxes*, 21.2; Hofstetter 1978: 190.
[101] Griffiths 1987; Llewellyn-Jones and Robson 2010: 12–17.
[102] Hofstetter 1978: 154; Briant 2002a: 254.   [103] Plutarch, *Life of Artaxerxes*, 21.3.
[104] Llewellyn-Jones and Robson 2010: 17–18.

2.3 The Persian Wars (490–479)

The Persian Wars were part of the wider process of the expansion of the Persian Empire into Europe and the ways in which communities and individuals tried to oppose or take advantage of this expansion.[105] Unfortunately, the fact that effectively all our evidence for these wars comes from the Greek side means that we have to be particularly careful to reconstruct a balanced account. The conquests of Cyrus the Great had brought Persian power to the Aegean coast of Asia Minor; Dareius I and his son, Xerxes, attempted in a series of campaigns to expand their empire across the sea into Greece, Thrace and the Black Sea region.[106] The expedition against the Scythians in 513 might have been unsuccessful, but by 500 the Thracian polities, the Macedonian kingdom, and the Greek poleis on the coasts of Thrace and Macedonia were under Persian control.[107] The communities and individuals that faced imperial expansion had a range of options of how to respond: some decided to resist, even in the face of likely annihilation; others decided that resistance was futile, and that the only course was to negotiate a settlement with the conqueror, or, even better, to use the conquest as an opportunity to settle old scores with neighbours and enemies, or expand their own sphere of influence; finally, individuals could see imperial expansion as an opportunity to win power and prestige, either by using Persian power in order to become rulers of their communities, or by leading opposition to Persian expansion.

This complex range of strategies was the cause of the Ionian revolt (499–494), the prelude to the Persian Wars (490–479).[108] We have seen how the Greek poleis of Asia Minor were often ruled by tyrants who relied on Persian support in order to dominate their communities.[109] One of the most telling indications of this mutual support concerned the Scythian expedition of Dareius I, in which the Ionian tyrants were trusted with guarding the bridge of boats that allowed Dareius to cross the Danube and attack the Scythians. According to Herodotus, when during the Persian invasion of Scythia the Scythians suggested to the Ionians guarding the Danube bridge that they should destroy it and thus annihilate the Persian army and win freedom for themselves, the Ionian tyrants refused, fearing that the destruction of the Persian Empire would also mean their

---

[105] For the account below, see Lazenby 1993; Balcer 1995; Burn 2002; Cawkwell 2005; Wallinga 2005.

[106] Briant 2002a: 139–61.   [107] Fol and Hammond 1988.   [108] Georges 2000.

[109] Austin 1990.

own demise as rulers;[110] their loyalty was even rewarded with possessions in Thrace (p. 120), showing how non-Persians could benefit from Persian expansion. Persian support for tyrants also meant that opponents of tyrants could see themselves as opponents of Persian rule; at the same time, individuals and communities outside the Persian Empire could try to use Persian power for their own benefit.[111] In 500 a group of exiles from the Greek island of Naxos asked Aristagoras, the tyrant of Miletus, to support their attempt to return home by force. Aristagoras managed to broker a deal with the Persians to send an expedition that would simultaneously conquer Naxos for Persia and restore the exiles to power.[112] But the campaign failed, allegedly through treason. At that point Aristagoras' relationship with the Persians became very strained, and he decided to instigate a revolt by taking advantage of the anti-Persian and anti-tyrannical feelings of the Greeks of Asia Minor.

The Greeks deposed their tyrants and sought allies; the revolt was soon joined by the Carians, who inhabited southwest Asia Minor, and by the Greek communities in Cyprus. Aristagoras tried to convince the Spartans to help, but he succeeded in getting support only from the Athenians and the Eretrians, who sent a few ships. The Greek force was successful in getting all the way to Sardis, the seat of the Persian satrap, where they failed to take the acropolis, but burned the famous temple of Artemis. At that point the Athenian and Eretrian forces left for home; but they had participated in a sacrilege and the Persians would not forget it. The war dragged on for many years, until finally in 494 the Ionian navy was crushed in the sea battle of Lade near Miletus and the revolt was over. The Persians re-conquered the cities, but the most memorable result of the revolt was the complete destruction of Miletus, the largest and most famous city of Ionia. This made a huge impression upon the whole Greek world.[113]

After crushing the revolt, the Persians were bent on punishing Athens and Eretria, which had supported the Ionians, and on extending their empire. Accordingly, they sent messengers to the Greek cities to ask for submission in the form of earth and water. Many Greek communities concurred, but the Athenians and the Spartans replied by throwing the sacrosanct messengers from a cliff and into a well, respectively. The first Persian expedition to punish Athens and Eretria took place in 492, but it was abandoned when the land forces encountered strong resistance from the Thracian tribes and the fleet was allegedly annihilated by the turbulent sea in the north Aegean. In 490 another force was sent, this time straight to

[110] 4.137.   [111] Gillis 1979.   [112] Herodotus, 5.30–1.   [113] Herodotus, 6.21.2.

Athens and Eretria through the Aegean; Eretria was conquered and destroyed, and its inhabitants were moved into forced exile deep within the Persian Empire. When the Persian forces landed at Marathon, it seemed that the fate of Athens would be no different. But the Athenian general Miltiades managed to choose a battlefield where the Persians were not able to employ their numerous and strong cavalry. In the battle the Athenians kept their centre weak, but strengthened their flanks and by means of a fake retreat managed to encircle the Persians and inflict a very heavy defeat on them. This was a significant victory for the Athenians, which saved their city and their democracy.[114]

The Persians were not ready to accept defeat. But the death of Dareius I in 486 and a number of rebellions under his son and successor, Xerxes, meant that preparations for a new campaign in which the king would participate personally did not start again until 484. It is important to note again that there were Greeks who were counting on the Persian invasion to settle their scores with other Greeks and to take account of the role they played in convincing the Persians to plan the expedition.[115] When it became clear to the Greeks that a large-scale invasion was inevitable, a number of communities decided to collaborate to face this threat. It is remarkable that the vast majority of Greek communities did not participate in this common front; there were around a thousand Greek communities at this point of time, but only thirty-one of them were finally represented on the victory monument at Delphi that commemorated the final Greek victory at Plataea.[116] Many Greek communities were under the rule of the Persians and in fact participated in the war on the Persian side. Despite the Greek attempt to lure these Greeks to abandon the Persians, or at least to fight without conviction, there were very few defections and in most of the cases the Greeks on the Persian side fought valiantly against their Greek compatriots. On the other hand, many Greek communities decided to stay neutral in the conflict and wait to see how things would turn out before taking sides. This was the case with the Cretans and the Corcyraeans,[117] but most notoriously with the citizens of Argos in the Peloponnese.[118]

The participation of many Greek states in the Greek alliance often had more to do with local Greek rivalries than with any overall national attachment or antipathy to the Persians. This cut both ways. For some of those Greek communities who fought with the Persians that was not merely the result of necessity: they saw in the Persian invasion a great opportunity to

---

[114] Cawkwell 2005: 88–9; Billows 2010; Krentz 2010.   [115] Herodotus, 7.6.
[116] *SIG*³, 31; translated in *Fornara*, 59.   [117] Herodotus, 7.168–9.   [118] Herodotus, 7.150.

settle old scores and advance their position vis-à-vis their old Greek enemies. The Thessalians saw in the Persian invasion an opportunity to defeat their Phocian enemies, and a similar motive applies to the Thebans, who were the most active Greek collaborators of the Persians. Conversely, according to Herodotus some Greek states, like the Phocians, participated in the Greek alliance primarily because their enemies collaborated with the Persians.[119]

Nevertheless, the decision of a number of Greek communities to fight together against the common enemy was something unprecedented and impressive in itself. Three of the most important Greek allies had been engaged in constant hostilities with each other. Only a few years before, the Spartans had invaded Attica twice; and Athens and Aegina had been in constant warfare for decades. In fact, it is possible that the famous Athenian fleet which saved the Greeks in Salamis was originally created for the war with Aegina; had that war not existed, it is likely that the Athenians would never have allocated so many resources to creating this fleet and the Greeks would have been defeated! Therefore, the agreement between these fiercely antagonistic states to fight the war jointly and to accept the leadership of Sparta on both land and sea was a significant achievement.

To understand the Persian Wars we have first to underline the significant differences between the compositions of the two forces. The Persian army was based on the great skill of their cavalry and their light-armed troops, in particular the archers; in contrast, the Greeks had effectively no cavalry or archers of any great worth. Their strong point was the hoplite phalanx, a force consisting of heavily armoured infantrymen fighting in line and not in single combat. In the case of the navy, the Persians depended on the skill of their main contingent, the Phoenicians, who were able to outperform the Greeks in naval drills. What about numerical superiority? The earliest Greek accounts present the Persian force as immense: a victory epigram immediately after the wars speaks of a Persian army of 3 million,[120] while Herodotus himself calculated more than 5 million.[121] These numbers are clearly absurd, and they were the result both of the Greek dread of the vast Persian Empire, and of the wish to magnify the Greek achievement by stressing the enormous size of the defeated enemy force. There is nevertheless no doubt that the Persian army and navy were much larger than the Greek forces; but they were not large enough for the Persians to be able to employ their land and sea forces independently. This is best seen in the case of the Persian navy: the Persians did not split their naval forces at any point

---

[119] 8.30.   [120] Herodotus, 7.228.   [121] 7.184–7.

in the campaign, although it would have been clearly to their advantage; this was obviously because had they done so, they would have lost their numerical superiority.

The main problem with the Greek strategy was finding the right place to stage a defence; it was early on agreed that they stood no chance in open combat with the Persians. The Persian cavalry and archers would have annihilated the Greek infantry before it could come to close combat, while Persian numerical superiority would have decided the battle in their favour. Only a confined space, where the Persians would be unable to employ their cavalry and their full force, could give the Greeks a chance of winning. The same applied to naval battle: only in a confined space, where the Phoenicians would not be able to take advantage of their lighter ships and their superior skills in drilling, would the Greek navy stand any chance. Therefore, the aim was to find such a confined place of defence both for the army and for the navy. For the Peloponnesians, who made up the preponderant part of the land forces, such an ideal place would be the Corinthian isthmus. A wall across the isthmus would be easy to defend, and the navy could stay nearby and help the land forces. But this effectively meant abandoning the allies who lived outside the Peloponnese, and in particular the Athenians. And it was also, as Herodotus pointed it out, a rather stupid idea.[122] If the Persian navy was free to roam the seas, it would be in a position to land forces anywhere in the Peloponnese, and the wall at the isthmus would be of little help. Only if the Persian navy was neutralised or defeated, would there be a serious prospect of Greek victory.

The alternative scenario was to find a place that would offer a good defensive position and would also protect the allies outside the Peloponnese. An initial plan to make a stand at the northernmost point of the entrance to Thessaly was abandoned when it was discovered that the Persians could easily bypass it by taking an alternative route to southern Greece. When the Greeks abandoned that plan, the Thessalians immediately abandoned the Greek alliance and joined the Persians.[123] It was then decided that the next best choice was Thermopylae; this is a pass in central Greece where communication between the north and the south was restricted to a small passage between the sea and high mountains. The narrow pass could be held by a small force and the Persians would not be able to employ their cavalry or take advantage of their numerical superiority. At the same time, the cape of Artemision opposite Thermopylae provided an ideal position for the Greek navy; it would make

---

[122] 7.139.   [123] Herodotus, 7.172–3.

communication between the army and navy easy, the navy could provide supplies for the army by sea, and the Greek army and navy could fight together and help each other. The plan of joint army–navy action at Thermopylae and Artemision was thus well thought out and stood a good chance of success.

Nevertheless, it failed. Within three days of its appearance, the Persian army had annihilated the Greek force and killed its leader, the Spartan king Leonidas, while the Greek navy after a rather inconclusive series of clashes had abandoned Artemision and sailed to the south. Both the sea and land routes for Attica were completely open; this was effectively a total catastrophe. But this is not the way the ancient Greeks presented Thermopylae and the way they handed down its memory to posterity. Thermopylae is still remembered as an heroic stand of a few courageous fighters ready to give their lives for their country and their values against an innumerable host of slavish barbarians. What, then, did really happen? The Peloponnesians sent 4,000 soldiers, 300 of whom were Spartans under Leonidas. Along with hoplites from other Greek allies, there were 7,100 soldiers in total. The fleet at nearby Artemision had about 300 ships, which would mean a force of tens of thousands of sailors and marines. Why were there so few people in Thermopylae? Probably because the Spartans and the Peloponnesians, who were at the time also celebrating the Olympic Games, thought that this advance force would be sufficient to keep the pass for some time and the reinforcements would have time to arrive after the celebrations. This was a terrible miscalculation. The Greek forces were able to hold the pass for the first two days with success; but when a local called Ephialtes guided the Persians through a path over the mountain that led to the rear of the Greek force holding the pass, all was effectively lost. The Greeks put up an heroic fight and the Spartans under Leonidas chose to stay and die rather than retreat, as was their custom.[124] Thus, the road to the south was now completely open for Xerxes and subjugation seemed inevitable. The Persian forces arrived in evacuated Attica and burned Athens and its temples in retaliation for the burning of the temple in Sardis in 499.

The Greek navy was now stationed in the straits of Salamis opposite Athens. It was an ideal position to fight the Persians, since the confined space would not allow the Persians to take advantage of their superior numbers and skill. But why did the Persians accept the situation and fight at Salamis? Greek tradition has it that Xerxes was fooled by a secret message from Themistocles, the leader of the Athenian forces, to the effect that the

---

[124] Albertz 2006; Cartledge 2006.

Greeks were about to flee and he should block their flight and force them to fight.[125] But it would have been in the Persian interest to allow the Greek fleet to move to the isthmus, where the naval battle would take place in the open sea. The Persians needed the fleet to support the forthcoming attack at the isthmus, and the Persian fleet could not move to the isthmus and leave the Greek fleet in its rear. The sailing season was drawing to a close, and soon, if there was no battle, the Persian army and navy would have to retreat to Thessaly to over-winter.[126] Thus, the Persians decided to force a battle and in this they miscalculated completely. The battle was a clear Greek victory.[127] Xerxes decided at this point to return to Asia and entrust the continuing operations to Mardonius; the Persian navy would retreat with him to guard the Hellespont and ensure the safe passage of the king, while the Persian army would retreat to Thessaly for the winter.

There was no longer a sea threat to the Greeks, but the Persian army was not defeated. In the spring of 479, Mardonius tried to woo the Athenians into abandoning the Greek alliance and ally itself with Persia by offering extremely generous terms. In front of the Spartan and Persian ambassadors the Athenians refused to do so and opted to fight for the common cause; their answer, according to Herodotus, is very interesting in also giving what is effectively a definition of Greek identity:

For there are many great reasons why we should not do this, even if we so desired; first and foremost, the burning and destruction of the adornments and temples of our gods, whom we are constrained to avenge to the utmost rather than make pacts with the perpetrator of these things, and next the kinship of all Greeks in blood and speech, and the shrines of gods and the sacrifices that we have in common, and the likeness of our way of life, to all of which it would not befit the Athenians to be false.[128]

This Athenian refusal to abandon the Greek alliance was crucial, as Herodotus would recognise many years later.[129]

Despite the brave Athenian reply, the Spartans were reluctant to send out a military force to face the Persians and stop them from invading Attica for a second time. This clearly shows how fragile the balance of the Greek alliance was; in the end, and after the second devastation of Attica, the Spartans had no option but to lead a combined Greek force of around 40,000 infantry to the Boeotian city of Plataea, where the decisive battle took place in the

[125] Herodotus, 8.75. [126] Cawkwell 2005: 106–10. [127] Strauss 2004. [128] 8.144.2.
[129] 7.139.

summer of 479. Each side was stationed on opposite banks of the River Asopus; for many days neither side was willing to give battle, because no one was willing to cross the river and give battle on the side whose terrain favoured the plans of the opponents. Finally, after the Greek retreat under Persian pressure to the hills close to Plataea, the Persians, under the impression that the Greeks were retreating without formation, attacked and were ultimately defeated. Tradition has it that on the very same day as the battle of Plataea the Persians were also defeated by the Greek naval force at Mycale in Asia Minor. A much-reduced Greek fleet was convinced by Ionians who were ready to revolt to advance from Delos to Samos. Mycale was on the opposite coast of Asia Minor, and there a land battle took place between the Greek and Persian forces in which the Greeks were victorious. Victory meant that the Greek cities of Asia Minor could now be set free from Persian control. The Persian offensive of 480/79 led to outcomes which were opposite to those envisaged.

2.4 The effects of the Persian Wars (479–431)

There is little doubt that Greek history would have developed in a very different way if the Persian Wars had had a different outcome, or if they had not happened at all.[130] We can start by asking two essential questions: how did the Greeks try to account for their victory? And what were the effects of the Persian Wars? Given the odds, it seemed a miracle that a small, perennially quarrelling alliance was able to defeat the forces of a great empire. The Greeks devised a number of explanations, which we shall also examine in Chapter 5 (pp. 191–3). It was possible to explain the outcome in traditional terms as a religious transgression of the hubristic Persians. It was also possible to give a political explanation: the Greeks saw their struggle as a fight to secure their freedom from Persian domination. Until that time freedom was a concept which described the legal and social status of individuals; but in the course of the Persian Wars and their aftermath freedom was transferred from a description of personal status to the condition of the community at large. Furthermore, the Greeks attributed their miraculous victory to the great political differences between Persian monarchy and Greek polities. The Persian Empire was seen as the tyranny of a despot who ruled autocratically over slavish subjects; thus, the concept of tyranny as political slavery was now transferred to describe oriental

---

[130] For the effects of the Persian Wars, see Bridges *et al.* 2007.

monarchies. On the contrary, the Greeks were able to fight valiantly because they were not ruled like slaves, but were free citizens who cared for the good of their communities.[131]

It was also possible to locate the Persian Wars within a narrative of the long-term conflict between Greeks and Barbarians. The Persian Wars were seen as but one episode in a story that had started with the Panhellenic expedition against Troy. This interpretation is already attested immediately after the wars in the poetry that commemorated the Greek victory, as we shall see in Chapter 5 (pp. 189–90). This use of myth was evidence of a crucial transformation. Until that time the Panhellenic world consisted of diverse communities whose unity was maintained by a literature based on Panhellenic myth and written in shared literary dialects, and by Panhellenic shrines and festivals. The Panhellenic community existed in the distant past, when heroes from all over Greece had joined together on expeditions like that against Troy, and in a separate present, when Greeks joined together to worship the gods and participate in games. By linking the heroic past with the present, the Persian Wars had brought into existence a third level of the Panhellenic world as a political community united in a common purpose: the fight against a common enemy. The problem was that this Panhellenic community was a project and not a given; the Greek world lacked a centre and was perennially ravaged by hostilities among its members. As at Troy under Agamemnon, or during the Persian Wars under Sparta, its unity and common action were impossible without a leader. Given the ambitions of Greek states, it was always possible to exploit the Panhellenic project as a means of achieving hegemony over the Greek world.[132]

The collapse of Persian expansion in Europe left a gap everywhere that communities and rulers tried to fill in different ways; but the common factor was the emergence of powerful states which came to exercise power over areas and resources unimaginable before. In the aftermath of the defeat of the Persian expedition to Scythia, the Royal Scythians managed to create a state that exercised power over a large number of non-Greek people and Greek communities in an area that stretched from the River Don to the Danube;[133] in Thrace, the Odrysian dynasty exploited the gap and created a state that exercised rule over an area that stretched from the Danube to the Aegean.[134] In the Aegean it was Athens that emerged as the big winner out of the gap left by the Persian defeat.

---

[131] Raaflaub 2004: 58–89.   [132] L. G. Mitchell 2007: 77–104, 169–94.   [133] Georges 1987.
[134] Archibald 1998: 93–125.

The war did not stop after the battle of Plataea, when the last vestiges of the invading army were extinguished; the Greek alliance immediately started a campaign to liberate the Greek communities of Asia Minor and the Thracian coast that were still under Persian control. For the first few months the Spartans remained the leaders of the campaigns, but after a while the harsh attitude of the Spartan regent Pausanias led the Greeks of Asia Minor to offer the leadership to the Athenians.[135] Athens made the most out of the kudos of the Persian Wars; it was the only Greek city that had defeated the Persians on its own at Marathon, and the city which had undergone the greatest sacrifices for the common cause. The Athenians had seen their country invaded and their city devastated twice in 480–479; even more, they had refused to abandon the Greek cause even when the Spartans were failing to protect Attica and Mardonius was offering extremely advantageous terms if the Athenians collaborated; and it was the Athenian navy that was crucial for the Greek victory in the Persian Wars and for taking the offensive against the Persians in the Aegean. For the Athenians, their role in the Persian Wars became the justification for the hegemonic role they assumed in the Panhellenic community and their right to rule other Greeks.[136]

In 478, the Athenians and hundreds of Greek communities on the Aegean coast and the islands created a new alliance, which modern scholars have called the Delian League because in the first few decades the treasury of the alliance and its meetings were held in the sanctuary of Apollo at Delos. This was a bilateral alliance between the Athenians, who would be the leaders, and the rest of the allies. In one of the most crucial developments in Greek history, it was agreed that the campaigns of the league would be funded by permanent contributions from each participant member. It was left to individual members to decide whether they would contribute ships or money, and an assessment of every state's contribution was undertaken by the Athenian politician Aristeides; within a few decades the Athenians had managed to transform the Delian League into an Athenian Empire in which they exercised direct control over other Greek and non-Greek states.[137]

The Athenian Empire would have been impossible without the Athenians learning from the imperial experience of the Persians. By 478 Greek communities knew of only three ways of exercising power over other communities: through conquest and the incorporation of foreign territory; through leadership of a hegemonic alliance of otherwise independent states; or through a metropolis exercising stronger control over its *apoikiai*. The

[135] Thucydides, 1.94–5.   [136] Thucydides, 1.73–4.   [137] Meiggs 1972; Ma *et al.* 2009.

Athenian Empire was completely novel in this respect: the establishment of permanent annual financial contributions; the imposition of garrisons and overseers on allied communities; the confiscation of land to support military settlers; and interference with the domestic autonomy of allies were all measures completely unknown to earlier Greek history. But they were standard practice in the Persian Empire that had been ruling most of Athens' new allies, and there is a good case to be made that in adopting such instruments of empire the Athenians were carefully learning from the Persians.[138]

The first decade of the Delian League was marked by significant successes in the war against Persia; the Athenians and their allies managed to dislodge all Persian garrisons from Thrace and the coast of Ionia. At some point in the 460s the Athenians faced the Persian forces on both land and sea at the Eurymedon River in Pamphylia and scored a major victory (see Figure 5); this victory essentially meant that no Persian navy could again sail into the Aegean for a long time to come (see p. 196). The result of the Eurymedon campaign was that many non-Greek communities from the south coast of Asia Minor, in particular the Lycians and Carians, became now members of the Delian League and paid tribute.[139] Later in the 460s, Egypt revolted against Persia and it took many years before the Persians were able to re-establish their authority.[140] The Athenians became allies of the Egyptian rebels and sent many expeditionary forces, which were however defeated in the end. But it is clear that the Athenians were willing not only to think big but were capable of doing so, and they intervened in the whole of the eastern Mediterranean, as one of their many casualty lists testifies: it records members of the tribe Erechtheis who died in the same year fighting in places as close to Athens as Halieis, Aegina and Megara, to places as distant as Cyprus, Phoenicia and Egypt.[141] But it was not just Athenians that went round the Mediterranean in the course of these military encounters: one inscription from Samos records a dedication by Inarus, the Egyptian rebel pharaoh, of a statue to Leocritus, the leader of the sailors in the allied Greek force;[142] while another records how the Samians captured fifteen ships from the Phoenicians in the Egyptian campaign.[143]

After the defeat of Athens in Egypt, the Persians tried again to bring their navy into the Aegean during the 450s; but another defeat in 450 in the waters off Cyprus put an end to this attempt. After the campaigns of 450 we

---

[138] Raaflaub 2009.   [139] Rhodes 1992.   [140] Ray 1988.
[141] *IG* I³, 1147; translated in *Fornara*, 78.   [142] *IG* XII.6, 1, 468.
[143] *IG* XII.6, 1, 279; translated in *Fornara*, 77.

Figure 5 Attic red-figure oinochoe, manner of the Triptolemos Painter, *c.* 460 BCE.

no longer hear of any direct confrontation between Athens and Persia until the 410s. How should we account for this? There is an ancient tradition which posits that it was the result of the Peace of Callias, an Athenian diplomat who allegedly conducted the negotiations with Persia. According to this tradition, the Persian king renounced his control of the Greek cities of Asia Minor and was forbidden from bringing his navy into Aegean waters. Therefore, the Aegean became a closed Greek lake controlled by the Athenian navy. The problem is that we hear about this treaty only from the fourth century onwards, and some ancient authors thought that the text of this treaty was a forgery.[144] Whatever the case, it is certainly clear that the prospect of direct military confrontation between Athens and Persia was no longer on the agenda; some scholars have characterised this situation as a Cold War.[145]

---

[144] *Fornara*, 95; Meiggs 1972: 129–51.   [145] See Lewis 1992.

2.5 From the Peloponnesian War to Alexander (431–334)

The financial contributions of the allies, along with the combined Athenian and allied navy, enabled the Athenians to create the most powerful navy of the Mediterranean during the fifth century. Land warfare in ancient Greece was relatively cheap: campaigns were short, usually lasting only a few days, and the hoplite infantry had to provide their own equipment. In contrast, the significant cost of constructing and maintaining a fleet of triremes burdened the state; in addition, every trireme carried up to 200 rowers, who had to be paid for their service, and campaigns could last for months, as long as the sea was navigable; consequently, maintaining a fleet was extremely costly. Greek states could hardly maintain a large navy solely on the basis of their own resources; and no Greek state could compete with the resources of the Persian Empire. Accordingly, there were two options available for a Greek state that wanted to dominate the sea. One was to force or convince other Greek states to provide resources for the construction and support of such a fleet: this is precisely what Athens managed to do in the fifth century, and it was the war with Persia which enabled Athens to elicit and command the resources of hundreds of Greek communities around the Aegean. The other solution was even more radical: to elicit the inexhaustible resources of the Persian Empire in order to construct and maintain such a navy.

The latter option materialised for the first time when Athens, Sparta and their allies went into the Peloponnesian War (431–404). No other Greek state had access to the huge resources made possible by the Athenian tribute. Accordingly, when the Spartans and their allies entered the war, they were at a clear disadvantage: they did not have the financial means to compete with Athens in long-term warfare. Initially, the Spartans thought that if they invaded Attica and won a battle or two, they would force the Athenians to surrender or negotiate. However, once it gradually became obvious that this would not be the case, the Spartans started to look to Persia for the financial sources that would allow them to create and maintain the navy that was necessary to defeat Athens. This was a long-term factor in the Greek political system. No state could dominate for long without enormous financial and military support: and the opponents of the dominant state could overthrow it if they could find external support from Persia.

Sparta and Persia started negotiating; Sparta wanted money, while Persia wanted to take back what it had lost to the Athenian Empire during the fifth century: control of the Greek cities of Asia Minor. Ultimately, a deal was sealed: Persia would support Sparta in exchange for Spartan agreement to some kind of Persian authority over the cities of Asia Minor.[146] For some time, this collaboration was not very effective, because of intrigues between the different Persian satraps in Asia Minor and the Athenian attempt to negotiate with the Persians and obstruct Persian support for Sparta. But everything changed when in 407 the Persian king Dareius II sent his son Cyrus as overall commander of western Asia Minor. Cyrus formed a lasting relationship of friendship and trust with Lysander, the Spartan commander, and fully supported the Spartan war effort; in fact, when in 405 he went back to Persia to visit his dying father, he left all his treasures to Lysander personally, with permission to use anything needed to defeat Athens. This in fact happened in 404, when Athens finally surrendered unconditionally.[147]

But the cordial relations between Sparta and the Persian king would not last long. When Dareius II died, Cyrus did not succeed him; the new king was Cyrus' brother, Artaxerxes II. Cyrus returned to Asia Minor and immediately planned rebellion. He patronised the Greek cities of Asia Minor by supporting them against Tissaphernes, the Persian satrap of Lydia, who was trying to enforce the treaty with Sparta and exact tribute from the cities; he got the discreet, but firm, support of Sparta, which owed the defeat of Athens to Cyrus; and he used his Greek contacts in order to gather secretly a mercenary army that would allow him to defeat his brother and take the throne. He would give his Greek friends money to hire mercenaries in far-away places, or even use them for their own purposes; and when Cyrus was ready, in 401, he asked his friends to bring over the troops they had gathered. Cyrus' army marched all the way from the coast of Asia Minor to modern-day Iraq, where it finally met the army of his brother at the battle of Cunaxa. The Greek soldiers were victorious against their opponents, but Cyrus attempted to win a clear victory by killing his brother personally and was himself killed in the attempt; Artaxerxes secured the victory and his throne.[148]

The day after the battle, the Greek mercenaries found themselves isolated in enemy territory, thousands of miles away from Greece: after an heroic march through Mesopotamia and northern Asia Minor, they finally reached the Black Sea coast. From there they gradually returned to the Propontis, and they entered the service of the Thracian prince Seuthes, before finally crossing back to Asia Minor and joining a Spartan anti-Persian expedition, which we shall examine shortly. The expedition of Cyrus and the return of

[146] Lewis 1977.   [147] Debord 1999: 203–32; Cawkwell 2005: 147–61.   [148] Briant 2002a: 615–30.

his mercenaries to the Aegean, also known as the expedition of the Ten Thousand, because the Greek mercenaries in Cyrus' army were roughly 10,000, were recorded in minute detail in an amazing work called *The Anabasis* or *March Upland of Cyrus*.[149] It was written by one of the leaders of the return trip, the Athenian Xenophon, an author to whose works we shall return often (pp. 221–2). The story of a large group of Greek mercenaries, who started in the service of a Persian rebel prince and ended up in the service of an anti-Persian force in Asia Minor, is a characteristic leitmotiv of fourth-century history.

A year after Cunaxa, Tissaphernes returned to Asia Minor with the king's order to subjugate the Greek cities that according to the treaty between Sparta and Persia belonged to him. The Greek cities appealed to Sparta to protect them and Sparta decided to accept. Casting aside their previous stance, they now presented themselves as the leader of a Panhellenic expedition to liberate the Greeks of Asia Minor.[150] Spartan commanders had some success in liberating Greek cities in collaboration with or in opposition to Greek dynasts who ruled some cities as Persian vassals. They also scored some initial successes in playing one satrap against the other and winning some non-Greeks as allies: the Spartan king Agesilaus collaborated with the disaffected Persian noble Spithridates and his forces, and procured an alliance with the Paphlagonian ruler, although these alliances ultimately broke down. But it was some important military factors that dictated that Sparta was unable to capitalise on its successes: the ability to fight the Persians in the open plains of Asia Minor necessitated cavalry forces to match the superiority of the Persians, as well as the ability to conquer cities by force, instead of resorting to long and costly sieges, which the Spartans were unable to undertake. Despite some attempts, the Spartans failed to meet these challenges.

The Persians quickly understood that their best way of defeating the Spartans would be to take advantage of the perennial divisions among the Greek states: Athens was always looking for a chance to reclaim its hegemonic role; while Corinth and Thebes, the erstwhile allies of Sparta, were deeply disaffected. Consequently, in 395 a quadruple alliance of Athens, Corinth, Boeotia and Argos proclaimed war against Sparta; the Spartans had no option but to order Agesilaus to retreat from Asia Minor and bring his forces back to Greece to face the anti-Spartan alliance. Meanwhile, Persia was rebuilding its navy, leadership of which was entrusted to the Persian satrap Pharnabazus together with Conon, the former Athenian general who

[149] Roy 1967; Briant 1995; Lane Fox 2004; Lee 2007.   [150] Xenophon, *Hellenica*, 3.4.3–4.

had gone into exile in Cyprus after the Athenian defeat in 404; the Persian navy faced the Spartans at Cnidos in 394 and won a crushing victory. This was a decisive sea battle, because it established Persian supremacy at sea: no Greek navy ever dared to fight against the Persians again. Conon used the Persian navy and Persian money in order to rebuild Athenian fortunes, and in particular to rebuild the Athenian walls, which had been destroyed after defeat in the Peloponnesian War. Athens was brought down through Persian money in 404 and had become a significant power again with the help of Persian money in 394![151]

The war between Sparta and its opponents dragged on for many years, until the Spartans realised that they could not win the war unless they abandoned the Greeks of Asia Minor to Persia and secured Persian support. In the end, they made an agreement with Persia which is known as the King's Peace or the Peace of Antalcidas, from the name of the Spartan who negotiated it. The Persian king made a proclamation at a conference of all Greek states in 387:

King Artaxerxes thinks it just that the cities in Asia should belong to him, as well as Clazomenae and Cyprus among the islands, and that the other Greek cities, both small and great, should be left autonomous, except Lemnos, Imbros, and Scyros; and these should belong, as of old, to the Athenians. But whichever of the two parties does not accept this peace, upon them I will make war, in company with those who desire this arrangement, both by land and by sea, with ships and with money.[152]

The threat of Spartan power backed by Persian gold and military power coerced all Greek states to accept it. The clause about the autonomy of the Greek cities was deceptive; Sparta merely used her authority and Persian backing to force the other Greek cities to dismantle any unions she disliked under the pretence of leaving every city independent. The Persian king got back the Greek cities of Asia Minor after about a century, and no Greek state would dispute this settlement till Alexander the Great destroyed the Persian Empire.[153]

The half century that separates the King's Peace from Alexander's invasion of the Persian Empire (334) is a complex but deeply fascinating period of interactions.[154] The Greeks universally accepted the Persian king as arbitrator of their affairs: the Greek states which were claiming hegemony over the Greek world were doing so with the support of the Persian king, while

---

[151] Hornblower 1994: 64–77; Debord 1999: 234–63.　[152] Xenophon, *Hellenica*, 5.1.31.
[153] Seager 1994.　[154] Starr 1975.

those Greek states that wished to undermine the status quo were equally trying to elicit Persian support and, in particular, Persian funding. What Persia had failed to do militarily with the Persian invasion of 480–479, it had succeeded in doing by diplomatic means in the fourth century. While Persia could offer unlimited financial resources, the Greeks could offer highly sought after manpower: primarily heavy infantry soldiers, but also professionals of various talents. There developed a complex interconnection between these various resources. The Persian Empire needed manpower not only for routine functions like garrisons and bodyguards, but in particular for important military campaigns in the eastern Mediterranean in order to quash rebellions of various forms.[155] Egypt revolted in 404 and remained independent till 343/2 despite various large-scale Persian campaigns to reconquer the land; Phoenicia and Cyprus revolted in the 340s;[156] and during the 360s a number of satraps in Asia Minor revolted from the central power, sometimes in collaboration and other times on their own.[157]

Greek manpower was accordingly highly sought after both by the Persian Empire and by its various opponents. This provided an excellent opportunity not only for individuals, but also for states: it was particularly common during this period for Greek states to send their generals and leaders as well as their citizen soldiers to serve as mercenaries on either side of the wars in the eastern Mediterranean, in order to procure money and political goodwill. In 375, Artaxerxes invited the Greek states to a conference concerning the Common Peace; his motive was to broker a deal that would end hostilities among the Greek states, in order to make available a large number of Greek soldiers that the Persian king wanted to employ in his campaign against Egypt.[158] Perhaps the most impressive case is that of the Spartan king Agesilaus, who in his old age was dispatched to fight abroad in order to procure money for a battered Sparta after its loss of Messenia in the 360s: after supporting in 364 Ariobarzanes, the Persian satrap of Lydia who had rebelled against the king, Agesilaus went to Egypt to help repel the imminent Persian invasion. After dabbling in Egyptian affairs by being instrumental in the coming to power of Nectanebo II, Agesilaus died in Libya on the trip back to Sparta, bringing with him 200 talents as a reward for his exploits.[159]

A second important factor was the growing interconnection between the political actors of the Mediterranean world. Within the Persian Empire, satraps and native rulers created their own links to the Greek world by

---

[155] Ruzicka 2012.   [156] Briant 2002a: 645–75, 681–90.   [157] Welskopf 1989.
[158] Diodorus, 15.38.   [159] Cartledge 1987: 314–30.

employing Greek mercenaries and other Greek professionals, maintaining relationships with various Greek states, and employing Greek practices for their own ends. In 368, Ariobarzanes sent his Greek emissary, Philiscus of Abydus, to convene a peace conference at the Panhellenic sanctuary of Delphi; the conference was a diplomatic failure, but Philiscus used Ariobarzanes' money to hire mercenaries whom he entrusted to the Spartans to use for their own ends; Ariobarzanes' dealings with Athens led to the grant of Athenian citizenship to both Ariobarzanes and Philiscus.[160] Straton, king of the Phoenician city of Sidon, was honoured by Athens for helping Athenian ambassadors reach the Persian king,[161] but later rebelled against Persia, probably during the troubles of the 360s. Straton's court was famous for its luxury, and he competed with the Cypriote king Nicocles to outdo each other in display; Straton made large-scale use of Greek entertainers, including courtesans from the Peloponnese, singers from Ionia, and singers and dancers from many other parts of the Greek world.[162]

But the most famous fourth-century family of native rulers and satraps is that of the Hecatomnids.[163] The Hecatomnid family had long maintained a powerful position in the Carian city of Mylasa; by 392/1 one of its members, Hecatomnus, had been appointed satrap of Caria by the Persian king, and the satrapy of Caria remained in the hands of Hecatomnus' children until Alexander's conquest. Hecatomnus was succeeded in 377 by his famous son Mausolus, married to his sister Artemisia, who ruled on her own for two years after Mausolus' death in 353. Rule was passed on to another brother–sister pair, Idrieus and Ada, and then to a third brother, Pixodarus, by which time the Hecatomnids had also been appointed satraps of Lycia.

We shall examine in detail the Hecatomnid role in glocalising Greek culture in Caria in Chapter 6 (pp. 257–60); here we are more interested in their relationship to the Panhellenic world. The Hecatomnids had no qualms about attacking and conquering Greek cities, but they were also able to take full advantage of the forms of diplomacy conducted by Greek communities in order to extend their power and prestige.[164] Miletus dedicated statues of Idrieus and Ada at Delphi,[165] while a relief from Tegea in Arcadia, probably carrying a local decree responding to a Hecatomnid benefaction, depicts Zeus of Labraunda, the chief Carian deity that appears on Hecatomnid coins, with Idrieus and Ada alongside him (see Figure 6).[166]

[160] Welskopf 1989: 26–44.   [161] *IG* II², 141; translated in *R-O*, 21.
[162] *FGrH*, 115 F114; Elayi 2005.   [163] Hornblower 1982; Ruzicka 1992.
[164] Hornblower 1982: 107–37.   [165] *Tod*, 161.   [166] Waywell 1993.

Figure 6 Stele of Zeus of Labraunda, Tegea, fourth century BCE.

The death of Mausolus provides a great illustration of the large-scale employment of Greek professionals by the Hecatomnids; his funeral was accompanied by typically Greek literary contests. There was a contest in oratory attended by eminent Greek intellectuals, such as the historian Theopompus of Chios and the orator Naucrates of Erythrae; but there was also a tragic competition, won by Theodectes of Phaselis with a tragedy entitled *Mausolus*, which was probably about a mythical ancestor of the Hecatomnid family.[167] But it was Mausolus' funerary monument, the famous Mausoleum of Halicarnassus, which attracted the most famous Greek artists of the time, as we shall examine in Chapter 6 (pp. 259–60).

We can best observe the interconnection between the Greek world and the world of empires during this period through a series of interrelated events.[168] In 357, the Athenians became engaged in the so-called Social War against their former allies Byzantion, Chios and Rhodes, whose revolt was supported, if not instigated, by Mausolus. The Athenians despatched the

---

[167] Hornblower 1982: 333–7.   [168] Welskopf 1989; Debord 1999: 375–99.

general Chares to take charge of the campaign, but with insufficient resources; in order to fund his campaign Chares had to support Artabazus, the
Persian satrap of Hellespontine Phrygia, in his revolt against the Persian
king Artaxerxes III and his other satraps. Chares scored some significant
victories against the loyalist Persian forces and ravaged the territory of
Persian potentates; at that point Artaxerxes intervened and ordered the
Athenians to recall Chares from helping Artabazus, or he would help the
allies against Athens: the Athenians had no choice but to end the Social War
in defeat.

This brings us to the fascinating family story of Artabazus, who was
appointed satrap of Hellespontine Phrygia around 363/2. Artabazus became
intimate with two Greek brothers, Mentor and Memnon from Rhodes, who
were leaders of his Greek mercenary forces. He married their sister and gave
each of them one of his daughters; the famous daughter was destined to be
Barsine, who married Mentor and, after his death, Memnon. After Chares'
withdrawal, Artabazus convinced the Thebans to send him a force of 5,000
citizens led by the general Pammenes, but he was defeated and found refuge
together with Memnon at the Macedonian court. Mentor went to Egypt,
where he served under the rebel pharaohs for many years, until he was
captured by the Persians. The Persians recognised his abilities and pardoned
him, and he served under them in the Persian invasion of Egypt. When the
re-conquest finished successfully in 343/2, Artaxerxes III asked Mentor
what he wanted as a gift, and Mentor requested the pardon of Artabazus
and Memnon; this was granted and Artabazus and Memnon returned to
Persian service. In 340 Mentor died. When Philip of Macedon commanded
his general Parmenion to stage an initial invasion of Asia Minor in 336,
Memnon, his erstwhile guest, successfully repelled the Macedonians.
Memnon's advice to follow a scorched-earth policy against Alexander's
invasion was not followed, but after the Persian defeat at Granicus in 334
he became chief of the Persian military forces, although he died a few
months later. Artabazus fought for the Persian king against Alexander,
but after the murder of Dareius III he switched allegiance to Alexander
and became an important official in Alexander's empire. His daughter
Barsine became a concubine of Alexander and gave birth to a son, named
Heracles. We see in this family saga the complex and changing relationship
between Persian aristocrats, Greek polities, Greek mercenaries, the
Macedonian monarchy and the Persian Empire.[169]

---

[169] Hofstetter 1978: 125–7, 129–31; Heckel 2006a: 55.

2.6 Macedonia and Alexander's conquests (334–323)

This story brings us to Philip and Alexander, the Macedonian kings who led a Panhellenic campaign against the Persian Empire that ended up creating a new world empire and changing the course of Mediterranean history in profound ways. The transformation of Macedonia from an unstable kingdom of limited power into the most powerful state in the Balkans was a feat accomplished in the course of Philip II's reign (359–336): by the time of his death, Macedonia was not only the hegemonic power over the Greek polities in the south, but also controlled Thrace from the Aegean to the Danube and other areas to the northwest of Macedonia through a complex system of alliances, vassalage and direct rule.[170] Part of this success was due to the ability to tap and develop the enormous resources of Macedonia and Thrace, a subject we shall come back to in Chapter 3 (pp. 119–25). But equally important was the ability to participate in and benefit from the system of interactions between the world of empires and other Mediterranean polities and the networks of mobile soldiers, professionals and intellectuals that crossed the Mediterranean.

This interconnected world is again best illustrated through a few connected stories. The saga of the families of Artabazus and Mentor has already been related, and a parallel case is that of Amminapes, an exiled Iranian noble who found refuge in the Macedonian court before returning to Persian service, playing an instrumental role in the Persian surrender of Egypt to Alexander, and entering Macedonian service once more.[171] It is worth remembering that the Aegean could be crossed in the opposite direction as well. One example concerns Amyntas, son of Antiochus, who fled Macedonia fearing for his life when Alexander came to the throne; he became a leader of Greek mercenaries in Persian service and advised Dareius III to fight Alexander in Syria; after defeat at Issos, he fled with 8,000 men first to Phoenician Tripolis and then to Egypt, where he claimed to have been appointed satrap of Egypt by Dareius, but failed in his quest and was killed.[172] On the eve of Philip's invasion of Asia Minor, Pixodarus, a member of the Hecatomnid dynasty and satrap of Caria and Lycia, offered his daughter in marriage to Arrhidaeus, Philip's retarded son. Alexander got wind of it and managed to get Pixodarus to make the marriage offer to himself by sending the Athenian actor Thessalus as an emissary, only to be rebuked

---

[170] Archibald 1998: 234–9.   [171] Heckel 2006a: 22.   [172] Hofstetter 1978: 13.

by Philip for his meddling.[173] The attempted marriage link between the Macedonian monarchy and a native dynasty of Asia Minor is notable, as is the role of mobile professionals like tragic actors in maintaining this interconnected world.

The final story concerns Aristotle, the famous philosopher. After Plato's death in 347, Aristotle left Athens and went first to Atarneus, a Greek city in Asia Minor opposite Lesbos, where he married the niece of the local tyrant Hermias. Hermias, a former slave and eunuch who originated from Bithynia, was educated by Plato in Athens and, according to the historian Theopompus, had managed to convince the city of Elis to send sacred envoys to announce the truce for the Olympic Games to him.[174] Hermias ruled as a Persian vassal, but when Mentor of Rhodes took command of the Persian forces in the area, he felt threatened and allied himself with Philip of Macedon; but he was defeated by Mentor and executed. After his death Aristotle accepted Philip's invitation to become tutor to his son Alexander. We shall examine in detail in Chapters 3 and 6 the role of these networks of mobile intellectuals; but for the time being, it is worth observing how a Greek intellectual such as Aristotle could move from Athens to the court of a Hellenised Persian vassal in Asia Minor and then to the Macedonian court, and how the very same people in various roles brought together the histories of the Persian Empire, the Greek cities of Asia Minor and Macedonia.

There is considerable debate among modern scholars with regard to the extent to which the emergence of Macedonia as a superpower during the reign of Philip was accompanied or facilitated by the adoption of Persian practices and techniques. While Persian influence on Macedonian material culture was limited,[175] there were some institutions, such as the importance of royal hunts or the royal pages, young members of the aristocracy educated at court, which were paralleled in both the Persian and the Macedonian monarchies; they could be either independent developments or Macedonian adaptations of Persian practices.[176]

At the same time it was Philip's and Alexander's ability to position themselves as leaders of a Panhellenic campaign that played an important role in the success of the enterprise. Macedonia was one of the border areas to the north of the Greek world: although Macedonian was a Greek dialect, many Greeks considered the Macedonians as Barbarians even in the time of Philip and Alexander.[177] When in the early fifth century the Macedonian king Alexander I had tried to participate in the Olympic Games, his Greek

---

[173] Ruzicka 2010.   [174] *FGrH*, 115 F250.   [175] Paspalas 2006.
[176] Cf. Kienast 1973; Briant 1994.   [177] Badian 1982.

credentials were disputed, although Alexander was successful in arguing that he descended from Argos (presumably because he was a descendant of Heracles, who originated from the Argolid);[178] at the same time, the epithet 'Philhellene' (friend of the Greeks) that was attributed to Alexander would imply that he was not seen as Greek. These aspects illustrate the means through which a state like Macedonia would come to be fully accepted as Greek: the use of mythology as a means of creating fictive kinship; participation in the Panhellenic Games; investment in Panhellenic sanctuaries; as well as the patronage of the mobile networks of Greek intellectuals, artists and other professionals. Famous tragedians like Euripides and Agathon and painters like Zeuxis had lived in the Macedonian court and worked for the Macedonian kings.[179]

Investment in Panhellenic sanctuaries or patronage of Greek intellectuals was not unique to the Macedonian monarchy. Similar phenomena can be observed for the Hecatomnids, or for the Lycian dynasts we shall examine in Chapter 6; Euripides' composition of a tragedy about the mythical ancestor of the Macedonian king Archelaus, at whose court he resided, is directly paralleled by Theodectes' composition of a tragedy about Mausolus' mythical ancestor.[180] What was unique to Macedonia was the ability of its kings to become recognised as leaders of the Panhellenic community in a campaign against the Barbarian enemy. The irony of the situation is that Panhellenic themes could be used both in favour of and against the Macedonian rulers. The Athenian orator Demosthenes was able to present Philip as a Barbarian who threatened Greek freedom and urged the unity of the Greek poleis against him;[181] he saw little problem in enlisting Persian support to fight against the new Barbarian threat from the north. At the same time, other Greek intellectuals, the most famous among whom was the Athenian rhetorician Isocrates, had long been calling for a Panhellenic campaign against Persia that would alleviate Greek social and political problems by exacting revenge and through the conquest and distribution of land to destitute Greeks.[182] Philip competed in the Olympic Games, presented himself as the protector of the Panhellenic shrine of Delphi, became accepted as a member of the Delphic amphictiony, and invested heavily in the Panhellenic shrines of Olympia.[183] Philip's espousal of the Panhellenic agenda allowed him to create the Hellenic League in Corinth in 337, which recognised him as its leader and duly declared war against Persia

---

[178] Herodotus, 5.22.   [179] Badian 1982.   [180] Hornblower 1982: 336.
[181] *Third Philippic*, 31.   [182] Too 1995: 129–50.   [183] Mari 2002: 76–202.

to avenge the wrongs of the Persian Wars.[184] After Philip's assassination in 336, it was his successor Alexander who took over the campaign and invaded Asia Minor in 334.

Alexander's invasion was heavily scripted according to Panhellenic themes: his first act after landing in Asia was to go to Troy to sacrifice to Achilles, a hero with whom Alexander identified strongly.[185] After overcoming the forces of the Asia Minor satraps in the battle of Granicus in 334, Alexander conquered the coast of Asia Minor and in 333 defeated the Persian king Dareius III at Issus in Cilicia. He decided first to conquer the Levant and Egypt instead of pursuing Dareius into Mesopotamia, and took Tyre and Gaza after long and difficult sieges. Alexander entered Egypt unopposed and followed the example of Persian kings like Cyrus by presenting himself as a liberator and adopting the role of the Egyptian pharaoh; but his decision to found a new city on the Egyptian coast, Alexandria, was a strong indication of an important novelty. In 331, Alexander defeated Dareius at Gaugamela in northern Iraq, and his success in taking the royal capitals of Babylon, Persepolis and Susa in the next few months sealed the fate of the Persian Empire. Alexander's decision to destroy Persepolis and his return to the Athenians of the statues of the tyrant slayers Harmodius and Aristogeiton, taken away by the Persians in 480, were clear indications of the Panhellenic aspect of his campaign; but the rest of Alexander's campaign, his defeat and punishment of the rebel satraps who executed Dareius and continued to resist him, his campaign into India, his return to Babylon, and finally his last arrangements and death in 323 would strike a very different chord.[186]

Alexander was creating a new structure and image for his rule which selectively accommodated the Persian past and present. He had already adopted the administrative structure of the Persian Empire with its satrapies and tribute before the conquest of Babylon, but now he confirmed the Persian satraps of Babylon and Susa in their positions and appointed other Iranians in similar positions. His adoption of elements of Persian garb, his receipt of *proskynesis* (prostration) from his non-Greek subjects and his (unsuccessful) attempt to impose the same on the Greeks and Macedonians, his incorporation of non-Greeks into the army and the court, and Alexander's wedding to two Iranian princesses along with the cross-ethnic weddings between Macedonian nobles and non-Greek women

[184] *IG* II², 236; translated in *R-O*, 76.   [185] Plutarch, *Life of Alexander*, 15.4–5.
[186] Lane Fox 1973; Bosworth 1988; Briant 2010.

brought Alexander into deep conflict with his Macedonian and Greek followers.[187]

Explaining Alexander's spectacular defeat of a great empire is not an easy task. It was long popular among modern historians to depict the Persian Empire as having been in continuous decline since the Persian Wars, ravaged by corruption at court, satrapal rebellions and the oppression of subject nations: an easy fruit to pick, once a determined and able commander rose to the task. This image of Persian defeat as a result of decline is no longer defensible.[188] In its place we have to posit a combination of factors of different gravity. There is no doubt that Persian military defeat was to an important extent the result of the military genius of Alexander. Sheer luck also played its role: Alexander was almost killed in the very first battle at Granicus, which would surely have ended the campaign prematurely, and the deaths of able Persian commanders like Memnon also played their role. Alexander's ability to tap the latest developments in military technology was equally important; without the advances in siege warfare initiated in the western Mediterranean and brought to the Macedonian army by the mobile professionals whom Alexander was in a position to hire, it would have been impossible to take cities by storm and conquer the vast Persian Empire in such a short period of time.[189] Ultimately, though, it was the range of strategies employed successfully by Alexander with regard to the communities and elites of the Persian Empire that guaranteed success. They ranged from the sheer application of large-scale terrorism in order to make surrender the only worthwhile choice, to the ability to forge alliances with local elites in Caria, Egypt or Babylonia through careful respect of their traditions and structures of power, and the selective cooption of the Iranian ruling elite within the new imperial structure.[190] It was Alexander's ability to replicate successfully the patterns through which the Persian kings had managed to create their own empire which played a crucial role in creating his own.

---

[187] Lane Fox 2007.   [188] Briant 2002b.   [189] Garlan 1974: 201–78.
[190] Bosworth 1996; Briant 2002a: 817–71.

3 | The world of networks and the world of *apoikiai*

3.1 A historical overview

Around 1000 BCE the Mediterranean world gives a strongly parochial appearance. Within the Aegean, most people produced and consumed local products, with limited evidence for the exchange of goods, ideas and technologies across cultures; people mostly lived and died where they were born, there being little evidence for human mobility. This was not the primeval condition of a primitive world; it was the result of the breakdown of a highly interconnected Mediterranean world during the Late Bronze Age (1500–1200). There is no better illustration of the interconnectedness of the Late Bronze Age Mediterranean than the bronze ingots in the shape of an oxhide, which can be found from Sardinia all the way to Cyprus and the Levant; the exchange of bronze had reached such levels that a standardised form in the shape of an oxhide was invented and widely adopted by various communities.[1] But this was all gone by the year 1000 and the world looked radically different.

This image of a Mediterranean world of small, isolated communities was gradually modified. New networks moving people, goods, ideas and technologies were being established across the Mediterranean. Archaeology provides hard evidence for the movement of goods: by 800 Greek pottery could be found from the Levantine coast of the eastern Mediterranean to Sardinia and southern Italy in the western Mediterranean; metal ware, jewellery, seals, vases and statuettes made of faience and alabaster produced by Syrian and Phoenician craftsmen were to be found in the Aegean as well as in the waters of the western Mediterranean.[2] Alongside the mobility of goods there was also the mobility of ideas and technologies. Many areas of the Mediterranean had never known the technology of writing, while in the Aegean the syllabic Linear B script vanished with the end of the Bronze Age world; during the eighth century the technology of alphabetic writing

---

[1] Gale and Stos-Gale 1986.

[2] Haider 1996: 60–79; Waldbaum 1997; Niemeier 2001; d'Agostino 2006; Ridgway 2006; Lane Fox 2008: 89–137.

expanded all over the Mediterranean through the Greek adaptation of the Phoenician alphabet, which was subsequently adopted by other non-Greek cultures for their own languages (pp. 227–9).[3] At the same time motifs, styles and iconographic elements from the artistic traditions of the Levant and northern Syria were being adopted and adapted in Greece as well as in the western Mediterranean.[4] This mobility of goods, ideas and technologies was predicated on human mobility. Homer's *Odyssey* offers us images of various forms of human mobility: the itinerant craftsman, moving from community to community in search of customers and patronage;[5] the Phoenician merchant, hopping from port to port and selling his trinkets and exotic items;[6] the Greek pirate, sailing in bands to attack the coast of Egypt and capture people and booty.[7] In Crete significant quantities of Near Eastern objects were likely produced by nuclei of resident Eastern craftsmen;[8] a Phoenician workshop is attested at Ialysus in Rhodes.[9]

These networks of mobility constitute a world in which Greeks and non-Greeks encountered and interacted with each other in different ways from the Panhellenic world and the world of empires we examined in Chapter 2. In the five centuries between 800 and 300 these networks expanded to cover the whole Mediterranean and the Black Sea, and intensified their impact on the lives of communities and individuals (Map 3); we shall devote the next section to examining their form and importance. But these networks also created the conditions for the emergence of another important world of interactions between Greeks and non-Greeks. Around 800 the small port of Kommos in southern Crete is a nice example of novel developments; a tri-pillar shrine, common in Phoenician settlements, but otherwise unattested in the Aegean, along with Egyptian faience figurines, illustrate the Phoenician frequentation of this crucial stepping stone in the passage from eastern to western Mediterranean.[10] The newly established interconnections between the eastern and western Mediterranean were no longer a matter of a few seasonal or one-off visits. By the eighth century the Phoenicians had established a settlement at Cypriote Cition opposite the Phoenician coast, as well as Carthage on the Tunisian coast and further settlements on the south coast of Spain.[11]

No better illustration of how the Mediterranean world was changing can be found than the emergence during the early eighth century of two settlements on opposite sides of the sea: Al Mina and Pithecusae. Al Mina

---

[3] Lejeune 1983; Woodard 2010.   [4] Akurgal 1968; Riva and Vella 2006.   [5] 17.382–5.
[6] 15.415–16.   [7] 14.192–359.   [8] Cf. Hoffman 1997.   [9] Coldstream 1969.
[10] Shaw 1989; cf. Hoffman 1997: 172–6.   [11] Gras *et al.* 1989; Aubet 2001; Niemeyer 2006.

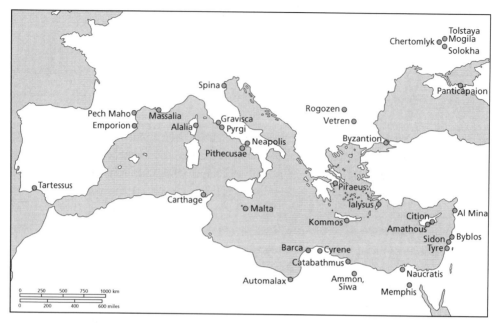

Map 3 The Mediterranean world

was a coastal site in northern Syria, serving the Aramaean kingdom in the interior of the Orontes River valley. The earliest strata of this site are dominated by Greek pottery, alongside Cypriote and Phoenician ceramics and north Syrian metal ware, ivory and seals; this shows that it was a commercial entrepôt for networks that extended from the Levantine coast into the Aegean.[12] Remarkably, a very similar range of objects is simultaneously attested at the settlement of Pithecusae, the island of Ischia in the bay of Naples. In both Al Mina and Pithecusae pottery from the Greek island of Euboea plays a very prominent role; in addition, later Greek literary sources describe Pithecusae as the earliest Greek settlement in the west, founded by Euboean settlers.[13]

Pithecusae is evidence of widespread human mobility: within a few years a community with thousands of residents emerged on the island. The evidence for the widespread processing of metals in this early community makes clear what a major purpose of its founders was: the importation of metals from Etruria to the north, and their processing and exportation to Greece and other metal-hungry areas.[14] While Pithecusae was founded by Euboeans,

---

[12] Hodos 2006: 37–40.   [13] Lane Fox 2008: 138–61.   [14] Ridgway 1992: 91–103.

it was at the same time a multicultural settlement.[15] Its international character is evident not only through the significant quantities of objects from the Levant, such as the Syrian Lyre Player seals and the Levantine aryballoi, it is, in fact, the epigraphic evidence that proves the existence of Semitic residents at Pithecusae. An amphora used for a burial carries three inscriptions in Aramaic: the first two identify its contents as '200 (units of liquid)' and as 'double (the standard quantity)', and clearly relate to the original use of the amphora as a liquid container. They must have been inscribed by the traders who exchanged this amphora, and it has been suggested that it could have been the Phoenician residents of Rhodes who dispatched the amphora to Pithecusae. But the third inscription is a Semitic religious sign which can only relate to the secondary use of the amphora as a grave container and must therefore have been inscribed locally. Two more inscriptions have been found on pieces of pottery, one of which was made locally.[16]

This original experiment in the bay of Naples quickly found innumerable imitators. Before the end of the eighth century Greek communities were already dotted along the coasts of southern Italy and Sicily. During the seventh century further settlements emerged in the western Mediterranean with the foundation of Cyrene in Libya, in the north Aegean islands and the coast of Thrace opposite, as well as in the Hellespont and around the Black Sea. In the sixth century Greek settlements expanded further to the west with the foundation of Massalia in southern France and Emporion in Spain. The standard Greek term for these settlements is *apoikia*, which means 'home away from home'.[17]

In order to understand what was happening across the Mediterranean we need to examine the wider phenomenon of Mediterranean redistribution and its networks. The Mediterranean ecosystem is characterised by the unpredictability of rainfall and the connectivity created by easy access to the sea. Faced with constant risk, individuals and communities have been perennially forced to devise strategies to deal with it. Overproduction is essential if one is to avoid the danger of starvation in the lean years; diversification of production is crucial in a world in which the diversity of micro-environments can lead to the failure of crops in one valley and their success in the next one; storage and redistribution are the means of ensuring that the surpluses created by overproduction and diversification are employed productively. The connectivity of the sea makes possible the extension of strategies of survival and success over very wide areas. This

---

[15] d'Agostino and Ridgway 1994.   [16] Ridgway 1992: 111–18.
[17] See general accounts of Greek *apoikiai* in Boardman 1999; Tsetskhladze 2006a, 2008.

does not mean that all areas of the Mediterranean world in all periods of their history constituted a highly interconnected world; but the ecology of the Mediterranean creates the background in which individuals and communities carved extended hinterlands and created networks that moved goods, people, ideas and technologies over very extensive distances.[18]

What was taking place around 800 and increasingly afterwards was the attempt by individuals and communities to control the processes of Mediterranean redistribution and connectivity. Settlements like Al Mina and Pithecusae were the earliest attested hubs of international mobility and redistribution, located in places of easy access, which in the Mediterranean tended to be ports. In the course of the archaic and classical periods innumerable such hubs emerged across the Mediterranean and the Black Sea. Communities and rulers could try to control and profit from these hubs: many communities established *emporia*, settlements for foreign traders with facilities for the exchange of goods, which were monitored and controlled by the host communities.[19] Around these *emporia* developed a cosmopolitan universe with fascinating economic, cultural and social interactions, which we shall examine in section 3.3 below.

An alternative range of strategies concerned controlling a landscape and its resources (e.g., staples, timber, metals) and the networks of mobility and connectivity which redistributed these resources. They could extend from the forcible appropriation of a resource through the creation of an organised and autonomous community of settlers to the successful insertion of opportunists into existing systems of control through intermarriage, diplomacy or cohabitation. The occupation of good agricultural land through the establishment of a Greek *apoikia* was one such strategy; but the many Athenians like Thucydides, who acquired rights to the Thracian silver mines through marriage into the Thracian aristocracy, are another facet of the same phenomenon.

The result was a world of connectivity and mobility within which we have to situate Greek *apoikiai*.[20] Early Greek *apoikiai* were the result of numerous private initiatives underwritten by widespread human mobility.[21] In fact, even during the classical period, when state-led colonisation was certainly the case, *apoikiai* drew their settlers from a variety of sources: to give one example among many, the Athenian *apoikia* of Amphipolis in Thrace included not only Athenian citizens, but also Greeks from other communities. The mobility of the Greek *apoikos* has to be set alongside

---

[18] Horden and Purcell 2000.   [19] Bresson and Rouillard 1993; Demetriou 2012.
[20] Purcell 2005.   [21] Osborne 1998.

the mobility of the trader, the pirate, the mercenary, the artisan, the diviner, the artist and the slave.[22] In contrast to the material culture of mainland Greek communities, where the majority of goods were produced locally, the material culture of Greek settlements overseas from the very beginning drew goods and ideas from a variety of different sources. From their very inception Greek *apoikiai* were a reaction to an expanding world of mobility and connectivity; they were not mere attempts to get away from home as a result of crisis, even if Greek accounts of colonisation tend to present them in such a way.[23] Many Greek *apoikiai* quickly became significant producers and exporters of agricultural staples; others played a significant role as mediators in the networks of redistribution, as we shall see.

Although Greek *apoikiai* were predicated on the world of networks and its mobility, the world of *apoikiai* had a character of its own. This world was characterised by a perennial contradiction.[24] On the one hand, Greek *apoikoi* were living among a variety of non-Greek communities in situations that ranged from conflict and subjugation to cohabitation, intermarriage and collaboration. In order to deal with this complex world, historians and archaeologists have utilised the concept of frontier societies.[25] This does not mean societies that are separated by a frontier, but societies that emerge and develop in situations of constant osmosis and interaction between different groups. The social, economic, political and cultural history of Greek *apoikiai* has to be situated within the frontier interactions with various non-Greek communities; the result was in many ways a highly hybrid and complex world. On the other hand, and at the same time, Greek *apoikiai* were highly conscious of being Greek communities and of being part of the Panhellenic world. In fact, the very process of creating *apoikiai* had a very important effect on the nature of Greek culture and its forms of interaction with non-Greeks. Section 3.4 will examine in detail this fascinating contradiction.

Before we move on to examine in detail the world of networks, the cosmopolitan universe of the *emporia*, and the frontier societies of the world of *apoikiai*, it is important to round off this brief historical overview by examining some important changes that took place in these worlds in the late archaic and classical periods. In the 250 years that followed the expansion of networks and *apoikiai* after 800 the Mediterranean world was an

---

[22] Giangiulio 1996. [23] For Greek accounts of 'colonisation', see Dougherty 1993.
[24] See the comments of Mairs 2008, 2011a. [25] Lepore 1968; *Confini e frontiera.*

anarchic system: the interactions between Greeks and various other groups and communities took place in innumerable local contexts and rarely affected significantly other areas outside these contexts. But between 550 and 450 the world of *apoikiai* and the world of networks experienced some profound changes which altered their form in important ways.[26]

The first of these developments was the growing interconnectedness between the different regions of the Mediterranean and the clash between opposing strategies and projects. Around 545 the Persian conquest of Asia Minor led the Phocaeans to abandon their city and resettle in an already existing settlement in Corsica. Their activities, which included piracy, led to a head-on confrontation with the Carthaginians and the Etruscans in a great naval battle which, despite the Pyrrhic victory of the Phocaeans, led to the dismantlement of their Corsican settlement, which was immediately succeeded by an Etruscan settlement.[27] Not only did events in the imperial world of Asia Minor lead to developments in the far west of the Mediterranean, but interconnectedness had reached a level in which Phocaean projects clashed immediately with those of the Etruscans and the Carthaginians.[28]

The second related development was the creation of superpowers among the communities of the world of the *apoikiai*. The process started in the western Mediterranean, with the emergence of both Carthage and Syracuse as large territorial states;[29] a related development took place in the Black Sea, with the emergence of the Bosporan kingdom which encompassed many Greek as well as non-Greek communities.[30] The first clash between Carthage and Syracuse took place in 480 at the battle of Himera, reputedly on the same day as the battle of Salamis. Their clash over rule in Sicily and the western Mediterranean would last for more than 200 years, until the final domination of both states by Rome during the Second Punic War (218–201). Greek, Phoenician and native communities in Sicily now had to position themselves in a new world defined by this bipolar clash; while this created new forms of ethnic polarisation, ethnic ties were constantly undercut by various other considerations, and people from the same ethnic group found themselves in opposite camps in the many wars that took place (pp. 106–7).

A third development was the emergence of powerful states among the non-Greek communities in various regions of the Mediterranean world. While during the archaic period Greek communities, groups and

---

[26] Malkin 2011: 38–41.   [27] Cristofani 1983: 63–89, 1996: 83–96.   [28] Gras 1997.
[29] Asheri 1988.   [30] Vinogradov [1980] 1997, [1987] 1997.

individuals in Thrace had only to deal with the local Thracian tribes, the emergence during the fifth century of the Odrysian state, which reached from the Aegean coast to the Danube, changed in important ways the forms of interaction between Greeks and non-Greeks.[31] The emergence of the Royal Scythians on the north coast of the Black Sea,[32] or of the league of the Lucanians in south Italy,[33] were similar developments with equally important results. Finally, the emergence of superpowers in the Aegean world, with Athens functioning as the quintessential example, was another important development of the period between 550 and 450. The almost simultaneous Athenian involvement in the creation of *apoikiai* at Amphipolis in Thrace and at Thourioi in southern Italy around 440 is a telling indication of a changing world; the Athenians' Sicilian expedition (415–413), at the instigation of the Elymian city of Segesta, is only the most famous example of a much wider phenomenon.[34]

3.2 Mobility of people, goods, ideas and technologies

After this brief historical overview, let us move to the world of networks and examine the mobility of people, goods, ideas and technologies. We have already examined the mobility of mercenaries, artists and entertainers employed by the world of empires, from Egypt to Persepolis; we could add religious specialists like the seer Symmachus from Achaean Pellana, who composed a poem for a local dynast at Xanthos of Lycia, or professionals like the Dorian gymnastic trainer who composed another poem for the same dynast.[35] What can we establish about the life of those mobile individuals whose activities supported the networks that linked Mediterranean communities together? Literary sources occasionally focus on such individuals: Herodotus presents two famous archaic merchants who crossed the Mediterranean from one side to the other. He narrates how Colaeus of Samos was blown off-track while sailing to Egypt and ended up passing the Straits of Gibraltar and reaching the famous mines of Tartessus in western Iberia, from which he derived a great profit; in the same breath he mentions another famous merchant, Sostratus of Aegina.[36] Miraculously, archaeological discoveries might have revealed Sostratus' activities at Etruscan Gravisca, an international port we shall examine below (pp. 94–5): a stone anchor was

---

[31] Archibald 1998; cf. Veligianni-Terzi 2004.　　[32] Rolle 1989.　　[33] Purcell 1994.
[34] Wentker 1956; Greco and Lombardo 2007.　　[35] *M-S*, 17.10.02–3.　　[36] 4.152.

dedicated to Aeginetan Apollo by a certain Sostratus, very likely the one mentioned by Herodotus.[37]

But it is normally the exceptional and accidental survival of rather mundane documents that allows us to glimpse the lives and conditions of these mobile individuals. Private letters and documents inscribed on small pieces of lead are particularly illuminating in this respect. From the western extremity of the Mediterranean comes a document from Pech Maho in western Languedoc in France. This document, dating to the middle of the fifth century, is inscribed on both sides; but while one side is inscribed in Greek, the other side is inscribed in Etruscan.[38] We can establish that the Etruscan text was inscribed first, because the Greek writer used the blank backside of the tablet to create his document and only inscribed the last word of his text around the already existing Etruscan text. The two texts are not related to each other; it seems that the Greek writer merely reused the back of a piece of lead already inscribed in Etruscan. The Greek text is a sales document, recording how the author bought a share of some boats from another individual:

(x) . . . bought a (some) boat(s) from the Emporitans. He bought . . . He passed over to me a half share at the price of two *octania* and a half. Two *hectania* and a half I gave in cash, and a personal pledge of one *trite*, and that final sum he received on the river. The advance payment (i.e. two *hectania* and a half plus one *trite*) handed over where the boats are moored, Basigerros, Bleryas, Golo.biur and Sedegon being witnesses. These were witnesses when I handed over the advance; but when I completed the sum of two *octania* and a half, .auaruas, Nalbe..n (and Heronoiios?) were witnesses.[39]

The text illustrates the mixed world in which these traders lived and worked.[40] The transaction took place probably between two Greeks; but all the witnesses to the transactions have Iberian names. That native Iberians could witness a transaction which is recorded in Greek is testimony to the strong links between these Greek traders and their local partners; but the ready availability of a document in Etruscan shows clearly that Greeks were not the only foreign traders in the area, and illustrates the connections between Greek and Etruscan traders. The mixed cargoes of the shipwrecks discovered in these areas, which contain Greek, Etruscan and Punic amphoras and other vases, further illustrate the evidence of the lead document.[41]

---

[37] Johnston 1972.   [38] Cristofani 1996: 83–96.
[39] *SEG* XXXVIII, 1036; translation from Rodríguez Somolinos 1996: 78.
[40] Lejeune *et al.* 1988; Ampolo and Caruso 1990; Chadwick 1990.
[41] Dietler 2007: 267–70, 2010: 131–56.

Next to traders we have to situate the mobility of artisans and other professionals. Thousands exercised their profession as itinerant specialists, or migrated to new communities, bringing in new techniques and starting new workshops. Many artists largely plied their trade as itinerants, crossing the Mediterranean in their incessant journeys. A revealing example is that of the fourth-century cithara player Stratonicus, who toured mainland Greece, Macedonia, the Greek *apoikiai* in Thrace, the Bosporan kingdom in the Black Sea, the Greek communities in Asia Minor, as well as non-Greek communities like Mylasa in Caria and Side in Pamphylia.[42] The Athenian sculptor Philistides left his signature on one of his works at the Carian city of Theangela,[43] while the best Greek artists of the time took part in the construction of the famous Mausoleum, the tomb of the Carian satrap Mausolus.[44] Others made the decision to migrate for good; Athenian potters migrated to southern Italy in the late fifth century and provided the impetus for the establishment of local workshops of red-figure pottery, with their own fascinating hybrid traditions (p. 111).[45] The role of Greek artisans in non-Greek settlements is nicely illustrated by a terracotta obelisk with a dedicatory inscription spread over its four sides, found at the native settlement of San Mauro Forte, 50 km to the northeast of the Greek *apoikia* of Metapontion in south Italy:

> Nicomachus made me;
> Rejoice Lord Heracles;
> The potter dedicated me to you;
> Give it to him
> that he should enjoy an excellent reputation among men.[46]

This dedication is evidence of the mobility of Greek artisans, as well as the penetration of Greek cults among the native communities. But it is also important to stress the poetic qualities of the dedication: the formula of the second line is found among the spurious fragments of Archilochus, while the formula of the fifth line is attested in the poetry of Solon. Artisans could transmit ideas alongside technologies and objects.

The mobility of people in the ancient Mediterranean was not necessarily voluntary. While traversing Anatolia towards the Black Sea on their way back to Greece, the Ten Thousand (pp. 66–7) come upon a river, whose passage is blocked by fighters from a local population unknown to the Greeks.

---

[42] Asheri 1983: 55–6; Gilula 2000b.   [43] Foucart 1890: 375–6.   [44] Hornblower 1982: 240–4.
[45] MacDonald 1981; Trendall 1989.
[46] *SEG* LII, 958; Dubois 2002: 125–8; illustrated in Pugliese Carratelli 1988: 19.

Figure 7 Silver drachma of Istria, fourth century BCE.

At this moment one of the peltasts [light infantry] came up to Xenophon, a man who said that he had been a slave at Athens, with word that he knew the language of these people; 'I think,' he went on, 'that this is my native country, and if there is nothing to hinder, I should like to have a talk with them.'[47]

The man manages to communicate with their enemies, and both he and the rest of the Greeks find out that the name of these people is Macronians; they finally negotiate a happy settlement. This former slave and current mercenary must have been sold as a child, since he could understand the language, but was not aware of his origins: the networks moving human cargo had brought him away from home, the networks moving mercenaries had accidentally brought him back.[48] This moving story is an excellent illustration of the interconnectedness of the ancient Mediterranean, but it also provides a link between the movement of people and the movement of goods, for slaves qualify as both.

A significant number, if not the overwhelming majority, of slaves in Greek communities were of non-Greek origins.[49] Many of them originated from areas where the Greeks had created *apoikiai*, and these *apoikiai* often played an important role in the networks of slave trade.[50] In fact, silver coins from Istria in the Black Sea with an unparalleled depiction of two youthful faces laid out in opposite directions (tête-bêche) have been interpreted as an illustration of the main export product of this Greek *apoikia,* in the same way that Cyrene depicted on its coins its silphium plant and Thasos an amphora of wine: the exports of Istria were nothing else than slaves (see Figure 7).[51]

---

[47] Xenophon, *Anabasis*, 4.8.4.   [48] Ma 2004: 330–2.   [49] But see Vlassopoulos 2010b.
[50] Gavriljuk 2006.   [51] Hansen and Nielsen 2004: 933.

It is unfortunate that for the archaic and classical periods it is only in Athens that we come across some evidence for the ethnic origins of non-Greek slaves and their role in social and economic life. A window on the make-up of the fifth-century Athenian slave population is opened through inscriptions that record the confiscation and sale of the property of some upper-class citizens and foreign residents involved in a religious and political scandal. The household of one of those involved, Cephisodorus, included slaves from Thrace and Illyria in the north, from Scythia and Colchis on the Black Sea, from Caria and Lydia in Asia Minor, from Syria and possibly even from Malta in the west: evidence of how the networks of moving slaves extended to the whole of the Mediterranean and the Black Sea.[52] Non-Greek slaves were used in the most diverse ways in Athens: from house servants,[53] agricultural workers[54] and miners[55] to skilled artisans,[56] managers[57] and bankers,[58] while Scythian archers were employed as public slaves in the role of policemen.[59]

The expansion of networks moving goods across the Mediterranean is captured in a passage from the fifth-century comedian Hermippus, which relates the range of goods available in a large commercial centre like Athens:

Tell me now, Muses whose home is on Olympus, about all the good things Dionysus brings here for men with his black ship during the time he is a captain on the wine-dark sea. From Cyrene there is silphium stalk and cowhides; from the Hellespont mackerel and every kind of salt-fish; from Thessaly barley meal and sides of beef . . . Syracuse supplying us with hogs and cheese . . . From Egypt comes hanging gear, that is, sails and papyrus ropes; and from Syria comes frankincense. Beautiful Crete furnishes cypress wood for the gods, while Libya has vast amounts of ivory for sale, and Rhodes offers raisins and dried figs that bring sweet dreams. He brings pears and goodly apples from Euboea, slaves from Phrygia, and mercenaries from Arcadia. Pagasae supplies us with servants and men with tattoos, and hazelnuts and shining almonds are provided by the Paphlagonians; for these are the accessories of a feast. Sidon again offers dates and wheat, Carthage blankets and embroidered pillows.[60]

We can observe the process by which goods entered the networks of Mediterranean exchange through a contemporary document of a very different nature: a register of toll dues paid over a number of months by foreign ships at an unknown location in Persian-ruled Egypt.[61] The register,

---

[52] *IG* I³, 421, I.33–49; Lewis 2011.   [53] Aristophanes, *Wasps*, 828.   [54] *IG* II², 1553.24–5.
[55] Lauffer 1955/6: 121–40.   [56] Lydus the potter: Canciani 1978.
[57] Sosias the Thracian: Xenophon, *Ways and Means*, 4.1.   [58] Pasion the banker: Trevett 1992.
[59] Bäbler 2005.   [60] K-A, 63; translated in Olson 2007: 435–6; Gilula 2000a.
[61] Translated in Kuhrt 2007: 681–703.

written in Aramaic, records the dues on imported and exported goods of thirty-six 'Ionian' and six 'Phoenician' ships. The ships largely imported to Egypt amphoras with wine and oil, presumably perfumed, metals (iron, bronze, tin), wool and cedarwood, as well as rarer goods, such as wooden supports or the Samian earth used for various industrial and medicinal purposes. After staying in Egypt for between seven and twenty days, the ships departed with their export cargo, on which they paid further dues; because of the nature of our documentation, the only recorded export product is that of natron, used again for a variety of industrial purposes, such as the production of faience objects.[62]

How should we understand this enormous mobility of goods? To start with, it is essential to remember that goods did not move solely through networks of trade; they also moved through networks of friendship or diplomacy. Homer's *Odyssey* has various stories about the 'social life of things': the silver basket that was given to Helen by Alcandre, the wife of Polybus from Egyptian Thebes;[63] or the silver mixing bowl with gilded rims that Phaedimus, king of Phoenician Sidon, gave to Menelaus, who in his turn gave it as a gift to Telemachus.[64] A fascinating story narrates how a pendant from Sicily was acquired by the Thessalian Scopas, who sent it to his friend Cyrus the Younger, the Persian overlord of Asia Minor in the late fifth century, who gave it as a gift to his Greek mistress Aspasia and then, following her suggestion, sent it to his mother Parysatis in Persia.[65] Flowing in the opposite direction, peacocks entered Athenian culture as gifts to Athenian envoys from the Persian kings,[66] and the same must have applied to Persian silverware found in Thrace.[67]

An essential aspect of Mediterranean networks was the search for raw materials and the exchange of surpluses between different regions. We have already mentioned the importance of metals in the expansion of networks and *apoikiai* from the eighth century onwards;[68] grain was another such commodity of crucial importance.[69] Already during the archaic period we have attestations of the importation of grain to the Aegean: while crossing the Hellespont in his invasion of Greece, Xerxes observed the ships bringing grain to the island of Aegina from the Black Sea.[70] The Aegean communities depended for grain imports from four main areas: Sicily, Egypt, Libyan Cyrene and the Black Sea. The profits from the large-scale exportation of cereals was the explanation for the fabulous wealth of some Greek *apoikiai*,

[62] Briant and Descat 1998.   [63] 4.125–7.   [64] 4.611–19.   [65] Aelian, *Various History*, 12.1.
[66] Cartledge 1990; Miller 1997: 189–92.   [67] Archibald 1998: 85; Zournatzi 2000.
[68] Treister 1996.   [69] Bresson 2007a.   [70] Herodotus, 7.147.

attested by the numerous magnificent temples of Sicily and the troves of precious objects from Black Sea cemeteries.[71] It was the ability to commercialise their products that gradually turned the miserable hamlets of semi-dugouts of fishermen and traders in the Black Sea into the organised Greek poleis with their institutions and public monuments.

On the other hand, without the constant and guaranteed supply of grain, the Greek communities of the Aegean would have been unable to sustain their expanded populations. A city like Athens with hundreds of thousands of inhabitants could not survive without maintaining the links with these crucial sources of supply. This led to important interdependencies, and the economic, social and cultural links between Athens and the Black Sea have been examined in impressive detail.[72] Equally important was the ability of Aegean communities to supply commodities lacking in other areas. Olive oil was a commodity highly sought after by both Greeks and non-Greeks in the northern Black Sea, but could not be cultivated locally for climatic reasons; the communities of the Aegean filled in the gap, as shown by the innumerable Aegean amphoras found all over the Black Sea.[73]

It would be a mistake, though, to think that the exchange of goods in the world of networks was merely the result of deficits and surpluses in different regions of the Mediterranean; consumption and fashion played an equally important role.[74] Most Mediterranean communities had their own wine production, but local productions had different features and qualities and they were desirable precisely for these reasons; the same applies to an extensive range of other products. Although Hesiod's Boeotia had its own wine production, Hesiod was fond of consuming the foreign Biblian wine during the summer.[75] Consuming foreign products with desirable qualities not available in local produce is probably a universal feature, but it was the immense expansion of the networks linking together Mediterranean communities from the eighth century onwards which made this practice available to large sectors of the population and for a wide range of products.

This complex movement of commodities in the ancient Mediterranean is best illustrated by the evidence of ancient shipwrecks, which preserve in almost their entirety the cargoes of ancient vessels.[76] An intriguing example is the shipwreck by the island Giglio, off the coast of Etruria, dating to around 590–580.[77] The ship must have started its voyage from the coast of Asia Minor and probably from Samos, given the Samian origin of the oil

---

[71] Fantasia 1993; de Angelis 2000, 2002.   [72] Moreno 2007: 144–208.
[73] Garlan 1999; Banari 2003: 88–174.   [74] Foxhall 1998, 2005.
[75] *Works and Days*, 589; West 1978: 306.   [76] Parker 1992.   [77] Cristofani 1996: 21–48.

lamps for the personal use of the crew. The table vases were primarily of east Greek and Corinthian production, while the unguent vases were Corinthian and Laconian, suggesting that the ship stopped at Corinth on its way west. But most of the amphoras, which contained wine, pine seeds, olives and resin used as a preservative, were of Etruscan manufacture, although there were also a few Samian and Clazomenian from Asia Minor, Corinthian and Laconian from mainland Greece, and even a Phoenician one. The cargo also contained a significant number of copper ingots. But most exciting is the evidence for life onboard ship. The presence of a helmet and arrowheads indicates the necessity of protecting the ship from pirates; but the evidence also includes a writing tablet and a stylus, a full set of vases for a symposion alongside the remains of a *kline* (bed) for reclining, and multiple fragments of pipes for playing music and singing. The Giglio wreck is a magnificent illustration of maritime routes: probably an Ionian ship from Asia Minor moving through central Greece to Etruria and probably heading for southern France, carrying a mixed cargo of products from various Greek and non-Greek areas. But it also illustrates the social and cultural activities, from writing to reclined drinking and singing in the symposion, which were practised and transmitted by agents of mobility like the Giglio crew.

This brings us to the last aspect of the world of networks: the mobility of ideas and technologies. Technologies and ideas like alphabetic writing, coinage, monumental building and sculpture criss-crossed the Mediterranean time and again: they were formulated by non-Greek communities in the eastern Mediterranean, adopted and adapted by the Greeks, and circulated further through the world of networks and the world of *apoikiai* to various non-Greek communities, which further adopted and adapted them. We shall return time and again to the globalisation and glocalisation of such ideas and technologies in the ancient Mediterranean, in particular in Chapter 6 (pp. 226–34), but for the time being let us focus on one illuminating example: that of funerary monuments.

During the archaic period there existed two different traditions of funerary monuments in Greece and in Asia Minor. Greek communities had adopted grave stelae as elaborate grave markers, and artists from various parts of the Greek world had developed various styles and iconographies for these monuments.[78] These grave stelae were very modest undertakings in comparison with those of various areas of Asia Minor, where it was common to construct tombs carved in the living rock on cliffs with often elaborate facades.[79] The movement of artists across the Mediterranean led to the movement of ideas

---

[78] Schmaltz 1983.   [79] von Gall 1966.

Figure 8 Funerary monument of Niceratus and Polyxenus of Istria, Attica, fourth century BCE.

and technologies as regards funerary monuments.[80] Artists in Asia Minor experimented with novel ways of constructing monumental tombs. One such solution, which we shall examine in detail in Chapter 6 (pp. 264–7), was the use of the architectural form of the Greek temple for a funerary monument; the Nereid Monument from Lycian Xanthos is the most famous surviving example (see Figure 39). But these experiments of artists working for non-Greek patrons in Asia Minor were carried back through these same networks into artworks commissioned in mainland Greece. A fourth-century funerary monument for Niceratus and his son Polyxenus from Istria, a Greek *apoikia* on the Black Sea, found at Callithea in Attica, consists of a podium decorated with an Amazonomachy frieze and a Ionic *naiskos* (small temple), within which were standing three male statues (see Figure 8). This is an exact equivalent of a grave monument like the Nereid Monument, if at reduced size. A form of monument based on glocalising Greek architecture in Asia Minor had found its way to an Athenian cemetery.

[80] Tsetskhladze 1998a.

But it was also possible to combine the Greek form of grave stele with the monumental tomb tradition of Asia Minor; the result was grave reliefs which take the form of a naiskos. The earliest naiskos grave reliefs, dating from around 450, have been found in Sinope, a Greek *apoikia* on the south coast of the Black Sea; there was a strong tradition of chamber tombs with architectural facades in Paphlagonia, the region in which Sinope was situated.[81] The stelae from Sinope represent the adaptation of a non-Greek tomb type into the traditional form of Greek grave stele. Like the monumental temple tomb, naiskos grave reliefs also found their way to Athens in the last few decades of the fifth century; by the fourth century they had become one of the most popular forms of Athenian grave monuments. These examples show the constant movement of ideas and technologies between the Greek *apoikiai* in Asia Minor and the Black Sea, the non-Greek communities of Asia Minor and the Greek communities of the Aegean.[82]

3.3 The cosmopolitan interactions of the *emporia*

Networks create and necessitate hubs: the expansion of networks moving goods, people, ideas and technologies led to the creation of *emporia*, hosting international communities of traders, artisans and other professionals, while at the same time being under the greater or lesser control of the host communities.[83] Let us start with the western Mediterranean and examine two *emporia* on the coast of Etruria: Gravisca and Pyrgi. Gravisca was a coastal settlement that functioned as the port of the Etruscan city of Tarquinia. Excavations have uncovered a sanctuary area with a number of buildings and a large number of dedications.[84] The dedications and the other findings from Gravisca testify to the international character of this *emporion*: they include transport amphorae ranging in origin from Asia Minor and the Aegean islands to Massalia and Carthage, as well as Greek statuettes and faience bottles depicting the Egyptian deities Horus and Bes.[85] Many of the dedicated vases bear Greek inscriptions to Greek deities, thus showing that this sanctuary was frequented by Greek traders who conducted their business in the port.

The inscriptions are mostly in the Ionic script, indicating that many of these traders came from the Aegean and Asia Minor, while a few are in the

---

[81] Summerer and von Kienlin 2010.   [82] Hagemajer Allen 2003a.
[83] Bresson and Rouillard 1993; Demetriou 2011, 2012.   [84] Torelli 1977.
[85] Torelli 1977: 398–404.

script of the island of Aegina, an important commercial community during the archaic period. Dedications were made primarily to Hera, Apollo and Aphrodite, deities particularly popular with the Ionian traders who frequented Gravisca; some of the Etruscan inscriptions were dedications to Turan, the Etruscan equivalent of Aphrodite.[86] One of the most intriguing finds is a Laconian *crater* (wine-mixing vase) with a dedication to Turan, which was recovered from the building in which Greek dedications to Aphrodite were also found. An Attic *scyphos* carried an Etruscan inscription with a dedication to Turan along with a Greek inscription with what is probably the name of the dedicator.[87] The sanctuary brought together Greek traders from various communities with Etruscans who dedicated Greek goods to what they saw as the Etruscan equivalent of the Greek deities.[88]

The complexities of cultural interactions in Gravisca are nicely paralleled in another Etruscan *emporion*, that of Pyrgi, which functioned as one of the ports of the Etruscan city of Caere. The Greek name of the settlement (Pyrgoi = towers) is already illustrative of its clientele. Excavations have discovered a sanctuary area similar to that of Gravisca with two main temples and various other buildings. Temple B dates to the late sixth century and takes the form of a Greek temple with columns on all four sides (*peripteros*). Adjacent to this temple the excavators discovered three golden tablets, which were originally fixed with nails to wooden doors. Two of the tablets are in Etruscan, while the third is in Phoenician.[89] All three of them refer in different ways to the dedication of another sacred building by Thefarie Velianas, the ruler of Caere, to a deity who is identified as the Etruscan Uni in the Etruscan tablets, but as the Phoenician Astarte in the Phoenician one.[90] The bilingual dedications testify to the importance of Carthaginians in this Etruscan port and illustrate the process of translating deities that we have also seen in Gravisca. Around the middle of the fifth century, Temple A was constructed to the north of Temple B. But while the plan of Temple A is typically Etruscan and pointedly differs from that of the adjacent Greek-style Temple B, its figured decoration is dominated by Greek mythology. The best preserved relief panel from the rear pediment of the temple depicts two violent scenes from the mythological cycle of the Seven against Thebes: the relief juxtaposes a depiction of Capaneus being struck by Zeus' thunderbolt with the famous Homeric scene of Tydeus

---

[86] Johnston and Pandolfini 2000: 71.   [87] Johnston and Pandolfini 2000: 21.
[88] Demetriou 2012: 64–104; but see Cristofani 1996: 49–57.   [89] Heurgon 1966.
[90] Cristofani 1996: 59–81.

Figure 9 Pediment of Temple A, Pyrgi, mid-fifth century BCE.

about to devour the brain of his fallen opponent Melanippus, and Athena in disgust withholding from Tydeus her intended offer of immortality (see Figure 9).[91]

If Pyrgi documents the complex interactions between Etruscans, Phoenicians and Greeks and shows the necessity of a non-Hellenocentric perspective, the same is no less the case with the *emporion* of Spina, situated in the estuary of the River Po on the Adriatic Sea.[92] Greek sources present Spina as a wealthy Greek *apoikia* during the classical period;[93] that this is grossly misleading is proven by the inscriptions that have been recovered in Spina. Out of around 200 inscriptions, 180 are in Etruscan, around twenty in Greek, and another ten in the language of the native Veneti; we have clearly to assume a triangulation between Etruscan and Greek settlers along with the 'natives'. That Spina was primarily an Etruscan settlement is proven not only by the clear preponderance of Etruscan inscriptions, some of which seem to

---

[91] Serra Ridgway 1990; Haynes 2000: 174–84.
[92] See Cristofani 1983: 95–103, 128–9; Camporeale 2000: 513–21.
[93] Hansen and Nielsen 2004: 334.

be of a public character (one apparent boundary stone reads 'I am the border'), but also by the Etruscan influence on the organisation of space and the division of land.[94] This *emporion* with Etruscan cultural preponderance on the Adriatic Sea is an important reminder that in the western Mediterranean the Greeks were not the only people familiar with traditions and techniques of 'colonisation'; nor were the Etruscans passive recipients of foreign merchants in their country.[95] The cemeteries of Spina have turned up a massive quantity of Athenian pottery covering most of the classical period, which is accompanied by inscriptions in the Attic alphabet and the use of Athenian lecythoi as funerary gifts, as in Attica.[96] Some of the Greek inscriptions are dedications to Apollo, Dionysus and Hermes, showing the cult of Greek deities as in other *emporia*, such as Gravisca.

The complex interactions that took place in an *emporion* like Spina can be illustrated through two examples.[97] According to Ps.-Aristotle, there was a tradition that Daedalus had arrived at Spina and left behind two statues made in the archaic fashion, one for himself and one for his son Icarus.[98] It is accordingly impressive to find in Spina a bronze bulla with two male figures on opposite sides, identified through Etruscan inscriptions as Taitle (Daedalus) and Vikare (Icarus).[99] A Greek myth was created concerning the local commercial settlement, and it was taken over and depicted by Etruscan artists. As an *emporion* in a lagoon area without stone resources, it is unsurprising that no monumental temples have been found in Spina and that houses were made of wood. But Spina was also wealthy, important and connected enough to dedicate an impressive treasury (*thesauros*) at Delphi.[100] This does not necessarily mean that Spina was a Greek polis, as there is evidence of other Etruscan cities dedicating treasuries at Panhellenic sanctuaries, as we have seen in Chapter 2 (pp. 40–1). But it is particularly important that an *emporion* with a predominant Etruscan presence would make the decision to dedicate a building in a Panhellenic sanctuary.

Let us move to the eastern Mediterranean and examine the case of Naucratis, the sole Greek *apoikia* in Egypt.[101] The discovery of large amounts of Greek pottery shows that the settlement was already in existence in the late seventh century during the reign of pharaoh Psammetichus I; however, a major reorganisation seems to have taken place during the reign of Amasis:

Amasis became a philhellene [friend of the Greeks], and besides other services which he performed for some of the Greeks, he gave those who came to Egypt the

[94] Gulletta 1994.   [95] Cristofani 1983.   [96] Johnston 1979.   [97] Berti and Guzzo 1993.
[98] *Mirabilia*, 836a.   [99] Camporeale 2000: 513–14, with fig. 329.
[100] Strabo, *Geography*, 5.1.7.   [101] See in general Möller 2000; Demetriou 2012: 105–52.

city of Naucratis to live in; and to those who travelled to the country without wanting to settle there, he gave lands where they might set up altars and make holy places for their gods.[102]

It seems that, contrary to what Herodotus suggests, Amasis in fact restricted the Greek presence in Egypt, by forcing Greek traders to trade in Egypt only through Naucratis; as he mentions in another passage, any Greek trader found in a mouth of the Nile other than the one leading to Naucratis had to sail back.[103] It was this restriction that led to the organisation of Naucratis as a settlement. The importance of the relationship between the Egyptian state and Naucratis is illustrated by a fourth-century hieroglyphic stele, in which the pharaoh Nectanebo grants 'the tithes from the gold and silver and whatever is produced' in Naucratis to the goddess Neith of Sais, for 'she is the mistress of the Ocean and it is she who bestows its bounty'.[104] The power of the Egyptian state could not be better illustrated than by a decree in hieroglyphic standing in the middle of the Greek settlement.[105] Scholars have posited the existence of an Egyptian settlement in Naucratis, but there is little evidence for the presence of Egyptians, although this is hardly surprising given that the residential quarters of the city have never been excavated.[106]

A decree from Rhodes towards the end of the fifth century grants the status of *proxenos* (representative in a foreign community) to an individual whose name has been lost in the text of the inscription, but whose father's name is Pytheas.[107] There have been two different restorations of his origin, either as Eg[yptian] from Naucratis or as Aeg[inetan] from Naucratis. The latter restoration has been suggested because scholars have been unwilling to accept that a Greek from Naucratis could be described as an Egyptian. But the assumption is certainly wrong; to give merely one example, the Greek *apoikoi* of Cyrene in Libya could be described as Libyans from Cyrene.[108] It is particularly interesting that the inscription also records the honorand's profession as an interpreter. While the mention of a profession is extremely uncommon in Greek public inscriptions, it was a common means of identification for Egyptians: this interpreter from Naucratis adopted an Egyptian means of identification.[109]

Naucratis provides fascinating evidence both for the hybrid results emerging out of the worlds of networks and *apoikiai*, as well as the formation of Greek identity within these same worlds. On the one hand, one encounters workshops producing objects in a variety of styles and iconographies.

---

[102] Herodotus, 2.178.   [103] 2.179.   [104] Translation from Gunn 1943: 58–9.
[105] Demetriou 2012: 121–2.   [106] Möller 2000: 185.   [107] *SIG*³, 110.
[108] Pausanias, 6.19.10; see Laronde 1990: 170.   [109] Bresson 1991.

Figure 10(a) Faience aryballus with cartouche of pharaoh Apries, Camirus, Rhodes, sixth century BCE.

Figure 10(b) Faience vase in the shape of warrior head, sixth century BCE.

One Naucratis workshop was producing objects in faience (see Figure 10); particularly interesting is the production of scarabs, traditional Egyptian objects widely glocalised across the Mediterranean from the archaic period onwards, in a variety of styles ranging from fully Egyptian to largely Greek. Equally interesting is the production of statuettes in Greco-Cypriote styles and iconographies, heavily influenced by Egyptian and/or Phoenician elements (pp. 215–16). Many of these hybrid scarabs and statuettes were widely exported to eastern Greece, whose communities were heavily represented in Naucratis.[110]

At the same time that they created hybrid objects, the Greek settlers in Naucratis were keen to stress their common Greek identity, as Herodotus reports when describing the Greek sanctuaries:

---

[110] Höckmann and Kreikenbom 2001; Höckmann 2007.

Of these the greatest and most famous and most visited precinct is that which is called the Hellenion, founded jointly by the Ionian cities of Chios, Teos, Phocaea and Clazomenae, the Dorian cities of Rhodes, Cnidos, Halicarnassus and Phaselis, and one Aeolian city, Mytilene. It is to these that the precinct belongs, and these are the cities that furnish overseers of the *emporion*; if any other cities advance claims, they claim what does not belong to them. The Aeginetans made a precinct of their own, sacred to Zeus; and so did the Samians for Hera and the Milesians for Apollo.[111]

The existence of the Hellenion, as well as the many dedications to 'the gods of the Greeks', illustrate how the experience of living in a Greek enclave in a foreign land could create, strengthen or redefine the sense of Greek identity; at the same time, the existence of separate polis sanctuaries, as well as the debate over which Greek cities had the right to administer the Hellenion, show once more the inherent disunity and multiformity of Greek identity.[112] An intriguing story is that of Rhodopis, a Thracian slave brought to Naucratis by Xanthes of Samos, where she was freed and worked as a courtesan; her success led her to dedicate a tithe of her fortune at Delphi, in the form of large iron spits.[113] A Thracian slave brought by the networks of mobility to the *emporion* of Naucratis in Egypt, where she adopted enough of Greek culture to be willing to make a dedication at a Panhellenic shrine: an excellent illustration of the interconnectedness of the four parallel worlds.

International *emporia* were not only to be found on the periphery of the Greek world. During the classical period one of the most important Mediterranean *emporia* was situated at Piraeus, the commercial port of Athens.[114] The Old Oligarch, a fifth-century source, describes eloquently the function of Piraeus as a hub of Mediterranean-wide networks and their effects on the host community:

If there should be mention also of slighter matters, first, by virtue of their naval power, the Athenians have mingled with various peoples and discovered types of luxury. Whatever the delicacy in Sicily, Italy, Cyprus, Egypt, Lydia, the Black Sea, the Peloponnese, or anywhere else – all these have been brought together into one place by virtue of naval power. Further, hearing every kind of dialect, they have taken something from each; the Greeks rather tend to use their own dialect, way of life, and type of dress, but the Athenians use a mixture from all the Greeks and Barbarians.[115]

---

[111] 2.178.   [112] Malkin 2011: 87–93.   [113] Herodotus, 2.134–5.
[114] Garland 2001; Demetriou 2012: 188–229.   [115] *Constitution of the Athenians*, 2.7–8.

Athens was a cosmopolitan society, where a significant proportion of the population consisted of non-Greeks, and one could encounter foreigners of the most diverse origins and status.[116] There were aristocratic exiles who had found refuge in Athens, like the Carian Tymnes, who was possibly a victim of the Ionian Revolt and who inscribed his tombstone in both Greek and Carian,[117] the Thracian prince Rheboulas, who was made an Athenian citizen,[118] or the Persian aristocrat Zopyrus.[119] At the opposite end of the spectrum one would encounter the thousands of slaves and freedmen we have already mentioned (p. 89). In between, there were countless foreign merchants, artisans, sailors and labourers, some of whom were visitors and passers-by, but many of whom were permanent settlers. Foreigners residing in Athens for more than a month, whether non-Greeks or from other Greek cities, had to register as metics (resident foreigners) and had obligations towards Athens as well as privileges. Xenophon condemns the fact that in the mid-fourth century many Barbarian metics were serving in the Athenian army:

The polis itself too would gain if the citizens served in the ranks together, and no longer found themselves in the same company with Lydians, Phrygians, Syrians and barbarians of all sorts, of whom a large part of our metics consists.[120]

A tombstone from the late fifth century was probably erected for one of those non-Greek metics who died fighting for Athens during the Peloponnesian War:

Mannes, the son of Orymas [or of the Orymaioi], was the best of Phrygians in broad-spaced Athens. This is his beautiful memorial. And, by Zeus, I have not seen a better wood-cutter than myself. He died in the war.[121]

A fourth-century Athenian decree honouring Straton, the king of the Phoenician city of Sidon, exempts merchants who are citizens of Sidon from the obligation to register as metics while visiting Athens for the purposes of trade.[122] The network between Athens and Phoenician cities is also attested by Athenian decrees bestowing honours on Phoenicians: one honours the Sidonian Apollonides, the son of Demetrius, following the recommendation of merchants and ship-owners,[123] while the other bestows the same honours on a merchant from Tyre and his father, who had conveyed grain to Athens and promised to do so in the future as well.[124] The presence of Phoenician

---

[116] Osborne and Byrne 1996; Bäbler 1998.   [117] *IG* I³, 1344; Bäbler 1998: 84–6.
[118] *IG* II², 349.   [119] Miller 1997: 24; Bäbler 1998: 101–3.   [120] *Ways and Means*, 2.3.
[121] *IG* I³, 1361; Bäbler 1998: 159–63.   [122] *IG* II², 141; translated in R-O, 21.   [123] *IG* II², 343.
[124] *IG* II², 342.

merchants in Athens is attested by numerous tombstones, many of which contain bilingual Greek and Phoenician inscriptions.[125] An interesting example of the mixed marriages that took place in the cosmopolitan milieu of Piraeus is the gravestone of Eirene from the Greek *apoikia* of Byzantion, who is commemorated by inscriptions in both Greek and Phoenician: the Greek metic Eirene must have married a Phoenician metic.[126] In the same way that cults played an important role for Greek merchants and sailors in *emporia* outside Greece, foreigners in Athens brought their own cults and built their own sanctuaries. A fourth-century Athenian decree bestows on merchants from the Phoenician settlement of Cition in Cyprus the right to buy land to build a sanctuary to Aphrodite, whose cult was closely associated with Cyprus; the decree mentions that a similar privilege had previously been bestowed on the Egyptians to build a sanctuary to Isis.[127] We shall explore the Thracian cults in Athens in Chapter 4 (pp. 144–5).

3.4 Frontier societies

Traditionally, historians have examined Greek *apoikiai* under the rubric of 'Greek colonisation'. According to this approach, in the latter half of the eighth century, for reasons which are not totally clear, but which probably included overpopulation, trade expansion and sociopolitical conflicts, Greek communities from mainland Greece started to send away colonies, originally to Italy and Sicily, but subsequently to the rest of the Mediterranean and the Black Sea. The colonists were inhabitants of the mother city (*metropolis*) under the leadership of a founder (*oecist*), who received a favourable oracle from Delphi, brought along the sacred fire from the metropolis, set up the new community, and received hero cult after his death.[128] The Greek colonies confronted in a variety of ways the native populations, which showed different degrees of acculturation and Hellenisation.[129]

There are various important problems with this traditional approach, which has come under significant attack in the last two decades,[130] although an overall alternative account has yet to be formulated.[131] The first set of problems concerns the decision to use the term 'colonisation' to describe

---

[125] Bäbler 1998: 115–55.   [126] *IG* II², 8440.

[127] *IG* II², 337; translated in *R-O*, 91; Simms 1989.   [128] Graham 1982: 143–52.

[129] Boardman 1999.

[130] Osborne 1996b: 79–92, 1998; Lyons and Papadopoulos 2002; Hurst and Owen 2005; Purcell 2005; Wilson 2006.

[131] The traditional account is still presented in Tsetskhladze 2006a.

these phenomena. Colonisation is a term with significant ideological ballast, and its employment can impose all sorts of implicit and explicit connotations. Modern scholars have tended to approach Greek colonisation on the basis of a rather limited conceptualisation of colonisation, which has been profoundly shaped by the experience of Western colonialisms in the last two centuries.[132] In contrast to these colonisations, which were undertaken by metropolitan national states in order to expand their territories and resources, Greek overseas settlements had a very different nature. With minor exceptions, Greek *apoikiai* were independent politically and economically from their metropolis, and retained only cultural and religious links. This is one of the reasons I have opted to use the transliterated term *apoikia* and avoid using the word 'colony'.

The generally positive attitude of Western scholars towards colonialism until the age of decolonisation after the Second World War meant that their accounts of antiquity were often conditioned in order to portray in a positive manner what they considered as the Greek equivalents of modern colonialisms.[133] Though this is hardly the case nowadays of course, it can still have very significant implicit connotations.[134] Talking about colonisation brings into mind images of confrontation with native populations which are less advanced technologically, socially and economically, and which are fated to be defeated and subjugated in the shorter or longer term. This can be a very misleading approach to Greek *apoikiai*.[135] The relationship between Greek *apoikiai* and their non-Greek neighbours could vary enormously, as we shall have the opportunity to observe. Although there are many examples in which the settlement of Greek *apoikiai* took place in collaboration with indigenous populations, there is no doubt that in equally many cases the Greek *apoikoi* exercised significant violence to expropriate land; there are a few cases in which Greek communities even managed to subjugate the indigenous population and turn them into dependent communities, as was the case with Heracleia and the Mariandynoi on the Black Sea, or Syracuse and the Cyllyrioi in Sicily. However, in the vast majority of cases the Greek *apoikiai* were simply not in a position to do anything of the sort, or even impose their terms on the 'natives'. In fact, many Greek *apoikiai* came under the protectorate of non-Greek communities and rulers, others became part of mixed Greco-Barbarian states, and a significant number were even conquered and/or destroyed by non-Greek communities. The Western colonisations of the

---

[132] Snodgrass 2005.   [133] de Angelis 1998; Shepherd 2005.   [134] Owen 2005.
[135] Malkin 2004.

last two centuries are very misleading models for understanding Greek *apoikiai*.

The traditional view presents Greek colonisation as a dramatic event: the sudden emergence of the colonists and their conquest and occupation of territory that previously belonged to native groups. Some Greek *apoikiai*, in particular the earliest ones in Sicily, were probably created in just such a way.[136] But there is clear evidence that many Greek *apoikiai* were created in rather different ways: the Greek *apoikiai* in the gulf of Taranto in southern Italy were the result of long processes of interaction between Greeks and native populations. Archaeological evidence shows that for more than a century Greek artisans and traders lived alongside local groups in mixed settlements, and it was only around the latter half of the seventh century that some of these settlements developed into Greek *apoikiai* with their own territories (Metapontion, Siris).[137]

Furthermore, we need to realise that 'colonisation' and mobility were not a uniquely Greek phenomenon, but a process which involved many different peoples in the western Mediterranean.[138] Modern scholars often make an exception to the uniqueness of Greek colonisation by recognising the parallel phenomenon of Phoenician colonisation.[139] But if 'colonisation' is the movement of groups of men able to carry arms and conquer territory, we must recognise that the creation of Greek and Phoenician *apoikiai* was part of a wider phenomenon which in the western Mediterranean also included other communities, such as the Etruscans or the various Oscan-speaking populations of Italy we shall examine below.[140]

These complex interactions, which both predate and postdate the emergence of Greek *apoikiai*, cannot be understood through a polar division between two static and closed entities of the Greeks and the natives; in most of the cases there rather existed a complex triangulation between various groups of Greeks and various groups of non-Greeks, some of which were locals and some of which were as much newcomers as the Greeks.[141] Scholars attempt to capture this complexity through the concept of the middle ground.[142] Instead of the dominance of one state or culture and the acculturation of the dominated, the concept of the middle ground refers to two things at the same time: on the one hand, a physical space which is in between different cultures, states and communities; on the other hand, a form of cultural dialogue in which people from different backgrounds attempt to reach

---

[136] Malkin 2002a.   [137] Yntema 2000.   [138] Gras 1995.   [139] Niemeyer 2006.
[140] Cristofani 1983, 1996.   [141] Hodos 2006.   [142] White 1991.

accommodation and create a mutually comprehensible world, often through creative misunderstanding of each other's values and ideas.[143]

An excellent example of the middle ground is the area of Campania.[144] From 800 onwards, the area showed a complex interaction between the 'native' communities, on the one hand, and various newcomers, on the other: Phoenician traders and sailors; Greek settlers who founded Cumae to the north and Poseidonia to the south; Etruscan settlers in communities like Nocera and Capua; and, finally, Campanian newcomers who gradually conquered the whole area from the fifth century onwards.[145] There is no better illustration of the Campanian middle ground between Greeks, Etruscans and Campanians than the inscribed vases found in graves in Campania: a tomb at Nocera contained a pitcher with an Italic inscription alongside an Etruscan bucchero cup inscribed with the Greek name Ariston; a tomb at Pontecagnano contained a bucchero cup with an Etruscan proprietary inscription alongside an Attic cylix inscribed in Greek; finally, a tomb at Capua contained a small drinking vase with an Etruscan inscription along with a bronze stamnos with an important Italic inscription.[146]

In order to examine these issues in more detail, we shall focus on two areas from opposite extremes of the world of *apoikiai*: Sicily and southern Italy, on the one hand, and the north coast of the Black Sea, on the other. These were the two major areas where Greek *apoikiai* emerged; the third major area, Thrace, is discussed as a case study in section 3.5 of this chapter.

From the late eighth century southern Italy and Sicily had witnessed the emergence of the earliest Greek *apoikiai* (Map 4).[147] Many flourishing and powerful Greek *apoikiai* emerged in southern Italy, alongside indigenous non-Greek communities such as the Messapians and the Peucetians, and non-Greek incomers like the Etruscans and the Lucanians.[148] The Greek *apoikiai* in Sicily coexisted with a variety of other communities and cultures; the Greeks had created settlements on the eastern and central coasts of the island, while the Phoenicians had contemporaneously settled the westernmost extremity; the interior of the island was occupied by various 'native' communities, from the Sicels in the east to the Elymians in the west.[149]

---

[143] Malkin 2002b; cf. Mairs 2011a.   [144] Malkin 2002b.   [145] Frederiksen 1984.
[146] Cristofani 1996: 108.   [147] Dunbabin 1948; Boardman 1999: 161–210.
[148] Greco 1992; de Juliis 1996.   [149] Asheri 1988; Hodos 2006: 89–157; Albanese Procelli 2003.

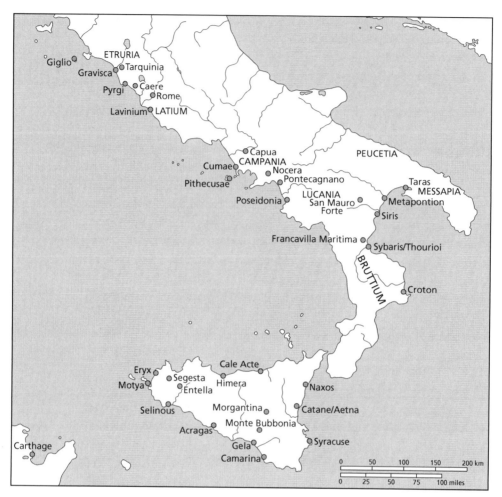

Map 4 Italy and Sicily

We can explore this complex world by focusing on Selinous, a Greek *apoikia* in southwest Sicily, located in an area that exhibited a close triangulation between the Greeks to the south, the Phoenician settlement of Motya in the west and the Elymian communities of Segesta and Eryx to the north. The relationships between these different communities could diverge significantly. Around 580 the Elymians defeated an alliance between Selinous and the 'colonising' expedition led by Pentathlus of Cnidos; in 510, the Spartan prince Dorieus attempted to create an *apoikia* at Eryx and was defeated by an alliance between the Phoenicians and Segesta; in 480, the Greeks of Selinous fought on the Carthaginian side against the Greek alliance of Syracuse and Acragas; in 416, hostilities with Selinous led Segesta to invite the Athenians to intervene in Sicily on its behalf; finally,

Selinous was conquered and destroyed by the Carthaginians in 409 and spent its fourth-century history under a Carthaginian protectorate.[150]

But interactions were not restricted to hostilities and warfare; we also know that there existed regulations for intermarriage between Selinous and Segesta.[151] Archaic inscriptions already attest the existence of Greek residents in the Phoenician settlement of Motya,[152] who fought in 397 alongside the Carthaginians against the Greek besiegers,[153] while many Carthaginians were living in sumptuous houses in Syracuse and other Greek *apoikiai*.[154] The Phoenician presence in Selinous in the fourth century is underscored by the multitude of Phoenician stelae dedicated in the sanctuary of Demeter Malophorus.[155] Selinous was keen to underscore its membership of the Panhellenic world, as shown by the construction of a *thesauros* in the Panhellenic sanctuary of Olympia.[156]

But Selinous was also a frontier society with a mixed population, as shown by a fifth-century Selinountian curse tablet recording a number of names that its author wished to be punished.[157] Some of the names are typically Greek, like Lycinus and Pyrrhus; one is Semitic (Magon), which is easily explicable given the proximity of Selinous to the Phoenician settlements; some are native Sicilian, like Apelus and Titelus, but others are Italic, like Rotylus, Caelius and Romis; finally, some seem to be of Asiatic origin, like Tamiras and Nanelaius, while a significant number are without parallels and therefore unclassifiable (Ecotis, Cadosis, Saris).[158] A simple distinction between Greeks and natives is deeply misleading here; we need to take into account the wider middle ground that included diverse groups of 'natives' and Greek and non-Greek settlers and immigrants.

Interactions also had significant cultural consequences. Segesta adopted the alphabet of Selinous to record its language, used Greek pottery and Greek-style terracottas extensively, while Greek artists and craftsmen worked in the construction of an impressive building in the form of a Greek temple for Segesta (see Figure 11).[159] The example of Segesta is not unique: archaeological excavations in inland Sicily have revealed a large number of settlements, whose material culture makes it often impossible to decide whether they were 'native' settlements which had glocalised elements of Greek culture, 'native' settlements with Greek settlers or Greek settlements with 'native' settlers. The settlement of Monte Bubbonia, situated 20 km inland from the Greek *apoikia* of Gela, is a characteristic example: a

---

[150] Hansen and Nielsen 2004: 220–4; de Angelis 2003.   [151] Thucydides, 6.6.2.
[152] *SEG* IV, 44.   [153] Diodorus, 14.53.4.   [154] Diodorus, 14.46.1.   [155] White 1967.
[156] Pausanias, 6.19.11.   [157] *SEG* XVI, 573; Dubois 1989: 49–52.   [158] Masson 1972.
[159] de la Genière 1978.

Figure 11 Temple of Segesta, fifth century BCE.

Greek-style *naiskos* together with an elaborately built subterranean chamber (*bothros*), Greek-style antefixes and votive terracottas, Greek vases, and
an orthogonally planned urban layout characteristic of Greek *apoikiai*
coexist with 'native' forms of graves and 'native' ceramics.[160]

The difficulty of separating Greek from non-Greek in terms of the material
culture of the frontier societies of Sicily is paralleled in the revealing biography of the 'native' Sicel leader Ducetius. He emerges for the first time in 461,
when he led the Sicel forces which, in collaboration with the Syracusans,
conquered and divided the territory of the Greek city of Aetna, which was
settled by the deposed Syracusan tyrants with their mercenaries. Ducetius
went on to refound his native city and create a new Sicel settlement, as well as
distributing lands within these settlements. He became the leader of a Sicel
alliance and in his plans for expansion he clashed with both native and Greek
communities, until he was finally defeated by the Syracusans and the
Acragantines, and was sent into exile to Corinth. In 446, following an oracle,

[160] Fischer-Hansen 2002.

he managed to return to Sicily as leader of an expedition to create an *apoikia* at Cale Acte on the north coast of Sicily, an *apoikia* which included both Greek settlers and native Sicels, and where Ducetius met his death in 440.[161] The example of Ducetius is not merely revealing of how often and how easily Greeks and non-Greeks could cross ethnic lines; it also illustrates how techniques of power such as land distribution and the creation of *apoikiai* could be employed by Greeks and non-Greeks alike, as well as showing that crossing the sea was not an exclusively Greek practice.

A different illustration of frontier societies in the western Mediterranean emerges from the results of the interaction between Greek *apoikiai* and another current of mobility: the gradual movement of Oscan-speaking groups of warriors and settlers from the sixth century onwards from their original heartlands in the mountainous parts of central Italy to the coastal areas. Those who moved to Campania on the Tyrrhenian coast, where they encountered Greek and Etruscan settlers alongside the 'native' Opici population, became known as Campanians;[162] those who moved to the southern coasts, where they encountered Greek settlers and the 'native' Oenotrians, became known as Lucanians and Brettians.[163] In the course of the fifth century the Campanians managed to conquer the Greek *apoikia* of Cumae and the Etruscan centres of Campania like Capua, while the Lucanians conquered the Greek *apoikia* of Poseidonia and large parts of the southern territories.

But this is not the whole story: the Campanians and Lucanians were not just conquerors and settlers who moved from the mountainous highlands to the nearby lowlands; they also entered the wider networks of Mediterranean mobility.[164] Their martial valour, along with the need to supplement the resources of their mountainous homelands, made them highly sought after as mercenaries in areas further afield. From the fifth century onwards Campanians start to appear as mercenaries in Sicily, sometimes employed by the Greek *apoikiai*, sometimes by the Carthaginians, and often changing employers with impressive rapidity.[165] Even more interesting is the fact that the Campanian mercenaries exploited the opportunities offered by a chaotic succession of wars in order to settle in the island and create their own autonomous communities. In the late fifth century some Campanians managed to convince the native Elymians in Sicilian Entella to accept them as fellow citizens, only subsequently to massacre them and make the

---

[161] Jackman 2006.   [162] Frederiksen 1984; Cerchiai 1995.   [163] Pontrandolfo 1982.

[164] For perceptions of the Oscan-speaking populations, see Dench 1995.

[165] Tagliamonte 1994: 124–64.

city Campanian;[166] other Campanians in the east of the island were given the city of Catane to settle and guard by the Syracusan tyrant Dionysius I.[167] The life of these Campanian communities in Sicily is beautifully illustrated by the minting of coins with the Greek legend Καμπανῶν (of the Campanians) and the fitting images of a galloping horse and a helmet,[168] or by a bronze weight from Camarina with the Greek inscription δαμόσια Καμπανῶν (public weight of the Campanians).[169] But most fascinating is to hear about Mamercus, one of the Campanian leaders, a skilled orator and a proud writer of poems and tragedies; his composition of an elegiac distich in Greek for the dedication of armour captured from his Syracusan enemies happens to survive:

> These bucklers, purple-painted, decked with ivory, gold, and amber,
> we captured with our simple little shields.[170]

As with the Thracian courtesan Rhodopis, who made a dedication at the Panhellenic sanctuary of Delphi (p. 100), the Campanian Mamercus composed in the genres of Greek literature in Greek. These non-Greeks encountered Greeks in the complex settings of cosmopolitan *emporia* and the frontier societies of Greek *apoikiai*, linked together by the world of networks; their participation in two levels of the Panhellenic world (Panhellenic sanctuaries, Greek literature) is an important indication for the processes of globalisation and glocalisation we shall examine in Chapter 6.

We can also follow the results of the expansion of Oscan-speaking populations in southern Italy, where in the last quarter of the fifth century Cumae fell to the Campanians and Poseidonia to the Lucanians.[171] A colourful passage attributed to the fourth-century scholar Aristoxenus presents an image of what happened to these Greek *apoikiai*:

We act like the people of Poseidonia, who dwell on the Tyrrhenian Gulf. It so happened that although they were originally Greeks, they were completely barbarised ... they changed their speech and their other practices, but they still celebrate one festival that is Greek to this day, wherein they gather together and recall those ancient words and institutions, and after bewailing them and weeping over them in one another's presence they depart home.[172]

The situation in Lucanian Poseidonia was infinitely more complex than Aristoxenus would suggest. On the one hand, there is evident continuity

---

[166] Diodorus, 14.9.8–9.   [167] Diodorus, 14.15.3.   [168] Tagliamonte 1994: 137–44.
[169] Tagliamonte 1994: 150–1, with tables xiv–xv.   [170] Plutarch, *Life of Timoleon*, 31.1.
[171] For the history of Poseidonia, see Pedley 1990.   [172] Athenaeus, *Deipnosophists*, 14.632.

in the maintenance of Greek cults and Greek temples, or in coinage which retains the images of the Greek period and the legend in Greek letters with the name of the city.[173] On the other hand, an Oscan dedication by a Lucanian magistrate found in the assembly place of the city shows the emergence of novel institutions run by the new rulers of the city. The influx of Lucanian settlers is shown by the changes in burial customs: weapons, which were typical in Lucanian burials but absent from the cemeteries of the Greek *apoikia*, start to appear in significant numbers.[174]

A particularly important phenomenon of this period in southern Italy is the creation of new forms of identity and new forms of material culture based on a hybrid mix of Lucanian, Greek and Etruscan elements and practices. One aspect of this phenomenon is the emergence from the late fifth century onwards of regional traditions of red-figure pottery in Lucania, Apulia, Campania and Poseidonia. Remarkable is the combination of cultural elements: from the Athenian red-figure technique and Greek-style iconographic repertoire to non-Greek vase shapes and the depiction of themes that represent Lucanian, Apulian and Campanian identities.[175] We can further follow this hybridity in the case of the painted tombs of Poseidonia.[176] Painted tombs were effectively non-existent in the Aegean Greek world before the emergence of the Macedonian tombs in the fourth century. But they were very common in Etruria,[177] and scholars have detected Etruscan influences in the famous Tomb of the Diver, an early fifth-century painted tomb at Poseidonia, which is so far a unique early example; the rest of the painted tombs appear about a century later in the aftermath of the Lucanian conquest. The major themes depicted are the return of the warrior; hunting; funeral games involving wrestling, boxing, duelling and horse racing; and funeral ceremonies and processions. The scenes depicting the return of the victorious rider, often accompanied by captives and booty and encountering a greeting female, are emblematic of the identity of the Lucanian aristocracy and are paralleled by depictions in the painted tombs of Campanian Capua and in other visual media (see Figure 12).[178] But they were created using iconographic schemes of Greek art, such as the libation scenes of women and warriors of Athenian pottery (pp. 178–9).[179] The parallel between the depiction of scenes depicting the departure of Persian warriors on Athenian vases (see Figure 23) and scenes

---

[173] Wonder 2002.   [174] Pedley 1990: 105–8.
[175] Trendall 1989; de Juliis 1996: 262–75, 302–9.
[176] Pontrandolfo and Rouveret 1992; Andreae and Schepkowski 2007.   [177] Steingräber 2006.
[178] Schneider-Herrmann 1996.   [179] Corrigan 1979: 365–90.

Figure 12 Fresco, Andriuolo tomb 86, Poseidonia, fourth century BCE.

depicting the homecoming of Lucanian warriors in Lucanian tomb paintings is particularly intriguing.

If Greek *apoikiai* like Poseidonia were conquered by non-Greeks, it is also important to examine some other Greek *apoikiai* from southern Italy which managed to create extensive territories incorporating non-Greek communities, and even to create hegemonic alliances that included Greek and non-Greek communities. The most famous case is that of archaic Sybaris, which was famed as having ruled over four nations and twenty-five cities.[180] This is shown by the coins of Greek and non-Greek communities of southern Italy which adopted the emblem of the bull that appears on Sybarite coins and which were in some kind of monetary alliance or subjection to Sybaris.[181] The interaction with non-Greek communities is also illustrated by the archaic text of a treaty that has been found in the Panhellenic sanctuary of Olympia:

Agreement was made between the Sybarites and their allies and the Serdaioi for friendship faithful and guileless forever. Protectors: Zeus and Apollo and the other gods and the city Poseidonia.[182]

[180] Strabo, *Geography*, 6.1.13; *Sibari.*   [181] Rutter 1997: 22–7.
[182] *SEG* XXII, 336; translated in *Fornara*, 29.

The Serdaioi were a non-Greek community of southern Italy, who minted their own Greek-style coins; the presence of Poseidonia, which was an *apoikia* of Sybaris, among the witnesses to the treaty shows the importance of the connection between metropoleis and *apoikiai*, while the display of this local treaty in the Panhellenic centre of Olympia testifies to the importance of the Panhellenic world we examined in Chapter 2. By and large, the vast majority of *apoikiai* in Sicily and Italy retained a strong sense of being Greek and of participating in the Panhellenic world.[183] This is exemplified not only by the *thesauroi* and the sumptuous dedications in Panhellenic centres like Delphi and Olympia, or the celebration of their athletic victories through epinician poems by famous mainland poets like Pindar; it is also illustrated by documents from the *apoikiai* themselves. The first Greek inscription to mention an Olympic victor dates from around 600 and consists of a dedication of a statue to Athena by the victor Cleombrotus.[184] The dedicatory inscription was found in Timpone della Motta in the territory of Sybaris, where a native settlement in Francavilla Maritima was succeeded by a Greek temple to Athena. This is an important illustration of the link between the Panhellenic world of festival competitions and the frontier societies of southern Italy.

We can now turn to the history of the two greatest *apoikiai* of the northern Black Sea: Olbia, in the estuary of the rivers Bug and Dnieper; and Panticapaion, the capital of the Bosporan kingdom, on the peninsula of Kerch (Map 5). Greek presence in the Black Sea starts in the seventh century.[185] The material culture of the earliest Greek settlers on the island of Berezan close to Olbia shows strong interactions with the native populations: the Greek settlers, mainly involved in fishing and the exchange of goods, adopted native architecture in building semi-dugout houses instead of traditional Greek houses, and used local hand-made pottery in addition to Greek vases.[186] By the late sixth century, though, Olbia and other Greek *apoikiai* in the Black Sea had adopted the typical outlook of a Greek polis: stone temples and public buildings, agoras, fortifications and Greek-style above-ground houses.[187]

Like all Greek *apoikiai* Olbia had to maintain a *modus vivendi* with its non-Greek neighbours.[188] The literary and epigraphic sources attest a system of diplomacy which took many different forms in the course of the

---

[183] *Grandi santuari*; Mastrocinque 1993.   [184] Dubois 2002: 23–7.
[185] Tsetskhladze 1998b; Bresson *et al.* 2007; Dana 2011b: 339–93.
[186] Cf. Solovyov 1999; Tsetskhladze 2004.   [187] Vinogradov and Kryžickij 1995.
[188] Braund and Kryzhitskiy 2007.

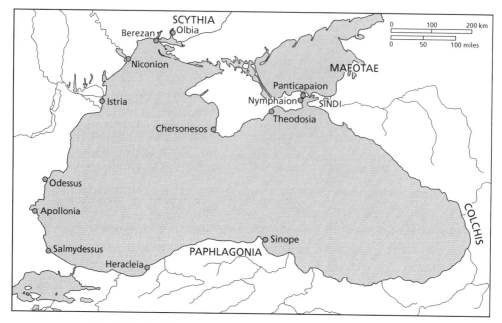

Map 5 The Black Sea

centuries. Several sources attest the payment of tribute to Scythians and other non-Greek groups, and Herodotus describes how the Scythian king Scyles used to reside for a significant part of the year in his stately home in Olbia, although his Scythian troops were obliged to camp outside the city.[189] Some scholars have posited a Scythian protectorate over Olbia and the other Greek cities of the northwest Black Sea.[190] Coins minted at Olbia bear the names of what are presumably Scythian kings, while coins of the Greek *apoikia* of Niconion bear the name of Scyles;[191] but it is a golden signet ring, inscribed in Greek with the name of Scyles, which shows the complexity of interactions between Greeks and Scythians, with Greek artists working for Scythian kings (see Figure 13).[192]

Like many Greek *apoikiai*, Olbia managed to acquire a significant rural territory along the rivers Bug and Dnieper, aptly called 'Greater Olbia'. Habitation and exploitation in the territory of Greater Olbia starts in the sixth century and comes to an abrupt end towards the beginning of the fifth; there follows a gap of half a century, but rural settlement re-emerges in the last quarter of the fifth century and reaches its greatest expansion towards the middle of the third century, to contract again forever afterwards.

[189] 4.79.   [190] Cf. Müller 2010: 48–57.   [191] Dubois 1996: 8–11.   [192] Dubois 1996: 11–14.

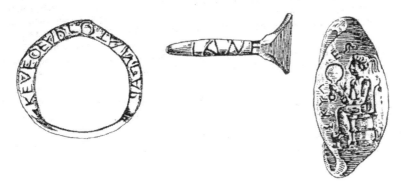

Figure 13 Golden ring of Scyles, Istria, *c.* 450 BCE.

Although it is far from clear how we should explain these changes, relation-ships with the non-Greek communities and states must have played a significant role in allowing or obstructing rural habitation and exploitation. Literary and epigraphic sources attest the existence of a mixed population in Greater Olbia, though archaeological evidence does not verify the existence of a mixed culture.[193]

Epigraphic evidence makes clear the presence of non-Greeks in Olbia; an individual with the non-Greek name Igdampaies made a dedication to Hermes,[194] while Anaperres, the son of Anacharsis, a non-Greek Scolotian, made the earliest attested dedication to Apollo the Healer.[195] Three persons with non-Greek names appear alongside many persons with Greek names on a curse tablet; they were all opponents of the curser in a judicial suit.[196] A fifth-century grave stele for Leoxus, son of Molpagoras, depicts a nude youth on one side and a young warrior dressed in Scythian clothes and carrying a bow and arrows on the other.[197] But at the same time in terms of its material culture and its institutional and social life, Olbia appears as a typical Greek polis, little different from one in the Peloponnese.[198] The vast majority of Ionian names in Olbian onomastics testify to the Milesian origins of the *apoikia*. If anything, Olbia appears abreast of the latest developments in Greek culture and society, from the spread of Orphic ideas and rituals to the development of novel administrative techniques like the control of currency.[199] The flat stone dishes, which appear both in female burials at Olbia and in Scythian burials on the steppe, and which

---

[193] Braund 2007.   [194] *SEG* XXX, 909; Dubois 1996: 126.
[195] *SEG* LIII, 788; Rusyayeva 2007: 100.   [196] *SEG* XLIV, 669; Dubois 1996: 172–3.
[197] *SEG* XLI, 619; Dubois 1996: 86–9.   [198] Kryzhitskiy 2007.   [199] Osborne 2008.

probably had some ritual meaning, are one of the rare examples of the presence of non-Greek practices in the material culture of Olbia.[200]

The situation was rather different in the Bosporan kingdom.[201] In this case the most important development occurred in the fifth century, when the Greek poleis on the two sides of the straits of Kerch (Cimmerian Bosporus) united first under the leadership of the mysterious Archaeanactidae, and then from 438 until the late second century under the dynasty of the Spartocids. We are left in the dark about the reasons behind these important developments; it has been suggested that it was pressure from the Scythians which led the Greek poleis of the Bosporus to unite under a powerful military leadership, but unification through military conquest is perhaps a more plausible scenario.[202] The origin of the Spartocids is equally mysterious; but there is no doubt that the non-Greek names borne by members of the dynasty are typical Thracian names (Spartocus, Paerisades). Some scholars have suggested that Spartocus, the founder of the dynasty, was a Thracian mercenary who took power in a military coup, while others have preferred to see him as a member of the native Cimmerian aristocracy which was Thracian in origin.[203] Whatever the case, the Spartocids created a complex state which included both the Greek poleis of the Bosporus and the Crimea as well as the non-Greek communities of the Kuban area, such as the Maeotae and the Sindoi. This double composition of the Bosporan state is reflected in the titulature of its rulers; an illustrative example is the following dedication by one of the Spartocid princesses:

> Comosarye, daughter of Gorgippus, wife
> of Paerisades, after vowing dedicated to
> the strong god Sanerges and Astara; Paerisades
> being *archon* of Bosporus and Theodosia
> and king of the Sindoi and all the
> Maitae and the Thateis.[204]

Paerisades' titulature portrays him as *archon* (ruler) of the Greek poleis of Bosporus (i.e., Panticapaion) and Theodosia, but as king of the non-Greek communities of the Sindoi, Maeotae and Thateis. The Bosporan state was not merely a composite state in which Greeks and non-Greeks were kept apart and ruled in different ways, as the titulature might suggest; the non-Greek name of the princess Comosarye and her dedication to two non-Greek deities, together with the use of the adjective 'strong' to describe

---

[200] Rusyaeva 2007: 100–1.   [201] Gajdukevič 1971; Hind 1994; Fornasier and Böttiger 2002.
[202] Vinogradov 1987; Müller 2010: 23–48.   [203] Gajdukevič 1971: 65–9.
[204] *CIRB*, 1015; translation from *R-O*, 65d.

deities,[205] which is very uncommon in Greek religion, illustrate a more complex phenomenon: the creation of a truly hybrid culture which mixed together Greek and non-Greek elements.

The hybrid nature of Bosporan communities is already reflected in their onomastics: in contrast to the purity of Olbian onomastics, the inscriptions of Panticapaion record a large number of non-Greek names.[206] We should not assume that everybody bearing a non-Greek name was non-Greek in origin, as non-Greek names could be assumed through marriage or guest-friendship (pp. 133–5); but the contrast with Olbia testifies to the significantly more widespread interaction with non-Greeks. But it is material culture that best attests the hybrid nature of Bosporan communities. Herodotus famously described how sumptuous burials under *kurgans* (tumuli) involving the sacrifice of horses and human beings was the tradition of Scythian rulers,[207] and archaeologists have discovered hundreds of such graves with impressive finds.[208] In contrast, burials in the necropoleis of Greek *apoikiai* were traditionally modest, the dead being buried in trenches or cists with a few pots as grave goods. But starting from the late fifth and extensively during the fourth century stone-built vaults covered by *kurgans* appear in the vicinity of Bosporan cities such as Panticapaion and Nymphaion. These stone tombs are effectively the petrification of the traditional Scythian *kurgan* burials, and there is little doubt that it was Greek artisans who had the necessary know-how to build such impressive monuments.[209]

It is, of course, impossible to ascertain the identity of the people who were buried in these stone vaults. Some of them, such as the Tsarski Kurgan in Panticapaion, are so impressive and so close to the Greek city that their identification as the graves of the Bosporan rulers has to be considered as a serious possibility. Most of the others which are close to Greek poleis could be the graves of Scythian nobles who lived in the Greek cities, people of mixed ancestry or Greeks following this new trend.[210] These hybrid tomb traditions were accompanied by the emergence of Greco-Scythian art: this artistic tradition followed Greek artistic styles, but created an iconography which represented Scythian life and identity. We shall examine this artistic tradition in more detail in Chapter 6 (p. 236) (see Figure 14).

---

[205] Ustinova 1999: 51–3.   [206] For example, *CIRB*, 114, 154, 171, 179–81, 193, 196, 200, 202.
[207] 4.71–2.   [208] Rolle 1989.   [209] Tsetskhladze 1998a.
[210] Fless and Lorenz 2005; Petersen 2010.

Figure 14 Golden comb, Solokha, fourth century BCE.

We have examined a range of different frontier societies in the world of *apoikiai* from Sicily to the Black Sea. Selinous played an important role as a transmitter of Greek cultural practices to its Elymian neighbours and finally came under the Carthaginian protectorate. Poseidonia, after being conquered by the Lucanians, exhibits a complex pattern in which some Greek cultural practices were maintained wholesale, while others provided the Lucanians with novel means of defining their identities. Olbia's material, social and institutional life largely presents an image of a typical Greek polis, despite its interactions with Scythian rulers and Scythian residents in the city and its territory. Finally, Panticapaion and the Bosporan kingdom created a hybrid Greco-Barbarian society with a deeply fascinating material culture. There was an enormous diversity in the forms of interaction between Greeks and non-Greeks as well as in their outcomes. This also applies to the extent of their interaction with the Panhellenic world; whereas Greek *apoikiai* in Sicily and Italy invested heavily in Panhellenic centres like Delphi and Olympia during the archaic and classical periods, there is not a single dedication from the *apoikiai* in the Black Sea.[211]

3.5 A case study: Thrace

The case of Thrace provides an excellent illustration of the issues raised above.[212] It allows us to perceive how Mediterranean redistribution (pp. 81–2) linked together the world of networks and the world of *apoikiai*; it illustrates the range of strategies pursued by individuals and communities concerning the very same region; it shows how ethnic and cultural lines were defined, redrawn or set aside in the frontier societies of the region; and, finally, it provides an illuminating example of how the four worlds were both parallel and interconnected (Map 6).

Some of the earliest fragments of Greek poetry, written by Archilochus during the seventh century, document his participation in the Parian *apoikia* on the island of Thasos opposite the Thracian coast, and the earliest Greek–Barbarian relations in the area. One fragment declares how the dregs

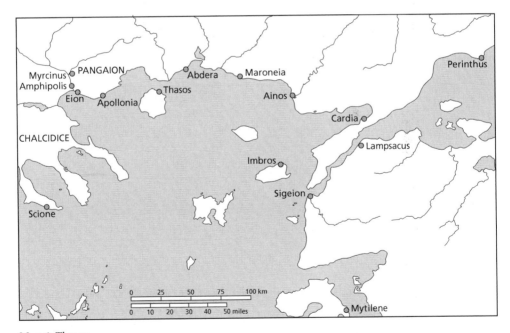

Map 6 Thrace

---

[211] For the limited evidence from the Hellenistic period onwards, see Dana 2011a.

[212] See the comments of Owen 2005.

of all Greeks gathered at Thasos;[213] another compares unfavourably the Thasian landscape with that of fertile Siris in southern Italy.[214] One of his most famous poems narrates how he lost his shield in a military engagement with a local tribe on the Thracian coast, where Thasos very quickly established secondary settlements and commercial outposts;[215] another reflects on his life as a soldier while drinking the famous wine of Thracian Ismarus.[216] What brought the Greeks to Thrace is vividly illustrated in a Herodotean passage which narrates how in the late sixth century the Persian king Dareius I decided to reward Histiaeus, the tyrant of Miletus, for his loyal support during the Persian campaign against the Scythians (pp. 53–4). Histiaeus requested the grant of a place in Thrace called Myrcinus, in the valley of the Strymon River. But the danger of making this grant was emphasised to Dareius by his general Megabazus, who was charged with the task of subduing Thrace for Persia:

Sir, what is this that you have done? You have permitted a clever and cunning Greek to build a city in Thrace, where there are abundant forests for shipbuilding, much wood for oars, mines of silver, and many people both Greek and barbarian dwelling around, who, when they have a champion to lead them, will carry out all his orders by day or by night.[217]

That, according to Herodotus, Dareius was convinced to effectively revoke the grant is sufficient proof of the seriousness of the arguments, further supported by the many later Greek efforts to follow in the steps of Histiaeus. Timber for shipbuilding, metals and manpower were the three crucial resources that the area had in abundance; Greeks, Thracians and imperial powers like Persia competed and collaborated with each other in order to procure them. We should also add agricultural products: Greek *apoikiai* in Thrace exploited in an intensive way the fertile soils that they managed to occupy. It is important to note the wide circulation of the amphoras of northern Greek *apoikiai* like Thasos, and the international reputation of the wines of Thasos and Maroneia. The productive exploitation of land by Greek *apoikiai* was not intended for mere subsistence; from early on Greek *apoikiai* were inserted into wider networks of redistribution of their valuable agricultural resources.[218]

One possible strategy was the creation of *apoikiai* that could occupy the land and control its resources. It was a strategy based on the employment of military force and dependent on the availability of sufficient manpower in order to defend the settlements and expand their territory and control.

---

[213] F102, *West.*   [214] F22, *West.*   [215] F5, *West.*   [216] F2, *West.*   [217] 5.23.2.
[218] Salviat 1986.

The sources record various Greek attempts from the sixth century onwards to follow such a strategy, from those of Histiaeus and his son-in-law Aristagoras to the various Athenian attempts from the beginning of the fifth century onwards.[219] It was only in 437 that the Athenians successfully managed to create the *apoikia* of Amphipolis in the lower Strymon valley; but this was possible only because the Athenians managed to mobilise sufficient manpower for their project, which included a minority of Athenian settlers and a majority of Greeks of various origins. It is important to emphasise that even military confrontation between Greeks and Thracians did not preclude other interactions. A funerary monument from this area depicting a horse rider and dating from around 500 records in Greek how the individual died while defending his beloved Eion, a local Greek *emporion*: the deceased bore the Thracian name Toces.[220] We cannot tell whether the man was a Thracian fighting for Eion or a Greek with a Thracian name, which would testify to links of marriage or guest-friendship between Greeks and Thracians (pp. 133–5); but it is significant that the man was a horse rider, given that Thracians were famous for their cavalry.

Nevertheless, the strategy of aggression and settlement was one that the Greeks could rarely put into practice. It was more common to establish networks and links with local non-Greek communities and rulers in order to exploit the resources of the area. The arguments used in the late 380s by the enemies of the *apoikia* of Olynthus in the Chalcidice, in order to convince the Spartans to intervene, portray vividly both the resources of Greek *apoikiai* and the ways in which they could interact with their non-Greek neighbours:

For what indeed is there to hinder such expansion, seeing that the country itself possesses ship-timber and has revenues from many ports and many *emporia*, and likewise an abundant population on account of the abundance of food? And further, mark you, they have for neighbours those Thracians who are under no king. They even now are paying court to the Olynthians; and if they should come under their sway, this also would be a great power added to the Olynthians. Then, if the Thracians were their followers, straightway the gold mines of Mount Pangaion also would beckon to them.[221]

Collaboration with the neighbouring Thracians could provide the Olynthians with not only manpower, but also access to the precious metal resources of the region.

---

[219] Isaac 1986: 13–34.   [220] *SEG* XXVII, 249; Isaac 1986: 5–8.
[221] Xenophon, *Hellenica*, 5.2.16–17.

Another illuminating window on this world is provided by a fourth-century inscription recently discovered near Vetren in Bulgaria.[222] The inscription records the oath sworn by a Thracian king to protect the privileges of the Greek *emporion* of Pistirus, along with various other privileges granted to members of Greek *apoikiai* in Thrace. There is some controversy over the localisation of the *emporion* of Pistirus.[223] The logical assumption would be that Pistirus was the name of the ancient settlement near which the inscription was found; but references in other sources situate a settlement of that name on the Thracian coast opposite Thasos; this identification is also strengthened by the reference to Greek merchants from the coastal cities of Thasos, Maroneia and Apollonia. Whatever the case, the Thracian king guarantees the security of property of the *emporitai*, with provisions forbidding the cancellation of debts owed by the Thracians, or the confiscation of land and pasture owned by the *emporitai*; the security of persons by provisions forbidding the seizure of the *emporitai*; the autonomy of the *emporion* by allowing the *emporitai* to settle their own disputes and by measures such as the pledge not to impose a garrison on the *emporion*; the limitation of financial exactions by forbidding the levying of road dues on the products transported between Pistirus, Maroneia and other *emporia*; finally, the king pledges not to kill, seize or capture the property of any citizen of Maroneia or of the citizens of Thasos and Apollonia residing at Pistirus. The inscription of Vetren throws light on what sort of issues could be at stake when Athens clashed with Thasos in 465 over the *emporia* on the Thracian coast, and engaged upon a two-year siege in order to subdue it.[224]

The role played by Greek *apoikiai* and non-Greek communities in the circulation of goods is nicely illustrated by local coinage.[225] The important role of the Greek *apoikiai* of Thrace in the circulation of the precious metals of the area is reflected in the copious coinage of Abdera, which started minting almost immediately after its foundation. Abderite coins were overwhelmingly silver octadrachms and tetradrachms; these were coins of very high value, and they were clearly not intended to facilitate everyday exchanges in the local level; they were produced for large-scale payments and large-scale trade. The Thracian communities which exploited the mines provided the bullion that was used for the coins of Greek cities like Abdera; but Thracian communities quickly adopted the practice of coinage and started striking their own coins, again in very large denominations. The Thracian coins use Greek legends and Greek iconography, although they

---

[222] *SEG* XLIX, 911; translated and commented in Demetriou 2012: 153–87.
[223] Tsetskhladze 2000.　　[224] Thucydides, 1.100.　　[225] Kraay 1976: 147–60.

often depict topics which seem to reflect Thracian traditions. Confirmation that the precious metals of the area entered international circulation through the striking of coins by the Greek *apoikiai* and the Thracian communities is provided by the abundant attestation of these coins in various sixth- and fifth-century hoards found in the Levant and Egypt.[226]

If some Greeks tried to create *apoikiai*, others tried to insert themselves into non-Greek communities and their structures of power and wealth, and create their own personal fiefdoms and bases in the area. Many Greeks from local *apoikiai* such as Abdera and Maroneia came to play a crucial role as intermediaries between Thracian rulers and Greek communities. Thucydides narrates how the Athenians in order to negotiate an alliance with the Thracian king Sitalces had to placate Nymphodorus of Abdera, his son-in-law.[227] Xenophon describes the role of Heracleides of Maroneia as the right hand of prince Seuthes; it is telling that Heracleides is charged with selling off the booty from the campaigns of Seuthes at the Greek *apoikia* of Perinthus.[228]

But Greeks coming from outside Thrace had an equally impressive success. Miltiades the Elder, an ancestor of the Athenian generals Miltiades and Cimon, managed to become ruler of a local tribe in the Thracian Chersonese;[229] the Athenian Alcibiades somehow acquired some forts on the Thracian coast, which he used to pursue his own agendas.[230] We also know of many Greeks and in particular Athenians who gained access to the significant resources of silver and gold in the area. Our earliest example is the Athenian tyrant Peisistratus,[231] and the list also includes the Athenian general Cimon and the historian Thucydides.[232] In the case of Cimon we are explicitly told that it was through the marriage of his father Miltiades to Hegesipyle, the daughter of the Thracian king Olorus, that he acquired his mine concessions. Given that Thucydides' father was called Olorus and was related to Cimon, it seems likely that it was through inheritance that Thucydides acquired his mines in this area; it is important to note how Greek–Thracian marriage links introduced a Thracian name into an Athenian family (pp. 133–5).[233]

How did these Greeks manage to contract such rewarding marriages? Because some Greeks could mobilise military manpower and put it in the service of Thracian rulers, this made them eligible for lucrative marriages which yielded forts and mines. A long fragment from a fourth-century Athenian comedy by Anaxandrides describes vividly the marriage of the

---

[226] Picard 2000.   [227] 2.29.   [228] *Anabasis*, 7.4.2.   [229] Herodotus, 6.34.
[230] Xenophon, *Hellenica*, 1.5.17, 2.1.25.
[231] Herodotus, 1.61–4; Aristotle, *Constitution of the Athenians*, 15; Lavelle 1992.
[232] Thucydides, 4.105.   [233] Isaac 1986: 31–4.

Figure 15 Inscribed silver bowl, Alexandrovo, fourth century BCE.

Athenian general Iphicrates to the daughter of the Thracian king Cotys, at whose service Iphicrates had put his expertise and men.[234] The passage reflects the keen interest in Athens concerning the actions of Athenian opportunists in Thrace and the wealth that could accrue to such individuals; but it also provides a window on the mobility of specialists. The flute player Antigenides, the singer Argas and the lyre player Cephisodotus, who performed at the wedding at Cotys' court, are only some of the mobile specialists who crossed the Mediterranean working for various Greek and non-Greek customers. Greek artisans working for Thracian rulers produced metal vessels which were an aesthetically and socially pleasing way of converting and storing the precious metals offered as tribute or gifts by Greek and Thracian communities to Thracian rulers. Such precious metal vessels have been found in many places in inland Thrace, the most famous of which is the fourth-century treasure of Rogozen. The ethnicity of the artisans is attested through the Greek inscriptions that many of these vessels carry (see Figure 15).[235]

We have seen the crucial role of manpower for both Greeks and Thracians in terms of controlling the resources of the area, and the importance of networks of mobility. Because our written sources are Greek, there is a danger of assuming that it was only Greeks who were mobilised by these networks and that mobility only brought people to Thrace, but not out of it. This could not be further from the truth. There was, of course, forced migration from the region, most obviously in the form of slavery. There were numerous Thracian slaves in Greek communities like Athens. Thracian maids and nurses were particularly common: the depiction of maids sporting tattoos on Athenian

[234] *K-A,* F42; Harris 1989.   [235] Zournatzi 2000.

vases was based on the fact that tattooing was a Thracian custom, and many real-life Thracian maids would have sported such tattoos.[236]

The fifth-century historian Charon of Lampsacus narrates a fascinating story about Naris, a Bisaltian Thracian, who was sold as a slave in the Greek *apoikia* of Cardia in the Thracian Chersonese; he became a barber and used to hear in his barbershop the Cardians saying that there was an oracle that one day the Bisaltians would attack them. He was also aware that the Cardians had trained their horses to dance to the music of flutes, in order to entertain themselves in their symposia. Naris escaped to the Bisaltians, became their leader and bought a slave flute-player girl from Cardia, who taught the Bisaltians how to play the flute; the Bisaltians subsequently used the flutes in order to confuse the Cardian cavalry and gain the victory.[237] This story shows clearly how complex the phenomenon of mobility was: Thracian slaves went to Greek *apoikiai*, but slaves moved in the opposite direction as well. Slaving could result in mobility for many other persons, as is nicely portrayed in an Athenian court speech concerning the disappearance and presumed death of the Athenian Herodes from a ship embarking from Mytilene on Lesbos and bound for the *apoikia* of Ainos on the Thracian coast. Herodes was travelling accompanied by certain Thracians who had come to negotiate the release of some captured Thracian slaves; the release would take place at Ainos.[238] The networks of mobility that moved Thracian slaves and Greek traders from Ainos to Mytilene could also move Thracian redeemers.

But it is primarily as soldiers and mercenaries that Thracians are attested as making a living abroad. Athens made a particular habit of employing Thracians as mercenaries, and the practice has left plentiful traces in our sources. Aristophanes draws a vivid image of the Odomantian hired soldiers and their strange appearance and practices;[239] Thucydides records, among many examples, 1,300 Thracian mercenaries who arrived at Athens in summer 413, too late to join the Sicilian expedition, but who subsequently brutally slaughtered the population of the Boeotian city of Mycalessus.[240] A late fourth-century Athenian inscription records various groups of mercenaries; the largest component is a group of forty-eight Thracians, two-thirds of whom bear Greek names.[241]

It should come as no surprise that the encounters between Greeks and Thracians in the worlds of networks and *apoikiai* had other significant

---

[236] Zimmermann 1980; Tsiafakis 2000: 372–6.   [237] *FGrH*, 262 F1.
[238] Antiphon, *On the Murder of Herodes*, 20.   [239] *Acharnians*, 153–72; Olson 2002: 119–25.
[240] Thucydides, 7.27–9.   [241] *IG* II², 1956; Rosivach 2000.

results. As one might expect, military encounters were crucial for the exchange, adoption and adaptation of military technologies. Thracian soldiers were particularly successful as light-armed infantry, with their characteristic crescent-shaped wicker shield called a *pelta*. It was the Athenian experience of employing as well as fighting against Thracian peltasts that led the Athenian general Iphicrates to re-organise Athenian light infantry into a potent military force using the *pelta*.[242] But even purely military encounters could have significant cultural effects. The Platonic Socrates narrates a revealing story, set in the aftermath of his return from the Athenian siege of the *apoikia* of Potidaea in Thracian Chalcidice:

> Such, then, Charmides, is the nature of this charm. I learnt it on campaign over there, from one of the Thracian physicians of Zalmoxis, who are said even to make one immortal. This Thracian said that the Greeks were right in advising as I told you just now: 'but Zalmoxis', he said, 'our king, who is a god, says that as you ought not to attempt to cure eyes without head, or head without body, so you should not treat body without soul'; and this was the reason why most maladies evaded the physicians of Greece – that they neglected the whole, on which they ought to spend their pains, for if this were out of order it was impossible for the part to be in order.[243]

The story is explicitly fictional, but there is little doubt that its verisimilitude is based on the recurrence of such encounters and the transmission of knowledge and practices through them.

In what ways were the complex relationships between Greeks and Thracians mediated? Let us look at two different examples in which Greek myth was used to mediate the relationship between Greeks and Thracians. We have already referred to the Athenian foundation of Amphipolis in the lower Strymon valley. The story was that the Athenians were given an oracle from Delphi that only if they managed to find and re-bury the remains of Rhesus on the site of Amphipolis would they finally succeed in planting an *apoikia* in the area after so many failures. Rhesus was a mythical king of the Thracians, whom Homer portrayed as a Trojan ally killed by Odysseus and Diomedes. The Athenians found the bones of Rhesus and brought them to Amphipolis, while successfully tricking the Thracians into a truce necessary to fortify their position.[244] We can see how a Thracian king in Greek myth was used to legitimise the Athenian attempt to confiscate land from the Thracians and create an *apoikia*.[245]

---

[242] Best 1969.   [243] Plato, *Charmides*, 156d–e; Brisson 2000; Murphy 2000.
[244] Polyaenus, *Stratagems*, 6.53.   [245] For the related cult, see Isaac 1986: 55–8.

A rather different use of Greek myth is portrayed by Xenophon, the leader of the Greek mercenary force of the Ten Thousand which the Thracian king Seuthes wanted to hire, when he narrates Seuthes' reaction on discovering that Xenophon was an Athenian:

Upon hearing these words Seuthes said that he should not distrust anyone who was an Athenian; for he knew, he said, that the Athenians were kinsmen of his, and he believed they were loyal friends.[246]

What Seuthes was probably referring to was the myth of Procne and Tereus.[247] According to the myth, Tereus had married the Athenian princess Procne who begat their son, Itys; Tereus then raped Procne's sister, Philomela, and cut out her tongue so that she would not be able to reveal the horrific truth to her sister. Nevertheless, she managed through embroidering a message on a robe to reveal the truth to Procne, who went on to kill Itys and serve him up to Tereus in order to punish him; all three of them were subsequently transformed into different birds.

It is probable that in the earlier versions of the myth there was no Thracian connection in this story, and Tereus was probably connected to Megara or to Daulis in Phocis; but in tandem with the wider process which saw the 'barbarisation' of various characters in Greek myths, as we shall see in Chapter 5 (pp. 186–90), Tereus became identified as a Thracian king. The earliest attestation of this new version of the myth was Sophocles' *Tereus*; it seems that a significant factor in the transformation of Tereus into a Thracian was the phonetic similarity of his name with that of Teres, the founder of the Odrysian kingdom of Thrace around the middle of the fifth century; the story was clearly taken seriously, for in a famous aside Thucydides protested against this identification.[248] What is important, nevertheless, is the use of Greek myth as a means of linking together Greeks and Thracians and of establishing mutual trust, as seen in Seuthes' reaction.

We have seen at various points how the world of networks and the world of *apoikiai* in Thrace became interlinked with the world of empires; a final point concerns the relationship between Thracians and the Panhellenic world. A fourth-century decree of Delphi grants the status of *proxenos* and the privileges of first consultation of the oracle (*promanteia*), first seat (*proedria*), priority of trial (*prodikia*) and exemption from taxes (*ateleia*) to Iolaus, Poseidonius, Medistas and Teres, the sons of the Thracian king Cersobleptes.[249] It is notable that while the last two Thracian princes bear Thracian names, the first two have typical Greek names, a fact that testifies

---

[246] *Anabasis*, 5.2.31.   [247] Patterson 2010: 53–9.   [248] 2.29.3.   [249] *FD* III.1, 392.

to the strong links between the Thracian court and the Greek networks we have been examining. But even more important is that these Thracian princes are inserted into the standard process of honouring Greeks for services rendered without any apparent concern for their Barbarian origin. We are not told what services lay behind this Delphic honorary decree; but the connection between the Thracian court and the Panhellenic centre is sufficient evidence of the interlinking between the four parallel worlds.[250]

[250] Mari 2002: 77–80.

4 | Intercultural communication

Chapters 2 and 3 have examined in detail the four parallel yet interconnected worlds within which interactions between Greeks and non-Greeks took place. The following three chapters will focus on the consequences of these parallel worlds for the social, economic, political and cultural history of the Mediterranean and the Black Sea during the archaic and classical periods. This chapter will focus on intercultural communication in the ancient Mediterranean: in what ways, in which contexts, and for what purposes did Greeks and non-Greeks attempt, succeed or fail to communicate, and what were the consequences of this intercultural communication? Because as historians we specialise in the study of particular cultures, we tend to believe that people within one culture think only in terms of their own culture; but intercultural communication poses very acute challenges to such a perspective. If one reads Egyptian texts and observes Egyptian images addressed to an Egyptian audience, the pharaoh was god on earth, on a level far above any other Egyptian, let alone non-Egyptian Barbarians; but the pharaohs who corresponded with other Near Eastern rulers and called them 'my brother' clearly had to think in very different terms when it came to intercultural communication.[1]

Let us start by exploring some examples of intercultural encounters and some forms of intercultural communication in the ancient Mediterranean. We have already come across the Greek and Carian mercenaries who became an important factor in the political and military history of Saite Egypt; their presence at the Egyptian capital of Memphis is illustrated by some fascinating 'bilingual' grave stelae, dating from the seventh and sixth centuries (see Figure 16).[2] These are stelae with two or more registers, which have been called bilingual because they combine registers decorated in typical Egyptian fashion with registers showing *ekphora* scenes which are typical of Greek art; they also carry inscriptions either in both hieroglyphic and Carian or only in Carian and rarely even in Greek. These immigrants, the result of processes of mobility and power put in motion by the empires of the East, chose to be commemorated with stelae which combined

---

[1] Kemp 1989: 223–7.   [2] Masson 1978.

Figure 16 'Bilingual' stele, Memphis, sixth century BCE.

Egyptian, Carian and Greek elements. How would such individuals participate in intercultural communication?

A second example comes from Athens: it is a fourth-century epitaph
found in the mining area of Laureion.

> Atotas the miner
> From the Black Sea Atotas, the great-hearted Paphlagonian,
> put to rest his body from the toils far away from his fatherland.
> Nobody vied [with me] in [my] art; I am from the stem of Pylaemenes,
> who died subdued by the hand of Achilles.[3]

Whether Atotas was a slave or a freedman at the time of his death is
impossible to tell; that he must have started as a slave miner is indisputable.
We are dealing with a person who was proud of his manual skill and of his
national origins. And what is most tantalising is that he was able to express his
national credentials in a language that could appeal to the Greek reader of this
epitaph. This Paphlagonian was clearly steeped in Greek culture. The epigram

---

[3] *IG* II², 10051.

uses Homeric expressions; Atotas is described as *megathymos Paphlagon*, which brings into mind the verse of the *Iliad*, in which Paphlagonians are described with exactly the same adjective; interestingly though, the Homeric version of the death of Pylaemenes is different from that of Atotas, since in the *Iliad* he is killed by Menelaus, a less important hero.[4] Clearly, Atotas combined a good knowledge of Greek mythology with national pride and his own version of mythical events.[5] How was the Paphlagonian miner Atotas able to acquire the necessary knowledge to portray himself in such characteristically Greek terms? What processes of intercultural communication do we have to assume in the course of this Paphlagonian's life in Athens?

4.1 Practices of interlinking

Ancient sources preserve a marvellous account concerning Demaratus, a Corinthian aristocrat who during the seventh century was sailing to Etruria in a ship of his own and selling Greek cargoes in Etruria and Etruscan cargoes back in Greece; when Corinth fell to a tyrant, Demaratus decided to migrate to the Etruscan city of Tarquinia and took with him, according to the legend, three artisans who taught their skills to the Etruscans. Demaratus used his established friendships to build a house and marry into the local aristocracy. He bestowed Etruscan names on his two sons and gave them both a Greek and an Etruscan education; one of his sons, Lucumo, migrated to Rome and became its fifth king under the name of Lucius Tarquinius Priscus.[6] This story illustrates a number of practices that created contexts for intercultural communication, from trade and guest-friendship to intermarriage and name-giving, which we shall examine in detail below.

4.1.1 Guest-friendship

Guest-friendship (*xenia*) is a practice that links together individuals from different communities through the exchange of gifts, hospitality and services.[7] The antiquity of the practice is attested by Homer; in a famous scene the Lycian Glaucus and the Achaean Diomedes encounter each other on the battlefield and, before fighting, introduce themselves. They suddenly discover that their grandfathers had been guest-friends; they then decide to avoid fighting each other, and renew the relationship through exchanging

---

[4] *Iliad*, 5.576–7.   [5] See Bäbler 1998: 94–7; Lauffer 1955/6: 200–4.
[6] Dionysius of Halicarnassus, *Roman Archaeology*, 3.46.3–5; Ampolo 1976/7.   [7] Herman 1987.

their armour.[8] Homer's description is echoed centuries later, when Xenophon described a negotiation in 394 between the Persian satrap Pharnabazus and the Spartan king Agesilaus in the course of the Spartan invasion of Asia Minor (pp. 67–8):

Pharnabazus mounted his horse and rode away, but his son by Parapita, who was still in the bloom of youth, remaining behind, ran up to Agesilaus and said to him: 'Agesilaus, I make you my guest-friend.' 'And I accept your friendship.' 'Remember, then,' he said. And immediately he gave his javelin (it was a beautiful one) to Agesilaus. And he, accepting it, took off and gave to the boy in return a splendid trapping which Idaeus, his secretary, had round his horse's neck. Then the boy leaped upon his horse and followed after his father.[9]

As the case of Glaucus and Diomedes suggests, the establishment of a guest-friendship was not a one-off; when Pharnabazus' son was exiled by his brother, he fled to the Peloponnese, where he received further benefits from Agesilaus.[10] Herodotus records the guest-friendship between Polycrates, the tyrant of Samos, and the Egyptian pharaoh Amasis and mentions the exchange of gifts as a means of sealing the friendly relationship.[11] These friendships could be very effective in diplomatic affairs. Lysander's friendship with the Persian prince Cyrus was crucial in ensuring that the Spartans always received sufficient financial support from Persia;[12] equally, the Spartans in 388/7 selected Antalcidas as their admiral, because they expected that this would gratify Tiribazus, the Persian satrap who was in charge of the peace negotiations; Antalcidas' success in controlling the Hellespont, a crucial step in the process leading to the King's Peace, was effected through collaboration with another of his friends, the Persian Ariobarzanes.[13] Guest-friendship was obviously not restricted to heroes, rulers and politicians: people constantly on the move, such as traders, sailors, artists and mercenaries, would have developed their own networks of friendships, which would have provided hospitality and support in a foreign and often hostile environment; that we rarely hear about them is merely the result of the nature of our sources.

4.1.2 Intermarriage

As in most historical periods, marriages across cultural and political divides were a common means of securing alliances and access to resources in the

---

[8] *Iliad*, 6.119–236.   [9] *Hellenica*, 4.1.39.   [10] *Hellenica*, 4.1.40.   [11] 3.39.
[12] Mitchell 1997: 118–19.   [13] Mitchell 1997: 126.

ancient Mediterranean. We have already examined the marriages between Thracian princes and Greek adventurers, such as Miltiades and Iphicrates (pp. 123–4); when the Thracian prince Seuthes wanted to secure the loyalty of Xenophon and the forces under his control, he promised him one of his daughters.[14] We have also examined marriages between Persian potentates and Greek adventurers, as in the case of the marriage of Artabazus' daughter successively to the Greek mercenary leaders Memnon and Mentor (p. 72). But foreign kings did marry Greek women as well: the pharaoh Amasis married a woman from Cyrene,[15] while the Scythian king Scyles was the son of a Greek woman from Istria; in fact, Herodotus attributes the Hellenising tendencies of Scyles to his Greek upbringing by his mother.[16]

Mixed marriages were not the preserve of the elite and a mere means of diplomacy; they also took place among the middle and lower classes in the multicultural centres we have explored in Chapter 3. We are in a better position to examine intercultural marriages among the lower classes than intercultural guest-friendships, because marriages can be recorded in epitaphs. We have already examined the case of Eirene from Byzantion marrying into a Phoenician family in Piraeus (p. 102); another Athenian funerary monument records the names of Attas (a typical male Phrygian name) and a Greek woman named [...]ora, the daughter of Diagoras;[17] a third records the Carian female name Ada along with a male called Micon, originating from the Greek city of Sigeion in the Hellespont.[18] Both monuments probably record couples from mixed marriages. Intermarriage between Greek *apoikoi* and 'native' populations was, of course, particularly common, and is nicely illustrated in the early Hellenistic ordinance of Ptolemy I for the *apoikia* of Cyrene in Libya, which is based on regulations dating back at least to the classical period: 'those men shall be citizens who are born of a Cyrenean father and a Cyrenean mother, those who are born of Libyan mothers from this side of Catabathmus and Automalax'.[19]

4.1.3 Name-giving

Closely related to the strong links created by guest-friendship and marriage was the practice of name-giving.[20] Guest-friends could bestow foreign names on members of their families in order to honour their foreign guests and stress the significance of the link; mixed marriages could result in names

[14] Xenophon, *Anabasis*, 7.2.38.   [15] Herodotus, 2.181.   [16] 4.78.
[17] *IG* II², 10898; *SEG* XIII, 184.   [18] *IG* II², 10575a; Bäbler 1998: 219–20.
[19] *SEG* IX, 1.2–3; translation from Laronde 1990: 178.   [20] Herman 1990.

from both Greek and non-Greek onomastic traditions being maintained within the same family. We have seen how two of the four sons of the Thracian king Cersobleptes bore Greek names (p. 127–8), as well as how Thucydides' father bore the Thracian name Olorus (p. 123). A sixth-century Athenian gravestone bears the following inscription: 'Stop and grieve at the tomb of the dead Croesus, slain by wild Ares in the front rank of the battle' (see Figure 27(b)).[21] This Athenian aristocrat was clearly named after the contemporary famous king of Lydia, possibly due to a guest-friendship, and a similar link can be postulated for the Corinthian tyrant who bore the name of the Egyptian pharaoh Psammetichus.[22] More ambiguous is the case of Psammetichus, the son of Theocles, the leader of the Greek mercenaries who left their graffiti at Abu Simbel during a campaign of another pharaoh called Psammetichus (p. 44). His father must have had an Egyptian connection, although in this case it is more likely that he was named in honour of the pharaoh, rather than as a result of a guest-friendship. The sixth-century Athenian potter named Amasis was either an Egyptian by origin, or more likely was named after some Egyptian connection in honour of the pharaoh Amasis.[23]

A late sixth-century magistrate of Eretria was called Scythes,[24] as was the father of an Athenian at around the same time,[25] and also a Thasian citizen in the fourth century:[26] we do not know what sort of connections with Scythia their names were supposed to evoke. Given that all these people were well-to-do citizens, it is rather unlikely that their connection to Scythia was the most obvious one: Greeks were in the habit of using ethnic names like Scythes, Lydus and Thraix in order to denote the foreign origin and outsider status of their slaves; ethnic names along with stereotypical foreign names like Manes or Tibeius were frequently given to Athenian slaves. However, a study of the totality of slave names reveals that the majority of Athenian slaves bore a name that did not distinguish them from Athenian citizens.[27]

At the same time, free non-Greek residents in Athens bore typical Greek names: it is extremely rare to come across free non-Greeks bearing foreign names. The only significant exception concerns the Thracian mercenaries listed in a late fourth-century inscription: even there only a third of them bear Thracian names, while two-thirds bear Greek names.[28] As with many Chinese people living abroad nowadays, non-Greeks in Athens preferred to use a Greek name in a Greek milieu. Most of them must have adopted Greek

---

[21] *IG* I³, 1240.   [22] Aristotle, *Politics*, 1315b26.   [23] Boardman 1987.   [24] *SEG* XXXIV, 898.
[25] *IG* I³, 658.   [26] Pouilloux 1954: 266, 279.   [27] Vlassopoulos 2010b.   [28] *IG* II², 1956.1–46.

names or translated their names in Greek, as we can establish in the case of the Phoenicians, because of their bilingual inscriptions. In a typical bilingual example, the Greek inscription mentions 'Artemidorus, son of Heliodorus, of Sidon', while the Phoenician text records 'this grave stele is for the memory among the living for Abd-Tanit, son of Abd-Shamash, of Sidon'.[29] This Phoenician had translated the Phoenician theophoric names of himself and his father into the equivalent Greek theophoric names, thus identifying Artemis with Tanit and Shamash with Helius. Both the translation and adoption of names were essential parts in the process of incorporation in a foreign society. In the same way that the Thracian Philonicus attested in fourth-century Athens bears a Greek name, while his father had the Thracian name Bithys,[30] the adoption of the Egyptian name Wahibre-em-achet was essential for the incorporation in the upper echelons of Egyptian society of the Greek son of Alexicles and Zenodote (p. 44).

4.1.4 Diplomacy

Diplomacy is the practice of establishing and maintaining links between rulers and communities; diplomatic relationships depend on a mix of good-will and trust, on the one hand, and awe and intimidation, on the other. Diplomacy requires mutual comprehension, and it is this practice which provides the best evidence for the use of interpreters and translators in antiquity. In 425/4 the Athenians captured at Eion in Thrace Artaphernes, an envoy of the Persian king on his way to Sparta. In his possession the Athenians found a letter from the king to the Spartans, which was written, according to Thucydides, in 'Assyrian letters', which must have meant Aramaic.[31] That the Athenians had no problem in translating the letter and finding out what the Persian message was is not particularly striking, given the existence of large numbers of foreigners in Athens, as we have already seen; that it was possible to translate a diplomatic dispatch in Aramaic in Sparta is much more interesting. We know that many of the communicators who mediated between Greeks and Persians were non-Greeks from Asia Minor, who spoke their own native tongues alongside Greek and Persian; particularly common are Carians, such as Mys, who served with the Persian general Mardonius, Gaulites with the satrap Tissaphernes and Pigres with the Persian prince Cyrus.[32]

---

[29] *IG* II², 10270.   [30] *IG* II², 8927.   [31] 4.50; Nylander 1968; Schmitt 1992.
[32] Asheri 1983: 20–2.

The means of establishing goodwill and trust depended to an important extent on the nature and status of the partners. An individual ruler often needed and had available means different from those available and needed by communities. A ruler could therefore employ practices that were also employed by private individuals, such as marriage and guest-friendship. We have already examined such cases as the marriages between Thracian rulers and Greek adventurers, or guest-friendships like that between Agesilaus and Pharnabazus. But it was possible to use such means to establish diplomatic relationships with communities as well, as in the case of the alliance between the pharaoh Amasis and Cyrene, which was sealed with Amasis' marriage to the daughter of an esteemed citizen of Cyrene.[33] It was also possible to establish diplomatic relationships by treating both partners as state entities of equal status, as seen in a treaty between Athens and three Thracian kings,[34] or that between the Greek *apoikia* of Phaselis in Lycia and the Carian satrap Mausolus.[35]

Nevertheless, because communities were not individual human beings like rulers, they often had to create their own communal means of establishing diplomatic relationships, even though these often developed out of practices employed originally by individuals.[36] Greek communities did not conduct diplomacy by dispatching citizens as ambassadors residing permanently at another community. Instead, Greek communities appointed as their representative in a foreign community (*proxenos*) a citizen of that polity: the Athenian *proxenos* in Sparta was a Spartan citizen representing Athenian interests. The position of *proxenos* was normally hereditary and grew gradually out of the personal guest-friendships among aristocrats; apart from its prestige, it also brought to the *proxenos* material benefits from the appointing community, including inviolability, easy access to its institutions, freedom from taxation, the right to buy land, etc.[37] But the greatest honour and privilege a Greek community could bestow, and a potent means in Greek diplomacy, was that of citizenship.[38]

It is important to stress that already from the archaic period the Greeks employed these means to create diplomatic links with non-Greek rulers and communities. We have already seen how the Delphians responded to the lavish gifts of Croesus through the bestowal of various privileges, which included citizenship for any Lydian who chose to go and live in Delphi (p. 43); this was a practice that continued into the classical period, as

---

[33] Herodotus, 2.181.   [34] *IG* II², 126, 127; translated in *R-O*, 47, 53.   [35] *TL*, 1183.
[36] Giovannini 2007.   [37] Herman 1987: 130–42.   [38] See for Athens, Osborne 1981–3.

we have seen with the similar grant to the sons of the Thracian king Cersobleptes (pp. 127–8). There are decrees from various Greek communities granting similar honours to non-Greeks, like that of the Boeotians for the Carthaginian Niobas.[39] But it is in the case of Athens where we have most information concerning the grants of *proxenia*, citizenship, and other honours and privileges to foreign rulers and potentates. We have already examined the *proxenia* for Straton the king of Sidon (p. 70) and the grant of citizenship to the Thracian prince Rheboulas, who came to reside in Athens and exercised his rights as a citizen there (p. 101). The most famous case is probably that of Sadocus, the son of the Thracian king Sitalces, who was given Athenian citizenship; a joke in Aristophanes suggests that he actually visited Athens, participated in the festival of the Apatouria and activated his citizenship.[40]

A recent study of the honours for foreigners bestowed by the Athenian democracy in the fourth century has shown that there was no significant difference between the kind of honours bestowed on Greek foreigners and those bestowed on non-Greek foreigners. Given that the Athenians did not use a standard formula for granting honours, but were very careful and discriminating about which honours to bestow on which individual, it seems clear that 'the ethnicity of the grant recipient did not influence the choice of honours to be given on any particular occasion'.[41] While the Athenians could employ the discourse of polarity on certain occasions in their diplomatic affairs, at the same time they had no misgivings in making Barbarian kings and potentates Athenian citizens.

This is nicely paralleled in the adoption of Greek diplomatic practices by non-Greek or Hellenised rulers in the course of the fourth century. While the Ionian city of Erythrae granted citizenship and *proxenia* to the Carian satrap Mausolus,[42] he in his turn appointed the Cnossians as *proxenoi* and granted them the fiscal privileges conventionally given to *proxenoi*.[43] There are two remarkable aspects of this inscription. The first is its formulas: while a typical Greek decree would start with the formula 'resolved by' (ἔδοξε) followed by the name of the community, in this decree the formula is followed by the names of Mausolus and his sister, wife and co-ruler Artemisia. The second is that, while the status of *proxenos* and its attending privileges was normally bestowed on a single or a few individuals, in this particular case the practice is reconfigured so as to include the whole

---

[39] *IG* VII, 2407; translated in *R-O*, 43.
[40] Aristophanes, *Acharnians*, 141–50; Olson 2002: 116–19.   [41] Hagemajer Allen 2003b: 218.
[42] *SIG*³, 168; translated in *R-O*, 56.   [43] *Labraunda*, 40; translated in *R-O*, 55.

community of the Cnossians. A similar development can be observed in the Bosporan kingdom: an inscription records King Paerisades and his sons bestowing *proxenia* and other fiscal privileges on Dionysius from Piraeus.[44] By the end of the classical period Greek diplomatic practices were applied to non-Greeks, and non-Greeks were reconfiguring Greek diplomatic practices for their own needs.

4.1.5 Commensality

Commensality, or eating and drinking together, is an activity which can create strong intercultural bonds. During the archaic period a particular form of ritualised commensality, whose key feature was reclined banqueting, spread from Assyria across the Mediterranean through Greece all the way to Etruria.[45] The Greek version of this form, the symposion, combined eating and drinking with singing, dancing, sex and intellectual discussion. It is in such a context of merrymaking that intercultural communication took place in particular ways. Literary sources provide fascinating vignettes of banquets involving Greeks and non-Greeks. Herodotus describes a banquet at Thebes before the battle of Plataea, in which a Persian and a Greek sat next to each other on every couch and in which a Persian predicted to his Greek co-diner the doomed outcome of the forthcoming battle.[46]

But non-Greek societies had their own forms of ritualised commensality, and the negotiation of different rules in intercultural banquets could take a variety of forms.[47] Xenophon describes a banquet at the court of the Thracian prince Seuthes, in which one of the Greek guests hungrily evaded the Thracian custom of passing up most of the food while keeping only a small part for oneself.[48] If the Thracian reaction to this Greek breach of etiquette was good-humoured, a different breaking of rules had tragic consequences. The Persian envoys to the court of King Amyntas of Macedonia behaved immoderately by Greek standards in the banquet provided by the king: they allegedly demanded the presence of respectable Macedonian women, something unthinkable in a Greek symposion, and their behaviour caused the Macedonian prince Alexander to plan their slaughter.[49] Another Herodotean story concerning the tragic end of the Scythian king Scyles is illuminating:

---

[44] *CIRB*, 1.   [45] Fehr 1971; Dentzer 1982; Murray 1990.   [46] 9.16.
[47] Athenaeus, *Deipnosophists*, 4.148–54d.   [48] *Anabasis*, 7.3.22–5.   [49] Herodotus, 5.18–20.

Now the Scythians reproach the Greeks for this Bacchic revelling, saying that it is not reasonable to set up a god who leads men to madness. So when Scyles had been initiated into the Bacchic rite, some one of the Borysthenites [i.e., citizens of Olbia] scoffed at the Scythians: 'You laugh at us, Scythians, because we play the Bacchant and the god possesses us; but now this deity has possessed your own king, so that he plays the Bacchant and is maddened by the god. If you will not believe me, follow me now and I will show him to you.'[50]

Herodotus does not explicitly describe the specific setting in which this encounter between Greeks and Scythians took place, but the symposion with its ethnographic reflections would provide an ideal setting. This is a setting of encounters between Greeks and non-Greeks in which taunts and assertions of superiority play an important role.[51] The Scythians taunt the Greeks in such encounters over their Bacchic revelries, and on this occasion a Borysthenite has found the opportunity to strike back by telling them about the actions of their own king.

Stressing polarity was not the only form of intercultural communication in a symposion; an early fifth-century *olpe* (jug), carrying an inscription painted before firing, provides a different perspective:

> Apollodorus loves Xylla;
> Volchas sodomised Apollodorus;
> Onatas loves Nixo;
> Hybrichus loves Parmynis.[52]

There is no doubt that the painting of this inscription on the vase before firing was intended as a deliberate joke to amuse the participants in a symposion who would handle this *olpe*. The names are a good indication of the mixed groups involved. Apollodorus, Onatas, Hybrichus and Parmynis are Greek names; but there are no Greek parallels for the female names Xylla and Nixo and they are presumably Italic, while the name Volchas is clearly Etruscan. Equally important is the findspot of this vase in a tomb at Fratte in Salerno, in an area of Campania under heavy Etruscan influence, as we have seen (p. 105).[53]

4.1.6 Travel, exchange and labour

We have explored in Chapter 3 the complex world of cosmopolitan centres, like those of the *emporia*: what forms of intercultural communication took place when Greeks and non-Greeks found themselves travelling with,

---

[50] 4.79.   [51] Braund 2008.   [52] *SEG* XXVII, 817; Dubois 2002: 72–3.   [53] Pontrandolfo 1987.

exchanging with or working next to each other? A tantalising example of such forms of intercultural communication is presented by a small ivory piece with a figure of a lion, which has been found in a cemetery of Carthage. The piece seems to be of Etruscan production and carries an Etruscan inscription, the beginning of which can be translated as 'I am a Punic from Carthage'; it apparently functioned as an introduction card for a Carthaginian merchant in Etruria, who finally took it to his grave when he returned home.[54] A vivid illustration of such intercultural encounters is provided by Xenophon:

> Once I had an opportunity of looking over the great Phoenician merchantman, Socrates, and I thought I had never seen tackle so excellently and accurately arranged. For I never saw so many bits of stuff packed away separately in so small a receptacle . . . I found that the steersman's servant, who is called the mate, knows each particular section so exactly, that he can tell, even when away, where everything is kept and how much there is of it, just as well as a man who knows how to spell can tell how many letters there are in 'Socrates' and in what order they come. Now, I saw this man in his spare time inspecting all the stores that are wanted, as a matter of course, in the ship . . .[55]

There is no way to tell, of course, whether Xenophon is here describing a real event; but there is also nothing to suggest that the event is not plausible, in particular given that the nationality of the ship and its sailors plays no instrumental role in the story or the wider context of the *Oeconomicus*, but is only thrown in as a casual detail. One wonders, to start with, in which language Xenophon imagined Ischomachus and the Phoenician mate conversing: did Ischomachus speak Phoenician? Or did the Phoenician sailor speak Greek? Were there Greek sailors aboard a Phoenician ship? Whatever the case, it is clear that Xenophon presents Ischomachus as clearly impressed not only by the size of the Phoenician ship, whose arrival in Piraeus is presented as a memorable event, but also by the tidiness and organisation aboard the ship. This is an occasion of intercultural communication in which a non-Greek manages to present successfully values and achievements that a Greek can appreciate.

Equally illuminating are two stories relating to the Ten Thousand, the international force of mercenaries put together in order to support a Persian prince's claim to the throne (pp. 66–7).[56] The first story comes from the aftermath of Cunaxa, when the Greek army is debating what plan to follow in order to survive and return home. Xenophon has already suggested that

---

[54] Cristofani 1983: 66, with fig. 40.   [55] *Oeconomicus*, 8.11–16.
[56] For intercultural exchanges among mercenaries, see Kaplan 2003.

the only way forward is to fight their way out of Mesopotamia and back into the Greek world, instead of capitulating or collaborating with the Persian king. His proposal was countered by a man named Apollonides, who spoke in the Boeotian dialect, and who proposed that negotiation with the king was the only option.[57] Apollonides' speech was met with a furious refutation by Xenophon, pointing out the treachery of the Persians and the futility of trusting them and concluding:

'In my opinion, gentlemen, we should not simply refuse to admit this fellow to companionship with us, but should deprive him of his captaincy, lay packs on his back, and treat him as that sort of a creature. For the fellow is a disgrace both to his native state and to the whole of Greece, since, being a Greek, he is still a man of this kind.' Then Agasias, a Stymphalian, broke in and said: 'For that matter, this fellow has nothing to do either with Boeotia or with any part of Greece at all, for I have noticed that he has both his ears bored, like a Lydian's.' In fact, it was so. He, therefore, was driven away.[58]

This is a characteristic example of the widespread practice of ethnography by ordinary people: notice the role in the encounter of the observation of Apollonides' dialect, his bored ears and the ethnographic knowledge that this is a practice associated with the Lydians. This incident shows that the experience of working together with people from different cultures did not necessarily counter, and could even inspire, xenophobic attitudes; the bored ears are evidence of a non-Greek custom, and accordingly Apollonides is immediately designated as a Barbarian and driven away.

But things are not so simple; if Apollonides was actually a Lydian, it is remarkable that he bore a Greek name and was able to pass as a Boeotian. The distinction between Greek and Barbarian was permeable enough for a non-Greek to be able to speak the language fluently enough to be taken as a Greek. But, in fact, we cannot be certain that Apollonides was indeed Lydian; it is possible that he might have come from Aeolis in Asia Minor, where a dialect similar to Boeotian was spoken (p. 37), and where proximity with Lydia meant that certain Lydian customs could be adopted by the local Greeks; or he might indeed have been a Boeotian who had spent time in Aeolis during the latest stages of the Peloponnesian War and adopted a Lydian custom.[59] Whichever of these three scenarios we opt for, it is obvious that the strict polarity between Greek and Barbarian often broke down in practice. The experience of working together could combine xenophobia

---

[57] *Anabasis*, 3.1.26.   [58] *Anabasis*, 3.1.30–2.   [59] Lane Fox 2004b: 204; Ma 2004: 336–7.

with the adoption of foreign customs and an attitude of nonchalance towards foreign people.

While at Cotyora on the southern Black Sea coast, the Greek army received ambassadors from Corylas, the king of the Paphlagonians, proposing a non-aggression pact; the ambassadors were then invited to dinner by the Greeks. After eating followed entertainment from the various contingents of the Ten Thousand:

After they had made libations and sung the paean, two Thracians rose up first and began a dance in full armour to the music of a flute, leaping high and lightly and using their sabres; finally, one struck the other, as everybody thought, and the second man fell, in a rather skilful way. And the Paphlagonians set up a cry. Then the first man despoiled the other of his arms and marched out singing the Sitalcas, while other Thracians carried off the fallen dancer, as though he were dead; in fact, he had not been hurt at all.[60]

After other Greek and non-Greek contingents of the Ten Thousand had presented their own dances as well, the Paphlagonians were really impressed by the military format of the dances.

Thereupon the Mysian, seeing how astounded they were, persuaded one of the Arcadians who had a dancing girl to let him bring her in, after dressing her up in the finest way he could, and giving her a light shield. And she danced the Pyrrhic with grace. Then there was great applause, and the Paphlagonians asked whether women also fought by their side. And the Greeks replied that these women were precisely the ones who put the King to flight from his camp. Such was the end of that evening.[61]

What we see here is collaboration between the various Greek and non-Greek elements of the Ten Thousand in order to provide entertainment, impress the Paphlagonian ambassadors with the spectacle and their martial valour, and to ensure the good relations with the Paphlagonian king that would be essential for their survival. Ethnographic display is here put into the service of forging diplomatic relations. Xenophon mentions that the Thracian dancer was singing a song about Sitalces, a contemporary Thracian king; this song could have been another source of ethnographic information through intercultural communication. It is also important that the dancing performances betray a prior process of cultural mingling; it is not accidental that the Mysian performed a Persian dance after having served in what was originally a contingent of a Persian army.

---

[60] *Anabasis*, 6.1.5–6.   [61] *Anabasis*, 6.1.12–13.

Finally, we should include pilgrimage and tourism, which bridge the gap between travel and our next practice, cult. We have particularly rich evidence from Egypt, where thousands of graffiti were left by Greeks and other foreigners, resident or visiting, on the walls of sanctuaries, tombs and other famous monuments. Such is the case of the Cypriote Cratandrus, the son of Stasinus, who along with his wife Themito, daughter of Morandrus, left a graffito in the Greek language, but using the Cypriote syllabic script, on a block of the pyramid of Cheops in Giza.[62] Places of international pilgrimage in particular were hotspots of intercultural communication. Herodotus presents a visit of some Cyrenaeans to the oracle of Ammon at the oasis of Siwa in the Libyan Desert; during that visit, the Cyrenaeans came to converse with the local king Etearchus (who interestingly bore a Greek name) and in the course of discussion the geographic issue of the sources of the Nile was raised, as a result of which the local king came to narrate a story he had heard in a different encounter at his court with members of a Libyan tribe.[63]

4.1.7 Cult

Cult was another practice that brought Greeks and non-Greeks together in a variety of different ways.[64] We have already seen how the Citian merchants and the Egyptians were granted by Athens the right to buy land to build temples to Aphrodite and Isis, respectively (p. 102). These cults were probably primarily for Citians and Egyptians, at least initially; but they were the means through which foreign cults like that of Isis found their way to and became established in Greek communities. We have other examples of foreign cults which raise very interesting questions about intercultural communication. The following fourth-century dedication derives from the mining area of Laureion:

The following members of the *eranos* dedicated [this] to [Men Tyrannos]:
  Cadous, Manes, Callias, Attas, Artemidorus, Maes, Sosias, Saggarius,
  Hermaeus, Tibeius, Hermus.

Thousands of slaves were employed in the mining area of Laureion; most of the dedicators in this inscription bear foreign names of various origins (Phrygian, Paphlagonian, Bithynian) or Greek names commonly borne by slaves, and are thus certainly either slaves or a mixed group of slaves and freedmen. Despite their non-Greek ethnicities, it is telling that they made a dedication in the Greek language and according to the standard Greek

---

[62] *ICS*, 371.   [63] 2.32.   [64] Mastrocinque 1993; Naso 2006.

formulas; they even described their association as an *eranos*, that is, a group whose activities are funded by joint contributions. There is some uncertainty concerning the restoration of the name of the deity addressed; if the restoration to Tyrannos (Lord) Men is correct, the dedication is for an Anatolian deity, who is described with the Greek adjective *tyrannos* (tyrant), something which is uncommon in the Greek religious ritual of the classical period.[65] These slaves created a world of their own, mixing various Greek and non-Greek elements.[66]

But we also have evidence for mixed cult associations that brought Greeks and non-Greeks together in a variety of ways. A fourth-century Athenian dedication is illustrative:

To the nymphs and all the gods, fulfilling a vow, the washers set up this tablet: Zoagoras the son of Zocyprus, Zocyprus the son of Zoagoras, Thallus, Leuce, Socrates son of Polycrates, Apollophanes, the son of Euporion, Sosistratus, Manes, Myrrhine, Sosias, Sosigenes, Midas.[67]

This is a dedication created by a cult group for people exercising the same profession: the dedicators are all washers, though of varying social status. Those with patronyms (father's name) are likely to be free, possibly even citizens, though Zoagoras and his son Zocyprus must have been Cypriote metics as they both bear typical Cypriote names; some of the other dedicators have non-Greek names (Manes, Midas) and are probably slaves or freedmen. Despite their different origins and social status, these washers joined together to worship a group of Greek deities closely associated with water, their means of livelihood.

The most fascinating example, though, is that of the cult association for the Thracian goddess Bendis that was officially created by the Athenian state at some point after the middle of the fifth century.[68] This was an important cult, as even in the fourth century the sacrifices to Bendis involved the third largest expenditure for buying animals, after the festivals of the City Dionysia and the Olympia. The opening of Plato's *Republic* commemorates what was likely the first celebration of Bendis' festival:

I went down yesterday to the Piraeus with Glaucon, the son of Ariston, to pay my devotions to the Goddess, and also because I wished to see how they would conduct the festival since this was its inauguration. I thought the procession of the locals very fine, but it was no better than the show made by the marching of the Thracian contingent.[69]

---

[65] *SEG* XXIX 163, XLII 152; Lauffer 1955/6: 185.   [66] Vlassopoulos 2011.   [67] *IG* II², 2934.
[68] Simms 1988; Planeaux 2000/1.   [69] *Republic*, 327a.

The passage goes on to describe an impressive performance of a torch race on horseback, which, given that normal Athenian torch races were on foot, was probably an innovation connected with the Thracian horse-loving customs of the goddess' devotees.[70] We must be dealing here with quite affluent Thracians, who could afford to own horses and exercise with them, and we have the votive dedication of one such Thracian: 'Daus dedicated this to Bendis, having won in the torch-race'.[71] A third-century inscription purports to describe the conditions of the establishment of the cult, 'since the people of the Athenians gave only to the Thracians among the other nations the right to buy land (*enktesis*) and to found a temple according to the oracle of Dodona', and sets out various regulations 'so that, if these things happen and the whole nation is of the same opinion, the sacrifices to the gods will take place and everything else that is appropriate according to the ancestral customs of the Thracians and the laws of the city'.[72]

If Athenians participated in a Thracian cult, Thracians could also learn about Greek cults through intercultural communication and participate in them. In the marble quarries of the island of Paros stands a fourth-century relief with an accompanying inscription: 'Adamas, the Odrysian, to the Nymphs'.[73] The Odrysians were one of the most powerful Thracian tribes, and Odrysian rulers from the fifth century onwards created a state that ranged from the Aegean to the Danube. We do not know what the status of this Thracian was, but given the strong links between Paros and its *apoikia* Thasos opposite the Thracian coast, the presence of a Thracian at Paros is not surprising. The relief represents the Nymphs among other deities who are difficult to identify, one of which is likely to be the Thracian goddess Bendis.[74]

4.2 Media and contents of communication

We have examined in section 4.1 practices which provided contexts for intercultural communication. But what was actually communicated in these contexts and through what media? We can roughly define three different media of communication. The first is oral communication, and most intercultural communication in antiquity must have taken this form. To this, we can add the importance of objects and monuments as media of communication. Objects and monuments could communicate through their icon-

[70] Parker 1996: 171.   [71] *SEG* XXXIX, 210.   [72] *IG* II², 1283.   [73] *IG* XII.5, 245.
[74] Berranger 1983.

ography or function; but they also had a 'social life', and the history of their past owners and creators was as important as the iconography or the objects themselves.[75] Finally, texts in their various forms did circulate across cultures and could become a means of intercultural communication. But the effectiveness of texts as means of intercultural communication depends not only on the extent of literacy, but even more on the extent to which they can be read either through translations or because they have been written in a lingua franca which is intelligible across cultural frontiers.

There exists very limited evidence for the translation of written texts across the frontiers of language and script during the archaic and classical periods. Even more, the archaic and classical periods stand in between two periods in which linguae francae were widely used for the dissemination of texts. During the Bronze Age, Babylonian, written in cuneiform script, had functioned as the lingua franca of written communication in an area extending from Iran to Egypt, the Levant and Asia Minor; and from the Hellenistic period onwards, as we shall see in Chapter 7, Greek came to function as the lingua franca of intercultural communication across the Mediterranean and the Near East (pp. 291, 310–11). During the period that we are examining here two languages came gradually to be employed over wide areas: these were Greek and Aramaic. In the case of Aramaic we do have some tantalising evidence for its use as a medium of intercultural communication by the Aramaic-speaking communities of Egypt. One papyrus records a variety of texts written in the Egyptian demotic script but in the Aramaic language: the texts belong to an Aramaic-speaking community that had its origins in south Syria. Exactly the opposite seems to be the case with the Bar Puneš text and some Egyptian cave inscriptions: these are written in Aramaic, but they seem to be translations of Egyptian stories and have an Egyptian setting.[76] To judge from the evidence we currently have, there seems to be little crossover between the texts written in Greek and those written in Aramaic; the connections that we do find are more likely to be the result of oral or material communication rather than established through written texts.[77]

It is accordingly primarily oral communication, as exemplified in the practices and contexts we have examined above, that will be the focus of our discussion.[78] This should not mean underestimating the role of objects as media of communication.[79] A popular theme in Mesopotamian art is the combat between the heroes Gilgamesh and Enkidu and the monster

[75] Appadurai 1986.   [76] Kottsieper 2009: 426–30.   [77] Henkelman 2006.
[78] López-Ruiz 2010: 30–8.   [79] Uehlinger 2000; Fless and Treister 2005.

Humbaba, depicted with a frontal grim yet grinning face. There is little doubt that it is this iconographic theme, transmitted through portable objects like seals and metal bowls, which is the prototype for the depictions by Greek artists of Perseus killing the frontally facing Medusa.[80] But can we also assume that the Mesopotamian myth was transmitted along with the images depicted on the objects?[81] This is often impossible to substantiate.

An excellent proof of the role of oral communication in the transmission of stories and knowledge is provided by the Etruscan illustrations of Greek myths. There were countless Greek vases transported to Etruria, as well as Etruscan-made vases and other objects, such as the famous Etruscan mirrors, which provided a major means through which Greek myths were transmitted and familiarised in Etruscan society.[82] But did the Etruscan artists who created these objects derive their knowledge of Greek myths from the visual representations on Greek vases and other objects of art? Or did they derive their knowledge from personal communication with Greek traders, artisans and settlers? There is no doubt that the former could be the case, but there are far too many examples which strongly suggest the significance of personal communication.[83] This is because some Etruscan depictions are closer to the forms of the myths as we know them from literary texts than they are to the forms of these myths in Greek artistic depictions. An archaic Etruscan *pithos* depicts the blinding of Polyphemus as described in the *Odyssey* far more literally than any previous depiction on Greek vases;[84] depictions of the ambush of Troilus in Etruscan art show features which are not represented in Greek art, but which are echoed in literary versions of the myth.[85] But why should we attribute all this to personal oral communication rather than to the Etruscan artists reading Greek literary texts? The proof is provided by the fact that in almost all cases the names of Greek gods and heroes in Etruscan are largely derived from the Doric dialect of Corinth,[86] and there is a long tradition regarding the presence of Corinthians in Etruria;[87] if Etruscan artists were reading Greek literature, which was written in a variety of dialects (pp. 37–8), one would have expected more diversity.

Communication clearly involved the exchange of information. Sailors and travellers were reliant on information about currents, winds, coasts, ports and hosts in order to navigate the Mediterranean; Greek ethnography developed out of the *Periploi*, pilot books that compiled information on the

[80] Burkert 2003: 66.   [81] Gufler 2002.   [82] Hemelrijk 1984; van der Meer 1995.
[83] Osborne 2009: 87.   [84] Snodgrass 1998: 89–100.   [85] Spivey and Stoddart 1990: 99.
[86] de Simone 1972.   [87] Ampolo 1976/7.

coasts and ports of the Mediterranean;[88] and traders exchanged information on routes, products and conditions. This information could range widely. There was obviously factual information necessary for traders, such as knowledge of the Egyptian regulations that prohibited Greek merchants from sailing into any mouth of the Nile except that leading to Naucratis.[89] There were stories about interesting but normal experiences, like Herodotus' story of how Greek and Phoenician wine amphoras were imported into Egypt, emptied of their contents and refilled with water to be re-exported to Syria,[90] or how the Egyptians sold to Greek merchants accursed bovine heads.[91] But there were also exotic tales about far-away places, ranging from believable stories about the silent trade of the Carthaginians,[92] to tall tales about the one-eyed men and gold-guarding griffins related by Scythians doing business at the end of the world through interpreters in seven languages.[93] The communication of information was not restricted to sailors and travellers; people involved in diplomatic relationships could be equally important vectors. The fifth-century historian Damastes of Sigeion claimed to have formed his view of the shape of the Arabian Gulf on the basis of information provided by Diotimus, the head of an Athenian embassy to Susa.[94]

Diplomatic relationships provided a major means through which the Greeks came to learn about the imperial powers, their rulers and their courts. There was a lot of ethnographic information exchanged, and that information could be used in a variety of ways. Herodotus reported how Hecataeus of Miletus, one of the pioneers of Greek ethnography, recited a list of the many nations under the rule of Dareius I in order to convince his Ionian compatriots that revolt against the Persians was futile;[95] on the opposite side, Xenophon described how an Arcadian ambassador to the Persian king reported back to his fellow citizens:

Antiochus, because the Arcadian League was less regarded, did not accept the royal gifts, and reported back to the Ten Thousand [the Arcadian assembly] that the King had bakers, and cooks, and wine-pourers, and doorkeepers in vast numbers, but as for men who could fight with Greeks, he said that though he sought diligently, he could not see any. Besides this, he said that for his part he thought that the King's wealth of money was also mere pretence, for he said that even the golden plane-tree, that was forever harped upon, was not large enough to afford shade for a cicada.[96]

---

[88] Dilke 1985: 130–44.   [89] Herodotus, 2.179.   [90] 3.6–7.   [91] 2.39.   [92] 4.196.
[93] 4.24–7.   [94] *FGrH*, 5 F8.   [95] 5.36.2.   [96] *Hellenica*, 7.1.38.

We can here see clearly how the political argument is based on an ethnographic account. Equally important was finding out about the customs of other people and accommodating them in order to achieve smooth communication and desirable results. This was, of course, particularly important in diplomatic relationships; Xenophon describes how the Persian satrap Pharnabazus accommodated Spartan customs during a negotiation we have already encountered (p. 132):

Apollophanes, after obtaining a truce and a pledge, brought Pharnabazus with him to a place which had been agreed upon, where Agesilaus and the thirty Spartans with him were lying on the ground in a grassy spot awaiting them; Pharnabazus, however, came in a dress which was worth much gold. But when his attendants were proceeding to spread rugs beneath him, upon which the Persians sit softly, he was ashamed to indulge in luxury, seeing as he did the simplicity of Agesilaus; so he too lay down on the ground without further ado.[97]

Thucydides, after describing the importance of gifts for the revenue of the Thracian kings, stresses a difference that would be essential knowledge for anyone conducting diplomacy with the Thracians:

For there was here established a custom opposite to that prevailing in the Persian kingdom, namely, of taking rather than giving; more disgrace being attached to not giving when asked than to asking and being refused. And although this prevailed elsewhere in Thrace, it was practised most extensively among the powerful Odrysians, it being impossible to get anything done without a present.[98]

Closely connected to the exchange of information was the exchange of words, expressions and manners of speech.[99] This is shown by the fact that most foreign loanwords in the Greek vocabulary belong to three distinct fields: those of economic practices; goods and objects; and imperial institutions.[100] Words involving economic practices include *mna* (1/60th of a talent) and *arrabon* (pledge); words for goods and products include *libanos* (frankincense), *byssos* (fine linen) and *kados* (wine jar); words related to imperial institutions include *parasagges* (a Persian measure of distance), while our word 'paradise' derives from the Greek word *paradeisos*, which is a Persian loanword describing an enclosed garden or park.[101] The transmission of words across cultures has fascinating repercussions. For example, one of the Indian names for India is Hindustan: why, then, do we say 'India' instead of 'Hindia'? This is because the modern Western terms for the country derive from ancient Greek; and the first Greeks to come across

---

[97] 4.1.29–30.   [98] 2.97.4.   [99] Hawkins 2010.   [100] Braun 1982a: 24–9.
[101] Tuplin 1996a: 80–131.

India, when part of it was conquered by the Persian Empire, were the Ionians, whose dialect was affected by psilosis (the loss of the aspirate sound h): hence, India, instead of Hindia.[102] The adoption of words and expressions could easily be followed by the customs and practices that these words expressed. The Phoenicians who lived in Greece accommodated Greek practices and abandoned their customary circumcision,[103] while the women of the Greek *apoikia* of Cyrene in Libya abstained from eating cow flesh because of their adherence to the Egyptian cult of Isis.[104]

The example of Cyrene presents an excellent opportunity to examine the transmission of cults and religious ideas through intercultural communication.[105] Like many other Greek *apoikiai* Cyrene quickly adopted a major pre-existing local cult: that of the Egyptian deity Ammon in the particular form in which he was worshipped at his oracle in the oasis of Siwa in the Libyan Desert. Cyrene's largest temple was dedicated to Ammon, and many Cyrenaeans bore the name Ammonius. Cyrene played a fundamental role in the transmission of the cult of Ammon to the Greek world, which occurred through a variety of different media. We have already seen how the sanctuary of Ammon in the oasis of Siwa was an international site of pilgrimage (p. 143); it is the only non-Greek oracle that was steadily frequented by Greeks during the archaic and classical periods. Pilgrims and visitors were one means of transmission; famous Greeks such as the Athenian Cimon and the Spartan Lysander visited the shrine. But the most famous pilgrim was undoubtedly Alexander the Great. In fact, it was believed in antiquity that a linguistic miscommunication was the cause of Alexander's view that the oracle had asserted his divine origin: the Libyan priest wanted to say in Greek 'oh paidion' ('oh, child') as a greeting to Alexander, but his mispronunciation was construed by Alexander as 'oh pai Dios' ('oh, son of Zeus').[106]

We should also remember the importance of objects. Ammon is prominently depicted on the coins of Cyrene, and in the course of the classical period other Greek cities such as Melos and Cyzicus depicted his image on their coins; their circulation would also transmit the image of the god. But we can also see the importance of the networks that linked *apoikiai* like Cyrene with the Panhellenic world. There was a statue of Ammon at Delphi dedicated by the Cyrenaeans and his cult was also present at Olympia. Pindar was one of those mobile intellectuals who composed poems for rulers and athletes from across the Greek world on the occasion of their

---

[102] Schmitt 2007: 373.   [103] Herodotus, 2.104.   [104] Herodotus, 4.186.
[105] For Cyrene, see Austin 2008.   [106] Plutarch, *Life of Alexander*, 27.5.

victories in the Panhellenic Games. Pindar situated his poems within the local political, social and cultural history of the homeland of the victor, and a communicative network was essential for accomplishing this. His poems for victors from Cyrene often mention Ammon; we also know that Pindar composed a hymn to Ammon for the Ammonians, the inhabitants of the area of the oracle, in which he identified Ammon with Zeus. It was through his Cyrenaean connections that Pindar found out about the deity; his attraction to the cult was expressed through the dedication in his homeland, Thebes, of a statue of Ammon, made by the famous sculptor Calamis.[107]

Let us bring this discussion to an end by looking more closely at the two cases of Greek myths and of stories about the great kings of the world of empires and their courts. Both were conduits of intercultural communication in the archaic and classical Mediterranean; but they also served as media by which various other ideas could be communicated. As we shall examine in detail in Chapter 5 (pp. 166–8), Greek myth was a very peculiar communicative system. Greek mythology, and in particular its heroic component, is unique in being located in space and time; the movements of Greek heroes in space and time link communities and individuals, found settlements and instigate feuds. At the same time, foreign heroes, like the Lycian Sarpedon or the Thracian Rhesus (p. 126), were an inherent and important part of this mythology.[108] There is nothing equivalent in the Mesopotamian or Egyptian mythologies, which are the only ones to offer sufficient evidence to judge. We have seen how a Paphlagonian slave like Atotas was able to use Greek myth to present his ethnic identity, because Paphlagonian heroes were present in Greek mythology (pp. 130–1); we have also examined the role of Greek myth in mediating the interactions between Greeks and Thracians, whether to legitimise the Greek appropriation of land or to cement a relationship of trust between Thracian rulers and Greek mercenaries (pp. 126–7). Herodotus reports the gifts of Amasis to the sanctuary of Athena at Lindos in Rhodes; eliciting those gifts was based on the myth that the Egyptian Danaids had founded the sanctuary in their flight from their Egyptian cousins.[109]

But there is another aspect of Greek myth which is equally important. This is its ability to incorporate local traditions through selective filtering as well as the opportunity it offered to non-Greek cultures to present their traditions to a broader, Mediterranean-wide audience. Herodotus alludes at various points to the myth of Io and her sojourn in Egypt.[110] Greek myth

---

[107] On the cult of Ammon and its expansion, see Classen 1959; Malkin 1994b: 143–68.
[108] Gehrke 2005.   [109] 2.182; Francis and Vickers 1984.   [110] 1.1–5, 2.41.

tells the story of how Zeus fell in love with Io, how Io attracted the wrath of Hera and how Zeus had to transform Io into a cow to escape Hera's wrath. But Hera sent a gadfly to sting and persecute Io, who then roamed all over the world till she reached Egypt, where she gave birth to Epaphus.[111] This is no doubt a Greek myth, which seemed to have more than one version;[112] but it is also clear that a Greek myth of a woman turned into a cow is linked here to the Egyptian tradition of Isis depicted as a cow and to Apis, an important deity of Memphis, where Greek presence was strong (pp. 253–4), depicted as a calf, with a name sounding similar to that of Greek Epaphus. The Greek mythic tradition brought Io to Egypt and then identified her through translation with Egyptian traditions about Isis and Apis. It seems that, when the world of mobility and empire brought Greeks to Egypt as mercenaries, traders and pilgrims, they identified one of their own mythical figures with a local one, and located Io's sojourn in Egypt. Greek myth was in a position to link with a local myth and incorporate it as part of a Greek mythical narrative. But the opposite is true as well. Greek myth was not merely a medium for certain interlinking practices; it was also already widely adopted by many non-Greek communities from Etruria to Lycia during the archaic period and incorporated within their own religious and cultural systems.[113] We shall examine in Chapter 6 the variety of ways in which Greek myth was glocalised across the Mediterranean.

If Greek myth had a privileged position in intercultural communication, the same applies to the imperial powers which shaped the eastern Mediterranean world in the archaic and classical periods. From Assyria, Egypt and Lydia to Persia, the imperial rulers and their courts exercised an enormous role not only in the lives of their subjects and enemies, but also in their imaginations and conversations. In the Mediterranean and the Near East countless stories circulated about these kings and their courts. But what is even more important is the emergence of complex literary narratives which used these rulers and their courts as settings for the most varied projects.[114] Unfortunately, with two major exceptions, the vast majority of these texts have been lost. The two major exceptions are Greek literary texts and those Jewish texts that survived because they became part of the Bible.[115] Otherwise, we have only fragmentary glimpses of this extensive literature, as in the famous text of Ahiqar, preserved on an Aramaic papyrus found at Elephantine in Egypt: it narrates the story of a

[111] Hicks 1962: 93–7; West 1984.   [112] Mitchell 2001.   [113] Malkin 1998.   [114] Dalley 2001.
[115] Wills 1990; Johnson 2004.

wise courtier of the Assyrian king who is unfairly condemned, but who secretly escapes execution only to be vindicated afterwards.[116]

It would be instructive to compare a Herodotean story with one from the Jewish texts that became part of the Bible.[117] The story of how Dareius I enquired about the diversity of human customs by asking the Indians present in his court how much he would have to pay them to bury their dead fathers and the Greeks to eat theirs is justly famous: the Indians found abhorrent what the Greeks considered normal and vice versa.[118] *I Esdras* has a parallel story in which three bodyguards attempt to convince Dareius as to what is the strongest thing, with the Jewish bodyguard Zerubbabel winning by convincing Dareius that the strongest thing is truth.[119] The authorial aims of these two stories could not be more different: Herodotus is using his in order to argue the relativity of human customs, whereas the author of *I Esdras* aims to glorify his religion and uses the story as a means through which Dareius is convinced to allow the re-erection of the Temple.[120] But in both cases there is a common theme of the Persian court as an arena of enquiry.[121] The theme of Ahiqar is clearly recognisable in the Herodotean story of Cambyses and his decision to execute his courtier Croesus.[122] But whereas in Ahiqar the travails of the hero largely provide a setting for the didactic part of the text, expressed in a series of proverbs and other gnomic statements, in Herodotus the same motif has been used in order to portray the mad tyrant that Cambyses 'was'. We need to recognise the international character of these motifs and settings, and the complex role they played in articulating the most disparate stories. Imperial rulers and their courts functioned as a means of intercultural communication in the most variable ways.

We have explored the popularity of Greek myth as a medium of communication and the imaginary potency of imperial rulers and their courts. But these two factors were by no means unrelated. We have already examined the presence of Greeks in the royal and satrapal courts of the Persian Empire (pp. 50–2). These Greeks did not merely conduct negotiations or formulate diplomatic documents;[123] there are good reasons to believe that they were instrumental in creating stories that allowed the Persians to comprehend the nature and views of their Greek subjects, opponents and allies, and to intervene in Greek affairs for their own benefit. We have already seen how Greeks could use mythology and genealogy in order to connect to

---

[116] Fales 1993.   [117] For Persian stories in Herodotus, see Reinhardt 1965.
[118] Herodotus, 3.38.   [119] *I Esdras*, 3–4.   [120] Gruen 1998: 161–7.   [121] Christ 1994.
[122] Herodotus, 3.36; West 2003.   [123] Lewis 1977: 14–15.

non-Greeks and derive benefits from such links (p. 151); but the process could work the other way round, as some stories in Herodotus manifest. Thus, Herodotus reports one of the stories that circulated in order to explain why the Argives did not participate in the Panhellenic campaign against the Persians:

Such is the Argives' account of this matter, but there is another story told in Greece, namely that before Xerxes set forth on his march against Greece, he sent a herald to Argos, who said on his coming (so the story goes), 'Men of Argos, this is the message to you from King Xerxes. Perses our forefather had, as we believe, Perseus son of Danae for his father, and Andromeda daughter of Cepheus for his mother; if that is so, then we are descended from your nation. In all right and reason we should therefore neither march against the land of our forefathers, nor should you become our enemies by aiding others or do anything but abide by yourselves in peace. If all goes as I desire, I will hold none in higher esteem than you.' The Argives were strongly moved when they heard this.[124]

Mythological stories that linked together Greeks and Barbarians could originate from a non-Greek initiative, although it is likely that this non-Greek initiative was formulated and expressed through Greek brokers. We have seen how the Greeks used the myth of the Trojan War in order to interpret the Persian Wars as one episode in the long struggle between Greeks and Barbarians (p. 61). It has been convincingly argued that the use of the Trojan War as a mythological exemplum through which to understand the Persian Wars is likely to be a Persian invention to justify their invasion. Xerxes' sacrifices at Troy were part of a propaganda campaign orchestrated by the Greeks in Persian service in order to justify the Persian invasion to the Greeks: Xerxes was only exacting revenge for the Greek destruction of Troy. This ingenious use of Greek myth was subsequently taken over and reversed by the victorious Greeks![125] This impressive example shows eloquently how complex were the media of intercultural communication and how varied its contents.

4.3 Patterns of communication

We have examined practices and contexts as well as the contents of intercultural communication; we have established that people from different cultures were talking to each other in the archaic and classical Mediterranean; but what were the patterns of this communication and how effectively did

---

[124] 7.150.   [125] Haubold 2007.

people communicate? Intercultural communication could often produce distorted results. One obvious case is the deception of the middleman. Herodotus provides a characteristic example when he credulously reports how the tourist guides at the Pyramids of Giza purported to translate the hieroglyphic inscriptions, recording (they said) how many onions were consumed by the workers who built the pyramids.[126] Hieroglyphic inscriptions did not actually record this kind of information, but to Herodotus this was confirmation of the power of kings who could mobilise such enormous manpower. Intercultural communication could also lead to creative misunderstandings. In the course of his march through Cilicia, Alexander the Great encountered what was purportedly the tomb of the Assyrian king Sardanapalus (Assurbanipal):

Sardanapalus' tomb was near the wall of Anchialus; over it stood Sardanapalus himself, his hands joined as if to clap, and an epitaph was inscribed in the Assyrian script; the Assyrians said that it was in verse. In any case the general meaning was: 'Sardanapalus son of Anacyndaraxes built Anchialus and Tarsos in one day; do you, stranger, eat and drink and be merry, since other human things are not worth *this*' – the idea being the hand-clap; and (it was said) the word 'be merry' had a less delicate meaning in Assyrian.[127]

It is, of course, unlikely that such an inscription would have been erected by an Assyrian king. But there was Assyrian presence in Cilicia before as well as during Assurbanipal's time, and the practice of erecting inscribed statues was common in the area; the gesture that the Greeks understood as clapping was used to express blessing by the Assyrians. Sardanapalus was a well-known figure in Greek discourses associated with bliss and effeminacy, and an epitaph similar to that described above was known to the Greeks long before Alexander's time. But while Greeks normally took the imperatives 'drink, eat and be merry' to imply a hedonistic and carefree attitude to life, this was by no means how it was interpreted by the non-Greek cultures of the area. This is shown by a fourth-century Greek inscription recently discovered in eastern Lycia, which links the expression with the idea of justice:

> Here I, Apollonius the son of Hellaphilus, lie dead.
> I worked justly, and while I was alive I had always a sweet life,
> eating and drinking and playing; go and hail.[128]

---

[126] 2.125. [127] Arrian, *Anabasis*, 2.5.3. [128] *M-S*, 17.19.03; Wörrle 1996/7.

Some of the expressions in this epigram are rather unusual in Greek, and would imply either that the deceased belonged to a native Hellenised family or that this Greek was influenced by local ideas and expressions. Clearly, not every Greek speaker understood the expression in a hedonistic manner. We cannot be certain exactly what the monument and its inscription encountered by Alexander were; but it is clear that local stories, local monuments and ideas attributed to famous non-Greeks were re-interpreted through a process of intercultural communication.[129]

Another example of how intercultural communication could fundamentally alter the content transmitted concerns Herodotus' confused description of Lake Moeris in Egypt.[130] It is in effect a transposition, in the form of a realistic geographical description, of the theological geography of the Egyptian *Book of the Fayum*.[131] But intercultural communication could also create stories that successfully combined elements from different cultural traditions. A nice example is a story concerning the pharaoh Amasis. Herodotus reports how Amasis would spend the mornings conducting state business, while the rest of the day he devoted to drinking and idleness. When criticised by his friends for behaving in a manner not fit for a king, Amasis explained that, just as a permanently strung bow would break, in the same way relaxation was necessary for a man's mental stability.[132] The motif of Amasis the merrymaker can be found in Egyptian literature: a Demotic tale about a sick skipper is presented as a story narrated to entertain Amasis during a hangover, after the pharaoh had consumed a large quantity of heavy wine despite the warnings of his councillors.[133] The story found in Herodotus clearly has an Egyptian basis, reflected in other Egyptian stories about the Saite kings who were fond of wine.[134] These examples should be sufficient to show the complex means by which stories employ different elements of intercultural communication.

Cultural contact and encounters between different groups do not lead to a single type of reaction; what we have to posit is a variety of patterns of intercultural communication. We can divide these patterns in two different ways: according to perspective and according to content. As regards perspective, stories can be told either from a Greek perspective (*interpretatio graeca*) or from a non-Greek perspective. In other words, stories can either try to translate the customs, values and history of one community into terms understandable by another, or explain them in terms native to the community from which the stories originate. As regards content, the stories can take as

---

[129] Burkert 2009.   [130] 2.149–50.   [131] Haider 2001.   [132] 2.173.
[133] Translated in Simpson 2003: 450–2.   [134] Lloyd 1988: 213–14; Quaegebeur 1990.

their subject issues that either focus on the differences between Greeks and non-Greeks (polarity), or on common, shared or universal values and ideas (universality). Of course, the division by content and the division by perspective are not mutually irreconcilable. A story can, for example, emphasise the differences between two cultures, while also trying to explain a custom of one culture in terms of the other. In practice, of course, things were often less clear-cut than the four patterns would suggest: but for heuristic purposes the four patterns can prove a very illuminating tool.

The first pattern of communication is the polarity model that we are so familiar with.[135] This pattern focuses on the obvious or perceived differences between groups and creates stories which emphasise these differences. Given that *nomos* is king,[136] every culture inclines to taking its own customs as being superior to all other; accordingly, there is a strong tendency in such stories to portray other groups as inferior. The stories concerning the Spartan messengers Sperthias and Boulis, who were sent by the Spartans in the late 480s to atone for their sacrilegious execution of the Persian envoys, are characteristic. The stories portray them lecturing the Persian satrap Hydarnes, who has only experienced subservience to the Persian king, on the value of Greek freedom, as well as refusing to perform the Persian custom of obeisance to the king (*proskynesis*), since Greek custom approved of obeisance only to the gods.[137] Equally characteristic is the story of the two banquets organised by the Spartan regent Pausanias after the battle of Plataea: the one was in the austere Laconian fashion, while the other was according to the luxurious Persian taste.[138]

In contrast to polarity, the second pattern of cultural communication appeals to common or shared denominators. Greek authors report various stories transmitted through intercultural communication which stress common or universal values. A typical example concerns Herodotus' story about the Egyptian soldiers who in the time of pharaoh Psammetichus rebelled and escaped to Ethiopia:

Psammetichus heard of it and pursued them; and when he overtook them, he asked them in a long speech not to desert their children and wives and the gods of their fathers. Then one of them, the story goes, pointed to his genitals and said that wherever that was, they would have wives and children.[139]

This is a story that examines the limits of male attachment to family and country, and one that could easily be understood by both Greeks and

---

[135] For polarity in Greek culture, see Lloyd 1966.   [136] Herodotus, 3.38.4.
[137] Herodotus, 7.135–6.   [138] Herodotus, 9.82.   [139] 2.30.4.

Egyptians.[140] The story of pharaoh Pherus is another good example. Pherus was punished with blindness for an offensive act; an oracle predicted that he would regain his sight if he washed his eyes with the urine of a chaste woman. Predictably, there was only a single chaste woman in the whole kingdom, whom the Pharaoh duly married, while exterminating all the unchaste ones.[141] Female lack of chastity is, of course, an issue of male concern in very different societies.[142]

Let us now move to patterns according to perspective. A third pattern tries to explain a culture and its particular features not in terms of understanding this culture's particular views, but by creating stories that attempt to explain the other culture by means that are comprehensible in the storyteller's own cultural terms: this would mean the *interpretatio graeca* of Egyptian customs or the *interpretatio aegyptiaca* of Greek customs. On the opposite side, the fourth pattern tries to explain a particular culture and its customs, monuments and history by means of this culture's own terms. Perhaps the best way to show the difference between the third and fourth patterns is to rehearse the various stories concerning the origins of the Scythian nation reported by Herodotus; he explicitly states that one story is told by the Greeks of the Black Sea area, while the other is related by the Scythians themselves.[143]

The Greek story seems a characteristic example of *interpretatio graeca*. While Heracles was driving the oxen of Geryon, he came to the land of Scythia, where he lost his mares and had to copulate with a half-woman, half-snake monster in order to get them back. This copulation produced three sons, Agathyrsus, Gelonus and Scythes. When Heracles was leaving, he gave the monster a bow and a belt and told her to give the land to whomever of the sons was able to draw the bow. Scythes, the youngest, was the only one who managed to draw the bow and thus became the ruler of the land and the ancestor of the Royal Scythians; Agathyrsus and Gelonus had to leave the land of Scythia and became the ancestors of the neighbouring nations of the Agathyrsi and the Geloni.[144] The origins of the Scythian nation are explained through the adventures of a famous Greek hero.

The Scythian tale narrates how Targitaus was the first man to appear in desolate Scythia; he had three sons, Lipoxaïs, Arpoxaïs and Colaxaïs. One day certain golden objects fell from the sky, which nobody could approach apart from the youngest brother Colaxaïs; his older brothers accepted this as a divine omen and conceded royal power to him. The story continues by

[140] But see Lloyd 1976: 129.   [141] Herodotus, 2.111.   [142] Aly 1921: 66, 255.   [143] 4.5, 4.8.
[144] 4.8–10.

showing how the different Scythian groups are descended from the three sons of Targitaus and finishes off by linking the miraculous golden objects with some Scythian rituals and customs.[145] It is obvious that this is a totally different kind of story from that propounded by the Black Sea Greeks. There are no figures of Greek mythology in the Scythian tale, and there are no links to any Greek tales or Greek concerns; it contains only native Scythian characters and is related to purely Scythian customs.[146]

Religion provides an excellent test case for exploring the various patterns of intercultural communication. The interlinking practices discussed above created a variety of contexts for intercultural communication through religion and cult. Making dedications to foreign deities opened up a variety of possibilities, and we have already examined some examples from the cosmopolitan universe of the *emporia* (pp. 94–5). Let us explore it further through three Greek dedications to Egyptian deities.[147] The first is an archaic bronze sheath depicting a devotee in front of Ammon, chief deity of Egyptian Thebes, and the goddess Mut. The sheath sports a bilingual dedication: while the hieroglyphic inscription mentions Ammon, the accompanying Greek inscription records a dedication by Melanthius to Theban Zeus (see Figure 17).[148] Ammon is identified through *interpretatio graeca* with Zeus, and we have already examined how the Libyan version of Ammon at Siwa was also identified by Greeks with Zeus (pp. 150–1). More adventurous is a statuette of Osiris in the form of Osiris-Lunus, with a Greek dedication by Zenes, the son of Theodotus, to Selene: in this case the lunar form of Osiris led to his identification with the Greek moon deity, even

Figure 17 Bilingual Greek dedication to Theban Zeus.

[145] 4.5–7.   [146] Ivantchik 1999.   [147] Vittmann 2003: 230–3.   [148] *SEG* XXVII, 1106.

though Selene was a female deity.[149] Different again is the case of a statuette of Isis suckling baby Horus, with an archaic dedication to Isis by Pythermus: in this case the Greek dedicator chose to identify the deity by her Egyptian name and avoided translating it into Greek terms.[150] In these three dedications, Greek devotees made diverse choices of intercultural identification: they could perform various acts of intercultural translation in Greek terms or decline it and adopt a deity in its Egyptian form.

We have explored the range of practices that created and facilitated intercultural communication, from guest-friendship and intermarriage through diplomacy and trade to commensality and cult. We have also examined the media of intercultural communication through oral and written communication, as well as through objects and monuments; we have also seen the diverse contents communicated through these media, from information and words to ideas and practices. Finally, we have discussed the patterns of intercultural communication and the choices facing people who tried, managed or failed to communicate across cultural, linguistic and ethnic divisions: whether to stress polarity or commonality and universality, whether to try to understand another culture in its own terms or to translate it in one's own terms. The next two chapters will focus on the diverse ways in which different cultures in the archaic and classical Mediterranean were shaped by the encounters and interactions in the four parallel worlds as filtered through intercultural communication.

[149] *SEG* XXVII, 1107.   [150] *SEG* XXVII, 1115.

5 | The Barbarian repertoire in Greek culture

It is time to examine the second of the paradoxes we set out in the Introduction: the paradoxical nature of Greek participation in the processes of globalisation and glocalisation and their effects on Greek culture. Chapter 4 examined in detail the contexts, patterns and content of intercultural communication in the ancient Mediterranean. Intercultural communication involved practices, ideas and stories which were transmitted across cultures. A series of texts translated and recorded in the Hittite language of the second millennium are known as the Kumarbi cycle and deal with the topic of divine succession in heaven. The myths describe how the deity Anu is confronted by his cup-bearer Kumarbi and flees to heaven, but has his genitals bitten off and swallowed by Kumarbi. Kumarbi becomes divine ruler, but has three fearful deities inside his body as a result of swallowing Anu's genitals. His attempt to prevent them from coming out fails after swallowing a rock, and the weather god Teshub emerges out of Kumarbi's body and eventually succeeds him as ruler. It is obvious that a version of this myth has been transmitted through intercultural communication and further adapted in the succession myth narrated in Hesiod's *Theogony*, where Cronus castrates Uranus, swallows his children and is finally defeated by his son, the weather god Zeus.[1]

The interaction with the Persian Empire that we examined in Chapter 2 had obvious effects on Athenian culture. Through trade, gift-exchange and war spoils, Athenian potters came across metal vase forms popular in Persia, such as the handless vases in the form of an animal head, adopted the shape in clay, but adapted it to suit Greek drinking customs by adding handles and a foot.[2] Another example is that of the parasol, a traditional status symbol for Near Eastern kings, who were often depicted served by parasol bearers in Assyrian or Persian art, which in the course of the first millennium was also adopted by the aristocracies of Asia Minor as a status symbol. From the later sixth century onwards the parasol was adopted as a status symbol in Athenian society, but its use was significantly

---

[1] Rutherford 2009; López-Ruiz 2010: 84–129.   [2] Miller 1997: 141–4.

adapted: in contrast to non-Greek practices, the parasol was restricted to the use by women, since its use by men was considered luxurious and effeminate.[3]

This adoption and adaptation of practices, ideas, objects and techniques between Greeks and non-Greeks should be taken as a constant result of intercultural interaction and communication in the four parallel worlds we have examined. In the last few decades numerous scholars have tried to identify elements, motifs, stories, similes and images which Greek authors and artists adopted and adapted from Near Eastern and other non-Greek cultures.[4] Observations range from noting parallels, which can be explained either by borrowing or by parallel developments, all the way to showing conscious reaction to foreign works.[5] Side by side with this scholarly approach though there also exists a voluminous scholarship which examines how Greek literature and art exemplify polarity and alterity towards other cultures; from Herodotus to Athenian tragedy and Greek art, scholars have explored how non-Greeks and their cultures are depicted as despotic, luxurious and effeminate, and how they provide the polar Other which serves to define Greek identity.[6] It is rather unfortunate that these diametrically opposed approaches exist side by side without any consistent effort to combine them or explain their contradictory coexistence. It is often stated or implied that the two approaches exemplify different periods. While, for example, Martin West has claimed to find an enormous range of Near Eastern parallels in Greek literature up to the time of Aeschylus, there seems to be little in comparison in Sophocles or Euripides.[7] Accordingly, it could be argued that borrowing from Near Eastern cultures was something that characterised the so-called 'Orientalising phase' of Greek culture during the archaic period; the clash of the Persian Wars and the development of a Greek identity in self-conscious polarity with non-Greek cultures is seen as a new phase where borrowing becomes less important or less apparent.[8]

There are major problems with these two divergent approaches. The approaches that focus on polarity in classical Greek culture fail to take into account the full range of ways in which Greek culture employed non-Greeks and their cultures; even during the classical period, polarity accounted for only a limited part of the surviving Greek literature and art.[9] The approaches that stress the openness of archaic Greek culture largely miss that polarity is already present from the very beginning of

---

[3] Miller 1997: 193–8.   [4] Burkert 1992, 2004; Morris 1992; West 1997; López-Ruiz 2010.
[5] See, e.g., Louden 2011.   [6] Hartog 1988; Hall 1989; Castriota 1992; Isaac 2004.
[7] West 1997: 544.   [8] Burkert 1992, 2004: 12–16; Morris 1992: 362–86.   [9] See now Gruen 2011.

Greek literature in the works of Homer. Furthermore, the privileging of the Persian Wars as the transformative event that separates the two periods is equally problematic. As we shall see, the two important changes that significantly expanded the Barbarian repertoire in Greek culture, and the means through which Greek authors and artists could employ the inter-actions with non-Greeks and the various Barbarian images, clearly preceded the Persian Wars. While there is no doubt that the Persian Wars had important cultural consequences, they largely intensified developments that had already started earlier and which were only partly related to the bolstering of Greek identity.

Given the fact that we cannot divide the Greek interaction with non-Greek cultures between archaic openness and classical polarity, we need an approach that is able to account *at the same time* both for the important role of non-Greek cultures in shaping Greek culture as well as for the crucial role of polarity and conflict in Greek cultural practices. It is here that traditional approaches of cultural interaction as a direct and unproblematic trans-mission of objects, ideas, similes and motifs are deeply inadequate. They are inadequate because they fail to take into account both the diversity of the Barbarian repertoire in Greek culture and the peculiar way in which Greek culture had already glocalised other cultures since the archaic period.

In order to understand what is peculiar about the Greek glocalisation of non-Greek cultures, we need to situate Greek culture within a spectrum of ways in which cultures relate to each other. Section 5.1 explores how we can situate Greek culture between the pole of self-referential cultures like Egypt, which eschew references to other cultures, and the other pole of cultures which make reference to foreign cultures a key aspect of their cultural repertoires. It then examines two important features which account to a large extent for the peculiar nature of Greek culture: the peculiar form of Greek myth; and the Greek textualisation of intercultural interactions and encounters in the four parallel worlds. The following two sections provide an alternative chronological account of the development of the Barbarian repertoire in Greek culture. Section 5.2 examines the diverse ways in which different genres of archaic Greek literature and art incorporated non-Greeks in their discourses and iconographies. While earlier scholarship has argued that Barbarians became an important part of Greek literature and art only after the clash of the Persian Wars and the creation of the polarised image of the Barbarian, section 5.2 documents the important roles already played by diverse images of Barbarians during the archaic period. This diversity was not abandoned after the Persian Wars, but remained an essential part of Greek literature and art in the classical and later periods, as sections 5.4, 5.5

and 5.6 will demonstrate. Section 5.3 examines two crucial transformations that occurred in Greek literature and art in the late archaic–early classical period and expanded immensely the Barbarian repertoire of archaic literature and art. The first was the textualisation of the oral world of the encounters and interactions in the four parallel worlds, which led to the emergence of new genres such as anthropology, geography and historiography; the second was the attempt in both literature and art to make the representation of the Barbarian one of their major pursuits. The legacy of archaic Greek literature and art, alongside the crucial transformations in textualisation and representation, created during the classical period an extensive Barbarian repertoire in which non-Greeks played a crucial role in Greek discourses on identities and moralities (section 5.4), models and utopias (section 5.5) and alien wisdom (section 5.6). Finally, section 5.7 examines some exceptions to the self-referential character of Greek culture and explores how they relate to the canonical forms of Greek literature and art.

5.1 The peculiar nature of Greek culture

While there is hardly any culture that is not affected by the exchange of practices, ideas and techniques, how do different cultures reflect on this process? Do adopted and adapted objects, techniques, ideas and practices become a means of relating and referring to other cultures, or do cultures eschew such a process? We could start by drawing a distinction between two extremes in the history of intercultural relationships. At the one extreme we can place cultures which construct and develop their literature, art and other cultural practices in explicit reference to other cultures. This reference can take a variety of forms. It can take the form of 'bilingualism', in which authors, artists, intellectuals and even a significant proportion of the population learn to operate in more than one written, spoken, visual or expressive language.[10] Educated Babylonians learned to read and write in both Babylonian and Sumerian;[11] during the Late Bronze Age scribes and intellectuals were conversant with a variety of local scripts and literatures as well as the Babylonian cuneiform script and its literature;[12] during the first millennium the Assyrians added Aramaic to the existing repertory;[13] and there is hardly a need to stress the bilingualism of Romans in both Latin

---

[10] Briquel-Chatonnet 1996.   [11] Hallo 1996: 154–68.
[12] Carr 2005: 17–61; van de Mieroop 2007: 192–205; Ehrlich 2009.   [13] Millard 1983.

and Greek.[14] Phoenician artists could employ both Egyptian and Greek styles and iconographies (pp. 271–3), and the case of Roman artists is even more impressive: they could produce free-standing sculpture in Greek style, historical and religious reliefs in Roman style, and villa paintings in Egyptian style and iconography.[15]

A second means of reference was through translations. The Babylonian Gilgamesh epic is the best known example of a literary work translated and adapted in various languages and scripts in the eastern Mediterranean,[16] while Latin literature commenced with the translation of Homer into Latin by Livius Andronicus.[17] Finally, reference can be expressed in locating a culture's imaginary universe in relationship to that of another. An obvious form of this is intertextuality, in which texts from one culture presuppose and refer to texts from another; Latin texts such as those of Virgil or Statius are in a direct intertextual relationship with the Greek text of Homer. But it can also take more diverse forms; Assyrian mythology is essentially an adaptation of the Babylonian mythical universe, while Etruscan mythology is unthinkable without the Greek.[18]

At the other extreme we find cultures defined by self-reference in their literature, art and other cultural practices. It is not that these cultures are not shaped by their interactions with other cultures; it is rather that they find means of eschewing the explicit recognition of these interactions and develop a self-referential mode of expression. Perhaps the best example in the ancient Mediterranean is that of Egypt; Egyptian art and literature largely lack 'bilingualism', translations and reference to the mental universe, texts or art of other cultures.[19] Instead, they develop a complex means of self-referentiality, in which reference is almost exclusively restricted to previous periods, styles, texts and monuments of Egyptian history.[20]

At first glance, Greek culture appears close to the self-referential model of Egypt. 'Bilingualism' was largely unknown; Greek authors like Aeschylus and Euripides did not operate in any language apart from Greek, and Greek artists like Polycleitus did not operate in any style and iconography apart from the Greek ones. Translations were effectively unheard of;[21] there was no intertextuality with non-Greek texts, and one will search in vain for a Greek story putting together, for example, Heracles and Isis. A comparison with the Hittites would make very clear what the difference is. We have

---

[14] Adams 2003; Wallace-Hadrill 2008: 38–70.   [15] Hölscher 2004; Elsner 2006.

[16] Tigay 1982; George 2003.   [17] Gruen 1990: 79–123, 1992.   [18] de Grummond 2006.

[19] There are, of course, a few exceptions, like the Egyptian tale about the Phoenician goddess Astarte: translation in Simpson 2003: 108–11.

[20] Assmann 2002.   [21] Most 2003.

already referred above to the Kumarbi cycle of myths recorded in texts in the Hittite language (p. 161). But the deities in the Kumarbi cycle have Hurrian names and were Hurrian deities, while these myths also include Mesopotamian deities, like Anu and Ea. Thus, Hittite texts make direct reference to the imaginary world of the Hurrians and the Babylonians.[22] Motifs from the Kumarbi cycle were undoubtedly adopted in the Greek theogonic myths concerning Cronus. But they were adopted in such a way that there is no reference to Hittite, Hurrian or Babylonian deities; the motifs have been completely assimilated and refer only to Greek deities. This shows eloquently the self-referential nature of Greek culture.

Nevertheless, Greek culture should be situated in between the two poles we have delineated above, because it developed two peculiar cultural strategies of enormous consequences. The first is that of Greek myth.[23] What is peculiar about Greek myth is its focus on heroes, a category that straddles the division between gods and mortals. While stories about gods are effectively universal, the development of heroic mythologies is much more circumscribed in world history. In the ancient Mediterranean and the Near East, heroic narratives are either unknown or of secondary importance in the mythologies of Mesopotamia, Egypt and the Levant, of which sufficient evidence survives to allow us to draw any conclusions.[24] It is three particular features of Greek heroic mythology which are important for our topic: its location in time; its location in space; and its dominance over Greek culture.

Greek myths were situated in time: they described the life, wars and adventures of a race of heroes who lived in a bygone age. This situation in time opened two alternative opportunities to Greek authors and artists working with the resources of Greek myth. On the one hand, the mythical world was an heroic world of the past which differed substantially from the present. Already Homer uses all his poetic skill in order to create historical distance between the heroic world and the present, by giving his heroes weapons of bronze, or by commenting on their superhuman qualities which no longer existed in the present.[25] Therefore, from the very beginning of Greek literature it was possible to depict the heroic world as an age separate and distinct from the contemporary world. On the other hand, the heroes were not simply a bygone race; they were connected through genealogical and cultic links with individuals, families and communities which existed in

---

[22] Hoffner 1998: 40–77.   [23] Cf. Konstan 1991.

[24] For a comparison, see Kirk 1970, 1974. For an anthology of translated Mesopotamian texts, see Foster 2005. For Egyptian texts, see Simpson 2003.

[25] Morris 1986: 89–91.

the present.[26] It was equally possible, therefore, to explore the ways in which the age of the heroes was related to the present.

Greek myth was also situated in space in a very different way from the myths of Mesopotamia or Egypt, where imaginary space was either unimportant or restricted to the area occupied by that culture. This meant an unparalleled potential expansion of Greek imaginary space; the events of Greek myth could be situated pretty much anywhere in either real or imaginary geography. Greek myths could be located with the Achaeans in Troy, with Bellerophon in Lycia, with the Argonauts in Colchis, or in the imaginary lands of the Phaeacians and the Ethiopians. Equally important, Greek myths included as an organic element foreign heroes: Trojans like Hector and Aeneas, Lycians like Glaucus and Sarpedon, Thracians like Rhesus, Ethiopians like Memnon, as well as peoples like the Hyperboreans and the Amazons. It is important to stress that these foreign heroes existed only in Greek myth and not in the native mythic traditions of Lycia or Thrace.[27] Greek myth was a closed system: it rarely incorporated foreign deities and myths in the way that the Etruscans depicted Greek deities alongside Etruscan ones (see Figure 31), or the Romans adapted the heroes of a Greek myth in their own myth of origins (p. 280). Nevertheless, the fact that Greek myth reserved an important role for foreign heroes, even if these heroes existed only in the Greek mythic tradition, is a factor of crucial importance that created a wide range of opportunities (pp. 267–8).

On the one hand, foreigners like Lycians and Thracians existed in the present as well as in myth. This made it possible to link the foreign heroes of myth with the foreign peoples of the present in a variety of ways that we shall have the opportunity to examine. One could use the genealogical mode in order to connect Greeks and non-Greeks in the present through the links created by the heroes of the past (p. 154);[28] or one could resort to modernising myth by using elements from the ethnographic present in order to portray and conceptualise the foreign heroes of the past (pp. 186–90). On the other hand, not all places and not all foreign heroes of myth had their counterparts in present reality; Trojans and Amazons could not readily be encountered in the present, and where exactly Ethiopia was supposed to be could be a matter of considerable debate. As with the dimension of time, this opened a wide vista of possibilities. It was possible to link these places and heroes to the present through genealogy, or through modernising the myths on the basis of the ethnographic present.

[26] See, e.g., Thomas 1989: 155–95.   [27] Erskine 2005.   [28] Gehrke 2005.

But it was also possible to maintain heroic space as a separate and distant imaginary space that was not reducible to the present, as we shall see (pp. 194–5).[29]

The third aspect concerns the dominance of myth in Greek cultural life;[30] Greek myth played a dominant role in Greek literature and art. Epic, lyric and tragedy were largely dominated by plots and themes derived from Greek myth; from the seventh century onwards Greek art was to a very large extent geared towards the depiction of myth, whether in vase painting or in sculpture.[31] What in other cultures existed as distinct and separate literary genres, in Greek culture was appropriated and incorporated within mythical narratives. I need only mention three genres: folktales, novellas and wisdom literature. By folktales I mean stories like that of Cinderella, which are normally not located in space and time, and where supernatural forces play an important role;[32] by novellas I mean stories portraying real-life people in a real-life setting;[33] and by wisdom literature I mean the collection of sayings and aphorisms which aim to teach about virtue and morality. All three genres were important in the cultures of the Ancient Near East; and all three genres are effectively absent from the Greek literature of the archaic and classical periods, with the partial exception of Hesiod's *Works and Days*.[34]

The reason these genres are effectively absent from Greek literature is that they have been incorporated within Greek mythical narratives, as is already evident in the *Iliad* and the *Odyssey*. The encounter between Odysseus and the Cyclops is a universal folktale that has been incorporated into a mythical narrative about a named hero, taking place at a specific time and a specific place. Odysseus' lying tales about his exploits in Egypt are novellas comparable to that of the Egyptian *Sinuhe*;[35] but while *Sinuhe* is an independent novella, the tales of Odysseus have been incorporated into a mythic narrative.[36] This dominant role of myth in Greek literature is one of the major reasons for the lack of Greek translations and intertextual relations to non-Greek literary texts. Translating texts would have been more likely if there had existed equivalent literary genres in Greek literature; but the incorporation of the equivalent genres within Greek genres based on mythical narrative made it less desirable and less feasible.

The second peculiar aspect of Greek culture is the way it relates to the interactions and encounters in the four parallel worlds. We have examined

---

[29] Mattison 2009.   [30] Buxton 1994.   [31] Giuliani 2003.   [32] Aly 1921; Hansen 2002.
[33] Trenkner 1958; Müller 2006.   [34] On which see López-Ruiz 2010: 48–129.
[35] Translated in Simpson 2003: 54–66.   [36] Hölscher 1988.

in Chapter 4 the patterns and processes of intercultural communication that were the results of these four parallel worlds. There should be no doubt that Persians, Thracians, Egyptians, Carians or Babylonians participated in intercultural communication and reflected on it as much as the Greeks.[37] This was a primarily oral universe in which countless stories, customs, information and ideas endlessly circulated. The Greek peculiarity was the textualisation of this oral universe through the development of literary genres which were based on the encounters and interactions of the four parallel worlds and the processes of intercultural communication.[38] Sailors from all societies developed stories and a stock of information which was crucial for navigating in foreign lands and waters; what was peculiar about the Greeks was the textualisation of this information and stories into a literary genre, the *Periploi*, descriptions of foreign lands from a coastal perspective, which further developed into the literary genre we would describe as anthropology.[39] Stories about mercenary soldiers abroad must have been common among Carians and Jews, whom we have encountered as mercenaries in Egypt (pp. 43–4). Greek authors textualised such stories in a variety of literary genres. We find such stories in the historical works of Herodotus and Ctesias; Xenophon used his own experience as a mercenary for a Persian pretender in order to compose the large-scale narrative of the *Anabasis* (pp. 221–2). Stories and discussions about the great kings and their acts circulated among all Mediterranean societies; the Greeks used such stories to create new literary genres, such as political theory, moral philosophy, or manuals for political and economic administration (pp. 200–6).

The textualisation of this oral universe of interactions and encounters had a momentous effect. Xenophon wrote the *Cyropaedia*, a work on the relationships between politics, morality and education, which took the form of a biography of Cyrus the Great, the creator of the Persian Empire (p. 222). There is hardly any example in Mesopotamian or Egyptian literature in which a foreign king is presented as the model of an ideal ruler. When Ctesias composed his *Persica*, he effectively presented to his Greek audience a history of the successive empires of the east, from the Assyrians to the Medes and the Persians (pp. 219–21). Works narrating the history of one's own community or its rulers had a long pedigree in Mesopotamia, and

---

[37] Skinner 2012.

[38] For the relationship between encounters in the middle ground and ethnographic writing in the Roman Empire, see Woolf 2011: 8–31.

[39] For the relative independence of the genre of anthropology within Greek and Roman literature, see Woolf 2011.

some kind of equivalent works could also be found in the Levant and Egypt.[40] But in none of these cultures is it possible to find a work which is devoted to the history of foreign peoples or states.

Greek culture was, therefore, self-referential in that it lacked 'bilingualism', translations or intertextuality; but the peculiar nature of Greek myth and the textualisation of intercultural encounters, interactions and communication provided two potent means through which foreign cultures fundamentally shaped Greek culture. These two phenomena were by no means unrelated. The location of Greek myth in space and time often shaped the way in which textualisation made use of the encounters and interactions in the four parallel worlds (p. 268). On the other hand, Greek myth was adapted and deployed in the most diverse ways as a result of these encounters and interactions and their textualisation (pp. 181–3). In combination, these two phenomena had a powerful effect: they created an extremely diverse and complex Barbarian repertoire. Non-Greeks and their cultures were not just strangers, enemies or Others, even though these images accounted for a significant part of the Barbarian repertoire. Non-Greeks and their cultures could also be depicted as utopian societies, whether because of their primitive simplicity (Scythia), archaic stability (Egypt) or sophisticated administration (Persia); they could provide models through which the Greeks could debate what an ideal society should be like (pp. 00–00), with a view to making practical reforms in politics, law, economics, education or warfare (pp. 200–6), as well as serve as means of debating morality and religion (pp. 196–200). Foreign cultures could be depicted as possessors of alien wisdom, the original source of Greek philosophical, religious and scientific ideas and discoveries (pp. 206–14). This Barbarian repertoire had a very important role in Greek culture, as this chapter will demonstrate. But it was also important for the role of Greek culture in the processes of globalisation and glocalisation in the ancient Mediterranean that we shall examine in Chapter 6.[41]

5.2 Ethnographies, mythologies, genealogies

At the beginning of Greek literature stand the *Iliad* and the *Odyssey*. The *Iliad* encapsulates in the narrative of Achilles' wrath the ten-year war between the Achaeans and the Trojans and their allies. Book II of the *Iliad* provides extensive catalogues of the contingents of warriors: on the

[40] van Seters 1983.   [41] For the Hellenistic and Roman periods, see Richter 2011.

Achaean side the *Catalogue of Ships* enumerates countless communities
from all over the heroic Greek world which sent contingents to Troy under
the leadership of Agamemnon,[42] while the catalogue of Trojan allies enumerates various people speaking other languages (*allothrooi*), who sent their
troops to help the Trojans, including Lycians, Carians, Thracians,
Paphlagonians, Phrygians, Mysians and Paeonians.[43] All Greek communities have sent their troops to the Achaean expedition; all non-Greek peoples
of Asia Minor and the north, whom the Greeks encountered during the
eighth century and later, were Trojan allies.[44] It is not unreasonable to
expect that the narrative will focus on a titanic struggle between the
Greeks and their national enemies, and this is one of the ways in which
the *Iliad* could be interpreted, as evidence from the classical period onwards
suggests. And yet the epic largely ignores the issue of cultural and ethnic
difference: Achaeans and Trojans are depicted as worshipping the same
gods, speaking the same language, accepting the same moral and social
values.[45]

Modern scholars have often interpreted this phenomenon by arguing
that in Homer's time (the eighth century) Greek identity was still inchoate
and the juxtaposition of all non-Greek people as Barbarians had not yet
taken place.[46] This is a misleading historical interpretation, as we have seen
in Chapter 2 (pp. 34–41); but it is also a misleading literary interpretation of
Homeric epic. We should not underestimate the poetic sophistication of
these epics. The themes and motifs that will later become the stock-in-trade
of the Greek depictions of the Other were clearly already present in Homer's
time and are also present in the poem. Homer mentions the Pygmies and
their battles with the cranes,[47] the Amazons[48] and the Ethiopians who live at
the edge of the world.[49] When he describes how the leader of *barbarophonoi*
Carians 'came to the war all decked with gold, like a girl, fool that he was',[50]
the theme of Barbarian effeminate luxury and Greek disapproval of it is
clearly present. When Homer describes how Zeus averted his gaze from the
battle of Troy in order to scan

> the land of the horse-breeding Thracians,
> the Mysians who fight in close formation, and the brilliant Hippemolgi
> who feed on milk, and the Abii, most righteous of men[51]

---

[42] 2.494–759; Anderson 1995.   [43] 2.816–77.   [44] Sourvinou-Inwood 2005: 24–63.
[45] But there might be some sense of linguistic distinction in the *Iliad*: Dickie 1996.
[46] Hall 1989: 13–47.   [47] 3.3–7.   [48] 3.182, 6.186.   [49] 1.423–4; 23.202–7.   [50] 2.872–3.
[51] 13.4–6.

the ethnographic description of foreign people is clearly something that was within his poetic grasp. Homer presupposes the existence of tales where ethnography played a crucial role; the proem of the *Odyssey*, where it is said of Odysseus that 'many were the men whose cities he saw and whose mind he learned',[52] is sufficient testimony to this. Homeric epic was not ignorant of cultural and ethnic difference in a world of unstable identities; it is instead the result of a poetic choice not to focus on cultural and ethnic difference, but on the kind of universal concerns which are common to all humanity or, to be more precise, to the mortal heroes of divine origin who are the subject of epic; the ending of the *Iliad*, with the reconciliation between Achilles and Priam, chooses clearly to focus on mortality as the common fate of all human beings.[53] Perhaps the best example of the poem's decision to focus on universal human concerns is its depiction of the Lycian allies of Troy. Instead of focusing on cultural difference, Homer opts to portray the Lycians pondering the same kind of questions that perplex the Achaeans: why should they go on fighting for Helen instead of going back home? What is a cause worth dying for and what sort of life makes it worth living? These are the sort of issues that Lycian Sarpedon's famous speech opts to address.[54]

If the Iliadic model chooses to focus on what is universal in human affairs, other works and traditions of archaic epic poetry process the Greek relationship to foreign people in different, but equally significant, ways. In contrast to the *Iliad*, the *Odyssey* has extensive references to the foreign peoples encountered by the Greeks during the Geometric and archaic periods. Various stories involve the Phoenician merchants who manufacture precious and elaborate objects,[55] sail the seas, exchange goods, and kidnap and sell slaves.[56] Equally interesting are the stories about Egypt:[57] Odysseus' lying tales about raids, piracy and life in Egypt[58] or Menelaus' tale of his visit and encounters in Egypt.[59] But like the *Iliad*, the poet of the *Odyssey* is not generally interested in exploring cultural and ethnic difference; instead, the poem opts to stress institutions like gift-exchange and guest-friendship that bring people from different cultures together.[60] But this is not to say that questions of alterity are not an important topic for the *Odyssey*. Interestingly, though, they are not explored in the 'realistic' encounters with Phoenicians or Egyptians, but in Odysseus' tales about the Cyclopes and the Phaeacians: the *Odyssey* explores alterity with regard to beings

---

[52] 1.3.   [53] Haubold forthcoming a.   [54] 12.310–28.   [55] 4.611–19.
[56] 14.285–300; cf. Winter 1995; Dougherty 2001: 102–21.   [57] Froidefond 1971: 15–68.
[58] Haft 1984.   [59] 4.120–32.   [60] For example, 4.611–19.

encountered only in myth. Odysseus' description of the Cyclopes is a master-piece of ethnographic description:

Thence we sailed on, grieved at heart, and we came to the land of the Cyclopes, an overweening and lawless folk, who, trusting in the immortal gods, plant nothing with their hands nor plough; but all these things spring up for them without sowing or ploughing, wheat, and barley, and vines, which bear the rich clusters of wine, and the rain of Zeus gives them increase. Neither assemblies for council have they, nor appointed laws, but they dwell on the peaks of lofty mountains in hollow caves, and each one is lawgiver to his children and his wives, and they reckon nothing one of another.[61]

All the standard elements of scientific Greek ethnography are already here: way of life, religion, political institutions. Clothing and diet are not present in this passage, but they are amply described when Odysseus and his comrades actually encounter a Cyclops: he wears animal skins; he drinks milk and is unfamiliar with wine; he is a cannibal.[62] This ethnographic description is the quintessence of alterity: the Cyclopes are presented as a polar opposite of everything which is considered normal in Greek society.

Equally interesting is the presentation of the society of the Phaeacians. On the one hand, Odysseus describes the orchard of King Alcinous, where trees grow fruit all year round and fruit never rots,[63] clearly building on the image of a Golden Age of plenty without the need for labour; equally miraculous are the famous ships of the Phaeacians, who can know the minds of men and move on their own without steersmen and rudders.[64] Alcinous' palace, covered in gold, silver and bronze, with golden and silver guardian dogs made by Hephaestus and golden statues of boys carrying torches, is another memorable marvel.[65]

A link between the Homeric heroic narrative and the Hesiodic poetic tradition that we will shortly examine is provided by the *Homeric Hymns*, a series of hymns to the major Greek deities composed in a Homeric idiom and metre during the archaic period. What is interesting from our point of view is their location of Greek deities within the geography of the Greek world and at the same time within a wider geographical framework. The *Homeric Hymn to Apollo* clearly aims to glorify Delos and Delphi, the major cult sites of the deity, and to link them with various other Greek communities; but at the same time the poet mentions how Apollo rules over Lycia and Lydia,[66] and Lycian Apollo would be of particular importance in Greek

---

[61] 9.105–16.   [62] 9.193–298.   [63] 7.112–21.   [64] 8.557–62.
[65] 7.86–102; for the Near Eastern sources behind the imagery of the palace, see Cook 2004.
[66] 179–80.

literature and religion.[67] Even more emphatic is the *Hymn to Dionysus*, where the poet mentions various Greek places as candidates for the place of his divine birth, only to put them aside and claim that his birth had taken place on the mountain of Nysa, a place 'far from Phoenicia, near the streams of Egypt'.[68] Equally important is the depiction of the exotic cult of the Mother of the Gods, which includes castanets, kettledrums and pipes;[69] although the poet does not actually mention the foreign origin of the deity, as will be the case with later literary works, the exotic character of the cult is a factor whose importance we shall examine below.

We have already examined in Chapter 4 how Homer presents stories which link together Greeks and non-Greeks: the encounter between Glaucus and Diomedes provides the setting for the narrative of how Bellerophon came from Corinth to Lycia, where he ended up marrying the daughter of the Lycian king and fathering the current generation of Lycian heroes including Glaucus and Sarpedon (pp. 131–2). But it is with the florescence of genealogical poetry during the archaic period that we meet a breathtaking effort to catalogue and order the mythical links of the world of heroes and through them of the whole Mediterranean and Near Eastern world.[70] This effort is already present in what was probably a later addition to Hesiod's *Theogony*, which narrates how Odysseus fathered through Circe Agrius, Latinus and Telegonus, who became the rulers among the Tyrrhenians (Etruscans);[71] this is a clear attempt to bring the world of the western Mediterranean within the imaginary Greek geography through heroic genealogy.[72]

This effort receives a monumental form in the text known as the *Catalogue of Women*, which was attributed in antiquity to Hesiod, but probably dates from the sixth century.[73] Within the genealogy of those descended from Inachus, the author narrates Io's sojourn in Egypt, where she gave birth to Epaphus and through him to Libye, Aegyptus and Arabus, who clearly stand as the mythical ancestors of the Libyans, Egyptians and Arabs. The list of Io's descendants also includes two rare examples of foreign deities who are incorporated into Greek mythic genealogy: Belus clearly stands for Baal, a generic name for many deities of the Levant; and Adonis is another generic name of Levantine deities. But far more important mythical figures are heroes such as Danaus, Perseus, Andromeda and Cadmus. These heroes are not explicitly described in the *Catalogue* as Egyptian (Danaus), Phoenician (Cadmus), Ethiopian (Andromeda) or as the ancestor of the

---

[67] Bryce 1990/1.   [68] 8–9.   [69] *Hymn to the Mother of the Gods*, 1–3.   [70] Bickerman 1952.
[71] *Theogony*, 1011–16.   [72] West 1966: 433–7.   [73] West 1985; Hunter 2005.

Persians (Perseus), as will be the case in later Greek literature and art. But given their position within Io's genealogy, this was hardly a radical step; in fact, this process can already be observed in the *Catalogue* in the case of Telephus, son of Arcadian Auge and Heracles, who is explicitly described as king of the non-Greek Mysians.[74] What is important is that these were heroes who bridged the worlds of the Greeks and the non-Greeks: Phoenician Cadmus was the founder of Thebes, and Egyptian Danaus was the ancestor of the kings of Argos, while the Argive Perseus would become the mythical ancestor of the Persians. Finally, it is particularly noteworthy how mythological genealogy could be linked with ethnography; the pursuit of the Harpies gives the author the opportunity to present a journey around the world which includes mythical people like the Hyperboreans and the Laestrygonians alongside the Scythians, who are ethnographically described as 'mare-milking'.[75]

A final epic text is worth mentioning. Aristeas of Proconnesus wrote a long epic narrating how his soul left his body and travelled in the far north and the steppes of Asia, providing an ethnographic description of the various peoples encountered there, and relating stories about other fabulous peoples that circulated in the area. The text, which probably dates to the early sixth century, became known as the *Arimaspea* due to its description of the fight between the one-eyed Arimaspians and the gold-guarding griffins.[76] It seems to have mixed descriptions of *mirabilia* and fabulous people with ethnographic accounts; the story of how the Arimaspians pushed out the Issedones, who pushed out the Scythians, who forced the Cimmerians to leave the Black Sea and invade Asia Minor, combines the mythical Arimaspians with an explanation of population movements in the archaic Black Sea region.[77] Although it is difficult to understand this text due to the nature of the surviving evidence, one passage is particularly striking. Here Aristeas describes what the life of sailors and mariners must have looked like in the eyes of steppe people who have never encountered the sea:[78]

> This too is a great wonder to us in our minds:
> men live on water, away from the land on oceans.
> They are miserable people, as they have a grievous lot:
> they have their eyes on the stars, but their life in the sea,
> ah yes, much raising their very hands to the gods,
> they pray, with their guts evilly thrown up.[79]

---

[74] *M-W*, F165.   [75] *M-W*, F150–7.   [76] *BNJ*, 35.   [77] *BNJ*, 35 F2.   [78] Bowra 1956.
[79] Translation from *BNJ*, 35 F7.

This ability and willingness to portray what the world would look like from the point of view of a different culture is one of the most important manifestations of the influence of the practice of ethnography in Greek literature and art; a text like Aeschylus' *Persians* (pp. 188–9), or the vase images of Persian domestic scenes we shall examine below (pp. 197–9), would have been impossible without the perspective explored in the *Arimaspea*. Equally important, though, is the willingness to use this outsider perspective in order to scrutinise, criticise and reform essential aspects of Greek culture. The image of steppe-dwellers ignorant of sea-life and its problems drawn here by Aristeas is at the origins of the Greek use of foreign iconic figures in order to criticise the 'corrupting sea'; Scythian Anacharsis, the noble primitive used to criticise the Greek corruption of trade and money, is one of the developments of this perspective, as we shall see (pp. 206–8).[80]

If we move beyond the heroic world of the epic, it is truly impressive to observe the vitality with which Greek poetry of the archaic and early classical periods engages with the interactions and encounters between Greeks and non-Greeks in the four parallel worlds; this becomes even more impressive given the deeply fragmentary preservation of archaic poetry.[81] Noteworthy is the variety of ways in which archaic Greek poetry builds on and reflects these experiences. These can range from a brief allusion to becoming the focus of a long narrative poem, and from expressing hostility and rejection all the way to admiration and respect.[82] Sappho makes a brief allusion when she states that she considers seeing Anactoria to be a finer sight than the powerful Lydian cavalry;[83] but Bacchylides devotes a substantial part of an ode to narrating how Apollo saved Croesus from the pyre after the Persian conquest of Sardis.[84] If Archilochus' fictional speaker dismisses the wealth of Lydian Gyges and his *tyrannis*,[85] Pindar presents Lydian Croesus as a benevolent king rewarded by Apollo for his piety.[86]

The struggles of the Greek communities of Asia Minor against the Lydians and Cimmerians are made the subject of poems by Mimnermus of Smyrna[87] and Callinus of Ephesus;[88] while the momentous effect of the Persian conquest of the Ionian cities is vividly expressed by Xenophanes:

> You should say something like this in the winter season,
>   when you are lying by the fireside on a soft couch
>   with your belly full of food,

---

[80] Skinner 2012: 64–8.   [81] Campbell 1983.   [82] Skinner 2012: 59–109.   [83] *L-P*, F16.
[84] *Odes*, 3.23–62.   [85] F19, *West*.   [86] *Pythian*, 1.94.   [87] *BNJ*, 578.   [88] Bowie 2001.

drinking sweet wine and nibbling on chickpeas;
'Who are you and where are you from? How old are you?
What age were you when the Mede came?'[89]

But equally interesting are references to political collaboration, as when Alcaeus mentions how he and his fellow exiles received financial support from the Lydians,[90] as well as to the life of mercenaries working for the empires of the East, when, for example, Archilochus mentions the proverbial Carian mercenaries[91] or Alcaeus talks of the majestic feats of his brother Antimenidas, who killed a giant enemy while serving in the Babylonian army.[92] The poets also reflect on the Greek presence in imperial centres: Sappho mentions a Greek girl who now 'shines among Lydian women',[93] Hipponax describes various Lydian monuments on the road from Lydia to Smyrna,[94] while Alcman stresses the prestige of the Lydian capital of Sardis:

He was no yokel,
no fool even among experts;
not of Thessalian stock,
no shepherd from Nether Wallop,
but from the centre of Sardis.[95]

Poets also reflect the interaction between Greeks and non-Greeks in the world of *apoikiai*: Alcaeus composed a hymn to the River Hebrus in Thrace,[96] while Archilochus mentions battles with Thracians[97] as well as diplomatic relations.[98] Hipponax wishes for his enemy to be captured and live as a slave at Salmydessus on the Black Sea, describing the local Thracians as 'top-knotted',[99] while also mentioning the sale of Phrygian slaves at Miletus;[100] Anacreon refers in many fragments to Smerdies, his Thracian love-boy.[101] Poets refer to travel to far-away lands, such as Solon at the Nile's mouth,[102] and mention the wide range of goods circulated by the networks we examined in Chapter 3: Anacreon refers to Thracian horses,[103] Archilochus to wine from Thracian Ismarus,[104] Hipponax to bread from Cypriote Amathous,[105] Xenophanes to the Lydian invention of coinage,[106] while Sappho mentions Lydian slippers[107] and comments on the recent importation of embroidered headbands from Sardis to the Greek cities of

---

[89] *D-K*, 11 B22; translation from the Loeb edition of Athenaeus, *Deipnosophists*, 54e.
[90] *L-P*, F69.   [91] F216, *West*.   [92] *L-P*, F350.   [93] *L-P*, F96.   [94] F42, *West*.
[95] F16, *Page*; translation from West 1993: 34.   [96] *L-P*, F45.   [97] F5, *West*.
[98] F93, *West*.   [99] F115, *West*.   [100] F27, *West*.   [101] F347, *Page*.   [102] F28, *West*.
[103] F417, *Page*.   [104] F2, *West*.   [105] F125, *West*.   [106] *D-K*, 11 B4.   [107] *L-P*, F39.

Ionia.[108] We can also see how issues related to Panhellenism are brought in by the poets: Xenophanes mentions how singers can spread the fame of an individual all over Greece,[109] and also castigates his Colophonian compatriots for learning useless luxury from Lydia;[110] Anacreon condemns drinking in Scythian style with din and uproar;[111] while Archilochus compares fellatio to the Thracian custom of drinking beer with straws.[112]

This constant reference in archaic Greek poetry to encounters and interactions with foreigners and their cultures is largely unparalleled in the literatures of Mesopotamia and Egypt; but it finds fascinating counterparts in the Jewish literature that has survived through its inclusion in the Bible. From the genealogies of peoples in *Genesis*[113] to the brilliant portrayal of the world of networks of goods and people in Ezekiel's *Lamentation over Tyre*,[114] there are impressive parallels to the way Greek archaic poetry refers to the four parallel worlds. The reason is not difficult to grasp: while Egypt and Mesopotamia were imperial cultures, the Greeks and the Jews were in their different ways both peripheral societies that were fundamentally shaped by their interactions with the wider imperial worlds.[115]

Let us finally consider the use of ethnography in Greek art and in particular in vase painting, which exhibited the greatest range of depicted topics. As in Homer, alterity is present in archaic artistic depictions, but is little connected with ethnography. The Other in archaic art is explored through depictions of mythical creatures which subvert established customs and rules in a variety of ways. These include depictions of Centaurs, half-human, half-animal creatures, fighting in a bestial way using trees and rocks against heroes fighting with civilised weapons; satyrs, again half-animal and half-human, engaging in bestiality and revelry and subverting civilised customs; and Amazons, female warriors who have usurped male prerogatives, fighting against male heroes like Heracles and Theseus.[116] But it is important to stress the limits of alterity in these depictions. There also exist good and civilised Centaurs, like Cheiron and Pholus, while Amazons are depicted with exactly the same weapons as the Greek heroes fighting against them. Nevertheless, by the sixth century ethnography enters the repertory of the Greek vase painters. Elements of foreign clothing and weaponry, such as the Scythian pointed cap and the Thracian fox hat, the Thracian cloak and the Scythian trousers, and the Thracian moon-shaped light shield (*pelta*), increasingly appear in vase depictions.[117] But by and large these

---

[108] *L-P*, F44.   [109] *D-K*, 11 B6.   [110] *D-K*, 11 B3.   [111] F356b, *Page*.   [112] F42, *West*.
[113] *Genesis* 10.   [114] *Ezekiel* 27.   [115] Carr and Conway 2010.   [116] Hölscher 2000.
[117] Raeck 1981.

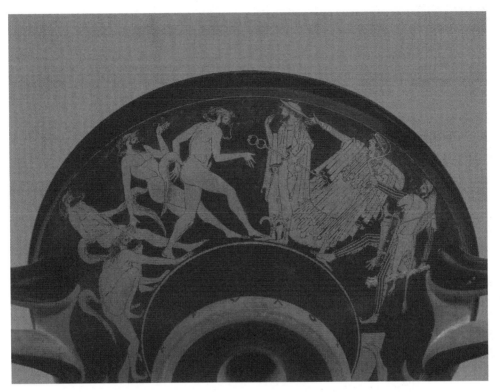

Figure 18 Athenian red-figure cylix by the Brygos Painter, *c.* 480 BCE.

ethnographic elements are not used to depict Scythians and Thracians as such, but in order to characterise or add detail to the depiction of particular groups, such as archers, riders or young warriors: Scythian costume is used, for example, to depict archers, even when these archers are Greek heroes like Heracles (see Figure 18).[118]

5.3 Transformations: textualisation and representation

Beginning in the last few decades of the sixth century two fundamental developments transformed the ways in which Greek literature and art utilised the encounters and interactions with non-Greeks and reflected on them. Until then some archaic poets had narrated the genealogies of heroes, while other poets had alluded to or mentioned interactions and encounters with non-Greeks. The first transformation was textualisation: the development of prose genres that made the world of interactions and encounters

[118] Lissarrague 1990; Ivantchik 2006; Osborne 2011: 141–5.

not a matter of passing reference or allusion, but one of their central concerns. The second transformation concerned the representation of the foreigner in Greek literature and art: the presence of Barbarian characters in Greek literature and the depiction of Barbarians in Greek art.

5.3.1 Textualisations

The people who created and developed the new prose genres originated primarily from the Greek communities on the coast of Asia Minor and the offshore islands (Hecataeus of Miletus,[119] Dionysius of Miletus,[120] Charon of Lampsacus,[121] Hellanicus of Lesbos,[122] Damastes of Sigeion[123]), although they also included a few intellectuals from mainland Greece, such as Acusilaus of Argos[124] and Pherecydes of Athens.[125] It is, of course, no coincidence that the development of new prose genres took place in Ionia. We have already seen the ways in which Ionian communities found themselves at the centre of developments in three parallel worlds: the world of *apoikiai*; the world of networks; and the world of empires.[126] A city like Miletus had created numerous *apoikiai* in the Black Sea and was one of the major participants in the *emporion* of Naucratis in Egypt. Her participation in the world of networks resulted in strong links with Greek *apoikiai* in the West like Sybaris; Herodotus reports how much the Milesians grieved on hearing of the destruction of Sybaris.[127] Alongside the other Greek poleis of Asia Minor, Miletus had also a long-term relationship alternating between war and alliance with the Lydian kingdom, until finally becoming a Persian subject on privileged terms. These expanded horizons meant that a city such as Miletus was a hotspot of intercultural communication: the port of Miletus must have been teeming with merchants, sailors and mercenaries full of stories about faraway places, strange natural phenomena, exotic products, foreign peoples, great kings, impressive exploits and bizarre customs.

But the crucial development was the creation of prose genres that processed these materials in novel ways. We can best understand the nature of this transformation by focusing on one of its pivotal figures: Hecataeus of Miletus. Hecataeus was the author of two revolutionary works: the *Periegesis*, or *Voyage around the Earth*, and the *Genealogies*. The sailors who were crossing the Mediterranean waters had developed a body of

---

[119] *FGrH*, 1; Fowler 2000: 110–46.   [120] *BNJ*, 15.   [121] *FGrH*, 262; Pearson 1939: 139–51.
[122] *FGrH*, 4; Pearson 1939: 152–235; Fowler 2000: 147–231.
[123] *FGrH*, 5; Fowler 2000: 67–72.   [124] *BNJ*, 2; Fowler 2000: 1–28.
[125] *BNJ*, 3; Fowler 2000: 272–364.   [126] Morris 2006: 75–8; Greaves 2010.   [127] 6.21.

knowledge that was crucial for their success: part of this process was the creation of oral and even written pilots, listing the ports and settlements that would be encountered by mariners sailing coastwise. Hecataeus transformed these pilots (*Periploi*) into a literary genre: the *Voyage around the Earth* described in clockwise fashion the whole Mediterranean world as seen from a coastal perspective. One aspect of this development was the invention of cartography.[128] It was hardly a coincidence that it was another Milesian, Anaximander, who was the first Greek to design a map of the whole world; the Milesian links to the four corners of the Mediterranean must have played a crucial role in this respect. Hecataeus revised Anaximander's map to make it accord better with empirical evidence than with abstract conceptual schemes.[129]

But the *Periegesis* was not a mere listing of settlements; it also utilised the ethnographic techniques available to Greek poets from Homer onwards in order to process and present in the literary form of an ethnographic account the information collected by Greek sailors, settlers, mercenaries and travellers on the countless foreign peoples they encountered across the Mediterranean. Hecataeus described how the Paeonians made their beer,[130] the dress of the Cissians and the Matienians[131] and the manner in which fugitive slaves who went to the Libyan city of Doulopolis managed to acquire their freedom.[132] The stories about encounters and interactions with non-Greeks were no longer restricted to oral communication or to passing allusions and references in poetry.

Hecataeus also exploited the extensive use of myth and genealogy in Greek poetry in order to trace the origins of people and the foundation of settlements and states; myth and ethnography were combined in order to create a literary universe which expanded immensely in both space and time. The name of the Phoenician city of Motya in Sicily was attributed to a woman who revealed to Heracles the people who stole the cattle of Geryon that he was bringing back to Mycenae,[133] while Canobus and Pharus in the Egyptian delta were named after Menelaus' pilot and look-out man, respectively.[134] Thus, settlements in Sicily and Egypt were located in time through Heracles' mythical travails in the western Mediterranean and Menelaus' visit to Egypt. Hecataeus also used the evidence of myth to argue that the Peloponnese was originally inhabited by Barbarians[135] or to narrate the unjust treatment of the native Pelasgians by the Athenians.[136] A work like

---

[128] Dilke 1985.   [129] *FGrH*, 1 T12.   [130] *FGrH*, 1 F154.   [131] *FGrH*, 1 F284, 287.
[132] *FGrH*, 1 F345.   [133] *FGrH*, 1 F76.   [134] *FGrH*, 1 F307–8.   [135] *FGrH*, 1 F119.
[136] *FGrH*, 1 F127.

the *Periegesis* included not only ethnographic descriptions of space, but also the temporal location of peoples and states through the medium of Greek myth. We should not underestimate the enormous significance of this achievement; thinkers like Hecataeus had created a literary and mental universe that, although it might be Hellenocentric, could incorporate every people and culture of the Mediterranean.

The *Genealogies* would have been equally inconceivable without the poetic works we have examined above. But the very opening words of the work express a fundamental intellectual shift:

Hecataeus of Miletus speaks as follows: I write down these things as they seem to me to be true, for the stories (*logoi*) of the Greeks are in my opinion many and foolish.[137]

Because of the dominant role of myth in Greek culture, the body of Greek knowledge in matters ranging from religion and politics to the understanding of the world and the past was expressed by poets through the medium of myth. From Hecataeus and his generation onwards Greek intellectuals became engaged in the project of a critical evaluation of received tradition, and developed an impressive repertoire of techniques and methodologies in order to deal with it.[138] One such technique already employed by Hecataeus was rationalisation:[139] he doubted that Aegyptus could have had fifty sons,[140] and he believed that the monster Cerberus guarding the passage to Hades was merely a snake with a deadly bite.[141] The rationalist critique of tradition could also be informed by the practice of ethnography. Another Ionian, Xenophanes of Colophon, developed a critical attitude towards the anthropomorphism of traditional Greek religion, and his argument was informed by ethnographic observation.[142] Horses, he claimed, if they could draw, would draw images of their gods in the image of horses, and cattle in that of cattle, and in the same way

> the Ethiopians say that their gods are snub-nosed and black,
> the Thracians that theirs have light blue eyes and red hair.[143]

But more important from our point of view was the realisation that one could critically scrutinise the 'many and foolish Greek tales' by means of comparison with the traditions of foreign cultures, which were older and/or had better recorded traditions. Herodotus narrates the famous story of how

---

[137] *FGrH*, 1 F1. The form of the pronouncement might owe a lot to the records of Near Eastern kings: Corcella 1996.
[138] Buxton 1999.   [139] Bertelli 2001.   [140] *FGrH*, 1 F19.   [141] *FGrH*, 1 F27.
[142] Heidel 1943.   [143] *D-K*, 11 B16; translation from Kirk *et al.* 1983: 168.

Hecataeus went to Egyptian Thebes and proudly traced his genealogy to the priests, claiming that he descended from a god in the sixteenth generation. But the Egyptian priests showed him the 345 statues of their predecessors, who had succeeded each other, father to son; they still could not trace any descent from a god even 345 generations back, thus showing that Hecataeus' claim was utterly ridiculous.[144] Hecataeus claimed on the basis of Phoenician usage that the correct spelling of Danae was Dana,[145] thus correcting Greek tradition on the basis of ethnographic information from a different culture.[146]

But it was equally possible to combine ethnographic information with Greek myth in a potent new mix. Hecataeus claimed that the Greek *apoikia* Sinope in the Black Sea was founded by a drunken Amazon; the Amazons were of Thracian origin,[147] and in Thracian the word for drunkards was 'sanapai', thus explaining the origins of Sinope's name.[148] In the same manner Hellanicus would argue that the name Italy derived from the native word 'vitulus', which meant bull; for, when Heracles was crossing Italy, he lost one of the bulls of Geryon, and the natives would answer Heracles' queries with their own word for bull![149] How later Greek authors could combine rationalisation and ethnography in order to scrutinise tradition can be seen in Herodotus' critique of the myth that the Egyptian pharaoh Bousiris sacrificed all foreigners, but was killed together with his followers when he tried to sacrifice Heracles. Herodotus wonders rationalistically how it would have been possible for a single man like Heracles to prevail over so many Egyptians; and he argues ethnographically that the nature of Egyptian sacrificial ritual would have made human sacrifice unthinkable to the Egyptians.[150]

Hecataeus' contribution to the textualisation of the encounters and interactions between Greeks and non-Greeks was twofold: he created a Mediterranean-wide literary universe, which incorporated ethnographic practice in a systematic manner and combined it with Greek mythology and genealogy; and he inaugurated the textualisation of a critical stance towards received tradition, in which foreign traditions and cultures could be used in order to scrutinise, correct or combine. The fragmentary state of our evidence makes it particularly difficult to assess the contribution of the intellectuals who stand between Hecataeus' work around 500 and Herodotus' *magnum opus* around 420. Although we know of the works of

---

[144] 2.143; cf. Heidel 1935; West 1991; Burstein 2009; Moyer 2011a: 42–83.   [145] *FGrH*, 1 F21.
[146] Nesselrath 1996.   [147] Dowden 1997: 99.   [148] *FGrH*, 1 F34.
[149] *FGrH*, 4 F111; Mele 2011.   [150] 2.45.

many intellectuals mentioned above, we cannot be certain how many of them predate Herodotus, how many were contemporaries and how many published their works only after Herodotus, or even in response to him.[151] For simplicity's sake we can follow the new developments through the works of Hellanicus of Lesbos, a contemporary of Herodotus who is likely to have published some of his works earlier than Herodotus.

Hellanicus worked within the ethnographic and mythographic genres created by Hecataeus; but alongside these we can observe two important additions to the tradition of prose textualisation. Hellanicus' *Priestesses of Hera at Argos* used the list of the successive Argive priestesses in order to create a chronological timescale within which events from universal history could be placed, starting from the deep recesses of mythical time and reaching up to the present. Within this timescale Hellanicus located the migration of the Italic peoples to Sicily,[152] the foundation of the *apoikia* of Naxos on Sicily[153] and the foundation of Rome by Aeneas.[154] Chronography, as this genre is called, allowed the synchronisation between the histories of different states and nations and laid the foundations for the emergence of universal history.[155]

Archaic poets mentioned or alluded to Eastern kings and to wars and encounters with non-Greeks; but in Hellanicus they are no longer merely mentioned in passing or alluded to, but have been brought centre stage through narrative.[156] Hellanicus told the story of how the Egyptian Amasis became the friend of the pharaoh by sending him a flower wreath, and how he ultimately became pharaoh himself;[157] and he narrated how Princess Atossa succeeded her father as king and proved to be a warlike and brave ruler who subjected many nations; in order to hide her gender, she communicated through written orders, and was the first Eastern ruler to wear a tiara and trousers and to institute the office of the eunuchs.[158] The countless stories that circulated orally through intercultural communication had now become textualised through the medium of Greek prose; we shall explore below the various ways in which Greek literature made use of these stories (pp. 200–22).

The combination of chronography and narrative that we can observe in authors such as Hellanicus led to a final development that is worth mentioning in this context. Many Greek historians concentrated on contemporary history, and they largely focused on Greek affairs, as one can observe in

---

[151] Drews 1973: 20–44; Fowler 1996, 2006; Luraghi 2001.   [152] *FGrH*, 4 F79.
[153] *FGrH*, 4 F82.   [154] *FGrH*, 4 F84.   [155] Möller 2001.   [156] Drews 1973: 20–44.
[157] *FGrH*, 4 F55.   [158] *FGrH*, 4 F178.

Thucydides or in Xenophon's *Hellenica*.[159] But when Greek historians began to write accounts that started from the distant past and reached up to the present, they created something novel. In antiquity there were works that traced the history of a nation from the distant past to the present: Livy's *History* or Josephus' *Jewish Antiquities* were precisely such narratives for Roman and Jewish history, respectively. When Greek historians wrote works of continuous narrative from the distant past to the present, they did not write Greek history; instead, they opted to write universal history, by including the history of Greek and non-Greek communities within a single account.[160] The first Greek historian to write such a work was, unsurprisingly, another Ionian: Ephorus of Cyme.[161]

We have seen how Greek intellectuals from the late archaic period onwards created a Mediterranean-wide literary universe which fused ethnography, mythology, critical scrutiny and storytelling. Although this literary universe was clearly Hellenocentric, we should also not lose sight of the appeal of its universality. This Greek literary universe was in a position to incorporate the foreign in a variety of complex ways. Let us for the time being focus on the ability of non-Greek authors to participate in this literary universe. A fascinating case is that of Xanthus, a fifth-century Lydian who wrote in Greek a work entitled *Lydiaca*, and to whom are also attributed works on the Magi and the philosopher Empedocles, the authenticity of which is, however, disputed.[162] The *Lydiaca* recorded various native stories about the history of Lydia; particularly interesting is the way in which many stories about Lydian kings and heroes were connected to places in the Levant, such as the story of how the Lydian prince Ascalus founded the Palestinian city Ascalon[163] or how Moxus the Lydian drowned Atargatis and her son Ichthys (Fish) in the lake of Ascalon,[164] a story related to aetiological tales of the fish cult of Atargatis.[165] But Xanthus also associates myths about Greek deities with features of the Lydian landscape, such as the story about how Typhon created the area known as the Catacecaumene (Burnt area) in east Lydia.[166] This is an example of the employment of Greek myth to account for non-Greek traditions and landscapes, and incorporate them within Greek imaginary geography.[167] Equally fascinating is how Xanthus employed standard methods and media of Greek prose writing and engaged in Greek intellectual debates. He used Homer to

---

[159] Tuplin 2007a.   [160] Vlassopoulos 2007: 226–9.

[161] Alonso-Nuñez 1990; Marincola 2007b.

[162] Pearson 1939: 109–38; Kingsley 1995; Schepens and Theys 1998.   [163] *FGrH*, 765 F8.

[164] *FGrH*, 765 F17.   [165] Cf. Lightfoot 2003: 65–72.   [166] *FGrH*, 765 F13.

[167] Robert 1962: 280–317.

interpret the movement of Phrygians into Asia after the Trojan War;[168] he employed Lydian etymologies to explain the origin of the names of foreign people, claiming that the Mysians' name derived from the Lydian word for the beech tree, which abounds on Mysian Olympus;[169] and he participated in the Greek debate on geology by recording his observations of fossils in Armenia and Phrygia.[170]

5.3.2 Representations

The second great transformation concerned the representation of the foreigner in Greek literature and art. We have seen how the narrative art of Homer already possessed the techniques for representing alterity in the case of the Cyclopes or the Phaeacians. Archaic poets mentioned or alluded to contemporary foreigners, but they do not seem to have moved beyond allusion and reference to actual representation; archaic artists used ethnographic elements from Thrace and Scythia to depict archers and riders, but they were largely unconcerned or unable to represent foreign people as such. But in the last few decades of the sixth century, and with much greater intensity in the course of the fifth century, artists and authors started to engage heavily in the project of representing the foreigner. Greek art now started to include images of non-Greek people depicted as such, while Greek literature included characters that were explicitly portrayed as non-Greeks. Modern scholars have argued that the Persian Wars played a fundamental role in this process: the 'invention of the Barbarian', it has been claimed, was a result of Greek victory and expressed the heightened sense of Greek identity through constructing a polar Other, which exemplified everything that was different from and inferior to Greek culture and values.[171] There is no doubt that the Persian Wars did play an important role in this process and that questions of identity were significant in the project of representing the foreigner in Greek art and literature. But the process had in fact started before the Persian Wars, and many of its aspects had little to do with bolstering a Greek sense of identity.[172] In other words, the representation of the foreigner was a complex process with multiple functions, which we shall try to explore below.

The representation of foreigners occurs in Greek visual art earlier than its appearance in literature. We have seen how archaic vase painters used ethnographic details in order to depict archers or riders in particular ways; but people wearing Scythian trousers or Thracian cloaks in these

---

[168] *FGrH*, 765 F14.   [169] *FGrH*, 765 F15.   [170] *FGrH*, 765 F12.
[171] Hall 1989; see also Hall 2006: 184–224.   [172] Osborne 2011: 124–57.

depictions were not normally meant to represent Thracians or Scythians. From the last few decades of the sixth century onwards there gradually appears an interest in representing foreign people as such. During the sixth century this largely takes place through the 'modernisation' of mythical depictions. In the depiction of a restricted range of Greek myths vase painters started to employ techniques in order to portray explicitly foreign characters. Vase painters depicted the followers of the Ethiopian hero Memnon as negroes, adjusting the depiction to accord with the ethnographic location of mythical Ethiopia to the south of Egypt;[173] to an even greater extent, vase painters illustrating the myth of Heracles and Bousiris adopted an ethnographic approach to depict Egyptians as foreigners through their distinctive clothing, shaved heads, circumcised genitals and the pharaonic uraeus on Bousiris' head (see Figure 19).[174] At the same time,

Figure 19 Athenian red-figure pelike by the Pan Painter, *c.* 470 BCE.

---

[173] Raeck 1981: 169–73; Bérard 2000: 395–402.　　[174] Miller 2000.

elements of Thracian and Scythian costume started to be attributed to the Amazons; while some Amazons could still wear Greek-style dress, in the same images artists started to use the Thracian *pelta*, the Scythian trousers or the Phrygian cap to depict other Amazons.[175] This is the beginning of the process of 'barbarisation' that ended in the depiction of some Amazons in Persian dress in the period after the Persian Wars.

It is obvious that the process of representing the foreigner started earlier than the Persian Wars; but there is little doubt that around the time of the Persian Wars we encounter an expansion of interest in representation, which cannot be coincidental. Instead of seeing the Persian Wars as the cause, we should rather see it as a catalyst that sped up an already existing process, heightened interest, and contributed new means and media for representing the foreigner in both literature and art. As we have commented above, it was rare for real historical figures and real events to play the central role in Greek literature and art; there are plenty of references to historical figures and events in literature, but they were practically never the central topic. It was rather myth or generic scenes and topics that played the central role; even epinician poetry, which celebrated historical individuals and events, focused primarily on myth as the medium for constructing its topic and expressing its message.[176]

The Persian Wars for the first time provided Greek authors and artists with the incentive to and means of representing historical figures and events in art and literature. We know that in 492 the Athenian tragedian Phrynichus presented a tragedy on *The Capture of Miletus*, concerning the failed Ionian revolt of two years earlier, for which he was fined by the Athenians for reminding them of their own misfortunes. In 476 the same poet presented *Phoenician Women*, which dealt with the Persian defeat at Salamis, and was this time victorious.[177] But we know hardly anything about these plays, and it is only with Aeschylus' *Persians* in 472 that we can observe for the first time the representation of the Barbarian in Greek literature.[178] The action takes place at Susa, where the Persian Queen-mother and a chorus of Persian elders are presented with the news of the Persian defeat at Salamis, summon the ghost of king Dareius I for advice, and finally receive Xerxes and lament with him. It is already impressive that all the characters presented are Persians, but the play also makes a concerted effort to present a convincing representation of the foreign Persians. Aeschylus uses some Persian terms and a long list of Persian names to give the impression of foreign speech, employs

[175] Shapiro 1983.   [176] Kurke 1991.   [177] Hall 1989: 62–9.   [178] Garvie 2009.

foreign clothing for the actors' costumes and explicitly refers to it, and uses ethnography to stress the cultural and political features of the Persians.[179]

Equally dramatic is the emergence in the visual arts of images depicting the Persians and the conflicts of the Persian Wars. Images of Persian warriors started to appear on vases in which artists pay meticulous attention to the depiction of their arms, clothing and footwear. There is little doubt that it was the direct observation of Persians during the wars that was responsible for this.[180] The earliest depictions of Persians are unambiguously derogatory: not only are they depicted as clearly defeated, but they are often shown in shameful flight or as being humiliated. Greek artists adopted the iconographic schemes used during the archaic period for depicting fights against monsters and evil-doers in order to depict the fights against the Persians. Interestingly, though, from the 450s onwards Greek artists abandoned these iconographic schemes and started to use the balanced-fight iconographies that were used during the archaic period to depict fights against Trojans or Amazons. It is normally evident that the Greeks will ultimately prevail, but the Persians are now depicted as worthy opponents who can stand their ground (see Figure 20).[181] There are even a few scenes in which the Persians are depicted as victorious![182]

We should turn our attention to a final aspect of the representation of the foreigner in Greek literature and art. We have already seen how during the archaic period Greek artists adjusted the depiction of a select number of myths in order to depict some mythical figures such as Bousiris, Memnon's companions or some Amazons as foreigners. In the aftermath of the Persian Wars we encounter a massive expansion of the use of myth in both literary and artistic media for the purpose of representing the foreigner. Our earliest evidence is the recently rediscovered ode of Simonides for the battle of Plataea.[183] Simonides compares the recent victory against the Persians and the valour of the Greek fighters with the Achaean conquest of Troy and the virtue of the great mythical heroes. A mythical event like the Trojan War could now be seen as a prefiguring of the recent Great Event; a further step was that of representing foreign heroes, depiction of whom in literature and art had so far eschewed issues of ethnic and cultural identity, as Barbarians. Given the dominance of myth in Greek culture, the reinterpretation of myth as a means of representing the Barbarian opened the full range of Greek literature and art to the exploration of issues related to the interaction between Greeks and non-Greeks; from tragedy to sculpture

---

[179] Hall 1989: 76–100.   [180] Bovon 1963.   [181] Muth 2008: 239–67.
[182] Raeck 1981: 124–7.   [183] Boedeker and Sider 2001.

Figure 20 Athenian red-figure hydria, fourth century BCE.

the representation of the mythical Barbarian became one of the major preoccupations of Greek authors and artists.[184]

We have so far explored the Barbarian repertoire of early Greek literature and art, and the important ways in which this repertoire was expanded and transformed by the revolutions in textualisation and representation. We shall now examine three broad areas in which this Barbarian repertoire was employed during the classical period: for exploring issues of identity and morality; for constructing models and utopias; and for utilising the inexhaustible resources of alien wisdom.

5.4 Identities and moralities

One major use of the Barbarian repertoire was the construction of polarised representations of non-Greeks as an incarnation of everything that was different and opposed to the values and customs that the Greeks held

---

[184] Hall 1989: 101–59; Castriota 1992.

dear; these representations could often reach the point of being xenophobic and jingoistic, and even similar, in some ways, to modern racism.[185] But in doing this the Greeks were merely unexceptional.[186] An examination of Egyptian and Mesopotamian literature and art reveals almost identical representations of the Other in the polarity mode.[187] What is particularly interesting about Greek culture, however, is the expansion of the Barbarian repertoire to encompass other modes beyond polarity.

One aspect of the Greek debate on identity is the definition of barbarism as a set of moral and cultural characteristics which are deemed opposite and/or inferior to Greek ones. These polarised constructions of identity and morality can be seen in the most diverse media. In art, a set of battle scenes between Order and Chaos, between Self and Other, became the stock themes for decorating public monuments and buildings like temples. To the archaic themes of the Amazonomachy, Centauromachy and Gigantomachy (Battle between the Giants and the Gods), the Persian Wars and their aftermath added depictions of battles between Achaeans and Trojans and battles between Greeks and Persians. On the Athenian Acropolis the metopes of the Parthenon present a famous example of the first four themes,[188] while the temple of Athena Nike presents a battle against Persians in triumphalist mode;[189] Panhellenic shrines like Olympia exhibited similar visual programmes; but we shall also see how these visual programmes were employed by non-Greeks (see Figure 36).[190]

It is also remarkable how many Greek literary genres engage with this debate using a variety of approaches. There is no doubt that upholding Greek moral superiority and condemning foreign barbarism is often at the forefront of the agenda of Greek authors. Perhaps the purest examples of the employment of the polarity mode can be seen in Athenian comedy.[191] Aristophanes presents various vignettes of ridiculed Barbarians, from the violent Odomantian mercenaries[192] and the sex-starved and boorish Scythian public slave[193] to the incomprehensible and uncivilised Triballian god;[194] Anaxandrides explains why an alliance between Athens and Egypt is impossible by showing that the animal gods so revered by the Egyptians were merely desirable delicacies for the Greeks,[195] while another

---

[185] Isaac 2004; cf. Tuplin 1999.   [186] Harrison 2000: 115.

[187] Müller 1972: 15–29; Fales 1982; Zaccagnini 1982; Loprieno 1988; Poo 2005; Michalowski 2010; Moers 2010.

[188] Castriota 1992: 134–75.   [189] Palagia 2005.   [190] Barringer 2008: 8–58.

[191] Long 1986; Willi 2003: 198–225.   [192] *Acharnians*, 153–72; Olson 2002: 119–25.

[193] *Thesmophoriazusae*, 1001–231; Hall 2006: 225–54.   [194] *Birds*, 1615–82.   [195] *K-A*, F40.

Aristophanic comedy presented the expulsion of corrupting foreign cults from Athens.[196] Similar examples can be found in Athenian tragedy, as we have already seen; the Phrygian slave depicted in Euripides' *Orestes* is a typical example of an effeminate, slavish Barbarian without honour or shame.[197] We can also mention examples from genres that stood between recital and drama; particularly interesting is the *Persians* of Timotheus of Miletus, a late fifth-century cithara song about the battle of Salamis, which presents a Phrygian drowning during the sea battle as begging for his life in broken Greek.[198]

Equally widespread is the presence of such themes in prose genres such as historiography. Herodotus' story of how after the battle of Plataea the Spartan king Pausanias refused to follow the example of the Persians at Thermopylae and mutilate the body of the Persian commander Mardonius is a clear example.[199] So is Thucydides' description of the massacre of the inhabitants of Boeotian Mycalessus by Thracian mercenaries, and his explicit comment about the savagery of the Barbarians.[200] The discourse of alterity even penetrated scientific genres, such as medicine. A fifth-century treatise *On Airs, Waters and Places*, traditionally attributed to Hippocrates, attempts to explain in scientific terms the purported effeminacy and lack of courage of the inhabitants of Asia: it is not only the climate, whose constancy induces indolence, but also the political and social effects of the institution of monarchy, which turn subjects into cowards.[201] Finally, it is hardly surprising that the discourse of Panhellenism is prominent in the genre of oratory. Particularly famous is the series of texts composed by the Athenian pamphleteer Isocrates, urging Greek states to put aside their differences and unite in a Panhellenic campaign against the Persian Empire, in order to avenge past wrongs and conquer land that could alleviate Greek social ills; the exalting of Greek identity and the denigration of the Barbarian enemy are a prominent feature of such works.[202] Perhaps the best summation of the polarised image of the Barbarian in Greek thought comes from Isocrates' *Panegyricus* of *c.* 380:

It is not possible for people who are reared and governed as are the Persians either to have a part in any other form of virtue, or to set up on the field of battle trophies of victory over their foes. For how could either an able general or a good soldier be produced amid such ways of life as theirs? Most of their population is a mob without discipline or experience of dangers, which has lost all stamina for war, and has been

[196] Delneri 2006: 73–124.   [197] 1370–1536; see Bacon 1961; Hall 1989: 101–59.
[198] Hordern 2002; Hall 2006: 255–87.   [199] 9.78–9.   [200] 7.27–9.
[201] 16; Thomas 2000: 86–98.   [202] Too 1995: 129–50.

trained more effectively for servitude than are the slaves in our country. Those, on the other hand, who stand highest in repute among them, have never governed their lives by dictates of equality, or of common interest, or of loyalty to the state; on the contrary, their whole existence consists of insolence towards some, and servility towards others – a manner of life than which nothing could be more demoralising to human nature. Because they are rich, they pamper their bodies; but because they are subject to one man's power, they keep their souls in a state of abject and cringing fear, parading themselves at the door of the royal palace, prostrating themselves, and in every way schooling themselves to humility of spirit, falling on their knees before a mortal man, addressing him as a divinity, and thinking more lightly of the gods than of men.[203]

Nevertheless, it is striking how Greek authors can often turn these ideas on their head in a variety of ways.[204] Some authors explore the rhetorical use of such arguments and attribute them to characters they want to discredit. In Euripides' *Andromache* Hermione introduces a whole anti-Barbarian tirade against Andromache, accusing her of lacking moral principles, and arguing that only a Barbarian woman would be willing to have children with the murderer of her husband and relatives; but the viewer can easily see how this rhetoric is self-serving and that Hermione is a disreputable character.[205] Even more challenging is Euripides' exploration of the same topic in *Iphigenia at Aulis*. He magnificently shows how the sacrifice of Iphigenia is forced onto the Achaean leaders by a series of political machinations, and how a shameless act is finally publicly justified as something necessary to defeat an imaginary Barbarian menace.[206]

Another option consisted in showing that the Greeks themselves could behave like Barbarians, or Barbarians according to Greek moral and cultural values; or to explore the extent to which barbarism and its opposite are unrelated to descent or culture, but embody a set of moral characteristics which can be exemplified by both Greeks and non-Greeks. It is particularly fascinating how again Greek myth provided Greek authors with the raw material for exploring such questions. The capture of Troy was early on represented as a bloodthirsty massacre accompanied by sacrilege and followed by the divine punishment of many Greeks for their atrocities.[207] Euripides' *Trojan Women* is the quintessential play exploring this theme: Andromache's cry 'oh Greeks, inventors of barbarian evils, why do you slay this child who never wronged anybody?' is a deeply moving depiction of the Greek ability to behave as Barbarians.[208] From the opposite side, Xenophon

---

[203] 150–1.   [204] Saïd 2002.   [205] Papadodima 2010: 16–26.
[206] L. G. Mitchell 2007: 16–19.   [207] Anderson 1997.   [208] *Trojan Women*, 764–5.

presents the Persian prince Cyrus behaving in a way congruent with Greek values and espousing such Greek ideals as freedom,[209] while Thucydides presents an Aetolian tribe as living in unwalled villages, speaking an incomprehensible language and even eating meat raw; the full range of polarised barbarism is used here against a Greek community.[210] Equally interesting is the way the discourse of polarity was used against the Spartans in order to describe them as anti-Greeks: already Herodotus stresses the similarity between Spartan and Barbarian customs, such as the elaborate royal funerals or the passing of certain professions from father to son, and the discourse would expand in later authors.[211] Even more radical are the views expressed by the sophist Antiphon, which negate the naturalness of the distinction between Greeks and Barbarians:

We understand the [laws?] of our neighbours, but not of those who dwell far off; it is in this way that we have become Barbarians to one another since by nature we are all equally equipped in all things to be either Greeks or Barbarians.[212]

We have stressed at the beginning of this chapter how Greek myth and the textualisation of the interactions between Greeks and non-Greeks constituted the two major aspects of the peculiar form in which Greek culture related to non-Greek cultures. They both provide good examples for exploring the complex ways in which Greek literature and art reflected on Greek and Barbarian identities. We have seen how Greek artists and authors started to use myth as a means of exploring the differences between Greeks and Barbarians, and how mythical heroes become barbarised in literature and art; but while the barbarisation of mythical figures in literature is related to their barbarisation in art, literature and art do not always follow the same paths, or have the same emphases; even within literary or artistic treatments, context and aim often result in very different treatments. Some mythical figures barbarise early in both literature and art: the Trojan heroes Priam and Paris are characterised as Phrygians in literature and depicted in oriental clothes in vase painting. But while Trojans in general can be described as Phrygians in literature, this is not necessarily the case in vase painting; in battle scenes between Achaeans and Trojans the Trojans continued to be depicted wearing identical clothes and carrying the same weapons as the Greeks.[213] Vase painters opted to retain an heroic model in depicting the Trojans in battle scenes, but to Orientalise Trojan figures in scenes which focus on luxury (Paris) or on the portrayal of an

---

[209] *Anabasis*, 1.7.2–4.   [210] 3.94.4–5.   [211] 6.58–60; Millender 1996.   [212] *D-K*, 87 B44.
[213] Erskine 2001: 79–83.

enthroned ruler (Priam).[214] By the middle of the fifth century, literary works had come to portray founder heroes like Cadmus, Danaus and Pelops as Barbarians: Pindar talks of Lydian Pelops,[215] Euripides presents Cadmus as Phoenician,[216] but most memorable is the depiction of Danaus as Egyptian in Aeschylus' *Suppliant Women*. But while Athenian vase painters started to depict Pelops as Barbarian during the fifth century, they were largely allusive in the case of Danaus, and consistently eschewed depicting Cadmus as a Barbarian. At the same time, it is probable that in monumental sculpture artists eschewed the depiction of Danaus, Cadmus and Pelops as Barbarians.[217]

This inconsistency reflects a wider phenomenon.[218] Myth could be used to depict alterity, as in the case of barbarised Trojans or Amazons, but it could also be used in very different ways. Even after the efflorescence of the oppositional image of the Barbarian Other in the fifth century, mythical genealogy remained a potent mode of conceptualising the relationship between Greeks and non-Greeks. We have already examined numerous cases in which Greek mythology was used in the real world to link Greeks and non-Greeks and to cement relationships (pp. 127, 130–1, 151); this was no less the case in literature. Genealogical links can often be seen as part of the background of the plot. The chorus of Euripides' *Phoenician Women* consists of women from Phoenician Tyre, who were sent as offerings to serve in Apollo's shrine at Delphi;[219] they find themselves at Thebes, and describe the impending civil war between Eteocles and Polyneices as a misfortune that Phoenicia would share, as they have common blood with the Thebans.[220] The explanation of this reference to shared descent had been provided earlier by Jocasta, who narrates how Cadmus left Phoenicia in order to found the city of Thebes.[221] In Euripides' *Helen* the Egyptian king Theoclymenus and his sister Theonoe are the descendants of the Greek deities Nereus and Proteus.[222]

Even more fascinating, though, is the way in which tragedians exploited the complexity of different modes of relating to Barbarians. In Aeschylus' *Persians*, a play which clearly emphasises the cultural and political differences between Greeks and Persians,[223] the queen reports a dream concerning two sisters subjugated by Xerxes, one symbolising Greece, the other Persia.[224] This complexity becomes central in Aeschylus' *Suppliant Women*,

---

[214] Miller 1995.   [215] *Olympian*, 1.23–4, 36–8.   [216] *Phoenician Women*, 5–6, 638–9.
[217] Miller 2005.   [218] Compare Lloyd 1966 on polarity and analogy.
[219] *Phoenician Women*, 203–25.   [220] *Phoenician Women*, 239–49.
[221] *Phoenician Women*, 1–9.   [222] *Helen*, 4–15.   [223] Harrison 2000: 51–91.
[224] *Persians*, 181–99; Gruen 2011: 19–20.

which makes a significant effort to stress the alien cultural and racial back-ground of the Egyptian Danaids.[225] When Danaus and his daughters ask the king of Argos for asylum on the basis of their descent from the Argive priestess Io, the king initially disbelieves their Greek descent given their dark skin and Barbarian culture;[226] but he is convinced by their story, and so are the citizens of Argos, who grant them asylum. Furthermore, Danaus ulti-mately becomes king of Argos and fathers the future line of Argive kings; Aeschylus presents a strong argument for the importance of shared myth-ical descent in the relationship between Greeks and Barbarians.[227] While polarity constituted a powerful mode of thinking about identity and mor-ality, shared kinship remained equally important; Greek myth could be used to explore and illustrate both modes.

We have explored above the beginnings of the textualisation of encoun-ters and interactions between Greeks and non-Greeks in literature; equally illuminating is the equivalent phenomenon in Greek art. The Persian Wars opened the floodgates for the representation of historical events and figures in Greek art. It is true that in the history of Greek art the mythical and the generic always dominated the overwhelming proportion of artistic produc-tion; but it is telling that a significant number of the few historical artistic depictions relate to the Persians and to the other empires of the East.[228] One of the earliest (*c.* 490) is the Athenian amphora depicting Croesus on the pyre after his defeat by the Persians (see Figure 21); but this was a story that was quickly viewed by the Greeks through a mythical prism, as is evident in Bacchylides' contemporary story that Croesus was transferred by Apollo to the land of the Blessed, or in other stories stressing Croesus' miraculous salvation from the pyre.[229] Closely connected to the Persian Wars is the depiction of the battle of Marathon in the Stoa Poicile,[230] as well as the famous Eurymedon vase, which alludes to the crucial Athenian victory at the river Eurymedon in the 460s (see Figure 5).[231] It depicts a nude Greek holding his penis moving towards a bending Persian: the Greek enunciates 'I am Eurymedon,' while the Persian says 'I stand bent over.' As Kenneth Dover phrased it, a summary of the image could be 'we buggered the Persians'.[232]

But as with myth, polarity is not the only mode employed; the Xenophantus lecythos, illustrating this book's cover, takes us to a very

---

[225] Vasunia 2001: 33–58.   [226] *Suppliant Women*, 277–90.   [227] Mitchell 2006.
[228] Hölscher 1973.   [229] Hölscher 1973: 30–1.   [230] Castriota 1992: 76–89.
[231] Schauenburg 1975.
[232] Dover 1978: 105; for the controversy surrounding the interpretation of this vase, see Gruen 2011: 42–4.

Figure 21 Athenian red-figure amphora by Myson, *c.* 500–490 BCE.

different world (see also Figure 22). This is a magnificent fourth-century lecythos created by the Athenian painter Xenophantus, deposited at Panticapaion in the Black Sea, and decorated in the red-figure technique along with relief appliqués, paint and gilding. It depicts a scene in which figures dressed in Persian clothes and labelled with Persian names, which include Dareius and Cyrus, hunt two boars, a deer and two griffins in a carefully drawn landscape: the realistic depiction of the hunt is thus combined with the inclusion of the mythical griffins.[233] But what is important about this vase is the depiction of an idyllic Persian hunt involving famous Persian kings, which portrays the Persians in a very different manner from that of the battle scenes or the Eurymedon vase.

The Xenophantus vase was part of a very significant expansion of the iconographic repertoire of Persian depictions. Early depictions of foreigners in Greek art are largely similar to those in the Near Eastern arts; they are primarily about fighting and defeating foreign enemies, while Near Eastern

---

[233] Miller 2003; cf. Franks 2009.

Figure 22 Red-figure lecythos by Xenophantus, Panticapaion, fourth century BCE.

Figure 23 Athenian red-figure lecythos by the Peleus Painter, *c.* 430 BCE.

arts also include depictions of foreign subjects and their exotic tribute (to which the Greeks could have little claim).[234] But in the course of the fifth century Greek artists started to expand the repertoire of scenes and situations in which foreigners, in particular Persians, could be depicted: hunting scenes, foreign symposia, Barbarian courts, musicians and dancers.[235] Notable here are the 'warrior departure' scenes. We have already seen how elements of Thracian or Scythian costume were utilised to portray secondary characters in scenes depicting the departure of the Greek warrior from his wife and family; but now it is the departing warriors themselves who are Persians (see Figure 23).[236]

These scenes raise the issue of models and utopias that we shall shortly explore; but they also explore issues of identity and morality which focus on universal or shared perspectives. Depicting a departing Persian warrior invites the viewer to ponder questions about the universality of warfare, military valour, death and family loss, and the connection between war and domestic life. The countless stories that became textualised in Greek literature explored similar concerns. What duties and obligations do human

[234] Moers 2010.   [235] Raeck 1981: 147–60; Sgouropoulou 2004.   [236] Raeck 1981: 138–47.

beings have towards each other? Which allegiance is most important? The typical Greek way of dealing with these issues is through recourse to myth. Myth is employed in order to think through these difficult moral problems; the myth of Antigone, who has to choose between obedience to the state and loyalty to her kin and to the unwritten law, is a typical example of how a Greek author like Sophocles tried to deal with the dilemma. Herodotus provides a very different way of dealing with this moral dilemma in a story drawn from the Persian imperial world. He narrates how Dareius I condemned the Persian noble Intaphernes and his male relatives to death, but gave the noble's wife the choice of saving one of the condemned; when she chose to save her brother, rather than her husband or sons, the surprised Dareius asked for an explanation; she replied that she could have another husband and other sons, but she could never have another brother, since her parents had died.[237]

The story of Psammenitus, the pharaoh deposed by Cambyses, the Persian conqueror of Egypt, is another illuminating example.[238] According to the story, when Psammenitus saw a parade in which his daughter was dressed as a slave going to fetch water and his son was being led to execution, he merely bowed to the ground; but when he saw one of his former companions begging, he broke into loud weeping. When Cambyses, who had staged the parade, enquired the reason for these strange reactions, Psammenitus answered as follows:

Son of Cyrus, my private grief was too great for weeping; but the unhappiness of my companion deserves tears – a man fallen from abundance and prosperity to beggary come to the threshold of old age.[239]

In both Herodotean passages, stories concerning non-Greeks are narrated in order to explore questions of identity and morality. But these are not stories that focus on polarity and alterity; they stress values which are presented as shared or universal. Textualisation could serve many different purposes within the repertoire of Greek culture.

5.5 Models and utopias

A second way in which the Barbarian repertoire was employed in Greek culture was in constructing models and utopias; we shall explore a range of levels at which this took place. One of the major results of the textualisation

[237] Herodotus, 3.119.   [238] Aly 1921: 81–2.   [239] Herodotus, 3.14.

of intercultural encounters and communication is the ubiquity of the casual employment of Barbarians in the most diverse genres of Greek literature. Plato refers casually to Lycurgus, Solon and Dareius as great lawgivers,[240] while Ps.-Aristotle states that wine makes even freemen insolent, and gives as an example the Carthaginian prohibition of wine-drinking during military service in order to argue that slaves should never be given wine.[241]

A second, more ambitious, stage in the employment of non-Greeks as models is the emergence of treatises and manuals which collected and classified information pertaining to a particular pursuit or field. These manuals made their first appearance in the later fifth century, but became ubiquitous in the course of the fourth; they covered a wide range of topics, from medicine and biology to military, financial and political affairs. Such manuals collected pertinent information from the whole Mediterranean world and from both Greek and non-Greek communities. The earliest extant military treatise is the fourth-century *How to Survive Under Siege* by Aeneas the Tactician.[242] It is based on an extensive collection of stories used to illustrate various military stratagems and measures. While most of them relate solely to communities in mainland Greece, some stories originate from the world of *apoikiai* and their interaction with non-Greek populations, like Abdera in Thrace and the Triballians[243] or Cyrene and Barca in Libya.[244] Other stories concern Greeks or foreigners in Persian service, like Athenodorus of Imbros,[245] Timoxenus of Scione[246] or the Egyptian admiral Glos,[247] or conflicts between Greek communities and imperial powers, like that between Barca and Amasis[248] or Sinope and the Persian satrap Datames.[249]

But the most impressive series of manuals and treatises collecting information is associated with Aristotle and his school.[250] A treatise titled *Oeconomica* was traditionally attributed to Aristotle, but seems to have been written in the last few decades of the fourth century. Its second book is a collection of fiscal stratagems for the raising of money and resources by states and rulers in times of crisis.[251] The majority of the stratagems relate to Greek communities, but, again, a substantial number relate to non-Greeks; there are stories about the Persian satraps Mausolus[252] and Datames,[253] and the Thracian king Cotys,[254] as well as Greek mercenaries in the service of foreign rulers, like Chabrias and the pharaoh Taus,[255] or Iphicrates and Cotys.[256]

---

[240] *Phaedrus*, 258c.   [241] *Oeconomica*, 1344a31–3.   [242] Whitehead 1990.   [243] 15.9–10.
[244] 16.14.   [245] 24.3–14.   [246] 31.25–7.   [247] 31.35.   [248] 37.6–7.   [249] 40.4.
[250] Ostwald and Lynch 1994: 616–31.   [251] van Groningen 1933; Zoeppfel 2006.
[252] 1348a3–34.   [253] 1350b16–33.   [254] 1351a24–31.   [255] 1350b34–1351a16.
[256] 1351a17–22.

Aristotle and his students also initiated a massive project of collecting evidence about the history, customs and constitutions of contemporary communities; ancient scholars attributed to Aristotle works on the constitutions of 158 communities, overwhelmingly Greek, but also including some non-Greek communities like the Lycians.[257] It is not clear whether accounts of other non-Greek communities, such as the Thracians and the Lucanians, were covered by separate *Constitutions* or were part of an apparently separate collection of *Barbarian Customs*, which comprised an equally impressive register concerning non-Greek communities ranging from the Carians to the Etruscans and the Romans.[258] It is on the basis of this enormous collection of evidence that Aristotle composed his monumental *Politics*. Non-Greek communities are regularly considered in its explorations. Asking the question what is the best sort of life, Aristotle examined the answer that the pursuit and maintenance of power should be the aim of a state's laws by providing an extensive ethnography of Greek and non-Greek states whose laws furthered this aim, including the Spartans, Cretans, Persians, Carthaginians, Macedonians, Scythians and Iberians.[259] Discussing the institutions necessary for an ideal community, he attributed the idea of the division of the citizens into classes to the Cretan Minos and the Egyptian Sesostris and the institution of common messes among citizens to the Oenotrians in Italy.[260]

But the Barbarian repertoire was not restricted to providing useful examples or convenient stratagems. We have already explored how foreigners provided Greek authors with the dramatic setting in which to explore questions of identity and morality (pp. 199–200), and the same applies to political questions. Herodotus provides two illuminating examples. The first is the famous Constitutional Debate: Herodotus presents a debate among the seven Persian notables who conspired to kill the usurper of the throne about the form of constitution they should adopt.[261] Otanes speaks in favour of democracy, Megabyzus praises aristocracy, while Dareius defends monarchy and carries the day, ultimately winning the competition to become king as well.[262] It is highly unlikely that Persian grandees could have been using the categories of Greek political thought or have debated democracy decades before its emergence in Athens; but it is telling that Herodotus is keen to defend the historicity of the debate by claiming that the overthrow of tyrannies and the establishment of democracies in Asia Minor by the Persian general Mardonius in 493 proves that the Persians could have

---

[257] Hose 2002: 130–5.   [258] F604–11, *Rose*; Hose 2002: 250–2, 259–61.
[259] *Politics*, 1324a5–b25.   [260] 1329b.   [261] Pelling 2002.   [262] 3.80–8.

held such a debate.[263] What is important is that Herodotus or his sources were willing to imagine how the Persians would have debated during a political crisis; the Persian crisis provided a majestic setting in which to present the claims in favour and those against the various constitutional forms. Equally telling is Herodotus' tale about the emergence of political authority in Media. He describes an anarchic society, in which the Medes decide to entrust Deioces with the judging of their disputes due to his renown for justice, and narrates how Deioces manipulated the Medes into appointing him as ruler, and used bodyguards, monumentality and a refined court protocol in order to establish his absolute power.[264] Again, non-Greeks provide Greek authors with a setting for thinking about the origins of political power and the trappings of political authority.[265]

The belief that the success of a political system depends on educating existing rulers to adopt and practise the right kind of values is effectively universal: one can find it in various forms in the literatures of Mesopotamia, the Levant and Egypt, ranging from 'Mirror of Princes' homilies to lamentations and prophetic elenchus of lapsed rulers; similar forms can also be attested in Greek literature, from Hesiod's critical advice to the *basileis* to Isocrates' admonitions to Cypriote or Macedonian rulers.[266] What is rather unique in Greek political thought is the exploration of ways to construct a novel and ideal political community.[267] Greek thinkers pursued this aim through three complementary strategies: first, the identification of existing human communities that could function as models of emulation; second, the discovery of imaginary communities in mythical space and/or time, which were inaccessible to ordinary humans, but were miraculously discovered and described as real communities; and, third, the delineation of theoretical and practical schemes for constructing an ideal community.[268]

One way in which foreign communities become models is by being assimilated to the classifications of Greek constitutional theory. Greek thinkers distinguished between good and bad versions of constitutions based on the rule of one (monarchies and tyrannies), the few (aristocracies and oligarchies) and the many (democracies and ochlocracies). Carthage is the most characteristic example of this assimilation.[269] Aristotle offered an extensive discussion of the Carthaginian constitution in comparison to those of Sparta and Crete, based on the common view that they possessed the best constitutions as well as sharing many similar features. He described

---

[263] 6.43.3.   [264] 1.96–101.   [265] Meier *et al.* 2004.   [266] Gray 1998: 159–77.
[267] Vlassopoulos 2010a: 117–23.   [268] Hansen 2005.   [269] *BNJ*, 744.

the Carthaginian constitution as a mixture of democratic, oligarchic and aristocratic features, and praised its stability, as proven by the loyalty of the lower classes and the lack of rebellions and tyrannical coups. His main criticism concerned the preponderant role of wealth in Carthaginian politics, which often trumped merit as the criterion by which citizens were elected to office.[270]

Equally important is the role of foreign communities within some key preoccupations of Greek political thought. One such preoccupation was the issue of leadership: what are the properties of a good leader and in what ways and conditions can he lead his comrades and subjects successfully? Leadership was one of the key topics of enquiry in the work of Xenophon, and the *Cyropaedia* (Education of Cyrus) opens with an explicit description of its *aporia*. Observing that among all living beings man is the one who is least willing to obey its leaders, Xenophon states that it is natural that the case of Cyrus the Great should be particularly relevant, as he was able to create an empire and rule over willing subjects who lived far away and belonged to the most diverse nations.[271] We shall have more to say about the *Cyropaedia* and other similar works below (p. 222); but it is telling that the founder of the Persian Empire could be chosen as an illustration of the properties of the ideal ruler.

Another quest concerned administration. Greek communities had developed only elementary and rather fragile systems of public administration; accordingly, the imperial bureaucracies of Persia and Egypt exercised a strong influence on those Greek thinkers who were interested in problems of administration. Herodotus had provided a description of the Persian imperial taxation[272] and courier systems,[273] while Heracleides of Cyme offered a detailed description of the organisation and logic of the Persian palace system.[274] Two examples from Xenophon provide excellent illustrations of how Greek authors could make theoretical points by using the Persian system as a model. Xenophon makes the wider point that the division of labour leads to specialisation and a higher degree of excellence in the individual tasks; he then uses as his example the palace kitchen of Cyrus the Great, where the specialisation of cooks in preparing particular dishes explains the excellence of the food served.[275] Xenophon's *Oeconomicus* is a work about the ideal management of an estate; the Persian king is presented by Socrates as an ideal model of administration with regard to both agriculture and warfare. He describes the incentives

[270] *Politics*, 1272b24–1273b26.   [271] 1.1.1–6.   [272] 3.89–97.   [273] 5.52–4; 8.98.
[274] *FGrH*, 689 F1–4; Lewis 1997: 332–41; Lenfant 2009.   [275] *Cyropaedia*, 8.2.5–6.

offered by the Persian king to encourage officials to protect and advance agriculture, as well as to promote the careful management of land in the royal paradises; characteristically, when Socrates' interlocutor expresses disbelief that the Persian king would ever bother about agriculture, Socrates replies with the textualisation of a story about how the Spartan commander Lysander visited Cyrus the Younger in his paradise and was told that the beautiful trees had been personally planted by Cyrus.[276]

Another important Greek topic for discussion concerns the best distribution of tasks among the citizen body and the role of the state in creating the best life for its citizens. Greek thinkers who were attempting to devise an ideal polity were profoundly inspired by the example of non-Greek communities, where the population was divided into hereditary occupational castes. The best example of a caste system the Greeks knew about during the archaic and classical periods was that of Egypt, while the Indian system would become more influential from the Hellenistic period onwards.[277] The earliest preserved description of the Egyptian caste system is by Herodotus.[278] The division of the citizen body into castes of warriors, artisans and cultivators presented important advantages in the eyes of Greek thinkers: it allowed specialisation and the optimal performance of tasks; it enabled the ideal lawgiver to allocate each citizen to the profession to which his inherent nature made him most appropriate; it stopped corruption emerging from citizens' prioritising the pursuit of wealth, and allowed the dissociation of ruling from wealth.[279] Plato's famous utopian model in the *Republic* is clearly indebted to such ideas, and in the *Timaeus* he explicitly attributes it to Egypt.[280]

Another topic explored was state intervention to create the best citizen body. With the exception of Sparta, Greek communities did not have public systems of education. Accordingly, Greek authors who recognised the importance of education in shaping the best form of citizens could use as models non-Greek communities which did possess such systems; one example is Xenophon's presentation of the Persian system of court education as a model for emulation.[281] Equally important was state regulation of social life. Xenophon maintained that, while Athenian laws only punished wrongdoers, Persian laws were superior in their proactive concern to reward good behaviour.[282] Plato's *Laws* argued that, given the educative role of art, it is dangerous to leave it to the artists' whim to determine the form and

---

[276] 4.4–25.   [277] See, e.g., Parker 2008: 87–90.   [278] 2.164–6.
[279] Froidefond 1971: 237–48, 295–302.   [280] 23d–24b.   [281] *Cyropaedia*, 1.2.1–16.
[282] *Oeconomicus*, 14.6–7.

content of art, but rather the community should legislate about it. To support this thesis, Plato used the example of Egyptian art, explaining that the Egyptians long ago established and consecrated standards from which the artists were not allowed to deviate, and this explains why Egyptian artworks have followed exactly the same styles and forms for thousands of years.[283]

Finally, we can approach the issue of utopias: the depiction of ideal communities that are situated either faraway in time or faraway in space.[284] The depiction of foreign communities as utopias is already inherent in Homer, as we have seen in the case of the Ethiopians, who host the gods, or the Phaeacians; but both the Ethiopians and the Phaeacians are inaccessible to ordinary mortals, and only poets with their special gifts could describe such communities (pp. 172–3). In the course of the classical period utopian communities could now be situated in the ethnographic and historical present.[285] Herodotus provides a memorable description of Ethiopian society in the course of his account of how the Persian king Cambyses attempted and failed to conquer them.[286] The Ethiopians lived to the age of 120 by drinking milk and eating meat provided miraculously by the Table of the Sun, and they despise the trappings of civilisation, such as purple cloaks, golden jewellery and perfumes. Equally interesting is the way in which intellectuals developed the utopian image of another faraway nation, the Scythians.[287] The fourth-century historian Ephorus of Cyme is credited with a powerful presentation of the Scythians as a utopian society.[288] He decried other historians for presenting Scythians as only cruel and barbarous, claiming that other Scythians could be used as models of good conduct due to their just lives. The Scythians are not only presented as vegetarians who abstain from killing any living creature, but, because they do not engage in money-getting, they are also shown as frugal and just, they are invincible to their enemies, and they have everything in common, including their wives and children.[289]

5.6 Alien wisdom

When Herodotus visited the Black Sea, there was one Scythian he knew about already: this was the famous Anacharsis, about whom various stories circulated among Herodotus' Greek contemporaries. Herodotus appears

---

[283] 656d–657a; Davis 1979.   [284] Dawson 1992; Romm 1992: 45–81.
[285] Cf. Campbell 2006: 61–111.   [286] 3.17–25; Asheri *et al.* 2007: 417–25.
[287] Kindstrand 1981.   [288] Moreno 2007: 192–206.   [289] *FGrH*, 70 F42.

surprised that the Scythians seemed to know nothing about this famous Scythian; his explanation was that the Scythians refused to acknowledge him, because they abhorred the adoption of foreign customs and Anacharsis was guilty of this particular sin. He narrates how Anacharsis travelled around the world and became famous for his wisdom, and how on his return trip to Scythia he stopped at the Greek *apoikia* of Cyzicus in the Sea of Marmara, became initiated into the cult of the Mother of the Gods, and vowed to introduce this cult to Scythia. When the Scythians found out, he was killed by his own brother, the king.[290] Herodotus also narrated, as we have seen (pp. 138–9), how the Scythian king Scyles met a similar death a few generations later for introducing the cult of Dionysus.[291]

The story of Anacharsis is instructive on many levels. We do not know whether Anacharsis was a historical individual; Herodotus claims to have been given Anacharsis' royal Scythian genealogy by Tymnes, the chief official of the Scythian king Ariapeithes.[292] But even if this were the case, the Anacharsis of Greek literature has little to do with a historical Scythian prince; rather, Anacharsis is one among many foreign characters in Greek literature who became famous for their particular kind of wisdom. Some foreign sages, like the Egyptian Amasis (p. 156) or the Persian Zoroaster,[293] were individuals who existed in their own national traditions; others, like Abaris, existed only within the Greek imaginary universe. What is important to stress is that by the fifth century the figure of the foreign sage was well established in Greek culture: Herodotus already reports on Anacharsis, Amasis[294] and Abaris[295] as well-known sages, while his contemporary Xanthus of Lydia was the earliest author to mention Zoroaster in Greek literature.[296]

These foreign sages became major figures of Greek literature primarily from the Hellenistic period onwards: Anacharsis became the author of *Epistles* and a central character in the dialogues of Lucian,[297] while various Greek works attributed to Zoroaster date from the Hellenistic period onwards.[298] But we can already trace the beginnings of this phenomenon during the classical period. Abaris was a Scythian who, according to Pindar, visited Athens on the occasion of a plague in the time of Croesus[299] and travelled around the world on an arrow; a poem *On the Arrival of Apollo among the Hyperboreans* and a *Theogony* were attributed to him, and might have existed already during the classical period, but hardly any evidence

---

[290] 4.76.   [291] 4.78–80.   [292] 4.76.   [293] West 2010.   [294] 2.173–4, 3.40–3.   [295] 4.36.
[296] *FGrH*, 765 F32; Kingsley 1995.   [297] Kindstrand 1981; cf. Richter 2011: 164–76.
[298] Bidez and Cumont 1938; Beck 1991.   [299] F270, *Snell.*

about them has survived.[300] Heracleides Ponticus, a student of Plato from
Heracleia in the Black Sea, was one of the earliest Greek authors to make
figures like Abaris major characters in philosophical dialogues with a
historical setting.[301] His *Abaris* expressed beliefs on the existence of gods
and the transmigration of souls;[302] another of his dialogues was apparently
named after Zoroaster,[303] while a third presented a Persian magus circum-
navigating Africa and visiting the court of the Syracusan tyrant Gelon.[304]

   This last work emphasises an important way in which foreign sages
feature in Greek literature: foreign sages can be presented as visiting
Greece and conversing with Greek sages and rulers; alternatively, Greek
sages can be portrayed as visiting foreign countries and learning their
wisdom or displaying their own. Herodotus is already familiar with stories
about Solon's visit to the court of Croesus and his display of wisdom,[305] as
well as his visit to Egypt and his adoption of Egyptian laws that he brought
to Athens;[306] he is equally familiar with Anacharsis' visit to Greece and with
stories concerning his pronouncements about the Spartans.[307] But it is
primarily in the fourth century that such stories become the focus of literary
works. Other students of Plato created works in which foreign sages played
an important role; particularly notable is the role of Persian sages and their
Zoroastrian beliefs.[308]

   Equally interesting for our subject are the cults that led to the death of
Anacharsis and Scyles; the Scythians allegedly killed them because they
considered the Mother of the Gods and Dionysus as typical Greek deities,
whose cults were unfit for Scythians to take part in. The Herodotean irony is
that both deities and their cults were constantly described by the Greeks
themselves as being of foreign origin. Herodotus explicitly comments that
the nature of Dionysiac cult was different from that of normal Greek cults
and therefore must have been an introduction from Egypt,[309] while
Euripides presents Dionysus in the *Bacchae* as a foreign newcomer from
Asia.[310] The orgiastic cult of the Mother is equally often depicted in Greek
sources as a foreign import.[311] We are thus faced with a paradox: what is
typically Greek in the eyes of Herodotus' Scythians can at the same time be
described as a foreign cult by the Greeks. In the same way that the image of
the foreign sage is an inherent feature of Greek culture, the image of the
foreign deity and cult is equally pregnant with meaning; it is the combination of these two themes that we shall explore in this section.

---

[300] *BNJ*, 34.   [301] Gottschalk 1980; Schütrumpf 2008; Fortenbaugh and Pender 2009.
[302] *Wehrli*, VII F73–5.   [303] *Wehrli*, VII F68.   [304] *Wehrli*, VII F69–70.   [305] 1.30–3.
[306] 1.30; 2.177.2.   [307] 4.77.   [308] Horky 2009.   [309] 2.49.   [310] 1–42.
[311] Roller 1999: 121–34.

At this stage it is inevitable that one should pause to ask the question: to what extent do traditions about foreign sages and foreign deities reflect a real historical process? Can we really believe that Greek intellectuals learnt their wisdom on visits to the East, or that all Greek deities came from Egypt? Scholarly views have been largely polarised between those who categorically negate any historical veracity behind the traditions of alien wisdom[312] and those who largely accept, in one form or another, the historicity of the tradition.[313] We have already examined in Chapters 2 and 3 the mobility of people, goods and ideas, and the plurality of encounters and interactions, while Chapter 4 has explored the processes of intercultural communication. In the light of all this, it makes little sense to deny that the Greek traditions of alien wisdom reflect in some way real historical processes. However, the peculiarly self-referential character of Greek culture means that we cannot posit a straightforward relation of imitation or adoption, as we can in the case of some of the cultures we examined at the beginning of this chapter.

A good illustration of this complexity is one of Herodotus' most famous claims. He argued that the Egyptian taboo against burial in woollen garments was taken over by the Pythagorean and Orphic doctrines,[314] and that certain Greeks (presumably the same Pythagoreans and Orphics) had taken over the concept of metempsychosis from the Egyptians.[315] This is an interesting example of the complexity of interactions that underlies such statements of alien wisdom. While there are obvious similarities in the wool taboo between the Egyptians and the Pythagoreans, the concept of metempsychosis is completely alien to Egyptian religion. Nevertheless, Egyptian art often represented souls as birds, and the Egyptian *Book of the Dead* included spells to enable the deceased to take any form they liked in order to avoid dangers and obstacles in their journey in the underworld. It is conceivable that there might be some connection between the Greek misunderstanding of these Egyptian depictions and spells and the Greek concept of metempsychosis.[316] Herodotus might have tried to accuse the Pythagoreans of stealing Egyptian doctrines and passing them off as their own, but the Pythagoreans by no means denied or tried to hide such links; the tradition of Pythagoras' visit to Egypt and his education by Egyptian priests is already attested by Isocrates in the early fourth century, and it would become further embellished in later times.[317] Neither is the visit of Pythagoras to

---

[312] For example, Hopfner 1925; Lloyd 1975: 49–60.
[313] For example, Burkert 1992, 2004; Kingsley 1994, 1995; West 1971, 1997.   [314] 2.81.
[315] 2.123.   [316] Lloyd 1975: 57–8; cf. Livingstone 2001: 157–8.
[317] *Bousiris*, 28–9; Livingstone 2001: 155–62.

Egypt improbable, given the strong connections between Samos and Egypt, nor is it impossible to derive the Greek doctrine of metempsychosis from a misunderstanding of some Egyptian spells and images.[318] But given that the concept of metempsychosis is, strictly speaking, completely alien to Egyptian culture, why did Greeks persist in portraying this idea as a loan from Egypt, instead of taking the credit for this novel idea?

This is the reason that it is essential to examine the filters and *topoi* through which the traditions of alien wisdom are utilised in Greek culture. One such *topos* is a cosmopolitan universe of civilisation, art and science. Many cultures have discourses about how civilisation, the arts and the sciences emerged, and how they reached their present state.[319] But in most cases these discourses attempt to explain how the arts and sciences emerged within one particular culture. What is peculiar about the Greek discourses is how the unit of analysis is the whole known human universe. There is also no doubt that most ancient cultures were affected by the international mobility of people, goods, ideas and technologies; the Greek peculiarity was to create a discourse which purported to investigate this very process.[320] One major assumption of this universalist approach is that a particular discovery or invention can have taken place only once; if it is attested more than once and in more places than one, then it must have been brought from the original place of discovery or have been handed down by the original discoverers. Given that the Greeks were keenly aware of the antiquity of many of the foreign cultures with which they were in contact, it is not surprising how often they were willing to attribute discoveries and inventions to non-Greeks. Hecataeus attributed the origins of the Greek alphabet to the Egyptian Danaus,[321] while Hellanicus attributed the first construction of iron weapons to the Scythian king Saneunus[322] and the discovery of the vine to Egypt.[323] Aristotle claimed that the theoretical sciences were first developed when people could afford leisure from making a living; accordingly, mathematical science was invented in Egypt, because there the priestly caste could devote its time to research.[324]

It should be noted that the Greek discourse of the discovery of the arts and the sciences only very partially matches the processes taking place in the real world.[325] Some Greeks attributed the importation of the alphabet to Greece to the Phoenician Cadmus,[326] and this surely reflects in some way the fact that the Greek alphabet did derive from the Phoenician; but other

---

[318] Kingsley 1994.   [319] Zhmud 2006: 33–4.   [320] Kleingünther 1934.   [321] *FGrH*, 1 F20.
[322] *FGrH*, 4 F189.   [323] *FGrH*, 4 F175.   [324] *Metaphysics*, 981b20–5.
[325] Zhmud 2006: 40–2.   [326] Herodotus, 5.58; Edwards 1979.

Greeks attributed its introduction to the Egyptians, as we just saw, or even to Greek mythical heroes like Palamedes.[327] The Greek discourses are informed by the real processes, but they primarily express a Greek *topos*, which is willing to attribute priority and debts to foreign cultures. The importance of this *topos* for the history of interactions between Greeks and non-Greeks can hardly be overestimated; for it provided a means through which most foreign cultures could position themselves favourably within Greek culture, and even claim a position of superiority. We shall examine in Chapter 7 how in the Hellenistic period Jewish authors could make effective use of this *topos* in order to situate Jewish tradition within Greek culture, and even claim a position of priority and superiority (pp. 315–16).

A second *topos* was predicated on the first: Greek authors could claim privileged access to alien wisdom in order to give authority to the views they expressed. The claim that Pythagoras had been educated in Egypt was an authorial strategy that aimed to give authority and credibility to a Greek view by means of appeal to alien wisdom, even if the concept of metempsychosis did not exist in Egyptian culture. The antiquity of Egyptian civilisation, the continuity of tradition established by its archives, and the apocryphal and inaccessible knowledge secreted by temples and priests were the major tropes through which Greek authors employed the image of Egypt in their authorial projects.[328] We have already seen how the antiquity of Egyptian civilisation could be employed in order to scrutinise and correct Greek traditions in the case of Hecataeus (pp. 182–3); Herodotus also used Egyptian and Phoenician traditions about Heracles in order to correct the Greek chronology of Heracles and to distinguish between a divine and an heroic Heracles.[329]

Plato employs the image of Egyptian archives and their apocryphal knowledge in order to give legitimacy to his notorious tale of Atlantis.[330] The setting is Solon's visit to the Egyptian city of Sais and his conversation with the priests of Neith. As in the similar story of Hecataeus, Solon's attempt to present Greek myths and genealogies is ridiculed by an old Egyptian priest, who famously claims that all Greeks are children, and goes on to narrate the story of the primeval Athenians and their struggle with Atlantis, which story Solon subsequently brings back to Athens.[331] The Athenians did not know anything about primeval Athens and Atlantis because deluges and catastrophes had broken the stream of tradition; but

---

[327] Stesichorus, F213, *Page.*   [328] Assmann 2001.   [329] 2.43–4.
[330] Froidefond 1971: 284–94.   [331] *Timaeus*, 21c–25e; *Critias.*

in Egypt, the morphology of the land had prevented the catastrophic loss of memory, and old stories had been preserved by the priests. It is impressive to note what care Plato has taken to give verisimilitude to the story. The city of Sais is related to Athens, as the founder goddess Neith is the Egyptian equivalent of Athena,[332] and the presence of Greek names in an Egyptian tale is the result of Solon's translating the Egyptian names into Greek ones.[333] A different example is the Egyptian tale that Plato uses to illustrate his argument concerning the inferiority of writing to oral debate. Plato depicts the Egyptian god Thoth, the inventor of arts, presenting his inventions to Ammon, the king of the gods, and defending their utility for mankind. Ammon accepts his other arguments, but contests Thoth's defence of writing by arguing that writing can only weaken memory and cannot substitute the exchange of arguments in oral debate.[334]

Finally, let us deal with the third *topos*: the construct of the foreign deity in Greek culture. As we have seen in Chapters 3 and 4, and as we shall further explore in Chapter 7, the transfer and adoption of deities and mythologies across cultural boundaries was a potent and long-term process in the ancient Mediterranean. What is of interest here is not the actual process of adoption, as in the case of Libyan Ammon that we have already examined (pp. 150–1), but the depiction and characterisation of deities as explicitly foreign. Like the other *topoi* we examined above, this could take a variety of forms. Foreign deities could be adopted and assimilated as well as depicted as foreign at the same time. We have seen how during the fifth century the Athenian state adopted the cult of the Thracian deity Bendis (pp. 144–5). Since the Thracians had not yet developed an iconography of deities, the depiction of Bendis in Greek art was shaped by Greek deities perceived to be similar or equivalent to Bendis. In this case, it was Artemis that provided Bendis with the main elements of her iconography; but at the same time Bendis' Thracian dress served to identify the goddess as explicitly foreign (see Figure 24).[335]

More complex was the case of the Mother of the Gods and her consort Attis.[336] In the case of the Mother it is likely that there was a conflation between, on the one hand, Greek deities that could play this role, such as Gaia (Mother Earth) or Rhea, the mother of Zeus and the Olympian gods, and, on the other, the Phrygian deity Matar, whose epithet kubileya became Cybele, the alternative name of the Greek Mother. As we have already seen with regard to the *Homeric Hymns*, the Greek cult of the Mother involved

[332] *Timaeus*, 21e.   [333] *Critias*, 113a.   [334] *Phaedrus*, 274c–275c; Froidefond 1971: 272–84.
[335] Gočeva and Popov 1986.   [336] Roller 1999; Lancellotti 2002; Borgeaud 2004.

Figure 24 Votive relief to Bendis, Athens, fourth century BCE.

ecstatic music and mysteries (pp. 173–4), while her Greek iconography came to depict her as a deity enthroned among lions and holding a *tympanum* (drum). While some elements of the Greek iconography could be traced back to the Phrygian cult, the depiction of the *tympanum* as a standard divine attribute served to depict the deity as quintessentially exotic. Equally interesting is the case of the divine escort Attis, who does not seem to be attested as a deity in Phrygia, and who is absent from the early Greek references and depictions of the Mother. It is only in the latter half of the fourth century that Attis emerges in Greek literature and art; Greek artists depicted him as a shepherd with the typical costume of Oriental characters such as Paris and the Amazons that we examined already (pp. 194–5).[337]

But the *topos* of the foreign deity was not restricted to deities who were indeed foreign; it could be equally applied to Greek deities in order to define and characterise particular aspects of their function. From early on the Greeks developed narratives that depicted Dionysus as a foreign deity, even though accounts differed concerning his origins: some posited

---

[337] Roller 1994.

Thrace, others Asia Minor and yet others Nyssa in Ethiopia. Accordingly, and given the negligible presence of Dionysus in Homer, modern scholars had long taken the Greeks at their word, and considered Dionysus as a foreign deity who had entered Greece only at some point during the archaic period. It was only the discovery of Linear B tablets that mentioned Dionysus which proved that the god had existed in the Greek pantheon since the second millennium.[338] The depiction of Dionysus as a foreign ecstatic deity is memorably accomplished in Euripides' *Bacchae*:

> I, the son of Zeus, have come to this land of the Thebans – Dionysus, whom once Semele, Kadmos' daughter, bore, delivered by a lightning-bearing flame . . . I have left the wealthy lands of the Lydians and Phrygians, the sun-parched plains of the Persians, and the Bactrian walls, and have passed over the wintry land of the Medes, and blessed Arabia, and all of Asia which lies along the coast of the salt sea with its beautifully-towered cities full of Greeks and barbarians mingled together; and I have come to this Greek city first, having already set those other lands to dance and established my mysteries there, so that I might be a deity manifest among men. In this land of Greece, I have first excited Thebes to my cry, fitting a fawn-skin to my body and taking a thyrsos in my hand, a weapon of ivy.[339]

It is the combination of an ecstatic ritual with a secret rite that promised a better afterlife which stands behind the use of the *topos* of the foreign deity in the case of Dionysus. Ecstatic rituals, although an essential feature of Greek culture, raised unavoidable questions of identity and morality; the Greeks could imagine such rituals as typical of effeminate Barbarians and described the deities of those rituals as foreign. Herodotus' stories about the Scythians' unwillingness to accept the ecstatic Greek rituals of Dionysus and the Mother, which the Greeks themselves could at the same time describe as foreign, brilliantly reveals the inherent paradox. On the other side stand the Greek mystery cults: secret rites requiring initiation which promised a better afterlife. Mystery cults seem equally typically Greek, as there is hardly any evidence for such cults among non-Greek Mediterranean religions.[340] Nevertheless, the Greeks recognised the antiquity of non-Greek religions, and in particular that of Egypt, where participation in the cult was largely restricted to the priests, and where the cult of Osiris, the ruler of the Underworld, aimed to ensure a happy afterlife. It is likely that it was through Greek influence from the Osiris myth and cult that Dionysus became associated with secret rites and the afterlife.[341]

---

[338] Burkert 1985: 161–7.   [339] 1–26.   [340] Burkert 1987: 2–3.   [341] Burkert 2004: 71–98.

5.7 Canons and exceptions

Let us conclude our discussion by examining some exceptions to the general rule postulated above concerning the self-referential character of Greek culture and its lack of phenomena such as 'bilingualism' and translations. To understand better these exceptions we should draw a distinction between traditions and practices which became canonical and those that did not. Within every culture certain traditions and practices can acquire a canonical form that effectively determines, often very strictly, the limits and the means of what can be done and in particular how. When during the eighth century Greeks started to construct temples as a special form of architectural buildings housing the statue of a divinity, there was wide variation in what Greek temples looked like and the materials from which they were constructed. In fact, in certain areas of the Greek world, like Crete, temples followed a completely different tradition which often borrowed heavily from Near Eastern models, as, for example, the temple of Prinias with its wall reliefs influenced by Syrian architecture.[342] By the sixth century, though, Greek temple architecture had become canonical; Greek temples had acquired a particular design (a cella surrounded by columns with specific forms), were constructed of stone, and their sculpted decoration was primarily presented in pediments, metopes and friezes. Once Greek temples became canonical, there were few ways in which their architecture could be further influenced by foreign artistic styles. It is, of course, a very different story when the form of the Greek temple was glocalised by non-Greek communities, a topic we shall examine in Chapter 6 (pp. 264–6).

It is accordingly with regard to those forms of Greek literature and art where no canons existed, or where they developed late, that we can see references to foreign styles, themes and genres. One illuminating example is the Greek production of objects made of faience, a technology with a long Egyptian tradition. During the seventh and sixth centuries there existed faience workshops at Naucratis and Rhodes, producing scarabs, unguent vases and figurines. Many of these objects adopted Egyptian forms, styles and iconographies, such as the monkey-shaped vases; but even more telling is the use of cartouches with pharaonic names and even hieroglyphic inscriptions on objects in Greek shapes and iconography. Particularly interesting are the aryballoi, small spherical flasks used as unguent

---

[342] Beyer 1976; Marinatos 2000: 71–9.

containers, and vases in the shape of helmeted warriors (see Figure 10). In this case, the intention to create an Egyptian reference on Greek objects could not be more explicit. Here, therefore, we can see Greek artisans creating objects in foreign styles and traditions and with reference to foreign cultures.[343]

But we can also find a few occasions in which even canonical forms of Greek art and literature could refer to non-Greek styles, genres and themes. Although Greek vase painting is largely restricted to Greek styles and iconographies, we can occasionally find examples of foreign reference. This is in particular the case with references to Egyptian art and its styles and iconography.[344] An Athenian *hydria* uses a type illustrated in the Egyptian *Book of the Dead* in order to depict a funerary *prothesis* scene, while a famous Laconian cup, depicting King Arcesilas of Cyrene weighing silphium, adapts the scheme used in the *Book of the Dead* for depicting the weighing of the souls (see Figure 25). A sixth-century Caeretan hydria parodies the Egyptian iconography of the pharaoh triumphing over his enemies, in order to depict Heracles defeating Bousiris and his Egyptian followers who are about to sacrifice him. Following the Egyptian scheme, Heracles is depicted as much larger than his enemies, whom he tosses about, but the scheme is employed mockingly in order to depict the defeat of the pharaoh and his subjects. The myth of Bousiris and Heracles is also a good example of the way in which Greek vase painting could occasionally refer to the schemes of Persian art too. During the fifth century Greek vase painters moved from depicting the scene of Heracles' aborted sacrifice at the altar into depicting a procession bringing Heracles to Bousiris, who is now portrayed in the style of the enthroned Persian king; both the procession and the throne scene on Greek vases are direct references to common iconographic themes of Persian art.[345] Some scholars have argued that a similar influence of Persian iconography can be detected in the Parthenon frieze: the procession of cavalry and sacrificial victims, a theme practically absent in earlier Greek art, might be an Athenian adaptation of the delegations of subjects bringing gifts to the Persian king, as depicted in the famous Apadana reliefs of Persepolis.[346]

'Bilingualism' and translations were rare in archaic and classical Greek literature, but a convincing case can be made for the fourth-century astronomer and mathematician Eudoxus of Cnidos.[347] After studying with Plato at Athens, Eudoxus received a letter of reference from the Spartan king

---

[343] Webb 1978.   [344] Miller 2000: 417–20.   [345] Miller 2000: 430–8.   [346] Root 1985.
[347] Lasserre 1966.

Figure 25(a) Laconian cup by the Arcesilas Painter, *c.* 560 BCE.

Figure 25(b) The 'weighing of the conscience' vignette from the papyrus of Ani, *c.* 1250 BCE.

Agesilaus for pharaoh Nectanebo (p. 69). The pharaoh gave him access to the priests of Heliopolis, where Eudoxus spent a year and a half with them, even shaving his beard and eyebrows in the Egyptian manner. This immersion in the Egyptian environment is displayed in the deep knowledge of Egyptian customs and theology visible in his works; it is this immersion that made possible Eudoxus' translation into Greek of an Egyptian work entitled *Dialogues of Dogs*.[348]

But the case of Eudoxus is largely unparalleled in archaic and classical Greek literature. We should rather be looking in a different direction if we want to observe the enormous influence that interaction with non-Greeks had on Greek culture. Greeks rarely translated or behaved in a 'bilingual' mode; by the sixth century they had developed a literary culture with its own genres which functioned like a closed system. But the creation of new genres in Greek literature is a different story. It is impressive to observe the ways in which the Persian Empire and the various experiences of those who came into contact with it had a profound effect on Greek literature by inspiring the creation of novel literary genres. Let us start our discussion with the case of Scylax of Caryanda.[349] Scylax was a Carian who was entrusted by Dareius I with a mission to explore the Indus River in preparation for the Persian annexation of India.[350] Carian Scylax wrote an account of his Persian-sponsored exploration of India in Greek, one of the earliest recorded Greek travel accounts and the earliest description of India in Greek literature.[351] It is particularly interesting to note how the travel account is interspersed with ethnographic descriptions of various forms. Scylax reports all the fabulous stories about the Sciapods (Shade-feet) and Winnowing-fan-ears,[352] but he also engages in ethnographic descriptions of the political and social aspects of the Indian kingdoms.[353]

Scylax was also credited with another work in Greek titled *Affairs Concerning Heracleides, the King of Mylasa*.[354] Heracleides was a Carian ruler who played a leading role in the Carian resistance against the Persians during the Ionian revolt (p. 54); after the defeat, he seems to have retreated to mainland Greece, where he valiantly took part on the Greek side in the battle of Artemision. Thus, if Scylax wrote one of the earliest works of Greek ethnography as a Persian employee, he also authored a work about one of the leaders of anti-Persian resistance. Modern scholars have argued that Scylax's book on Heracleides was the earliest work of Greek

---

[348] Griffiths 1965.   [349] *BNJ*, 709.   [350] Herodotus, 4.43.   [351] Parker 2008: 14–18.
[352] *FGrH*, 709 F7.   [353] *FGrH*, 709 F5.   [354] Schepens 1998.

biography;[355] but the scanty remains do not allow us to verify whether it provided a full biography by covering the whole life of Heracleides or merely narrated certain events relating to him. There is no doubt, however, that the earliest Greek prose work devoted to a historical individual was written by a Carian who had served the Persian Empire, about another Carian who had brilliantly opposed it.

A different author originating from a Greek polis in Caria had an even more profound effect on Greek literature. Herodotus from Halicarnassus was born a subject of the Persian Empire and became the 'father of history' by writing a work on the great deeds (*erga*) of Greeks and Barbarians and the conflicts between them, in particular the Persian Wars.[356] In many ways, Herodotus was indebted to the drastic developments that transformed Greek literature through the textualisation of the interactions in the four parallel worlds and the representation of the foreigner in Greek literature and art. His recounting of countless tales from the experiences of Greek mercenaries, intellectuals, merchants, exiles and their interactions with non-Greeks,[357] his ethnographic presentations of so many Mediterranean and Near Eastern cultures,[358] and his constant exploration of cultural and political difference and the search for Greek identity[359] stand out so vividly nowadays to an important extent because we have lost all the earlier and contemporary Greek prose on which Herodotus grounded himself (pp. 180–5).[360] But it is on the construction of his historical narrative that the Persian Empire had the most profound impact. This is obviously because the Persian Wars was the first event in Greek history which seemed important enough to rival the great events of heroic myth and demand its preservation in word through narrative. But it is even more so in terms of the solution that Herodotus found for organising his historical narrative. Biographies of kings and their achievements were standard in Near Eastern literatures, as were accounts of battles and wars; but Herodotus' brilliant idea was to use a series of successive biographies of Lydian (Croesus) and Persian kings (Cyrus, Cambyses, Dareius, Xerxes) as the narrative skeleton through which he could present the ethnography and great feats of non-Greeks, as well as their conflicts with the Greek world.[361]

Another Greek from Caria, Ctesias of Cnidos, served as a doctor at the court of the Persian king Artaxerxes II (404–358).[362] His *Indica* made him both famous as the author of the most influential ethnographic presentation

---

[355] See, e.g., Momigliano 1971: 29–38.   [356] Bakker *et al.* 2002; Asheri *et al.* 2007.
[357] Vlassopoulos forthcoming a.   [358] Bichler 2000; Dorati 2000.
[359] Hartog 1988; Pelling 1997; Munson 2001.   [360] Drews 1973; Fowler 1996; Luraghi 2001.
[361] Payen 1997.   [362] Wiesehöfer *et al.* 2011.

of India and notorious for the presumed unreliability of his account;[363] but it is with his other famous work that we are more concerned here. The *Persica* was a large work in twenty-three books, which narrated the history of the Assyrian, Median and Persian empires down to 398.[364] Modern historians often complain about the unreliability of his historical account, and there is no doubt that in comparison with the historical methods of data collection and verification employed by earlier historians, such as Herodotus and Thucydides, Ctesias' work is largely wanting.

But this should not obscure the great innovations heralded by this work. The first was the very idea of writing a continuous large-scale narrative about the history of foreign nations. It might seem to us something self-evident, but we should not forget that there is simply nothing equivalent in the earlier literatures of the ancient Near East. Even among Greek authors, Herodotus might have used the reigns of Persian kings as a skeleton on which to structure his account, but he never wrote a history of Persia. Equally important was Ctesias' conception of his task. Despite the title, one quarter of the work was devoted to the Assyrian and Median empires. The unifying link that brought Assyrian, Median and Persian history together was the idea of the succession of empires. This was an extremely important concept, destined to be made famous by Daniel's dream in the Bible;[365] the Macedonians and the Romans were later included in the succession list, which could be endlessly expanded into the future.[366] The idea of organising world history as a succession of empires became extremely popular in the Middle Ages and continued to shape historical imagination up to the eighteenth century.[367]

But how could the history of these empires be written? Despite his claim to have consulted Persian archives, Ctesias largely eschewed the use of documentary sources. Instead, he used the innumerable oral novellas about life at court as the skeleton for a continuous historical narrative. One could compare in this respect the way the Jewish author of the book of *Kings* used novellas about kings David and Solomon in order to construct his historical account.[368] But equally fascinating is the way Ctesias reworked these stories in order to ask questions about moral and social issues. One of his stories narrated how the brave Median Parsondas abhorred Nanarus, the satrap of Babylonia, simply because Nanarus was a eunuch and tried to vilify him to the Median king. Nanarus managed to capture Parsondas and

[363] Parker 2008: 28–33; Nichols 2011.
[364] Lenfant 2004; Llewellyn-Jones and Robson 2010; Stronk 2010.   [365] Millar 2006: 51–66.
[366] Fabbrini 1983.   [367] Vlassopoulos 2007: 20–2.   [368] Llewellyn-Jones and Robson 2010: 66–8.

punished him by forcing him to dress and live as a transvestite singer in his court, until Parsondas was rescued and returned to the Median court. The narration poses in vivid dialogue two challenging moral questions: Nanarus asks Parsondas why he tried to harm him, although he had suffered nothing from him and for the sole reason that he was a eunuch; the Median king challenges Parsondas by asking him how he could bear to live ignominiously as a transvestite, instead of making an honourable end to his life.[369]

Xenophon was another Greek connected to the Persian Empire, as we have seen in Chapter 2 (pp. 66–7). Despite the variety of modern assessments of his intellectual achievement, there should be no doubt that he was one of the most innovative spirits in Greek literature of the fourth century, and it is hardly surprising that the Persian Empire loomed large and in various ways in his oeuvre.[370] The *Anabasis* is Xenophon's eye-witness account of the expedition of 10,000 Greek mercenaries in the service of the Persian rebel prince Cyrus from Asia Minor to Mesopotamia and their successful return to Greece after the defeat and death of Cyrus, written probably many decades after the events took place.[371] On one level the *Anabasis* is the most characteristic product of the textualisation of the interactions between Greeks and non-Greeks in the four parallel worlds. It gives an account of the everyday experiences of the Greek mercenaries on the march; it includes accounts of battles, marches, ambushes and looting against and with non-Greeks; diplomatic negotiations, drinking, eating and dancing with non-Greeks, as well as ethnographic observations on the foreign landscapes and the customs of the people encountered. Although we have seen many examples of the textualisation of these experiences and encounters, all previous examples fade in comparison with the amazing detail of this account; scholars are still puzzling how Xenophon managed to keep a record of the distances between the various stops of the march decades after the event.[372] Why all this detail?

The answer is partly that Xenophon liked to experiment by incorporating within one work elements from different genres, as in the case of the *Anabasis*, which combines historiography, ethnography and military treatise.[373] But primarily it is because the *Anabasis* is Xenophon's exploration of what it means to be a leader of men. The stories of the *Anabasis* provide a concrete illustration of the qualities needed to rule soldiers, motivate comrades, persuade audiences, take the initiative, create and maintain friend-

---

[369] *Persica*, F6b; translated in Llewellyn-Jones and Robson 2010: 151–6.   [370] Hirsch 1985.
[371] Briant 1995; Lendle 1995; Stronk 1995; Lane Fox 2004a; Lee 2007.   [372] Roy 2007.
[373] For a literary approach to the *Anabasis*, see Flower 2012.

ships, conduct diplomacy and survive in extreme circumstances. And it is telling that Greeks and non-Greeks are presented in both positive and negative roles; the duplicitous Persian satrap Tissaphernes[374] finds his counterpart in the Greek mercenary Menon, while the flattering portrait that Xenophon paints of himself is balanced by his eulogy of the qualities of Cyrus the Younger.

The same willingness to experiment with new literary forms that mix different genres and the same strong interest in the problems of leadership is manifested in Xenophon's other great Persian-related work, the *Cyropaedia* or *Education of Cyrus*.[375] This is a work which examines the education of an individual in the art of ruling through a narrative of the life of Cyrus the Great, the creator of the Persian Empire. The *Cyropaedia* mixes together historiography, biography, ethnography, political utopia, philosophical dialogue, technical writing and novella. There are good reasons to believe that, as Xenophon explicitly claims, various Persian stories and songs about Cyrus have been reworked and reframed within the structure and aims of the work.[376] Particularly interesting is a series of novellas which Xenophon craftily interspersed through the main narrative of the story, the tragic love story of Pantheia and Abradatas being the most famous of them. Novellas concerning court or love stories were particularly prominent in the eastern Mediterranean and beyond, but hardly developed in Greek culture, where the dominant role of myth had incorporated novelistic elements within mythical narratives, as we have seen (p. 168). In the case of Ctesias and Xenophon, we see two different ways in which such Persian stories could be used by Greek authors: Ctesias uses them as the skeleton for constructing a historical narrative of successive eastern empires, while Xenophon reworks them into an exploration of the relationship between politics, education and morality. A different opportunity, that of reworking such stories so as to create Greek novels as independent literary works, occurs only from the Hellenistic period onwards, as is seen in works like the *Ninus Romance* about a legendary Assyrian king.[377]

This chapter has examined in detail the peculiar form in which Greek culture glocalised non-Greek cultures. We have seen that, despite a few exceptions, Greek culture took a self-referential stance: Greek authors did not imitate non-Greek genres, translate non-Greek works or create intertextual links with them; Greek artists did not imitate foreign styles and

---

[374] Danzig 2007.   [375] Due 1989; Tatum 1989; Gera 1993; Gray 2011.   [376] Tuplin 1996b.
[377] Braun 1938; Reichel 2010.

iconographies. Explaining precisely why this was the case is a complicated question. But an essential part of the answer is the peculiar form of the Panhellenic world we have examined in Chapter 2 (pp. 34–41). Because the Panhellenic world had no centre and was characterised by enormous diversity, its cultural unity could exist only through some very peculiar practices and at different and often contradictory levels. Greek myth, and the literature and art that were dominated by it, were an essential level of the cultural unity of the Greek world. What linked the Greeks together were the heroic genealogies that created shared kinship, the movement of heroes from one place to another, the joint expeditions in the mythical past. These myths were celebrated in works which were composed in shared literary dialects and they dominated every genre of Greek literature and art.

This dominance of myth in Greek culture meant that various genres that existed independently in other cultures, such as the folktale, the novella or wisdom literature, in Greece were incorporated in mythical narratives, rather than existing as independent genres. As a result, the translation of foreign folktales, novellas or wisdom stories lacked an immediate entrance point into Greek literature; they could be introduced only through filtering and incorporating either in mythical narratives or through the novel Greek prose genres that textualised the encounters and interactions with non-Greeks. The dominance of Greek myth in, for example, the iconography of temples is another reason why phenomena like the depiction of foreign deities in Etruscan temples in Pyrgi (pp. 95–6), or Lycian heroa in Limyra (p. 266), are largely absent from Greek art.

Nevertheless, this self-referential attitude was accompanied by the development of a Barbarian repertoire in Greek culture which constitutes a phenomenon of great historical significance. It was significant because of the immense expansion of the imaginary universe of Greek literature and art. Greek myth contained as one of its inherent features the concept of foreign heroes and foreign space; Greek myths could be located almost anywhere across the known world and provided a potent means through which foreign people and foreign cultures could find a place within a framework that was Hellenocentric and universalist at the same time. The same applies to the textualisation of the interactions with non-Greeks. Political and moral thought, practical manuals and treatises, historiography and anthropology, and philosophical and religious works were framed within an imaginary universe that could incorporate almost the whole known world. The stories of sailors and traders could be textualised to create an ethnographic account of all Mediterranean communities and their location within a universal chronological framework; the encounters of a group of mercenaries could be textualised as the exploration of the moral, political, military and ethnographic issues that is the *Anabasis*.

Equally important was the expansion of the roles and functions that non-Greeks and their images could play within Greek culture. The depiction of foreigners and Others and the employment of alterity and polarity are a practically universal phenomenon that appears among the most diverse cultures. Unsurprisingly, they also play an important role in Greek culture; not only that, but the Greek invention of the opposition between freedom and Oriental despotism or the image of Oriental luxury and effeminacy came to play a very significant role in world history through their reception by the modern West. But we also need to recognise the significance of the various other ways in which non-Greeks are present in Greek culture. The diversity of interactions and encounters with non-Greeks in the four parallel worlds led to the diversity of the Barbarian repertoire: presenting foreign sages as possessors of alien wisdom, Persian kings as ideal rulers or non-Greek communities as utopias is a peculiar aspect of Greek culture and a phenomenon largely absent from the older Mesopotamian and Egyptian cultures, from which we have sufficient evidence to judge. Greek myth is employed not only to explore polarity, but also to explore kinship with the Barbarians. The Athenian vases depicting the departure of Persian warriors is a characteristic example of the ability of Greek culture to see an issue from the point of view of a foreigner; the Scythian Anacharsis or the Egyptian stories employed by Hecataeus are typical examples of the use of the Barbarian as a means of internal self-criticism.

This diversity of the Barbarian repertoire reflects to an important extent a historical conjuncture: the diversity of the four parallel worlds and the interactions between Greeks and non-Greeks. Greeks employed thousands of Barbarian slaves, but thousands of Greeks worked for foreign kings; Greeks fought against Barbarian empires, but also gave citizenship or Panhellenic honours to Barbarian kings and rulers; Greeks encountered communities with primitive material cultures as well as great ancient civilisations of enormous power and wealth; encounters in the world of *apoikiai* ranged from the hybrid frontier societies to stressing the Greek identity of *apoikiai* through participation in the Panhellenic world. Had Greek culture developed outside the interdependence of the four parallel worlds, the expanded Barbarian repertoire might have never developed. But at the same time there were inherent features of the peculiar nature of the Panhellenic world which explain why Greek culture was in a position to turn the diversity of encounters and interactions into the diversity of a Barbarian repertoire employed widely in literature and art.

The self-referential and Hellenocentric character of Greek glocalisation, alongside the universal scope and diversity of the Barbarian repertoire in Greek culture, played a particularly important role in two historical processes that we shall examine in the next two chapters. The globalisation of Greek culture and its glocalisation by non-Greek cultures in the archaic and classical periods is the subject of Chapter 6. The processes of Hellenistic globalisation and glocalisation form the subject of Chapter 7.

6 | Globalisation and glocalisation

The Introduction sketched two fascinating conundrums in the study of Greek–Barbarian relationships. The first was the peculiar way in which Greek culture filtered its interaction with and debts to non-Greek cultures through the construction of a Barbarian repertoire. The second was the significant impact of Greek culture during the archaic and classical periods on many cultures and societies of the eastern Mediterranean. How are we to explain the fact that the Greek periphery influenced so deeply the much larger, older, wealthier and more powerful world of the empires of the East? Chapter 5 dealt with the first conundrum; this one will deal with the second. As the Introduction suggested, the best way to understand our conundrum is by situating it within the processes of globalisation and glocalisation in the ancient Mediterranean. We shall therefore examine how Greek culture was part of the processes of globalisation and how non-Greek communities around the Mediterranean glocalised various aspects of it in diverse ways. The following discussion of glocalisation and globalisation is largely focused on archaeological, numismatic and epigraphic evidence; the reason for this selection is not merely their intrinsic interest, but the fact that the non-Greek literatures of the archaic and classical periods have almost completely vanished, with the obvious exception of the Jewish texts included in the Old Testament.

6.1 Illustrating globalisation

Let us start with some concrete examples that illustrate the processes of globalisation in the archaic and classical Mediterranean. Out of a vast number of possible examples, let us concentrate on three: script, coinage and monumental sculpture and temple-building. In all these cases we can perceive a common pattern: these were all ideas and technologies which were created or had their origins among the non-Greek societies of the eastern Mediterranean and the Near East. During the archaic period the Greeks adopted the Phoenician alphabet, the Lydian invention of coinage, and the Egyptian techniques for making monumental sculpture and temples, and adapted them to suit their own needs and interests. At the same time, the expansion of the world of networks, which came to encompass the whole Mediterranean, and the world of *apoikiai* brought these new technologies and ideas to many other communities around the Mediterranean, which adopted and further adapted them. By the end of the classical period, there had developed across the Mediterranean a material and cultural *koine*, of which these ideas and technologies formed an essential part.

6.1.1 Alphabetic writing

Around 800 the Greeks borrowed the alphabetic Phoenician writing system which had developed since the second millennium on the Levantine coast, in order to write down their own language. They adapted the Phoenician alphabet, whose signs denoted only consonants, by using certain signs representing consonants that did not exist in the Greek language in order to represent vowels. In some Greek communities the name for a scribe was rendered by the word 'phoenicistes', attesting the Phoenician origin of the Greek alphabet.[1] The adaptation proved extremely popular, and within a short period most Greek communities acquired their own local alphabetic version, sometimes with significant differences in letter forms.[2] Some non-Greek communities, such as the Aramaeans and the Jews, adapted the Phoenician alphabet independently from the Greeks to create their own scripts;[3] but many other communities across the Mediterranean, from Carians and Lycians in the east to the Etruscans, Sicels and Romans in the west, adopted and adapted the Greek glocalisation of the Phoenician alphabet to record their own languages.[4] It is not an accident that this adapted form of the Phoenician alphabet is attested for the first time in the western Mediterranean: a flask found in a grave at Osteria del Osa, a community in the vicinity of Rome, carries the fragmentary inscription EYΛIN and dates to around 770. It is unclear whether the inscription is in Greek (in which case it might represent the word *eulinos* and comment on the weaving abilities of the deceased female), or in Latin or another non-Greek language; if the latter, it is evidence for the rapidity with which the Greek alphabet was adopted by the Italic populations to record their own language.[5] The

[1] Jeffery and Morpurgo Davies 1970.   [2] Wirbelauer 2005; Woodard 2010.   [3] Sanders 2009.
[4] Lejeune 1983; Baurain *et al.* 1991.   [5] Lane Fox 2008: 136–7.

interconnectedness of a world in which the earliest adaptation of the Phoenician alphabet is attested in a community of Latium hardly needs to be stressed.

However, even more interesting is the differential spread of the cultural practices for which writing could be used.[6] Some of the uses of writing were effectively universal in the ancient Mediterranean: indications of ownership, dedications to divinities or epitaphs. Others, such as the recording of commercial transactions, must have been very widespread, but the use of perishable materials, such as papyrus and leather, makes it difficult to generalise; we have examined above the customs register from Elephantine (pp. 89–90) and the Pech Maho lead tablet (p. 86).[7] But it is with the more variegated practices that interest lies. One of the earliest Greek inscriptions comes characteristically from Pithecusae; a Rhodian cup carries the following inscription in verse: 'Nestor's cup is good to drink from; but he who drinks from this cup, forthwith him will seize desire of fair-garlanded Aphrodite'.[8] The inscription alludes to the famous description of Nestor's cup in the *Iliad*,[9] as well as being evidence of the use of writing to record verses or poetry in a sympotic context.[10] The fact that so many of the earliest Greek inscriptions are in verse has even prompted scholars to argue that the adaptation of the Phoenician alphabet was motivated by poetry, and in particular by the wish to record the Homeric epics.[11]

What is certainly the case is that the use of writing to record verses, or to allude to a sympotic context on imperishable materials, was a Greek innovation; there are hardly any comparable examples in contemporary or subsequent Phoenician, Aramaic or Hebrew inscriptions. But the practice was clearly adopted by the non-Greek cultures of Italy and Sicily; a sixth-century Attic cylix cup from Sicilian Morgantina carries the Sicel inscription 'pibe' (drink), clearly alluding to the sympotic context; other Italic inscriptions are in verse.[12] While most non-Greek cultures of Asia Minor adopted their alphabet from the Greeks, the practice of inscribing verses is largely absent from them. It is only in Lydian that one finds some inscriptions in verse; it is remarkable that the verses attested in Lycian inscriptions are in Greek rather than Lycian.[13] What implications does this have for the production and communication of poetry?

---

[6] de Hoz 2010.   [7] See also Dana 2007.   [8] *SEG* XIV, 604; Dubois 1995: 22–8.
[9] 11.632–7.   [10] Lane Fox 2008: 157–8.   [11] Powell 1991.   [12] Watkins 1995.
[13] Eichner 1993.

The recording of communal decisions in public inscriptions in imperishable materials for public display was another Greek innovation, as the thousands of Greek decrees demonstrate.[14] When Carian communities came to adopt the practice during the fourth century, they had to decide whether to adopt the Greek language of the practice as well or to innovate by using their own language and script. While a few of the communal inscriptions are in Carian, the majority are in Greek, together with some fascinating bilinguals we shall examine below (pp. 256–9).

6.1.2 Coinage

Since the beginnings of history the exchange of goods has been based on barter or the use of certain goods as media of exchange. In the Near East metals, and in particular silver, had already come to play the role of money in the third millennium in the form of metal ingots that would be cut and weighed to pay for the equivalent commodities. Silver as bullion was used by highly complex Near Eastern economies for hundreds of years, and in fact continued to be used even after the invention of coinage.[15] Around 600 in western Asia Minor there emerged the first forms of coinage: pieces of metal of the same weight, stamped with an image to guarantee their weight, purity and acceptance as money. The first coins were struck from electrum, a natural alloy of gold and silver, which is quite common in the region. Traditionally, the invention of coinage is attributed to the kings of Lydia and was quickly adopted by the Greek poleis of Asia Minor.[16] Around 550 the first coins in silver and in gold emerged, traditionally attributed to King Croesus of Lydia, although a significant number of these coins were minted by the Persian kings that succeeded Croesus; it is even possible that they minted all of these series.[17] The Persians continued the practice of minting, but only in the western part of their empire, where the use of coins had become common; the gold coins depicting an image of the Persian king as an archer (darics) became an international coinage highly popular in Greece and the rest of the eastern Mediterranean, until replaced by the gold coins of Philip of Macedon.[18] The new idea of striking silver coins was spread quickly by the networks of communication and exchange over the whole Mediterranean; it was instantly adopted in Asia Minor by the Greek poleis and by the Carians and Lycians; within a short period of time it appeared in mainland Greece, southern Italy and Sicily, Thrace and Macedonia, and

[14] Rhodes and Lewis 1997.   [15] le Rider 2001: 1–39.   [16] le Rider 2001: 41–100.
[17] le Rider 2001: 101–21.   [18] Carradice 1987b; *L'Or perse.*

Figure 26 Silver tetradrachm of the satrap Mazakes imitating an Athenian 'owl', fourth century BCE.

around the Black Sea. During the fifth century coinage was gradually adopted in Cilicia and Phoenicia, and later on by Carthage and the Phoenician communities in Sicily, as well as non-Greek communities in southern Italy.[19]

Coinage provides an excellent link between identity, power and circulation. It is obviously evidence of the circulation of goods in the ancient Mediterranean, and of the complexity and interconnectedness of Greek and non-Greek economic activities. On the one hand, one of the most characteristic illustrations of the wide circulation of Athenian coins all over the Mediterranean world is the creation of imitation coins in various areas of the eastern Mediterranean, such as Gaza or Egypt, where we even have imitations of Athenian 'owls' with a Demotic legend bearing the name of Artaxerxes III, the penultimate Persian king (see Figure 26).[20] On the opposite side, it has long been known that the Greek *apoikiai* in Sicily minted coins not only of 1/6th of a drachma (obols), but also coins of 1/5th. These were coins which were equivalent to a *litra*, a native Sicilian weight measure based on the use of bronze as a means of circulation; clearly, exchange with native communities was important enough to require the creation of such subdivisions.[21]

But coinage was not merely a technology to ease circulation, for early on coins became a medium for displaying communal identity.[22] The use of legends with the name of the community, images with puns on the name of

[19] Kraay 1976.   [20] Buttrey 1982; Mildenberg 2000.   [21] Kraay 1976: 204–38.
[22] Skinner 2010.

the community,[23] or images depicting the cults, myths or products of these communities was a display strategy that could be ignored by non-Greek issuers or adopted in manifold ways. Some non-Greek communities used legends in the Greek language to inscribe their identity, as was the case with the various sixth-century Thracian issues;[24] others used their local writing systems and languages to display their identity proudly, for example, the city of Segesta in western Sicily employing inscriptions in its Elymian language;[25] some communities alternated, sometimes using legends in their local script and language and others in Greek, like the Lucanians;[26] finally, others used a range of international scripts and languages, as in the use of Aramaic alongside Greek legends in Cilicia.[27] Some non-Greek coins merely copied the standard iconography of the Greek coins which circulated widely in their respective area, like the coins of Campanian communities which copied the coinage of Neapolis;[28] others used elements of Greek iconography in order to construct their own local visual imagery, as on the coins of various Thracian tribes.[29] Others adopted the concept of the coin as a visual display of identity, but used non-Greek iconographic traditions to achieve this aim; Phoenician coinage is an example of this practice.[30] Needless to say, a complex mixture of different traditions could also be the case, and we will have the opportunity to examine below the fascinating example of Cilician coins (pp. 268–70).

6.1.3 Monumentality

Before 700 monumental buildings and monumental sculpture in stone were largely unknown in Greece and most areas of the Mediterranean world. Although potters could create truly monumental funerary vases, artisans could create only small statuettes a few centimetres long, while buildings were small and made of perishable materials. As a result, wealth, power and ideology were expressed primarily through small, portable objects, like the cup of Nestor and the bronze bowls described in Homer and discovered by archaeologists. It was the expansion of networks that took place around that time that brought Greeks into a Mediterranean area with a long tradition in monumental sculpture and architecture: Egypt. We have already examined the presence of Greek and Carian mercenaries (pp. 43–4) and the creation of Naucratis during the seventh century (pp. 97–100); it was precisely in the

---

[23] For example, the coins of Selinous have depictions of parsley, the Greek word for which is *selinon*.

[24] Picard 2000.   [25] Kraay 1976: 220.   [26] Stazio 1987: 172.   [27] Casabonne 2004.

[28] Kraay 1976: 200; Rutter 1979.   [29] Kraay 1976: 139–41.   [30] Jigoulov 2010: 71–112.

Figure 27(a) Egyptian statue, seventh century BCE.

same century that stone temples and monumental statues in stone (the *kouroi*) emerged in the Greek world.[31]

Egypt provided Greek artisans and artists with the technologies necessary in order to work hard stone like marble and to construct monumental buildings with heavy materials. But it also provided them with the idea of using hard stone and monumental size in order to express wealth, power and ideology in a permanent and publicly visible manner.[32] The fluting and proportion of Egyptian columns and the creation of seas of columns around important buildings provided models for the Doric columns and the monumental temples that emerged in Ionia, an area with strong links to Egypt as we have seen (p. 180).[33] The similarities between the *kouroi* and Egyptian statues are obvious: they both have the left foot forward and the hands down at the side; but Egyptian statues normally wear kilts, whereas *kouroi* are nude, and they have a back rest and an unfinished screen between the legs,

[31] Whitley 2001: 156–64, 213–30.   [32] Tanner 2003.   [33] Bietak 2001.

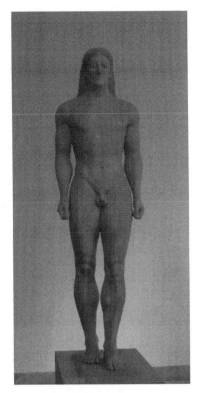

Figure 27(b) Kouros of Croesus, Attica, sixth century BCE.

whereas *kouroi* are fully carved and free-standing (see Figure 27).[34] Even more, scholars have argued that some Greek sculptors made use of the Egyptian canon in the design of *kouroi*. The Egyptian canon aimed to achieve consistency in the proportions of the sculpted human body by using a grid divided into twenty-one and a quarter squares: the eyes, for example, were always represented in the twenty-first square, while the knees were in the seventh.[35]

We have the rare opportunity to be able to link these processes and the world of networks with the name of a specific individual. We are told that Rhoecus was the architect of the dipteral temple of Hera on Samos, one of the earliest monumental temples of Ionia. Rhoecus also built a monumental stepped altar for the Heraeum, the earliest of its kind in the Aegean. Stepped altars had a long pedigree in Egypt, and it is no accident that the earliest

[34] Tanner 2003: 132.   [35] Guralnick 1978, 1985, 1996; cf. Carter and Steinberg 2010.

known Greek stepped altar has been found in the sanctuary of Aphrodite in Naucratis. We are told that Rhoecus visited Egypt in order to study the Egyptian sculptural canon, and a dedication of a bowl to Aphrodite by a Rhoecus that has been found in Naucratis is convincingly attributed to the architect.[36] According to the historian Diodorus, Telecles and Theodorus, the two sons of Rhoecus, created a statue (*xoanon*) of Apollo Pythios, one half of which was constructed by Telecles at Samos, while the other half was constructed by Theodorus at Ephesus; when the two halves were joined together, they made a perfect match, because they were both designed on the basis of the Egyptian canon.[37]

Greek sculpture and Greek temples came to look very different from those of Egypt; but as Jeremy Tanner has put it:

> it was Egyptian techniques of design which permitted archaic Greek sculptors to materially encode the culturally specific 'Greek' iconographic meanings which those statues embodied, and also to mobilize those meanings to greatest effect through the impressive monumentality of the images in which they were instantiated.[38]

In the course of the archaic and classical periods, the new monumental sculpture and temples were further globalised across the Mediterranean world through the agency of Greek artists and artisans, and glocalised in a variety of different ways by non-Greek communities. One of the best preserved Greek temples is the building in the form of a Doric temple at Segesta, an Elymian non-Greek community in the far west of Sicily (see Figure 11).[39] From the nearby Phoenician colony of Motya comes a brilliant Greek-style marble statue of a charioteer clothed in a rather unusual high-belted costume (see Figure 28).[40] We have already examined the different glocalisation of Greek-style temples and sculpture in Etruscan *emporia* such as Gravisca and Pyrgi (pp. 94–7), and we shall shortly examine the equivalent phenomena on the opposite coast of the Mediterranean, in the Persian-ruled Levant and Asia Minor.

We have explored a range of ideas and technologies in order to trace the processes of globalisation across the Mediterranean; before examining some of the outcomes of these processes in detail, however, it is essential to explore the patterns of glocalisation: in what ways did Mediterranean communities glocalise the traditions and practices spread by the processes of globalisation?

---

[36] Davis 1981; Tanner 2003: 131.   [37] 1.98.5–9.   [38] Tanner 2003: 139.   [39] Mertens 1984.
[40] Smith 2007: 130–6.

Figure 28 Charioteer statue, Motya, mid-fifth century BCE.

6.2 Patterns of glocalisation

Glocalisation can take a wide variety of forms. The most obvious one is the complete adoption of a foreign cultural practice in its original form. Non-Greek communities could adopt the form of the Greek temple for their own sanctuaries or the practice of public inscriptions recording the decisions of the community. Sometimes non-Greek communities would adopt the practice of public inscription along with the Greek language in which the Greek practice was expressed, while on other occasions they would adopt the practice, but use their own scripts and languages for recording the decisions. We shall see below how Carian and Lycian communities followed both strategies in glocalising this Greek practice (pp. 256–64).

A second pattern of glocalising strategies concerns the modification of globalised cultural practices in order to suit the tastes or needs of the glocalising communities. One variety of this strategy is the glocalisation of a cultural practice through its application in a novel context or for novel ends. It was possible to adopt the form of the Greek temple to construct the temples of a non-Greek community, as the Carians did; but it was also possible to adopt the architectural form of the Greek temple for different kinds of monument, more important to the glocalising culture. We shall see how the Lycians glocalised the architecture of the Greek temple for their grave monuments (pp. 264–6).

Another variant is the creation of cultural forms and codes which are constructed in such a way that they are meaningful and can be interpreted at the same time by people from different cultural backgrounds.[41] The Black Sea offers some fascinating examples of this strategy. Since the emergence of Greek *apoikiai* in the area during the seventh century, Greek artisans had created objects in the Greek styles and forms they brought over from their homelands or acquired through continuous participation in the world of networks. These objects were, of course, consumed by the Greek inhabitants of the *apoikiai*, but a significant proportion of them was acquired and consumed by the Scythians and the other non-Greek communities with which the Greeks of the Black Sea interacted. But starting from the fourth century onwards we observe a novel phenomenon: the creation of objects in accordance with the dictates of Greek artistic style, but with depictions of Scythian themes and customs.[42] Typical objects of this art are a golden pectoral from Tostaya Mogila depicting scenes from Scythian nomadic life,[43] a golden comb from Solokha depicting a Scythian rider fighting against two Scythians on foot (see Figure 14),[44] a silver vessel from Solokha depicting Scythians hunting a lion[45] and a silver amphora from Chertomlyk showing Scythians controlling horses.[46] In other words, Greek and/or Scythian artists used the conventions of Greek art in order to create an art for/about the Scythians.

A third broad pattern of glocalising strategies involves the intermingling of two or more cultural traditions. At one extreme, one can find the juxtaposition of different cultural traditions in the same objects and monuments. We have already referred above to the 'bilingual' stelae from Memphis (pp. 129–30); despite the proficiency of the artists who created these stelae in both Greek and Egyptian artistic traditions, the two styles and iconographies remain side by side without any real attempt at intermixture (see Figure 16). At the other extreme is hybridity: the creation of new cultural forms which fuse elements from different cultural traditions in a

---

[41] Fehr 1997; Ashton 2001; Stephens 2003; see also Barash 1996.

[42] Rostovtzeff 1922: 101–12; Boardman 1994: 192–217; Jacobson 1995; Fless and Treister 2005; Daumas 2009.

[43] Jacobson 1995: 115–19.   [44] Jacobson 1995: 158–62.   [45] Jacobson 1995: 196–200.

[46] Jacobson 1995: 209–13.

new original mix. The Creole languages of the New World, which combine elements of syntax, grammar and vocabulary from both European and African languages into a new linguistic system, are a characteristic example of hybridity. We shall see below how Phoenician artists mixed Egyptian and Greek styles and iconographies (pp. 271–2), how Lycian art expressed a hybrid interaction of Greek, Persian and Egyptian elements (pp. 264–7), and how Cilician coinage glocalised Greek, Persian, Aramaic and Babylonian iconographies and scripts (pp. 268–70).

It is possible to observe the full range of these patterns in the glocalisation of Greek culture in Etruria. What is particularly important in the Etruscan case is our ability to observe that glocalisation was a two-faced process; we can observe not only how Greek artists and professionals glocalised Greek culture for the Etruscans, but also how the Etruscans glocalised Greek culture on their own account. The Etruscans developed a voracious appetite for Greek pottery, and the overwhelming proportion of known Athenian pottery of the sixth and fifth centuries has been found in Etruscan cemeteries, rather than in Athens or Greece.[47] One side-effect of this large-scale export of Athenian vases to Etruria is that certain Athenian potters decided to create products specifically targeting the Etruscan market. The most famous example is the sixth-century workshop of Nicosthenes, 96 per cent of whose products have been found in Etruria,[48] and which made pots that imitated the shapes of native Etruscan bucchero pottery, even to the extent of creating different shapes for different markets in Etruria.[49]

Even more interesting from our point of view is the case of another sixth-century workshop known as the 'Perizoma group'. This workshop innovated by adapting the iconography of its vases in a way that could be meaningful and appealing to the Etruscans who bought its products. Thus, the typical scenes with Greek athletes were adapted by depicting the athletes wearing loin-cloths, something uncommon for Greek athletes who exercised naked, but common in Etruscan depictions, like those in the Tomba delle Olimpiadi in Tarquinia (see Figure 29). Even more striking, the typical rowdy scenes of a Greek symposion, which depict females only as entertainers or prostitutes, are adapted through the depiction of respectable and clothed women, as was common in Etruscan symposia.[50] The scenes illustrated on the vases of the Perizoma group are typical of the Greek artistic repertoire and are depicted in typical Greek style; we can hardly describe these images as hybrid. But these images are adapted in order to

---

[47] Spivey 1991; Osborne 2001.   [48] Osborne 1996a: 31.   [49] Tosto 1999.   [50] Shapiro 2000.

Figure 29 Athenian black-figure stamnos by the Michigan Painter, *c.* 520–500 BCE.

'see them double', to make them meaningful and appealing to a non-Greek audience.

If Athenian potters show evidence primarily for the glocalising adaptation of cultural practices, Etruscan artists employed the full range of glocalising strategies. They could resort to the wholesale adoption of Greek cultural practices and forms. A fascinating example in which we come face to face with direct adoption concerns the relationship between an Athenian cup found in Vulci in Etruria and an Etruscan cup of almost exact size and shape (see Figure 30). The Etruscan cup copies the two scenes with satyrs depicted on the Athenian cup, but omits one figure from each of the two scenes depicted on the Athenian cup. We can clearly observe in this example how an Athenian cup imported to Etruria was copied by an Etruscan artist in both iconography and style.[51]

This example opens the wider topic of the Etruscan glocalisation of Greek mythology and the iconography developed for depicting Greek deities.[52]

[51] Plaoutine 1937.   [52] de Grummond 2006.

Figure 30(a) Etruscan red-figure cup, fifth century BCE.

Figure 30(b) Athenian red-figure cup by the Oedipus Painter, *c.* 500–450 BCE.

Figure 31 Etruscan mirror, Atri, *c.* 500–475 BCE.

Etruscan bronze mirrors were particularly popular media for the depiction of myth. We can find faithful copies of Greek myths as depicted on Greek media like Athenian vases, but we can also find depictions of Etruscan myths within which Greek heroes and deities have been incorporated. A nice example is a fifth-century mirror depicting Heracles abducting a female figure called Mlacuch, both identified by inscriptions; some Etruscan myth stands behind the depiction, but it is telling that a Greek hero plays a key role within it (see Figure 31).[53] A final example of the hybrid pattern of glocalisation is an early fifth-century carnelian scarab that depicts a falling man holding shield and spear. He is identified by an Etruscan inscription as Capaneus, one of the Seven against Thebes, who was struck by Zeus' thunderbolt. This object is a glocalised hybrid of Egyptian, Greek and Etruscan elements: the scarab is a typically Egyptian object, globalised across the Mediterranean since the archaic period; but the depicted myth is Greek, while the inscription and the design of the scarab are Etruscan.[54]

---

[53] van der Meer 1995: 43–6.   [54] Richter 1948.

6.3 Currents of globalisation

In order to understand the globalisation of Greek culture in the archaic and classical periods we have to situate it among other currents of globalisation. The process of globalisation put into motion by the great empires, the networks moving goods, ideas and technologies, the diasporas created by mobility and migration, and the reformulations of identities and communities did not globalise only elements of Greek culture; it also globalised aspects of other cultures which must be taken into account.[55] It is beyond the limits of this book to give a detailed account of non-Greek currents of globalisation. For our purposes here a look at four other currents will be sufficient to make the point: the Egyptian, the Phoenician, the Aramaic and the Persian. These currents had different contents and intensities and, what is most important, were put into motion by different actors and processes.

During the archaic and classical periods the Egyptian current moved through objects which were overwhelmingly carried by non-Egyptians. In contrast to the situation in the Hellenistic period, there is little evidence for the presence of Egyptians outside Egypt during the archaic and classical periods.[56] We have encountered an Egyptian community at Athens building a temple to Isis in the late fourth century (p. 102), but the presence of this community in Athens is barely visible, and there is very little evidence of other such communities in the rest of the Greek world and the wider Mediterranean world. We also find hardly any evidence for the establishment of Egyptian-style cults or the creation of Egyptian-style buildings and monuments, such as we shall encounter in the Hellenistic period (pp. 307–9). The Greek glocalisation of Egyptian technologies in temple-building or sculpture depended on Greek presence in Egypt, not on Egyptian presence in Greece; the implications of this for the way in which Egyptian culture was glocalised are evident. It was primarily through the circulation of portable objects, such as scarabs, statuettes and vases made from faience and alabaster, that Egyptian culture was globalised during these periods. Thousands of these objects have been found in the Near East, in Greece, and in Italy and the western Mediterranean.[57] The Greeks and other people across the Mediterranean created their own glocalised versions of these objects; but it is primarily the Phoenicians, whose proximity to Egypt led to close political, economic and cultural relations, who were the main actors in glocalising

---

[55] For the comparative case of Indian, Muslim, Chinese and other currents in southeast Asia between 1000–1800 CE, see Gunn 2011.

[56] Lloyd 2007; but see Abdi 2002: 138–9.   [57] Hölbl 1979, 1986; Skon-Jedele 1994.

Figure 32 Phoenician bronze bowl, Amathous, eighth century BCE.

Egyptian culture and spreading its globalisation across the Mediterranean.[58] The famous Phoenician metal bowls, found across the Mediterranean and carrying narrative scenes in Egyptian-style iconographies, are a particularly telling example (see Figure 32).[59]

This brings us to the Phoenician current of globalisation, which was formulated in contexts very similar to those of Greek globalisation. Like the Greeks, the Phoenicians were deeply shaped by their interaction with the world of empires, in particular those of Egypt, Assyria and Persia, under whose domination they spent almost all of their historical existence.[60] They were key players in the networks of mobility that crossed the Mediterranean, and they had their own traditions in the creation of *apoikiai* in the western Mediterranean.[61] We have already examined the complex triangulations between Greeks, Phoenicians and Etruscans (p. 105), and equally fascinating are the interconnections between Phoenicians, Greeks and Iberians in Spain.[62] The obvious example of Phoenician globalisation is script and language; we have already examined how Greeks and other Mediterranean cultures glocalised the Phoenician alphabet,[63] but equally interesting is the story of the Phoenician language. In Cilicia, during the

[58] See, e.g., Lembke 2004.   [59] Markoe 1985.   [60] Markoe 2000; Moscati 2001; Jigoulov 2010.
[61] Aubet 2001.   [62] Dietler and López-Ruiz 2009.   [63] Baurain *et al.* 1991; Sanders 2009.

eighth and seventh centuries, local rulers employed the Phoenician language as a means of communication, normally alongside their native Luwian language, in bilingual public inscriptions or on seals. Given that the Phoenicians did not have any political influence in this area, it was their presence as traders, professionals and intellectuals which led to the glocalisation of their language and script by Cilician rulers.[64]

This provides a contrast with Aramaic globalisation. The Aramaeans were originally desert nomads who, in the course of the first millennium, came to occupy a large part of Syria, where they created their own principalities.[65] They developed their own cultural traditions in close interaction with the Phoenicians, whose alphabet they adapted for their own Semitic language. From the ninth century onwards the Aramaean states were gradually conquered by Assyria, which employed a policy of mass forced migrations of Aramaean populations to Assyria.[66] Due to this policy, Assyria acquired a very large Aramaean population, leading to the Assyrian adoption of the Aramaic language and alphabetic script alongside its own Assyrian language in cuneiform. Consequently, the expansion of the Assyrian Empire led to the expansion of the Aramaic language and script over a very extensive area of the Near East.[67] When the Persians created their own empire, they adopted Aramaic as one of the major languages of official communication. As a result of this, documents in the Aramaic language can be found in areas from Asia Minor through Egypt to Afghanistan, where it was primarily used as a global lingua franca, as well as in areas like Syria and Mesopotamia, where it was the primary language of the population.[68] There also developed a global Aramaic literature, exemplified by the famous Ahiqar text attested in the Jewish military colony in Egyptian Elephantine (pp. 152–3).[69] In contrast to the multifaceted Phoenician-style globalisation, the globalisation of Aramaic and its presence in areas like Lycia or Lydia was primarily the result of its role in the world of empires. This leads on to Persia and imperial globalisation, which demands a discussion of its own.

6.4 Imperial globalisation

The Egyptian and Phoenician currents of globalisation moved through the mobility of goods, people and ideas that characterised the decentralised

---

[64] Röllig 1992; Salmeri 2004: 189–90. [65] Lipiński 2000; Daviau *et al.* 2001. [66] Oded 1979.
[67] Millard 1983. [68] Greenfield 1985. [69] Kottsieper 2009.

world of networks. A very different form of globalisation was the result of the world of empires: we have examined in Chapter 2 the complex multi-ethnic structures of power created by the Persian Empire, the creation of an imperial diaspora and the large-scale employment of a multicultural and multilingual force of soldiers, administrators, entertainers and artisans (pp. 47–52). These imperial structures and the processes put into motion by the world of empires created a particular form of globalisation that we can call imperial globalisation.[70] In order to understand the particularity of imperial globalisation in the archaic and classical periods, it is essential to look at two different examples from other periods.[71]

The first time the eastern Mediterranean and the Near East had experienced an imperial world-system and its attendant globalisation was between 1500–1200. During this period there emerged a concerted system of inter-linked great powers, which included Assyria, Babylonia and Elam in Mesopotamia, the state of Mitanni in Syria, the Hittites in Asia Minor and the pharaonic state that ruled Egypt and a significant part of the Levantine coast.[72] This interlinked system of great powers is revealed to us through the archives of international diplomacy that have been discovered in the Egyptian capital of Amarna.[73] These archives provide a first significant testimony of imperial globalisation. From western Iran to Cyprus and Egypt people conducted their international diplomacy using a simplified form of the Babylonian language in its cuneiform script; the Levantine vassal states of Egypt did not communicate with their overlord in their native tongues or in Egyptian, but in Babylonian cuneiform.[74]

This international system of communication depended on the existence of scribes skilled in the international language and script, as well as the various local ones. The complexity of this system of communication on many levels is no better illustrated than through the archives of the city of Ugarit in northern Syria, where documents have been found in Sumerian, Babylonian, Hittite and Hurrian written in syllabic cuneiform, Hurrian and indigenous Ugaritic written in alphabetic cuneiform, and a few texts in the still undeciphered Cypro-Minoan syllabic script.[75] The education of these scribes in the international cuneiform system depended on learning and memorising some key texts of the cuneiform canon; this led to an international circulation of canonical Babylonian texts like the epic of Gilgamesh, their translation into other languages and scripts, and their glocalising

---

[70] For the concept of imperial globalisation, see Magee and Thompson 2010.

[71] For a comparative perspective on imperial repertoires, see Burbank and Cooper 2010.

[72] Liverani 2001; van de Mieroop 2007.   [73] Moran 1992; Bryce 2003.

[74] van de Mieroop 2007: 22.   [75] van de Mieroop 2007: 193.

adoption and adaptation in local literatures by, for example, the Hittites or the Levantines.[76] We can see the simultaneous development of two literary traditions: an international one in Babylonian and various local ones in native languages and/or scripts.[77]

Globalisation and glocalisation also affected material culture, but in rather different ways. We can again distinguish between, on the one hand, various local styles, which were based on a creative mixture between native artistic traditions and the glocalisation of elements taken from other traditions, and, on the other, an emergent 'international style', which was used for various precious objects consumed by the different courts and elites. But in contrast to language, literature and intellectual culture, where the cuneiform script and Babylonian literature provided the basis for a global *koine*, in the case of material culture no single artistic tradition functioned as a model. The artists who created precious objects in the 'international style' adopted and adapted elements from various artistic traditions to create a hybrid novel style.[78]

A very different example of imperial globalisation can be seen in the case of the Roman Empire.[79] The variety of ways in which the Roman Empire influenced the material, social and intellectual life of the societies that came under its control have traditionally been examined under the label of Romanisation. The last two decades have witnessed a significant debate on the nature of Romanisation. Scholars have rightly questioned the interpretation of Romanisation as a process of civilising the uncouth Barbarians; they have questioned whether Romanisation can be seen as a single process rather than as a variety of distinct if related processes; they have challenged the standard top-down perspective in which Rome imposed its culture on its Barbarian subjects, and they have examined the ways in which native societies adopted and adapted elements of Roman culture for their own aims.[80] There is also little doubt that Romanisation was not a unidirectional process in which the imperial centre transformed the provinces, but a complex interaction which involved the simultaneous and interactive transformation of both centre and periphery.[81]

What is important from our point of view is the existence of a cultural and social package along with institutionalised practices which enabled the multifaceted process that modern scholars call Romanisation. This Roman cultural and social package consisted of various elements, of which we can focus on two. On the one hand, there is the model of the city, with its

---

[76] Carr 2005: 47–61.   [77] van de Mieroop 2007: 203.   [78] Feldman 2005.   [79] Woolf 2012.
[80] Millett 1990; Woolf 1998; Mattingly 2011.   [81] Wallace-Hadrill 2008: 441–54.

standardised public buildings and services (forum, basilica, baths), and its government by annually elected magistrates and a council selected on the basis of wealth.[82] On the other hand, we can see cultural practices for expressing power, wealth and success, both for individuals and for communities. This involved the monumentalisation of space (villas, cemeteries, public buildings), the systematic use of inscriptions for public display (the epigraphic habit), the competitive use of wealth for public purposes (evergetism), a canonical system of public and private honours, a classical education, and attitudes towards consumption and the body. The emergence and formulation of this set of cultural and social practices around the time of Augustus were crucial for what Richard Hingley has described as 'globalising Roman culture'.[83] Equally important as this social and cultural package was the existence of institutionalised practices, such as the expansion of Roman citizenship, the provincial assemblies and the imperial cult, which allowed the emergence of an imperial Roman identity on top of the various local and regional ones.[84] The coins of the cities of Asia Minor, which display the heads of Roman emperors on one side and various symbols of local identity on the other, are an excellent illustration of this Roman imperial identity.[85]

The Persian imperial system was closer to that of Rome than it was to the second-millennium Near Eastern imperial system, in that a vast interlinked area was ruled by a single imperial power, rather than by a system of interacting states. Nevertheless, the form of imperial globalisation that we can link to the Persian Empire is far closer to that of the second-millennium empires than it is to that of Rome.[86] Some aspects of Persian culture became globalised as a result of the Persian Empire; although, as we shall see, by and large the Persian Empire created a context in which non-Persian currents of globalisation were widely glocalised within the Empire.[87] Scholars might disagree on how to define Romanisation; but no one has ever debated Persianisation, because there was simply no such thing.[88] There was no canonical set of social and cultural practices adopted, adapted and glocalised by the different subject societies within the Persian Empire; nor can we find evidence of institutionalised practices which created an imperial Persian identity in parallel with the various local ones.[89] We have already mentioned how the Persian Empire, instead of using Persian as its means of

---

[82] Laurence *et al.* 2011.   [83] Hingley 2005: 72–90; Wallace-Hadrill 2008.
[84] Price 1984; Ando 2000, 2010.   [85] Butcher 1988.
[86] For a modern comparative perspective, see Subrahmanyam 2006.
[87] Delemen 2007; Ivantchik and Licheli 2007; Nieling and Rehm 2010.   [88] Tuplin 2010.
[89] Wiesehöfer 1996: 56–9.

communication, as the later Hellenistic empires would do with Greek, globalised widely the Aramaic language and script. The use of Aramaic in classical Asia Minor would have been unthinkable without the Persian Empire; but it is telling that it is Aramaic and not Persian that was globalised by the Persian Empire.[90]

The genius of the Persian Empire, and the explanation for its success, lay in its ability to use local power structures and cultural practices in order to support Persian interests; the Persians had the ability to present their empire in local terms instead of imposing a Persian model on subject communities.[91] This is best illustrated through the example of Cyrus the Great, the creator of the Persian Empire. The so-called Cyrus cylinder is a typical Babylonian cuneiform document presenting Cyrus as restoring legitimate Babylonian kingship and cultural practices.[92] The Bible, for its part, presents Cyrus as the king who acted as an instrument of the divine will of the Jewish God in ending the Babylonian captivity and allowing the Jews to return to Judaea.[93] Thus, in both Babylonia and Judaea Cyrus had successfully inscribed Persian power within local idioms and cultural practices.

A different example is the case of Persian art; it was a quintessentially court art, an iconographic and ideological programme primarily displayed in the palaces and tombs of the Persian kings, and whose primary audience were the imperial courts and their visitors.[94] There seems to have been very little effort to expand the visual presence of Persian kings in the imperial provinces through such means as monumental epigraphy, sculpture or architecture, as the Assyrian kings did through their reliefs and inscriptions, and the Roman emperors through inscriptions, sculpture and architecture.[95] A rare exception is the famous relief depicting Dareius I and his defeated opponents with its accompanying trilingual inscription on the Behistun rock in Media; copies of the inscription have been found in Babylon and among the Jewish military colony in Egyptian Elephantine.[96] Another case of local elites within the Persian Empire glocalising elements from Persian court culture is the fortress of Meydancıkkale in mountainous Cilicia. One of the fragmentary Aramaic inscriptions found in the fortress mentions Persian kings; but it is the relief panels which imitate the Persepolis reliefs with processions of subjects bringing tribute, which

---

[90] For the similar role of Persian in the Mughal Empire in India, see Alam 1998.
[91] Root 1991.   [92] Translated in Kuhrt 2007: 70–4.   [93] Kuhrt 2007: 82–5.   [94] Root 1979.
[95] Jacobs 1987: 15–23.   [96] Translated and illustrated in Kuhrt 2007: 141–58.

provide a unique example of the glocalisation of Persian court iconography in monumental sculpture.[97]

This Persian peculiarity had a double consequence. On the one hand, it meant that Persian imperial iconography and ideology were primarily communicated through small portable objects, such as coins and seals, and, accordingly, it was more often glocalised in such media than in monumental art. One such example is the case of pyramidal stamp seals, which were common in Mesopotamian culture for centuries and which normally depicted cultic scenes. But from the sixth century onwards such seals start to spread outside Mesopotamia and to depict iconographic themes outside the Mesopotamian repertoire. Some of these seals carry images which are standard in Persian imperial iconography, such as the royal hero killing a lion or Persian-style sphinxes; but a few of these also carry Lydian inscriptions, showing that they were created by Lydian artists probably at the satrapal capital of Sardis. The Persian Empire enabled the globalisation of a Mesopotamian seal form and of Persian iconography, which was glocalised by Lydian artists among others.[98]

On the other hand, elites and communities within the Persian Empire did not have immediate and permanent access to an imperial art and ideology which was primarily expressed in the imperial courts; accordingly, their artistic programmes developed through glocalising a wide range of different cultural traditions and practices.[99] Among the communities of Asia Minor that were under Persian imperial rule there emerged a widely attested iconographic repertoire that was used primarily in funerary monuments and provided a means of expressing the self-perception and identity of the local elites who sponsored these monuments. The repertoire included themes based on the lifestyle of these elites, such as hunting, banqueting and fighting, as well as themes that stressed their power and majesty, such as sacrificial and audience scenes.[100] The style of these monuments could diverge widely, from the employment of local artistic styles to the adoption of Greek styles. Equally wide was the range of iconographic traditions which were glocalised in Persian-ruled Asia Minor. Depictions of city landscapes and city sieges, as, for example, they appear in the monuments of Lycia, glocalised the iconographic tradition of Assyrian palace reliefs depicting victorious campaigns of conquest, as well as a Greek artistic style for their depiction.[101] Audience scenes, depicting enthroned local dynasts and their

---

[97] Casabonne 2004: 151–65. For a possible reflex in the Nereid Monument, see Tuplin 2010: 165.
[98] Boardman 1970; Root 1998.   [99] Starr 1977.
[100] Fehr 1971; Gabelmann 1984; Fornasier 2001; Seyer 2007.   [101] Childs 1978.

subjects paying homage, could be influenced by the iconographic tradition of Persian imperial art to a greater or lesser extent.[102]

In order to understand the peculiar nature of imperial globalisation in the archaic and classical Mediterranean we can look in more detail at three satrapal capitals of the Persian Empire: Dascyleion, Sardis and Memphis. All three were already important before the Persian conquest: Sardis was the capital of the Lydian kingdom, and Dascyleion apparently one of its provincial centres, while Memphis was an ancient city that had functioned as capital of Egypt in many periods of its long history.

Dascyleion was situated next to Lake Dascylitis in a region known as Hellespontine Phrygia; it was close to the often unruly area of Mysia to the south and to Greek cities such as Cyzicus on the coast to the north. The satrapal capital hosted a multilingual and multicultural population. A significant part of its population were Phrygians, as attested by the inscriptions found:[103] a fifth-century Athenian bowl carries a Phrygian graffito; a marble block re-used in a grave carried a Phrygian inscription;[104] while a stele depicting a funerary banquet carried another Phrygian inscription for someone with the typically Anatolian name Manes.[105] This stele is part of a wider group, many examples of which have been found in Dascyleion and the surrounding area; they consist of a shaft, often more than three metres high, crowned by an anthemion and decorated with scenes depicting hunts, banquets or a funerary cortege.[106] Anthemion-crowned grave stelae have also been found on the Greek island of Samos and at Sardis; they were part of the artistic *koine* of coastal Asia Minor, which crossed ethnic and cultural boundaries. It is telling that, with the exception of the Manes stele with the Phrygian inscription, all other inscribed stelae carry inscriptions in Aramaic; these were clearly the gravestones of individuals who had come to Dascyleion as soldiers, professionals and bureaucrats serving the Persian administration. The inscriptions record west Semitic names that could have belonged to Jews, Aramaeans or Arabs, showing that these individuals had come to Dascyleion from very far away; particularly interesting is the stele for Elnaf, son of Ashay, which mentions the Babylonian deities Bel and Nabu (see Figure 33).[107] The presence of Greeks and Lydians alongside these other ethnic groups is attested by graffiti on both local and imported pottery.[108]

---

[102] Gabelmann 1984; Jacobs 1987.   [103] Bakır 1997.   [104] Bakır and Gusmani 1991.
[105] Gusmani and Polat 1999.   [106] Nollé 1992.   [107] Lemaire 2001.
[108] Bakır and Gusmani 1993.

Figure 33 Funerary stele of Elnaf, Dascyleion, fifth century BCE.

The material culture of Dascyleion gives ample evidence for its multicultural character.[109] Excavations have uncovered significant amounts of Athenian, Corinthian, Laconian, east Greek, Lydian and Phrygian pottery.[110] A monumental fifth-century building had a facade made out of Proconnesian marble, using Ionic column capitals and other decorative details of Ionic architectural style; the facade had at least one large window, a rare element in contemporary Greek architecture.[111] While the Persian satraps were obviously happy to employ Greek architects and builders for a Greek-style building whose function is unclear, there is also clear evidence for the importance of Persian culture in Dascyleion. Particularly interesting are the reliefs depicting Persian priests (*magi*) in a religious ceremony or in front of a building (see Figure 34):[112] in Dascyleion one could encounter worshippers of Persian, Babylonian and no doubt Phrygian, Lydian and Greek deities as well.

---

[109] Bakır 2001b.   [110] Tuna-Nörling 2001; Gürtekin-Demir 2002.   [111] Ateşlier 2001.
[112] Nollé 1992: 35–40, 93–6.

Figure 34 Relief with Persian *magi*, Dascyleion, fifth century BCE.

Sardis became the most important centre of the Persian administration in Asia Minor; unfortunately, the excavations of the city have not yet revealed the strata of the Persian period, and as a result our discussion will be dominated by epigraphic sources.[113] The inscriptions of the city open a fascinating window onto its multicultural character. The Lydian language obviously had a major role, but the presence of the satrapal court meant that Aramaic was widely used by both the imperial diaspora and the local population. A bilingual Lydian–Aramaic funerary inscription for a certain Manes is particularly interesting. This was a Lydian who chose to have his funerary monument inscribed in both the native tongue and the language of the imperial power.[114] The Aramaic text is dated in the tenth year of Artaxerxes, emphasising Aramaic's presence as the medium of imperial administration; no such reference is made in the Lydian text, which is dated in the month Bacchius, named after the Lydian equivalent of the

---

[113] For Persian Sardis, see Dusinberre 2003.
[114] *Gusmani*, 1; translated in Dusinberre 2003: 229, No. 9.

Greek god Bacchus (Dionysus). Equally interesting is the instruction that any violation of the grave would be punished by Artemis of Ephesus and Artemis of Coloe. There are multiple references to Artemis of Ephesus in other funerary inscriptions from Sardis, showing the important role played by the cult of a nearby Greek city, and we have seen how the Lydian king Croesus sponsored the construction of her famous temple in Ephesus (p. 43). Two other Lydian inscriptions record bequests by a priest with the Persian name Mitridastas, son of Mitratas.[115] The Carian immigrants in Sardis used their own script, as attested by many graffiti,[116] but particularly interesting is the use of Greek as a language of communication. A fourth-century Lydian–Greek bilingual records a dedication to Artemis by an individual with the Lydian name Nannas; his father's name is recorded as Bakivas in the Lydian inscription, but translated as Dionysicles in the Greek.[117] A Greek inscription re-inscribed in Roman times records the dedication of a statue to Zeus of Baradates by Droaphernes, the Persian sub-governor of Lydia; it is particularly notable that a Persian governor in Lydian Sardis would dedicate a statue bearing a Greek inscription.[118]

This ethnic *mélange* of a city like Sardis is illustrated by a fourth-century Greek inscription of Ephesus, towards the end of Persian rule.[119] There was a cultic connection between Ephesian Artemis and Sardis, and the inscription records the punishment of citizens of Sardis for a sacrilege committed against Ephesian sacred envoys. The inscription records forty-six Sardians, often along with their profession and their father's and grandfather's name. As expected, many of them have solely Lydian names (Moxus, son of Atas) or non-Greek names widely attested in Asia Minor (Daus); very common is a combination of Lydian and Greek names in the same family (Pytheus, son of Carous), but one also encounters individuals with purely Greek names (Musaeus, son of Heracleides), as well as people with Persian names like Mithradates and Sisines, while one individual is explicitly designated as a Carian (Pactyes, son of Manes).[120] The high number of individuals with Greek names in the satrapal capital of Sardis is telling, but needs to be situated alongside the Persian and Carian names.

[115] *Gusmani*, 23–4; translated in Dusinberre 2003: 230–1, Nos 13–14.
[116] Pedley 1974; Adiego 2007: 27–9.
[117] *Sardis*, 85; translated in Dusinberre 2003: 235, No. 49.
[118] *SEG* XXIX, 1205; translated in Kuhrt 2007: 865–7; Briant 1998c.
[119] *SEG* XXVII, 733; translated in Dusinberre 2003: 235–7, No. 54.   [120] Masson 1987.

Memphis was an ancient city that had long served as the capital of the pharaohs of Egypt; in fact, the very Greek name for the country (*Aigyptos*) derives from one of the Egyptian names of Memphis, 'Hekaptah', the 'palace of the spirit of Ptah', the chief deity of Memphis.[121] By the first millennium it had become a multiethnic city as a result of the processes of the world of empires: the Saite pharaohs had established the Greek and Carian mercenaries of their guard at Memphis, while the Persians made it the satrapal capital of Egypt and established their court and its functionaries there. The Greek community established at Memphis in Saite times continued its life in the new circumstances of the Persian Empire. The life of Greeks in the Egyptian milieu of Memphis is nicely captured in a fourth-century Greek curse tablet, recording a curse by a woman named Artemisia against her husband.[122] The name of the woman's father is Amasis, another example of Greeks named after Egyptian pharaohs (p. 134); the curse is not addressed to a Greek deity, but to Oserapis, the bull of Apis, whose cult was extremely important at Memphis and would expand to the whole Mediterranean from the Hellenistic period onwards (pp. 307–9).

Greek participation in Egyptian cults is also shown by a fifth-century plaque painted in Greek style and found in nearby Saqqara, which illustrates a procession related to the Apis cult.[123] While a stray fourth-century stele with an interesting metrical epitaph in Greek comes from Giza in the area of Memphis,[124] a whole cemetery of the Greek community has been found at nearby Abusir; one of them was buried together with a papyrus of Timotheus' *Persians*, a work presenting the Persians in a derogatory way, as we have seen (p. 192)![125] All foreign communities at Memphis had their own national shrines: the Greeks had a Hellenion, the Carians had one that was probably dedicated to Zeus of Labraunda, while the Phoenicians had a temple of Astarte.[126] In fact, a third-century papyrus records a petition to a Ptolemaic official to approve the grant of offerings to the Phoenician–Egyptian temple of Astarte, in the same way that offerings were given to the Carian and Greek cults at Memphis.[127]

But the best illustrations of Memphis' character are the funerary stelae and sarcophagi created for its multicultural population. These funerary monuments come in many forms. Some are typically Egyptian stelae, but erected for foreigners, as recorded in the hieroglyphic inscriptions or through inscriptions in the language of the respective foreigners; many

---

[121] Thompson 1988: 3.   [122] *UPZ*, I 1; translated in *Rowlandson*, 37.
[123] Illustrated in Boardman 1994: 162.   [124] Merkelbach 1970.   [125] Smoláriková 2000.
[126] Thompson 1988: 88–97.   [127] Thompson 1988: 90–1.

such stelae and sarcophagi were created for Aramaeans.[128] Sometimes the foreign ethnicity of the deceased is stressed by depicting the dead person with non-Egyptian facial characteristics; thus, a stele for a Persian follows Egyptian iconography, but presents the deceased in Persian guise.[129] Other stelae are 'bilingual': they normally have two or three registers which are executed in two different iconographic and artistic styles. Some registers are executed in an Egyptian style depicting traditional Egyptian iconographic themes related to death and the afterlife, such as the dead person in front of the enthroned Osiris, or scenes of homage to the Apis bull. Other scenes follow the Greek tradition of funerary iconography, depicting a *prothesis* scene (the laying out of the dead body with the accompanying dirge of mourners) familiar from Athenian Geometric monumental vases.[130] Most of these bilingual stelae were erected for Carians, often combining Egyptian hieroglyphs and Carian alphabetic inscriptions in a single sentence (see Figure 16).[131] But one also encounters a 'bilingual' stele with a Greek inscription recording the epitaph of a Greek woman,[132] or a stele with a Greek-style *prothesis* scene erected for a Persian dignitary.[133]

What should have become clear from our discussion of imperial globalisation in the archaic and classical Mediterranean is the complexity of the process. Instead of seeing the Persianisation of the communities and cultures under the Persian Empire, we observe processes of globalisation and glocalisation that drew on a variety of different currents and resulted in a variety of outcomes: Phrygian, Lydian, Greek and Aramaic inscriptions alongside Greek-style architecture and Mesopotamian and Persian deities at Dascyleion; Lydian, Carian, Aramaic and Greek inscriptions recording dedications and epitaphs mentioning Greek deities and Persian officials at Sardis; Greek, Carian and Phoenician temples alongside Greek reverence for Egyptian deities; and 'bilingual' Egyptian- and Greek-style stelae erected for Carians, Greeks and Persians at Memphis. What is particularly interesting from our point of view is the important role of Greek cultural practices in the processes of globalisation and glocalisation of communities under the Persian Empire. We shall now move on to examine in detail four such areas: Caria and Lycia in Asia Minor; Cilicia in between Asia Minor and the Levant; and Phoenicia in the Levant (Map 7).

---

[128] Porten and Gee 2001.   [129] Mathieson *et al.* 1995.   [130] Höckmann 2001; Labudek 2010.
[131] Masson 1978; Kammerzell 1993.   [132] Gallo and Masson 1993.   [133] Vittmann 2003: 148.

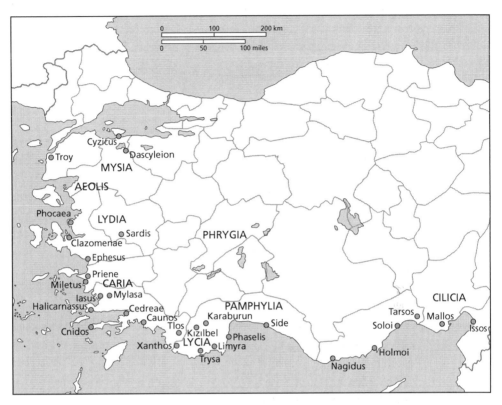

Map 7 Asia Minor

6.5 Greek-style glocalisation in the Persian Empire

Caria is an area that extends from the multiple gulfs and coasts of southwest Asia Minor to the mountainous inland regions, bordering Phrygia to the northeast, Lycia to the southeast and Lydia to the northwest. It was a multicultural area par excellence, including the Greek communities on the coast, such as Miletus, Halicarnassus and Cnidos, whose origins could go back as far as the second millennium;[134] the inland Carian communities; and a range of mixed Greco-Carian settlements. Greek authors distinguished between the Greek *apoikiai* in Caria and those settlements that were bilingual or described the inhabitants of a city like Cedreae as *mixo-barbaroi*.[135] But there was also heavy intermingling between Greeks and Carians even in the coastal Greek communities. Many Carian inscriptions

---

[134] Vanschoonwinkel 2006a, 2006b.   [135] Asheri 1983: 23.

have been found in the coastal city of Iasus,[136] while a fifth-century Greek inscription from Halicarnassus, recording the names of purchasers of confiscated properties, illustrates the mixed population of the city: the names of the inhabitants are almost equally divided between Carian and Greek, and it is very common for the same family to include both Greek and Carian names.[137]

Lycia was a mountainous coastal area bordering Caria to the east, Pamphylia to the west and Pisidia to the north. Although Greeks called Lycia after what seems to have been the name of the region during the Bronze Age, they were aware that the Lycians called themselves Tremilae (Trm̃mili). In contrast to Caria, there was very limited Greek presence in Lycia. The only Greek settlement was Phaselis, an *apoikia* of Rhodes on the east coast of Lycia, an area rather separated from the main centres in western and central Lycia.[138] The glocalisation of Greek culture was achieved primarily through the artisans, intellectuals, traders and artists that the networks of mobility brought to Lycia: people like the Athenian artist Theodorus, who constructed a monument at Tlos;[139] Symmachus from Achaean Pellana, a seer who composed a poem for a Lycian dynast; and the Dorian gymnastic trainer (*paidotribes*), who composed another poem for the same dynast.[140]

The difference in the ways in which Caria and Lycia glocalised Greek culture can already be seen in the ways they employed Greek language. There are numerous archaic and classical Greek inscriptions in Caria and Lycia; but local languages apart, non-Greek languages like Aramaic are effectively absent from Caria and have a limited presence in Lycia, compared to Dascyleion, Sardis or Cilicia.[141] Moreover, while Greek–Carian bilingual inscriptions are rare, Greek–Lycian bilinguals are comparatively common: there are bilingual epitaphs, dedications, public documents and even literary compositions/poems. Finally, the form of the Greek language attested in the two areas is rather different: the Greek used in Caria is largely based on the Ionic spoken in the influential Greek communities of Caria, such as Miletus and Halicarnassus, whereas the Greek of Lycia is a form of Attic Greek that would eventually become the Greek *koine* language from the Hellenistic period onwards. These differences can be explained by different kinds of Greek–non-Greek interaction. Caria was an area with both Greek and Carian communities and a significant mixed and bilingual

---

[136] Adiego 2007: 145–50.   [137] *SGDI*, 5727; Blümel 1993.
[138] Hansen and Nielsen 2004: 1140–1.   [139] *TL*, 25.   [140] *M-S*, 17.10.02–3.
[141] Lemaire and Lozachmeur 1996.

population; the Greek used by Carians was primarily that spoken by the overwhelmingly Ionian Greeks of Caria. Lycia did not have large Greek communities, and the Greek of Lycia was the form of *koine* largely based on the Attic dialect that was employed by the people that networks of mobility brought to Lycia.[142]

Caria and Lycia had a similar pattern of political and social organisation. In both areas there were a multitude of self-organised communities, whose activities are illustrated by the fact that they minted their own coins; but at the same time there existed dynastic families, which normally had as their basis a particular settlement, but, depending on the circumstances, could extend their power over other communities and dynasts.[143] In Lycia it was the dynasts from the city of Xanthos who long dominated Lycian affairs; but it was in Caria that a local dynastic family, the Hecatomnids of Mylasa, came to be appointed in the early fourth century as Persian satraps, and thus came to rule the whole of Caria and in the course of time Lycia as well.[144]

What is impressive about the Hecatomnids, a Carian dynasty ruling under Persian sovereignty, is the fact that their political and cultural programme was almost exclusively based on a glocalised form of Greek culture. This development took place decades before Alexander's conquest and the subsequent Hellenistic monarchies, and it shows therefore that the widespread globalisation of Greek culture was not merely the result of Greek rule over non-Greek communities from the Hellenistic period onwards, but a much more complex phenomenon that is in need of explanation. The coinage of the Hecatomnids always carries Greek legends, as well as a depiction of the important Carian deity of Zeus of Labraunda, with his characteristic double axe.[145] The Hecatomnids inaugurated a large-scale construction project in the major Carian sanctuaries such as Labraunda, Sinuri and Mylasa; dedications of Greek-style statues with Greek inscriptions and Greek-style temples are telling examples of the wholesale glocalisation of Greek culture. But there is also intriguing evidence for the adaptation of Greek practices to new ends; the use of elaborate Greek inscriptions on the architrave of temple buildings, naming the Hecatomnids as constructors and dedicators, is unparalleled in the Greek world (see Figure 35).[146] Yet Hecatomnid glocalisation was not exclusively Greek; one of the Greek-style buildings in Labraunda had as corner acroteria two Persian-style bearded sphinxes.[147]

[142] Brixhe 1993b.   [143] Marksteiner 2002.
[144] On Caria, see Hansen and Nielsen 2004: 1108–37. On Lycia, see Bryce 1986; Keen 1998.
[145] Kraay 1976: 273–5.   [146] Hornblower 1982: 274–5.   [147] Carstens 2010.

Figure 35 Reconstruction of the Andron, Labraunda, fourth century BCE.

It is a telling indication of the wider perspective of the Hecatomnids that Mausolus took the decision to move his capital from the inland Carian city of Mylasa to the coastal Greek city of Halicarnassus. This decision was accompanied by the traditional Greek practice of synoecism, which involved the unification of a number of settlements into a single community, whether in mere political terms or also involving the actual physical translocation of the population from their old settlements into the new centre. Mausolus synoecised a number of Carian settlements of the Halicarnassian peninsula into his new capital; while the old settlements did not disappear, undoubtedly a significant part of their population moved to Halicarnassus.[148] Making a Greek polis into a satrapal capital necessitated some significant modifications, though; the prominent role in the city's landscape of the Hecatomnid palace and the Mausoleum, Mausolus' funerary monument, make the point clear.

---

[148] Hornblower 1982: 78–105.

The Hecatomnids promoted the glocalisation of the model of the polis, alongside the use of the Greek language and the Greek form of communal decree as a means of public communication. Mylasa presents itself in its Greek decrees as a polis, whose citizens are divided into three tribes and meet in assemblies to pass decrees. We find decrees in the Greek language and in the standard format of Greek public decrees employed by Carian communities either for matters relating to the Hecatomnid dynasty or for their own affairs; while some Carian communities like Mylasa call themselves a polis, others use a variety of other Greek terms to describe their communal structure.[149] This is the glocalisation of a Greek practice in its original format; but we have also seen in Chapter 4 how Mausolus modified the format of Greek decrees from that of a communal decision into that of a ruler's proclamation, and how he adapted the Greek institution of *proxenia* (p. 137). It would be misleading nevertheless to imagine that the glocalisation of Greek epigraphic practices led only to the abandonment of the Carian language in favour of Greek. A fascinating recent discovery concerns a bilingual fourth-century decree from Caunos, granting the status of *proxenos* to two Athenian citizens. It is telling that the Carian text precedes the Greek, as well as that a Greco-Carian community uses a Greek epigraphic practice and employs a Greek institution (*proxenia*).[150]

But Mausolus' most famous achievement is, of course, his tomb: the Mausoleum of Halicarnassus, one of the Seven Wonders of Antiquity.[151] It consisted of a massive podium supporting a cella surrounded by Ionic columns; it had a pyramidal roof, on top of which rested a four-horse chariot. The building was decorated with both relief and free-standing sculpture: the three reliefs included an Amazonomachy, a Centauromachy and a Chariot frieze; the free-standing sculpture came in three sizes, two of which were one-third and two-thirds larger than life size, depicting a sacrifice, hunting and a battle between Greeks and Persians. The Mausoleum is a monument which glocalises many different traditions. The sculptures were in Greek style, created by some of the most famous Greek artists of the time: Scopas, Bryaxis, Timotheus and Leochares.[152] The Mausoleum combines a building in the form of a Greek temple with a pyramidal roof probably inspired from Egypt, where Carian presence had long been strong. The glocalisation of the Greek temple for a funerary monument had taken place in nearby Lycia a few decades before the Mausoleum was constructed; in fact, the Mausoleum seems to have been

[149] Hornblower 1982: 52–78.   [150] CC; Adiego 2007: 154–6.
[151] Clayton and Price 1988: 100–23; Jenkins 2006: 203–35.   [152] Hornblower 1982: 223–74.

Figure 36 Amazonomachy relief from the Mausoleum of Halicarnassus, fourth century BCE.

inspired by the famous Nereid Monument from Lycian Xanthos, which we shall examine shortly. The iconography of the Mausoleum is a combination of two different traditions. On the one hand, there are the themes of sacrifice and hunting so prominent on the funerary monuments of Asia Minor under the Persian Empire, as we have seen in Dascyleion and we shall also see in Lycia and Phoenicia; on the other, it is particularly striking that the typical themes of depicting alterity in Greek art, such as the Amazonomachy, the Centauromachy, and the battle between Greeks and Persians, are here employed on the monument of a Carian dynast who served as a Persian satrap (see Figure 36)![153]

Lycia had a special position in Greek myth; given the prominent role of Lycian heroes like Glaucus and Sarpedon in the *Iliad*, it is not difficult to see why Greek myth was so early and keenly glocalised by the Lycians, as we shall see. Mythical genealogy Greek-style also played an important role in linking together Greeks and Lycians. Already Homer had Glaucus reporting how he and Sarpedon were descended from the Greek hero Bellerophon, who married the daughter of the Lycian king after killing the Chimaera monster with the help of the winged horse Pegasus and defeating the Amazons and the Solymi.[154] Herodotus in the fifth century narrates an alternative story in which Sarpedon is a Cretan prince forced to flee the island after a quarrel with his brother Minos, who leads the Termilae into

---

[153] Hülden 2001.   [154] *Iliad*, 6.119–236.

Figure 37 Silver kantharos vase with Lycian legends, fourth century BCE.

settling Lycia; the change of name from Termilae to Lycians was due to the Athenian Lycus.[155] Herodotus' relative Panyassis composed verses narrating the descent of the founders of Lycian cities from Tremiles.[156] A good example of Lycian globalisation of Greek myth and iconography is a silver double-head vase allegedly found in Egypt (see Figure 37). The lip and high top of the vase are decorated with Greek-style reliefs, depicting Athena, Aphrodite, Paris in Phrygian garb and probably two other figures, Hermes and Hera, in what is obviously a Judgment of Paris scene. The figures are inscribed, but the legends are in the Lycian language: Aphrodite and Paris are named in accordance with the Lycian pronunciations of their names, but Athena is identified with the Lycian deity Malija.[157]

The Lycian glocalisation of Greek culture is different from that of Caria. It shows much stronger evidence of the strategies of adaptation and hybridity, and less of wholesale adoption, which is the case in Caria; alongside the Lycian glocalisation of Greek myth and Greek artistic styles, one also sees

[155] 1.173.   [156] *EGF*, 23.   [157] Barnett 1974.

Figure 38 Silver stater of Pericles of Limyra, fourth century BCE.

the glocalisation of Persian and even Assyrian themes and iconographies.[158] The Lycian glocalisation of Greek and Persian culture is attested in personal names: many Lycian potentates bore Iranian names (Harpagus, Erbbina, Mithrapata), a result of mixed marriages with the Persian imperial diaspora, of guest-friendships or even of accommodating onomastic fashions. More surprising is the much wider presence of Greek names; perhaps the most fascinating case is the fourth-century dynast of Limyra bearing the name Pericles, whose beautiful coins represent the earliest human portraits in Lycian art (see Figure 38).[159]

This Lycian form of glocalisation is already illustrated by two sixth-century painted tombs from the uplands of northern Lycia. Tomb II in Karaburun depicts a banquet scene, with the dead person reclining along with servants wearing Iranian trousers, and a procession scene with the dead man wearing Iranian costume in an elaborate wagon.[160] These are stock scenes of Anatolian iconography that developed in Persian-ruled Asia Minor, as represented by the stelae in Dascyleion and in other examples of Lycian art. A contemporary tomb from nearby Kızılbel adds different elements. The scenes largely represent the standard themes of Anatolian art: hunting, banqueting, processions, arming and departure of warriors, and audience in front of a ruler, as well as sporting activities in the form of boxing. It is possible that some of the scenes have a narrative character or that the stock themes are linked in depicting a narrative, even a mythical one: the depiction of a ship with warriors and of some mysterious blue male figures might refer to local myths. But what is particularly interesting is the depiction of Greek myths: one scene shows the decapitation of Medusa by

---

[158] Asheri 1983; Jacobs 1987.   [159] On Lycian names, see Colvin 2004.   [160] Jacobs 1987: 29–32.

Perseus and the emergence of the boy Chrysaor and the winged horse Pegasus out of Medusa's head; another scene might represent Troilus' killing by Achilles. Already in the sixth century in the interior valleys of Lycia we come across representations of Greek myth; and it is conceivable that the selection of the myth might have a particular Lycian connection, as Pegasus was used by Bellerophon to kill the Chimaera, a myth situated in Lycia and often depicted in later Lycian art, as we shall see.[161]

The Lycians did not glocalise the Greek practice of inscribing communal decisions, as the Carians did in various ways. The one exception to this rule is telling in many ways. It concerns the famous trilingual inscription from Xanthos, recording in Lycian and Greek the decision of the community of Xanthos to institute a new cult and the related provisions, along with a letter in Aramaic from the satrap approving the decision of the community. The satrap is Pixodarus, a brother of Mausolus and member of the Hecatomnid dynasty, which by that time had been appointed as satraps of both Caria and Lycia; given the ways the Hecatomnids had glocalised Greek language and Greek epigraphic habits in Caria, the decision of the Xanthians to glocalise the Greek epigraphic practice would appear to be a result of Hecatomnid influence.[162]

It was a different form of Greek inscription that was glocalised in Lycia: a number of Lycian monuments bear Greek poems composed for the Lycian dynasts that dedicated them.[163] The Inscribed Pillar of Xanthos is a late fifth-century funerary pillar with two Lycian texts of 138 and 105 lines and a Greek text of twelve lines; on top of the pillar was an enthroned statue of a dynast standing upon his burial chamber, whose exterior was decorated with reliefs. The two Lycian texts are historical accounts narrating military confrontations with the Athenians also reported by Thucydides, and other achievements of the deceased dynast.[164] The Greek text is a poem composed for the Lycian dynast, celebrating the fact that 'since Ocean separated Europe from Asia no Lycian has ever yet raised such a stele', and mentioning how he conquered many cities with the support of Athena and killed seven Arcadian hoplites in a single day; the six shields depicted on the relief alongside a falling warrior holding a seventh illustrate this feat.[165] The Inscribed Pillar is a practically unique inscribed historical account in Lycian; but equally fascinating is how it combines a message of

[161] Mellink 1998.
[162] Translated in Kuhrt 2007: 859–63; see also Asheri 1983: 107–23; Briant 1998b.
[163] Asheri 1983: 85–105.
[164] *TL*, 44; partial translation and illustration in Kuhrt 2007: 339–41; Thonemann 2009.
[165] *M-S*, 17.10.01.

confrontation and victory against the Greeks with its expression in Greek poetic diction, and the Near Eastern format of the enthroned dynastic statue with the Greek style of the reliefs.

Two other early fourth-century Greek poems were inscribed on dedications made by the dynast Erbbina in the sanctuary of Leto near Xanthos.[166] The one commemorates, alongside a Lycian inscription, the dedication of a bronze statue to Artemis; the interpretation of the Lycian deity of this sanctuary as the Greek Leto and the dedication of a statue to a deity identified in both the Greek and the Lycian inscriptions as Artemis, Leto's daughter, are particularly noteworthy. The other is an epitaph for Erbbina in hexameters, recording his conquests and dedications of monuments. It is interesting that the text glocalises both Greek and Persian elements in praise of a Lycian dynast. The poem mentions how Erbbina sought an oracle from Delphi before dedicating the monument to Leto and compares his achievements favourably with those of Achilles and Hector; the Trojan War register could be used not only for Panhellenic causes, but also to praise a Lycian dynast. But he is also praised for his pre-eminence in wisdom, bowmanship, courage and horsemanship, recalling the chief Persian values as described by Herodotus.[167] A final example consists of two hexameters recording the dedication of an altar to Zeus by Pericles, the dynast of Limyra.[168] Alongside these poems and their emphasis on Greek as a language of communication, we should also place many bilingual epitaphs and dedications in both Lycian and Greek;[169] it is important to note the relatively large number of texts in Greek compared with the tiny number of texts in Aramaic.[170]

Lycian art is another field in which to observe the processes of globalisation and glocalisation. The style of Lycian art is effectively exclusively Greek; but the artists who worked in Lycia glocalised a variety of Greek and non-Greek iconographies in order to create an art that is uniquely Lycian. This art is dynastic; the Lycians did not invest in monumental temples or public buildings, but in the construction of elaborate tombs which monumentalised the pre-eminent position of the Lycian elites.[171] Elaborate grave monuments start to appear from the sixth century onwards; the earliest, the pillar tombs in which the burial chamber stood on top of a pillar, the sarcophagi, and the rock-cut tombs that imitate the form of the Lycian house, take forms that are typically Lycian;[172] but already from the

---

[166] *M-S*, 17.10.02–3.   [167] Cf. Savalli 1988.   [168] *M-S*, 17.15.01.
[169] Bryce 1986: 71–88; Schweyer 2002: 209–74.   [170] le Roy 1982/3.
[171] Jenkins 2006: 151–85.   [172] Demargne 1958; Deltour-Levie 1982; Schweyer 2002.

Figure 39(a) Nereid Monument, Xanthos, fourth century BCE.

archaic period the Lycians glocalised Greek style and iconography for the reliefs that decorated these monuments. Around 400 a novel development took place: the use of the architectural form of the Greek temple for the grave monuments of Lycian dynasts. The most famous of them is the Nereid Monument of Xanthos, today in the British Museum (see Figure 39(a)).

The iconography of these funerary monuments consists of three elements: depictions of Greek mythology; narrative scenes of battles and sieges; and thematic scenes depicting hunting and banqueting. We can observe the range of choices through examining some of the most famous Lycian monuments. The Nereid Monument's iconography is largely restricted to the repertoire of the Anatolian art of Persian times: banquets, hunts, sacrifices, battles and city sieges are the themes adorning the friezes of the Monument. The dynast for whom the Monument was built is depicted seated under a Persian parasol, wearing Persian clothes and holding a Persian rhyton in a banquet scene (see Figure 39(b)). The glocalisation of Greek elements is seen in the artistic style, the employment of the form of Greek temple for a tomb and the free-standing

Figure 39(b) Nereid Monument, Xanthos, fourth century BCE.

female statues of the Nereids, the daughters of Poseidon that were placed between the columns of the Monument.[173]

A different example is the fourth-century monument of Pericles, dynast of Limyra in eastern Lycia; here the glocalisation of Greek culture is dominant (see Figure 3). Pericles' own name, with its Athenian connotations, makes the strong links of his monument to Athens less surprising. Like the Nereid Monument, Pericles' monument takes the form of a Greek-style temple; but instead of normal columns there are Caryatids (columns in the form of a female statue), imitating the Caryatids of the Erechtheion on the Athenian Acropolis. Equally interesting are the friezes depicting processions of cavalry and infantry that decorated the long walls of the building; influence from the famous Parthenon frieze is more than likely. On top of the front pediment stood a sculptural group with Bellerophon killing the Chimaera; a Greek myth with a Lycian setting is here displayed prominently on a Lycian monument.[174]

---

[173] Demargne and Childs 1989; Jenkins 2006: 186–202.   [174] Bruns-Özgan 1987: 81–91.

In between these two examples, in terms of both geography and glocalising strategies, is the fourth-century heroon of Trysa, in the inland of
central Lycia.[175] This heroon is a walled enclosure with sarcophagi for the
dead, an altar for funerary rituals, and facilities for holding funerary
banquets. The interior walls and the exterior walls at the short entrance
side carry friezes with relief sculpture. The friezes include themes from
Greek mythology, such as the Calydonian boar hunt or Odysseus' slaughter of the suitors. Remarkable is the presence, as on the Mausoleum, of
depictions of a Centauromachy and Amazonomachy, typical themes of
Greek alterity used here on the monument of a Lycian dynast; and
particularly important is the depiction of Bellerophon, a Greek hero who
had mythic links to Lycia. The friezes also include the typical themes of
Asia Minor dynastic art: city siege, battle on the coast, hunts and banquets.
Apart from Greek and Anatolian iconographies and styles, the Trysa
heroon also glocalises other traditions: the exterior lintel of the doorway
is decorated with Persian-style winged bulls, while the interior lintel
carries depictions of the Egyptian god Bes.[176]

Cilicia is in many ways a crossroad of cultures, providing a middle ground
for the interaction of Mesopotamia, the Levant and Anatolia, as well as
Greece and Persia, as we shall see; it is no accident that by far the best
evidence for strategies of hybridity in the archaic and classical periods is to
be found precisely in this area. Its complexity is already reflected in the
range of scripts and languages present in the region. The majority of the
Cilician population spoke Luwian, an Indo-European language, as attested
by personal names and the use of the Hieroglyphic Luwian script in the early
first millennium; when Hieroglyphic Luwian disappeared around 700, no
alphabetic script was devised or adapted to write the Luwian language, and
as a result Luwian ceased to be written down.[177] By that time Phoenician
and Aramaic, two Semitic languages, were used for written communication
in the region, and by the classical period effectively all Cilician inscriptions
were rendered in the Aramaic script and language. This was in part the
result of imperial globalisation; the conquest of Cilicia by the Assyrian and
Persian empires, which used Aramaic as their means of communication in
the West, played an important role in its diffusion.

In Cilicia there were no Greek *apoikiai*, and the area was never under the
hegemony of Greek states, in contrast to Caria and Lycia, which were briefly
under Athenian control in the fifth century. Accordingly, we have to assume

---

[175] Oberleitner 1994; Barringer 2008: 171–202.   [176] Abdi 2002.   [177] Melchert 2003.

that the only Greek presence in the area consisted of the people involved in networks of mobility, and the people serving in the armies and bureaucracies of the Persian Empire. The evidence for the presence of Greeks in Cilicia is very limited, but particularly interesting are two fourth-century funerary stelae found in Soloi. Erected for people bearing Greek names, they take the form popular at contemporary Athens, raising questions about the presence of artists capable of executing such monuments.[178]

Already by the fifth century there were stories incorporating Cilicia within the imaginary geography of Greek myth; Herodotus reports that the original name of the Cilicians was Hypachaioi (sub-Achaeans),[179] and mentions the legend of the foundation of Posideion, on the borders between Cilicia and Syria, by Amphilochus, the son of the seer Amphiaraus.[180] But it is in relation to another legendary seer that we can best see how intercultural communication between Greek sailors, artists, mercenaries and artisans and the non-Greek populations of Cilicia could use Greek myth, while incorporating within it local traditions. Various Greek traditions reported how the seer Mopsus came to Cilicia, where he founded settlements and was buried after a deadly contest with another seer, in one version Amphilochus. Inscriptions from Cilicia dating before 700 attest local rulers who proudly proclaimed themselves belonging to 'the house of Muksas/Mopsu'; Greek visitors in the area had identified a famous local ruler with a seer of Greek myth, and a whole range of mythical narratives had developed around this identification. In fact, from the Hellenistic period onwards a Cilician city bore the name of Mopsuestia, Mopsus' hearth.[181]

Cilicia had a number of local communities, whose autonomous existence is attested by the minting of coins; however, it also seems that until the end of the fifth century Cilicia had no Persian satrap, but was ruled by native kings under Persian suzerainty. During the fourth century the revolts in Egypt and Cyprus and the Persian attempt at re-conquest made Cilicia particularly important strategically as a base for organising and training armies and launching naval campaigns; it seems likely that it was at this time that Cilicia was organised as a satrapy.[182] The coins struck by Persian satraps like Tiribazus and Pharnabazus in Cilician cities probably aimed to pay for the expenses of these military campaigns. These coins should be examined alongside those struck by Cilician communities from the fifth century onwards; they present an extremely fascinating illustration of the full range of glocalising strategies we have reviewed above.

---

[178] Casabonne 2004: 89–90.   [179] 7.91.   [180] 3.91.
[181] Scheer 1993: 153–271; Lane Fox 2008: 218–39.   [182] Casabonne 2004: 101–207.

Figure 40 Silver stater of Nagidus, fourth century BCE.

Coinage was an Anatolian invention, globalised through the world of networks and the world of *apoikiai*, and glocalised by various non-Greek communities of Asia Minor and the Levant from the fifth century onwards. The networks crossing and linking the Mediterranean are brilliantly illustrated on the Cilician coins; coins of Cilician Holmoi and Side in neighbouring Pamphylia offer the earliest representations of the statue of Athena in the Parthenon, while the coins of the Persian satrap Pharnabazus struck in Cilicia copy the famous head of the nymph Arethusa that appears on the coins of Syracuse in Sicily.[183] Many Cilician communities glocalised coinage in its pure Greek form. Not only do coins bear Greek legends with the name of the community as the issuing authority, but the iconography and the style are purely Greek; the coins of Nagidus, depicting Aphrodite and Dionysus with a Greek legend, are a typical example (see Figure 40).[184] Other Cilician communities chose to adapt the glocalised technique to their own traditions and ideologies; the coins of Mallos depict a winged deity holding a disc, whose iconography has earlier Luwian parallels.[185]

The coins of Tarsos provide a fascinating example of the glocalisation of a wide range of different traditions.[186] The legends were originally in Aramaic, but from 380 onwards switch to Greek, and there are also Greek iconographic elements, such as depictions of Athena, Aphrodite and Heracles. Some of the Tarsos coins depict the Mesopotamian deity Nergal, while coins struck at Tarsos also portray the Mesopotamian deity Anu.[187] It is Persian themes, though, which dominate the city's coinage. Alongside depictions of standing Persians and Persian archers are coins depicting a

---

[183] Casabonne 2004: 91.   [184] Casabonne 2004: 112–14.   [185] Casabonne 2004: 133–4.
[186] Casabonne 2004: 123–31.   [187] Mildenberg 1998: 31–4; Lemaire 2000.

Figure 41 Silver stater of Tarsus, fifth century BCE.

Persian rider on one side and a kneeling hoplite on the other; but most fascinating are the coins which glocalise standard iconographic themes of Persian art (the Persian king killing a lion), or visualise Persian religious and social ideologies (a figure in Persian clothes ploughing on one side and the Persian winged disc over a suckling cow on the other) (see Figure 41).[188]

While Tarsos' coins employ themes, styles and iconographies from a wide range of traditions, they do not usually produce a hybrid mix on the same coin, and as can be seen in other Cilician examples. A coin of Mallos with a Greek legend depicts the Persian king holding spear and arrow on the obverse and Heracles killing the Nemean lion on the reverse.[189] But it is with the coins struck by Persian generals in Cilicia that we observe the most fascinating examples of hybridity. On the coins struck by Tiribazus the obverse portrays a standing deity depicted in Greek style, probably representing the Ba'al (Lord) of Tarsos; an Aramaic legend carries the name of Tiribazus; while a variety of Greek legends name the different Cilician cities at which the coins were struck. The reverse shows Ahura Mazda, the chief deity of the Persian religion; but whereas in Persian art he is always represented in profile, here he is depicted Greek-style in three-quarter view and with a nude torso. The artist who designed these coins combined Greek and Aramaic legends and the depictions of Cilician and Persian deities in a Greek style (see Figure 1) (pp. 22–3).[190]

Phoenicia presents again a different story from that of Cilicia.[191] There are hardly any Greek inscriptions from Phoenicia, and Phoenician coinage

[188] Briant 2002a: 204–54.   [189] Casabonne 2004: 132–4.   [190] Casabonne 2004: 188–9.
[191] Elayi 1987, 1988a; Jigoulov 2010.

sports Phoenician legends and iconographic themes, although a few Greek themes are sometimes present. But it is in the case of Phoenician art that we see the full range of glocalising strategies in which Greek art and iconography play a very important role.[192] We shall be focusing on Sidon, an important Phoenician city of the time; we have already noted the diplomatic relationships between Athens and the Sidonian king Straton, as well as the presence of Sidonian merchants in Athens (pp. 101–2).

The sanctuary of Eshmun, a Sidonian deity often identified with Greek healing deities such as Apollo and Asclepius,[193] illustrates the impact of globalisation on Phoenician culture.[194] The monumentalisation of the sanctuary starts in the sixth century, when two podia and a typical Phoenician temple were constructed. During the fourth century there appear a marble propylon with Ionic columns and an Ionic temple; but excavations have also revealed Persian-style column capitals with bull-heads and Syrian column bases, which probably decorated the interior of the Ionic temple; like the Greek-style buildings at Carian Labraunda (p. 257), the temple sported Persian-style bearded sphinxes for acroteria. The dedications included Cypriote, Egyptian and Phoenician sculpture; but one of the most impressive finds from the sanctuary is a marble monument with two friezes of reliefs, the upper one showing an assembly of gods, the lower dancing nymphs and a satyr (see Figure 42). The friezes are in typical fourth-century Greek style, and the iconography is unambiguously Greek, with depictions of satyrs or Greek deities like Apollo and Athena.[195]

We can follow the employment of a range of different glocalising strategies in the case of the Phoenician sarcophagi discovered in the royal cemetery of Sidon. Anthropoid sarcophagi, funerary coffins made of stone in the form of the human body, were a typical form of Egyptian funerary art; in the archaic period we encounter Egyptian sarcophagi brought to Phoenicia, where they were re-used for royal burials. Phoenician artists started to glocalise anthropoid sarcophagi in their Egyptian form, but from the fifth century onwards they began to adopt Greek artistic styles for the depiction of the heads of the dead. Typical of this hybrid form are Egyptian-style sarcophagi with Greek-style heads, which at the same time sport the Egyptian box-beard (see Figure 43).[196]

Alongside the anthropoid sarcophagi are the box-shaped sarcophagi with gabled roofs, which started to appear from the fifth century onwards. These

---

[192] Boardman 1994: 49–58.   [193] Lipiński 1995: 154–68.   [194] Stucky 1993, 2005.
[195] Stucky 1984.   [196] Elayi 1988b; Ferron 1993; Lembke 2001.

Figure 42 Marble 'tribune', Eshmun sanctuary, Sidon, fourth century BCE.

sarcophagi are made out of white marble imported from Greece, and they are decorated with reliefs in a Greek artistic style using a complex iconography which combines Greek and non-Greek themes. The earliest of them, the so-called Satrap sarcophagus, has an iconography based on the Anatolian themes we have observed at Dascyleion or in Lycia: depictions of the dead ruler in Persian attire in scenes of banqueting, hunting or enthroned among his dependants (see Figure 44).[197] The so-called Lycian sarcophagus follows the form of Lycian tomb-house sarcophagi with curved gable roofs; but the Lycian form is accompanied by Greek iconographic themes, such as the depiction of the myth of Caeneus being battered into the earth by centaurs (see Figure 45).[198] The sarcophagus of the Mourning Women takes the form of a Greek-style temple, among whose columns mourning women are depicted, while the common Anatolian themes of the funeral procession and the hunt adorn the base and the top.[199]

[197] Kleemann 1958.   [198] Langer-Karrenbrock 2000.   [199] Fleischer 1983.

Figure 43 Egyptian-style sarcophagus, Sidon, fifth century BCE.

The most famous of all these sarcophagi, though, is the Alexander sarcophagus, traditionally interpreted as the final resting-place of Abdalonymus, appointed king of Sidon by Alexander the Great in the place of the pro-Persian king Straton.[200] The iconography contains the standard themes of Anatolian art, like hunting and battle-fighting, although in an interesting twist some participants are dressed in Persian and others in Greek clothes, presumably depicting Persians and Greeks/Macedonians. While the artist was working in a Greek artistic style, he was also familiar with standard themes of Persian imperial iconography: the concave part of the shield of one of the Persian warriors was painted with a depiction of the enthroned Persian king in audience with a courtier performing *proskynesis* (a ceremonial show of respect through bowing and blowing a kiss) (see Figure 46).[201]

---

[200] But see Heckel 2006b.   [201] von Graeve 1970.

Figure 44 Satrap sarcophagus, Sidon, fourth century BCE.

6.6 Explaining the 'Greek miracle'

How should we explain the impressive extent of the Greek current of globalisation? We have examined in previous chapters four parallel worlds: the Panhellenic world; the world of empires; the world of networks; and the world of *apoikiai*. Each of these four worlds accounts for some part of our explanation. The processes of Mediterranean redistribution played an important part. Aegean Greece was a peripheral area relatively poor in resources; engaging with the world of networks, with the world of *apoikiai* and with the world of empires were means through which Greeks could acquire resources, make a living or even grow rich and powerful. Rulers and communities across the Mediterranean and the Black Sea had a constant and ample supply of Greek merchants and sailors, artists and artisans, mercenaries, musicians and poets: from the rulers of Scythia and Thrace and the Lucanian communities of southern Italy to the rulers of Lycia, the cities of Cilicia or the kings of Egypt. It was the easy and constant availability of Greek manpower and its accompanying goods, ideas and technologies

Figure 45 Lycian sarcophagus, Sidon, fourth century BCE.

which to an important extent explain the intensity of Greek globalisation. There were Greek and not Egyptian verses on Lycian monuments, because it was Greek and not Egyptian poets and seers who were frequenting Lycian ports and courts.

The peculiar nature of the world of empires in the archaic and classical periods also played its role. The Persian Empire worked successfully through the imposition of a small Persian dominant ethno-class on top of local structures and communities which were maintained and functioned with minimum intervention; there was no effort to impose a Persian cultural and social package on subject communities or to use it in order to rule the empire. This created an open space in which individuals and communities within the Persian Empire glocalised a variety of different traditions and practices in order to construct or redefine local identities and to maintain or expand structures of power. From Caria and Lycia to Cilicia and Phoenicia we have seen how communities and rulers came up with different expressions of glocalisation, in all of which Greek culture played an important role, although in different ways. The availability of Greek manpower and the

Figure 46 Alexander sarcophagus, Sidon, fourth century BCE.

open space of the Persian Empire combined to enable the extensive glocalisation of Greek culture.

Nevertheless, it was also some inherent features of Greek culture which
account for our paradox. Greek culture was already the culture of an
international world; it was a system of practices, media and institutions
created in order to enable hundreds of different Greek communities spread
across the Mediterranean to communicate and share an identity.
Panhellenic shrines allowed the Greek world to assemble and materialise
once a year; but they were also arenas of display and loci of power and
recruitment that could be employed by non-Greek rulers and communities,
from Egyptian pharaohs and Lydian kings to Etruscan communities, Carian
satraps and Thracian rulers. A medium like Greek mythology used genealogy and a shared imaginary world in order to link together hundreds of
independent Greek communities spread across the Mediterranean; but due
to its location in space and time Greek mythology included foreign space
and foreign heroes among its inherent features. It was accordingly easy for

non-Greek communities to glocalise a medium of communication in which they already featured, often in very exalted roles.

Finally, it is important to note an important feature of Greek culture which was the result of the world of *apoikiai*. Participation in the world of networks was common to most Mediterranean communities, although in different degrees; but the experience and know-how of creating independent organised communities were effectively restricted to the Greeks in the eastern Mediterranean (the western Mediterranean with Phoenicians, Etruscans and Romans was a different story). Year after year Greeks from the most diverse origins joined together in order to create organised communities. Out of the enormous diversity of Greek political, social and cultural institutions and practices, the process of creating *apoikiai* made the model of a Greek community become abstract and canonical: a community with a citizen body divided into tribes, ruled by magistrates, council and assembly, equipped with a particular kind of public space (agora) and adorned with a particular kind of temple and public building (theatre, council house, gymnasion).[202] When the mercenary army of the Ten Thousand reached the Black Sea on their way back home, it was a multinational amalgam, including a predominant number of Greeks from the most diverse origins, as well as Thracians, Lydians and Mysians. When Xenophon toyed with the idea of using the army to create an *apoikia*, his comrades knew what he was talking about; had Xenophon succeeded, a typical Greek polis would have emerged out of this amalgam, as in so many other cases around the Mediterranean and Black Sea coasts.[203] This process through which Greek culture became abstracted and canonical was particularly important for its globalisation and glocalisation; it meant that Greek practices and traditions existed as a model abstracted from particular circumstances and conditions that could be easily adopted and adapted to new uses and environments. This is perhaps less visible in the archaic and classical periods, if we forget cases like that of Mausolus; but it was destined to have an enormous importance in the Hellenistic world, to which we now turn.

---

[202] Malkin 2011: 221–2. [203] *Anabasis*, 5.6.15–21; Malkin 2011: 210–11.

7 | The Hellenistic world

The Hellenistic period starts with the wars between Alexander's successors to divide the empire that he conquered and created. The result of these wars was the emergence of a number of states that stretched from the Balkans to modern Pakistan. The Hellenistic period traditionally encompasses the history of these empires and kingdoms from the death of Alexander the Great in 323 until the last of them, the Ptolemaic kingdom of Egypt, succumbed to Rome after the battle of Actium in 31. We have seen how already during the archaic and classical periods Greek soldiers, professionals, intellectuals and artists had served the rulers, satraps and grandees of the empires of the East (pp. 43–52). But the radical difference between the Hellenistic and earlier periods is that now these Greeks were members of a Greco-Macedonian ruling elite; the new empires and kingdoms were ruled by Macedonians, and their courts consisted primarily of Macedonian and Greek military men, administrators, artists, intellectuals and professionals of various skills. For the first time Greeks had come to rule over non-Greeks. This was an important difference and one of the reasons for which the Hellenistic period is being examined separately in this final chapter, rather than being incorporated within the discussions of the previous chapters.

It was Droysen's great achievement to conceive of the historical epoch created by the conquests of Alexander not as a period of decline, as earlier accounts did, but as a novel historical phenomenon characterised by the expansion of Greek culture as well as its mixture with Near Eastern cultures. The scholarly study of interactions between Greeks and non-Greeks in the Hellenistic period since Droysen's time has seen a series of complex changes.[1] Until the post-war period, scholarship was characterised by an unquestioned agreement with regard to the superiority of Greek culture in relationship to the cultures of the Near East. Some scholars chose to put the emphasis on the novel ideas, practices and identities that emerged out of the interaction between Greek and Near Eastern cultures. Others, influenced by the apparent similarity between modern colonial rule over Orientals and the Greco-Macedonian empires ruling over Near Eastern communities, chose

---

[1] See the discussion of Moyer 2011a: 11–36.

to emphasise either the 'positive' message of the spread of Greek culture over non-Greeks, or the 'negative' message of the corruption of Hellenism due to the intermingling between Greeks and Orientals. It was only in the aftermath of decolonisation that a new approach gradually became dominant. Instead of mixture and Hellenisation, scholars came to see Hellenistic societies as divided between a Greek and a native sector, each of which retained their own cultural traditions and identities in almost total segregation;[2] the native resistance to Hellenisation became a very important field of study.[3] While the new orthodoxy was a necessary corrective to earlier colonialist and Hellenocentric approaches, the polarity approach that envisioned categorically separate ethnic and cultural sectors has led to problems of its own. More recent scholarship in the last twenty years has challenged the polarity approach, while also recognising the inherent problems of the alternative approach that goes back to Droysen.[4]

Droysen famously argued that a mixture of Greek and non-Greek elements was the result of the emergence of the new Greek empires of the Hellenistic period. But this political interpretation is deeply misleading. We have seen that the deep interaction between Greek and non-Greek cultures and the globalisation and glocalisation of Greek culture by many non-Greek communities across the Mediterranean constitute a phenomenon that long preceded the Hellenistic period. By focusing on the archaic and classical periods and treating the Hellenistic period separately it was easier both to observe the important paradoxes we have been examining, and to study the continuities and changes brought by the emergence of Hellenistic empires ruling over non-Greeks.

In order to understand the relationships between Greeks and non-Greeks during the Hellenistic period we need to distinguish between two related, but nevertheless separate, phenomena. On the one hand, are the processes of globalisation and glocalisation that we have explored in Chapter 6. We have already seen how Greek culture was already a significant current among the globalisation processes of the archaic and classical periods, and how many non-Greek communities and cultures glocalised in different ways many aspects of Greek culture in order to pursue their own aims and construct their own identities (pp. 255–73). This globalisation and glocalisation of Greek culture radically expanded in the course of the Hellenistic period until, by the time of Augustus' political unification of the whole Mediterranean basin, the material and intellectual cultures of

[2] Préaux 1978.   [3] Beginning with Eddy 1961.   [4] Clarysse 1992; Ritner 1992.

the Mediterranean world from west to east consisted to an important extent of various glocalised versions of Greek culture.

There were obviously significant differences between the Carthaginian, the Roman, the Thracian, the Cilician, the Judaean or the Bactrian glocalised versions of Greek culture. It is equally important to remember that in Augustus' time there still existed cultural traditions which were minimally affected by Greek-style globalisation, as well as that the Greek current of globalisation was not the only one, and that there existed other currents (e.g., the Egyptian) which had an important share in the processes of Hellenistic globalisation and glocalisation. Nevertheless, the existence of a Mediterranean-wide global *koine* based primarily on Greek culture is a significant historical phenomenon in itself. What we must remember, though, is that the glocalisation of Greek culture across the Mediterranean is not tantamount to the Hellenisation of non-Greek communities and cultures. The adoption of a glocalised version of Greek culture by the Carthaginians or the Romans did not make them Greeks. It did make them participants in cultural practices whose terms and media were distinctly Greek; the Carthaginian Hasdrubal, who adopted the Greek name Cleitomachus and became head of the Platonic Academy, or the Roman Cicero participated in the Greek practice of philosophy on Greek terms. But at the same time, the glocalisation of Greek culture was a major way in which Carthaginians or Romans constructed their own, explicitly non-Greek identities. The Roman adoption of the Greek myth of Aeneas as a national charter is a clear example of the glocalisation of Greek culture: but the adoption of the *Trojan* Aeneas as an ancestor also makes it clear that the glocalisation of Greek culture aimed to shape a distinctly *Roman* identity.[5]

Related to, but distinct from, the globalisation and glocalisation processes is Hellenisation: the process through which individuals and communities came to identify themselves as Greeks and participate in the Panhellenic world we explored in Chapter 2. Obviously, the emergence of empires with a Greek ruling class played an important role in the process. State service and proximity to the ruler always facilitated access to power and wealth; where the ruling class and the state service were primarily (though not exclusively) Greek, many non-Greeks had strong incentives to attain power and wealth through acquiring the Greek language, Greek names, Greek education or Greek cultural practices. Although some non-Greeks pursuing such strategies became completely Hellenised, more common was the 'bilingual' phenomenon of people who inhabited both worlds and were able to switch

[5] Erskine 2001: 15–43.

registers depending on context and circumstances. The new Greek-ruled empires also affected significantly the process of Hellenisation by adapting and transforming the world of *apoikiai*. The patterns and traditions created by the decentralised world of *apoikiai* were now put into the service of the Hellenistic empires, which created *apoikiai* from the Balkans all the way to central Asia and India. These novel *apoikiai* had a significant impact on the relationship between Greeks and non-Greeks, and in particular in the areas of high concentration, such as northern Syria or Lydia, they played a decisive role in the Hellenisation of those areas.[6]

However, the process of Hellenisation was much wider than its empire-sponsored aspect. As we have seen in Chapter 2 (pp. 34–41), the Panhellenic world had created practices, such as the Panhellenic Games, and media, such as genealogical mythology, which played a crucial role in maintaining its unity and mutual communication. While these practices and media could be used in order to circumscribe a Panhellenic community and distinguish it from non-Greeks, they were also inherently expandable. They could be used to incorporate new groups within the Panhellenic community, while still maintaining the distinction between insiders and outsiders. We have seen how the Macedonian kings made use of such practices and media in order to be fully accepted within the Panhellenic world and even to become its leaders in a crusade against Persia (pp. 74–6); in a similar way, many non-Greek communities during the Hellenistic period would make use of these practices and media in order to become members of the Panhellenic community. It is no accident that the regions that became Hellenised earlier and deeper were precisely those regions where the glocalisation of Greek culture during the archaic and classical periods was most intense: Caria, Lydia, Lycia and Cilicia. This clearly shows the connection between the processes of globalisation and glocalisation, on the one hand, and the process of Hellenisation, on the other. Nevertheless, the two processes were and should be seen as distinct; a case study of the fascinating example of Hellenistic Jews will serve to underline this observation.

The above introductory comments are geared towards non-Greeks: how they glocalised Greek culture or how they became Hellenised. What about the Greeks themselves and their culture in the Hellenistic world? We have already examined in Chapter 5 the complexity and peculiarity of the Barbarian repertoire in Greek culture, and the multiplicity of ways in which foreigners and foreign cultures were present in and influenced

---

[6] Cohen 1995, 2006.

Greek culture. The Hellenistic period is in many ways the continuation and expansion of this Barbarian repertoire, rather than a story of abrupt changes. We have examined the role of alien wisdom in Greek culture: this pattern continued and was further expanded with the creation of an enormous literature written by, or more usually attributed to, foreign sages. Perhaps the one area in which continuity and expansion verge on becoming change concerns the role of networks and the related phenomenon of non-Greek currents of globalisation. It is only in the Hellenistic period that we can first observe the large-scale presence of non-Greek immigrants and travellers in the Aegean and mainland Greece. If the multicultural *emporion* of Athens is largely unparalleled in the archaic and classical Aegean, cosmopolitan places like Rhodes, Delos and Demetrias, and large foreign communities in many Greek cities, are typical of Hellenistic Greece. Related to this was the stronger presence of foreign currents of globalisation in Greek communities: the impressive visibility of Egyptian cults in Hellenistic Greek communities is one aspect of this phenomenon we shall examine in depth.

7.1 The new world of Hellenistic empires

Alexander's conquests created an obvious difference with the archaic and classical world of empires: there now existed an empire in which Greeks ruled over non-Greeks (Map 8). It is still disputed what role he envisaged for non-Greeks, and in particular Persians, in the new structure of power.[7] Whatever his plans, his death led to the dismemberment of his empire and to decades of incessant infighting among his former generals and successors. Fifty years after Alexander's death his empire was largely divided between three states: the old kingdom of Macedonia, which also maintained its interests and power in Thrace and mainland Greece; the Ptolemaic dynasty, which, based in Egypt, acquired and lost various other possessions in Phoenicia and Palestine, Asia Minor and Thrace; and the Seleucid dynasty, which inherited the overwhelming share of the old Persian Empire, extending from Afghanistan to the Aegean coast of Asia Minor.[8] In the course of time some Greek officers of the Seleucids managed to acquire independence and establish large kingdoms. In the far west the Attalids created a state based on Pergamon on the coast of Asia Minor, while in the far east the Greek satraps of Bactria (northern Afghanistan) created their own

[7] Bosworth 1980; Lane Fox 2007.   [8] Shipley 2000; Erskine 2003.

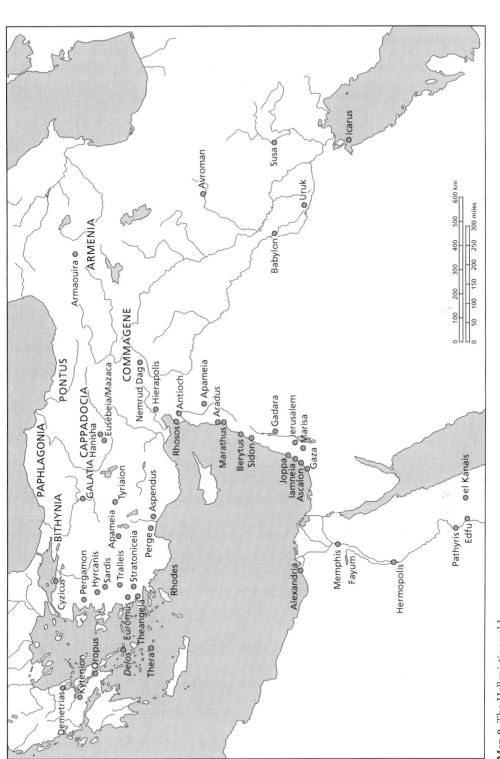

Map 8 The Hellenistic world

kingdom, as well as various Indo-Greek states which lasted for centuries.[9] Finally, a number of other kingdoms were created by former Persian satraps and native grandees, who took advantage of the chaos of the Succession wars to gradually acquire *de facto*, and ultimately *de jure*, independence: these included Pontus, Cappadocia, Paphlagonia, Bithynia, Armenia and Commagene.[10]

An initial way of describing the new Hellenistic empires is that they were the inheritors of the Persian Empire and its administrative traditions.[11] The Persians had created a world empire consisting of a wide range of pre-existing communities and states with their own structures and traditions, which were largely maintained; above them a dominant ethno-class, of overwhelmingly Persian make-up with the Persian king at its head, was the link that kept the empire together.[12] The Hellenistic empires in many ways followed the Persian solution, but substituted a Macedonian–Greek ethno-class for that of the Persians. There was thus both continuity and change: continuity in the maintenance of pre-existing structures, change in the emergence of a new ruling class.

Our best evidence for studying these pre-existing structures comes from Egypt and Mesopotamia, where papyri and clay tablets have managed to withstand the test of time. Egypt was, of course, the centre of the Ptolemaic Empire, while in some ways Mesopotamia was the heart of the Seleucid Empire. In both cases the Hellenistic kings had to deal with states that had existed for hundreds of years before they were conquered by the Persians and incorporated within a wider imperial structure. The Persians had largely maintained the power structures and bureaucracies of the Egyptian and Babylonian states; they adopted the traditional roles of kings in those countries and ruled as pharaohs in Egypt and as Babylonian kings in Mesopotamia. To an important extent, the Hellenistic rulers followed the example of the Persians; the cuneiform tablets from Mesopotamia and the Demotic papyri from Egypt can give the impression that little changed with the advent of the new foreign rulers. In fact, in both Babylonia and Egypt we can see Hellenistic rulers taking an active role in the maintenance and support of local traditions, and in particular the building and restoration of temples. From the second century onwards Ptolemaic kings were crowned at Memphis according to the traditional pharaonic ritual, while the Seleucid king Antiochus III was personally present at the New Year festival of Babylon in 205/4, in which the Babylonian king traditionally

---

[9] Holt 1999; Mairs 2011b.   [10] Facella 2006; Michels 2009.
[11] Sherwin-White and Kuhrt 1993; Briant and Joannès 2006.   [12] Briant 1988.

played an important role. The Ptolemies appear as pharaohs in Egyptian iconography, while Babylonian chronicles incorporated the Seleucid kings in their traditions.[13] It is tempting therefore to draw a picture in which non-Greek societies continued their traditions, coexisting with, but hardly affected by, the new imperial/colonial milieu of the Greek ruling elite; and there is little doubt that for many non-Greek people in Egypt or Mesopotamia this is what it must have looked like for a very long time.[14]

Let us move on to consider change. In Egypt, where surviving evidence allows us to follow the situation best, the Ptolemies created a basic distinction between Greeks and Egyptians. There existed two systems of law and two judicial systems, one for the Greeks and one for the Egyptians. Both systems were equally respected, and in 118 the Ptolemies enacted that in future what would determine which law would apply and which court would be sovereign depended not on the ethnic classification of the litigants, but on which language the contract was drawn up in; a Greek with a contract in Demotic would have to appear in an Egyptian court, while an Egyptian with a contract in Greek would have to appear in a Greek court.[15]

Nevertheless, the distinction between Greeks and Egyptians was not applied on an equal footing, as was only to be expected. As many studies have demonstrated, in both the Ptolemaic and the Seleucid empires, the vast majority of the upper echelons of the army, the bureaucracy and the court in Hellenistic kingdoms consisted of Macedonians and Greeks; non-Greeks were largely to be found among the regional elites and the lower echelons of the imperial armies and bureaucracies, although this changed in certain ways over time.[16] This overwhelming preponderance of Greeks among the ruling class was largely the result of ethnic and cultural preferences, rather than rules or laws of exclusion; nevertheless, the preferential position of Greeks could also be enshrined in law and affect a much wider group than the small numbers at the royal court. Taxation was an essential aspect of Hellenistic empires, and it is in the privileges and exceptions from taxes that we can observe distinctions between Greeks and non-Greeks. In Ptolemaic Egypt all males and females were obliged to pay the salt tax; the Ptolemies had granted exemptions to teachers, athletic coaches, actors and the victors in the games at Alexandria. The exempted groups were essential for the purveyance of Greek culture in Egypt and to demonstrate the priorities of the regime. All males were also eligible to pay the obol tax; Greeks, as well as

[13] Thompson 1988: 106–54; Sherwin-White and Kuhrt 1993; Huß 1994; Kuhrt 1996; Gorre 2009.
[14] Préaux 1978: 545–601; cf. Tuplin 2008.   [15] *COP*, 53.208–20; translated in *Austin*, 290.
[16] Habicht 2006: 26–40; Savalli-Lestrade 1998; Mehl 2003.

some other, but much smaller, privileged ethnically classified groups (Persians, Arabs), were exempt, and we also know that Greeks were exempt from corvée labour.[17]

But who were the people who were administratively classified as 'Greeks'?[18] Like the archaic and classical empires, the Hellenistic kingdoms required an enormous amount of manpower for their armies and bureaucracies. Greeks had long served in Egyptian and Persian armies and bureaucracies, alongside many other non-Greeks of various origins. This situation continued uninterrupted in the Hellenistic period; along with Greek and Macedonian immigrants, we also find large numbers from the non-Greek areas of Asia Minor, from Thrace, and in particular from Judaea and Palestine, including Jews and Idumaeans.[19] Because the administrative distinction drawn by the Ptolemaic bureaucracy was between the native Egyptian population and the newcomers, Jews or Thracians were classified as 'Greeks'. But the administrative classification as 'Greek' could also be accorded to Egyptian holders of certain administrative posts, such as scribes or policemen. A nice example is that of a family in which all the males have Egyptian names and have to pay the obol tax, except one, who bears the Greek name Pasicles, who serves as a policeman and is exempted from the obol tax.[20]

These examples show that it is misleading to see Hellenistic empires as divided between a Greek and a native sector leading their separate lives in isolation. What we must realise is that the new Hellenistic empires affected different aspects of different groups in different ways.[21] One of the major transformations effected by the Hellenistic empires was therefore the emergence of new groups with mixed cultural and ethnic origins and identities. These groups could range from high courtiers to lowly soldiers and village scribes. They were created through mixed marriages as well as cultural adaptation, that is, through the adoption primarily of Greek language, names, cultural practices and education by non-Greeks, but occasionally also in the opposite direction.

These mixed groups were the result of some structural phenomena of the new Hellenistic monarchies. The new imperial structures required communication between the Greek-speaking ruling elite and the mass of subjects who spoke non-Greek languages. In the higher echelons of the system it was essential to work with the native elites in order to maintain cooperation,

[17] Clarysse and Thompson 2006: 36–89.   [18] Goudriaan 1988.
[19] La'da 2002; Winnicki 2009.   [20] Thompson 2001; Clarysse and Thompson 2006: 123–61.
[21] Ritner 1992; for a similar argument with regard to the Roman Empire, see Terrenato 2005.

ensure loyalty and learn how to operate the already existing systems of administration. In both Egypt and Mesopotamia we can see how the first generation of Hellenistic rulers sponsored and worked closely with members of the native elites, and the interesting cultural interactions that this created.[22] In Egypt a famous example is that of Petosiris, a priest who lived under the Persians, Alexander and Ptolemy I, and whose tomb combines traditional Egyptian themes with Hellenising style and iconographic elements.[23] Another case is that of Senoucheri, born of a Greek father and an Egyptian mother, who served both as an Egyptian priest and as a counsellor of Ptolemy II. From the later second and first centuries many elite Egyptians figured among the court elite of the king's 'Friends', some of them setting up Egyptian-style statues of themselves bearing the Greek-style diadem of the courtier.[24] The process was paralleled in Seleucid Babylonia. We learn from a third-century building inscription how Anu-uballit, the governor of the Babylonian city Uruk, had bestowed upon him the Greek name Nicarchus by King Antiochus II; another third-century governor of Uruk also named Anu-uballit assumed the Greek name Cephalon, married a Greek woman and gave Greek names to his children.[25] An important result of this phenomenon was the emergence of native bilingual intellectuals who collaborated closely with the Hellenistic kings and who composed works in the Greek language, which presented the histories and traditions of their own cultures; the Egyptian Manetho and the Babylonian Berossus are the most famous of these intellectuals, and we shall further discuss them below (p. 306).

But these high courtiers and functionaries remain largely the exception among a ruling elite that was overwhelmingly Greek. It is among the lower functionaries and military men that we find the overwhelming majority of these mixed groups. Communication also required functionaries who were in a position to address the native subjects in their own tongue and the Greek rulers in theirs. The ability to speak and write in Greek was an essential skill for those Egyptians who wished to advance higher in their careers; and certain positions in the administrative and military sectors could lead to the bestowal of the bureaucratic identification as 'Greek', or any other privileged ethnic classification. Finally, mixed marriages were a prominent strategy for achieving social mobility; given the disproportion in numbers of Greek male and female immigrants to Egypt, it is obvious that many Greek males would have to marry Egyptian women (the opposite

---

[22] Legras 2002; Moyer 2011a: 88–91.   [23] Picard 1931.   [24] Moyer 2011b.
[25] Sherwin-White and Kuhrt 1993: 150–3.

seems to have happened very rarely). The children of such marriages acquired legal recognition as Greeks.

Members of these mixed groups usually had double names, both Greek and Egyptian. In fact, it has been shown that they tended to use their Greek name in their dealings with the state and other circumstances in the Greek milieu, while using their Egyptian names in their Egyptian milieu.[26] Their archives show that they composed documents in both Greek and Demotic, depending on the circumstances and the strategies to be followed.[27] This participation in two different milieus could also accompany them after death; a family at Edfu, whose members held both military and priestly offices, were recorded in both Greek- and Egyptian-style epitaphs and with both Greek and Egyptian names.[28] In particular, those Greeks who found themselves living in a largely Egyptian setting outside a large Greek community could quickly go native, and their progeny could be assimilated to their Egyptian community. The Greek cavalry commander Dryton, when posted to the Egyptian-dominated community of Pathyris, married a girl who was the offspring of an earlier mixed marriage; their children were largely assimilated to their Egyptian background, although they retained their legal classification as Greeks.[29] Neoptolemus, also known by the Egyptian name Onnophris, was the grandchild of a Macedonian cleruch and the offspring of a mixed marriage; he is recorded in a Demotic text dedicating himself to the Egyptian god Anubis.[30] Dionysius, the child of another such mixed marriage, even served as a priest of an Egyptian cult.[31]

It is particularly in the case of religion that the strongest interaction between Egyptians and Greeks can be seen. We have seen how Athenian comedians could ridicule the Egyptian cult of animals and the theriomorphic depiction of gods (p. 191); it is thus intriguing to come across a stele erected by members of a Greek gymnasion in Fayum, recording the dedication of a plot of land to the Egyptian crocodile god Sobek and depicting a crocodile; members of this quintessentially Greek institution were worshipping an Egyptian deity in the most un-Greek fashion![32] Alongside the interactions between Greeks and Egyptians, we should also place the triangulated interactions between non-Greek immigrants, Greeks and Egyptians. The large-scale immigration encouraged by the Ptolemies for their armies, bureaucracies and cultural projects brought as we have seen many non-Greeks to Egypt in the Hellenistic period. These non-Greek immigrants brought with them their cults and traditions. Thracians are

[26] Clarysse 1985.   [27] Clarysse 2010.   [28] Yoyotte 1969.   [29] Lewis 1986: 88–103.
[30] Clarysse 1992: 52–3.   [31] Lewis 1986: 124–39.   [32] *OGIS* I, 176; La'da 2003: 168.

seen worshipping their god Heron;[33] Syrians brought their cult of Atargatis;[34] while Idumaeans were worshipping their national god Qos.[35] The large numbers of Jews migrating to Egypt created their own communities and cults, which we shall examine below (pp. 313–14).

At the same time, we have seen how for taxation and other administrative purposes these non-Greek immigrants were classified as 'Greeks'. This administrative 'Hellenisation' was closely linked with a process of adopting various aspects of Greek cultural practices. Part of this process had to do with adapting to the dominant role of the Greek language in their new milieu. It is already indicative that the Thracian and Idumaean immigrants chose Greek language and Greek-style inscriptions to record the dedications and proceedings of their own cults and associations; when two Arabs in Memphis, Myroullas and Chalbas, write to Dakoutis, their third brother, in Greek instead of their native tongue, this shows eloquently the importance of Greek as a communicative medium, if not the linguistic Hellenisation of these Arabs.[36] The process is also paralleled in the adoption of Greek names. A late second-century dedication by a group of Idumaeans allows us to observe the names of three successive generations: 44 per cent of grandfathers, 88 per cent of fathers and all of the sons bear Greek names.[37] Participation in athletics was another aspect of the adoption of Greek cultural practices. A third-century inscription records victors in gymnastic, equestrian and military contests dedicated to King Ptolemy II and endowed by a Thracian named Amadocus; five Thracians are among the victors, the largest group along with five Macedonians.[38]

Papyrological evidence from Egypt allows us to glance at some examples of how relationships between Greeks and Egyptians were conducted on an everyday basis.[39] The Greek soldier Heracleides appeals to the king 'not to witness this outrage committed thus by an Egyptian woman against me, a Greek and one away from home'; he clearly thought that the ethnic argument would appeal to the king.[40] A camel driver complains to his Greek superior that he is mistreated and given only poor quality wine to drink, because he is a Barbarian and does not know how to speak/behave as a Greek (*hellenizein*).[41] These examples give the impression of a society divided on ethnic lines, in which the Greeks have the upper hand and can apply to the state apparatus to put Egyptians in their place. But the complexity of Ptolemaic Egypt is nicely illustrated by the case of Apollonius and

---

[33] Launey 1950: 959–74.   [34] Winnicki 2009: 175–6.   [35] Winnicki 2009: 296.
[36] *UPZ* I, 72; Thompson 1988: 86.   [37] *SB* I, 681; Winnicki 2009: 299–301.
[38] *SEG* XXVII, 1114; translated in *Austin*, 294; Bingen 2007: 86–9.   [39] Thompson 2001.
[40] *P.Enteux.* 79.9–10.   [41] *P. Col. IV*, 66; translated in *Austin*, 307.

Ptolemaeus, brothers who had joined the community of *enkatochoi* (religious detainees) in the Egyptian sanctuary of Sarapis in Memphis. In a letter to the authorities Ptolemaeus reports that he had been attacked by a group of people 'because I am Greek';[42] but he was also penning petitions for his Egyptian friends. His brother Apollonius used papyrus to record some of his dreams, but he recorded them in Demotic, as he seems to have dreamt in Egyptian; Apollonius was also reading translated Demotic texts, such as the *Dream of Nectanebo*.[43] Copying classical Greek literary texts to improve his handwriting, he records a passage from Euripides' *Telephus*, where Telephus laments his fate of being transported from Arcadia to Mysia, a Greek among Barbarians; Apollonius identifies with the feeling, effectively signing the passage with the words 'Apollonius the Macedonian ... a Macedonian I say'.[44] The very same people were reading classical Greek literature and a Greek translation of a Demotic tale, identifying as Greeks and dreaming as Egyptians.[45]

7.2 Globalisation, glocalisation, Hellenisation

We have already mentioned how one should distinguish between two closely related but nevertheless distinct processes of the Hellenistic world: the globalisation and glocalisation of Greek culture, on the one hand; and Hellenisation *tout court*, on the other. Let us first start with globalisation and glocalisation. We have examined in Chapter 6 how from the archaic period onwards, and increasingly during the fourth century, non-Greek communities in Asia Minor came to glocalise various aspects of Greek culture. We have seen among many examples how Mausolus, a Persian satrap as well as a Carian ruler, moved his capital to the Greek city of Halicarnassus, which he expanded through the Greek practice of synoecism, employed Greek professionals and intellectuals in his court, adopted the Greek language as his official medium of communication, and encouraged Carian communities to adopt the model of the Greek polis and its epigraphic habits (pp. 257–60). What we see in the aftermath of Alexander is not something completely novel, but an immense expansion and intensification of these processes. Expansion, because they now affected a much wider range of areas, reaching all the way to India and central Asia; intensification, because the depth and extent of these processes were greatly

---

[42] *UPZ* I, 8.14; translated in *B-D*, 138.   [43] *UPZ* I, 81.   [44] *P. Mil.*, I 15.
[45] Thompson 1988: 212–65; Legras 2011.

increased. The combination of expansion and intensification means that globalisation and glocalisation affected areas in highly different ways; in particular, there is a significant difference between areas of Asia Minor like Caria, Lycia and Lydia, where the strong presence of Greek-style glocalisation till the fourth century meant that they were radically transformed in the Hellenistic period, and areas where the novelty of Greek-style globalisation produced much more circumscribed results during the Hellenistic period.

Let us start with the globalisation of Greek language. A significant development of the Hellenistic period was the emergence of the *Koine*, a form of the Greek language based primarily on the Attic dialect, which developed out of the linguistic interactions of the world of networks and in the Hellenistic period gradually supplanted the local Greek dialects and became the lingua franca of the whole Mediterranean world.[46] If Carians, Lydians or Lycians had long been making use of Greek alongside their own languages as a means of communication or adopted Greek names (pp. 256–64), the eve of the Hellenistic period brings a rapid acceleration of both practices. Within a few decades, inscriptions in these native Anatolian languages cease completely. In Caria inscriptions in Greek were already very numerous before Alexander, but by the middle of the third century they have become the only means of communication; even more strikingly, Carian names start to disappear and are gradually replaced by Greek names.[47] One can also observe a tendency to Hellenise the names of Carian settlements, Hyromos becoming Euromus or Europus, and Syangela becoming Theangela.[48] The same picture can be observed in Lycia, where during the third century inscriptions in the Lycian language cease and Greek names come to account for 80 per cent of attested Lycians.[49]

The expansion of the Greek language did not take place in a void. By the late classical period a set of cultural practices and institutions, closely connected with each other, had come to be associated with the concept of Greek culture, in such a way that the orator Isocrates could already claim that the name of the Greek is no longer restricted to mere kinship, but also expresses a disposition: 'those are called Hellenes who share our education (*paideusis*) rather than our genetic inheritance (*physis*)'.[50] What these practices and institutions were can best be inferred from the list of people who were exempted from the Ptolemaic salt tax, as we saw above (p. 285): teachers in schools that taught Greek language and the canon of texts of Greek literature that were deemed classical for an educated man;[51] actors

---

[46] Brixhe 1993a.   [47] Blümel 1994.   [48] Bresson 2007b: 225.   [49] Colvin 2004.
[50] *Panegyricus*, 50.   [51] Morgan 1998; Cribiore 2001.

performing tragedies, comedies and other plays in theatres; coaches for the Greek practice of athletics in the institution of the gymnasion;[52] and victors in the institutionalised series of games, both in the old centres of the Aegean and in the new communities of the Hellenistic world. The expansion of Greek schools, theatres, gymnasia, and athletic and theatrical competitions across the Mediterranean and even further afield is an excellent illustration of the extent and degree of the globalisation of Greek culture. This expansion of Greek athletics is reflected in the emergence of gymnasia in Egyptian villages that had Greek settlers or in the cities of Asia Minor; an excellent illustration is an honorary stele erected by the members of a village around Cyzicus in the Propontis for an athlete with the Bithynian name Doidalses, lamenting that if it were not for his obscure origins, his achievements would be considered equal to those of Heracles.[53] Theatres did not merely host performances, but could also function as assembly places, and were closely connected to some of the most important cultural practices of the Greek world.[54] In the course of the Hellenistic period theatres spread across Asia Minor all the way to central Asia. But it is in particular in Caria and Lycia that theatres are most frequently attested: by the first century practically every Carian or Lycian community had its own theatre.[55]

7.2.1 The polis model

The major factor which expanded and intensified the globalisation and glocalisation processes in the Hellenistic world was the model of the polis.[56] Since the archaic period, the Greeks had accumulated centuries of experience in how to create an organised community. This accumulated experience became highly canonical; although Greek communities could differ among themselves significantly, the experience of creating *apoikiai* had abstracted a widely available mental model of how a Greek polis should be organised and what it should look like. A model polis should be run by a combination of council, assembly and magistrates; it should have a citizen body distributed in tribes, a particularly convenient way for mixing together and creating solidarities among *apoikoi* of mixed origins; it should possess certain public spaces and public buildings in highly canonical forms (agora, gymnasion, theatre, temple), which were essential for conducting the activities and practices for which a polis model was designed.

---

[52] Kah and Scholz 2007.   [53] *M-S*, 8.5.7.   [54] Chaniotis 1997: 224–6.
[55] See the map in le Guen 2003: 336.   [56] On the Hellenistic polis, see Gruen 1993.

In the course of the Hellenistic period this canonical model of the Greek polis was globalised and glocalised in an area that expanded from the western coast of Asia Minor to Pakistan and central Asia. It was heavily employed by the new Hellenistic states to advance their own aims: both by the Greek-ruled empires, like the Seleucids and the Ptolemies, and by the states created by local potentates and descendants of the Iranian imperial aristocracy. But it was also widely adopted and adapted by a great range of non-Greek communities.[57] The new poleis of the Hellenistic world generally emerged in three different ways. Some of them were native communities which were granted the right to be accepted as poleis and to be politically, administratively and culturally organised on the basis of the Greek polis model. Many non-Greek communities, such as the Phoenician city-states, the communities of Caria or the cities of Cilicia, had political and cultural structures that were very similar to those of the Greek poleis; perhaps the best indication of these similarities is that in Phoenicia, Caria and Cilicia coins were minted in the name of communities and city-states, although there also existed coinages in the name of dynasts and satraps. What we encounter in the Hellenistic period is the rapid adoption and adaptation of the organisational, political and cultural model of the Greek polis in non-Greek areas with similar structures.[58] In certain cases a pre-existing city would be recognised as a polis by a Hellenistic king, who would 'found' it by granting it a new dynastic name: Carian Tralleis was thus renamed Seleucia after Seleucus I,[59] while Phrygian Celaenae was renamed Apameia after his Iranian wife, Apame.[60] In other cases a number of pre-existing settlements would merge together to create a new community, often with the foundation of a new urban centre, a process that the Greeks called synoecism. This new community would adopt a polis model and usually a dynastic name as well; Stratoniceia in Caria is a characteristic example.[61]

On the other hand, there also existed regions, in particular in inland Asia Minor, where nothing equivalent to Greek poleis existed prior to the Hellenistic period, where villages predominated and cities were rare, and large areas were ruled by kings or as temple-states. In some of these areas Hellenistic kings introduced the model of the polis through their creation of *apoikiai*; but we can also find examples of local communities glocalising the polis model, as shown by a Hellenistic decree of the community of the Hanisenoi from Cappadocia, deep in the interior of Asia Minor.[62] The decree is in Greek and, in fact, adopts impeccably the standards of the

[57] Briant 1998a; Cohen 1995, 2006.   [58] Millar 2006: 32–50.   [59] Cohen 1995: 265–8.
[60] Cohen 1995: 281–5.   [61] Cohen 1995: 268–73.   [62] *Michel*, 546; Robert 1963: 457–523.

official Greek language of the time; the Hanisenoi have adopted Greek month names, Greek-sounding religious festivals (for Zeus Saviour and Heracles), Greek offices (*demiourgos, prytaneis*), and the institutions of Council and popular assembly. The fact that the community does not bear a dynastic name (as, e.g., the royal capital Eusebeia mentioned in the inscription) indicates that it was not a royal foundation or an implantation of Greek colonists; this fact is also established by the names mentioned in the decree, the overwhelming majority of which are Cappadocian. This was, in other words, a Cappadocian community that had come to adopt the Greek model of the polis along with the language of Greek politics; the titles of the offices show that the model originated from the Hellenised cities of Cilicia and Pamphylia to the south. The mention of the temple where the decree would be exhibited shows the long-term processes of globalisation at work. This was a temple of Astarte, a deity of Mesopotamian origins who seems out of context in inland Cappadocia. But Hellenistic Hanisa is the place known as Kanesh during the early second millennium, when Assyrian traders looking for metals had established a substantial *emporion* in the place.[63] The cult of Assyrian Astarte was a remnant of a previous current of globalisation that was now intermingling with the novel Hellenistic Greek current.

Other new poleis were in origin military settlements which in the process of time were organised as poleis. The community of the Macedonian Hyrcanians in Lydia is a particularly interesting example. A military settlement of Hyrcanians from central Asia established under the Persian Empire was joined by a military settlement of Macedonians established by some Hellenistic kingdom, and at some point it had developed into a polis.[64] An excellent illustration of the joining together of native communities with military settlements comes from a second-century inscription recording a letter of the Attalid king Eumenes II to the inhabitants of Tyriaion in Phrygia, approving their request to be granted 'a constitution, their own laws, a gymnasion and all the other rights that follow', and arranging for the setting up of a Council, magistrates and the distribution of citizens into tribes; the new polis would include the military settlers as well as the 'native' inhabitants.[65]

Finally, a small but important number of novel poleis were genuine foundations from scratch. Antioch in Syria and Alexandria in Egypt, respectively, the Seleucid and the Ptolemaic capitals, and the two most important cities of the eastern Mediterranean from the Hellenistic period

---

[63] Kuhrt 1998.   [64] Cohen 1995: 209–12.   [65] *SEG* XLVII, 1745; translation from *Austin*, 236.

till late antiquity, were novel foundations which necessitated a significant migration of settlers from Macedonia and Greece.[66] The foundation of dynastic cities had a long tradition in the Near East;[67] what was new in the Hellenistic foundations was the application of the model of the Greek *apoikia* in circumstances very different from those of its original inception.

The glocalisation of the polis model in coastal Asia Minor was a particularly intensified process, with consequences we shall explore later on. But it is no less interesting to explore the more circumscribed glocalisation of the polis model further away, in Mesopotamia, Iran and central Asia. It is illuminating to start with a settlement that was not in fact a polis, because of the similarities it shows to the wider process of glocalising Greek culture. This is the settlement on the island of Failaka, off the coast of Kuwait in the Persian Gulf, the ancient Icarus.[68] The settlement of the island goes back to the Neo-Babylonian period, but excavations have revealed a Hellenistic fortified complex housing a Seleucid garrison. Most of the objects found on the island are part of Mesopotamian material culture; but there are also three Greek-style temples, which, nevertheless, employ Persian-style bell-shaped column bases. Some Greek inscriptions have been found on the island, along with a non-Greek graffito; they record dedications to Greek divinities as well as a letter from the Seleucid satrap establishing a Greek-style athletic competition.[69]

The Seleucid Empire employed the polis model with varying intensity in its various domains to the east of Syria. Greek *apoikiai* were created in the old imperial capitals of Babylon and Susa. Some doubts exist about the name and the status of the Greek community in Babylon, but its importance is shown by the existence of a theatre,[70] a gymnasion and an agora.[71] The connections of the Greeks of Babylon to the wider Greek world is shown by the appointment of Dromon, the son of Phanodemus, who is described as a citizen of Babylon, as proxenos of the Aegean island polis of Andros.[72] A Greek *apoikia* named Seleucia-on-the-Eulaeus was established at Susa.[73] The Greek inscriptions from Susa open a fascinating window on the life of this community. One inscription records a dedication by a Greek to the Anatolian goddess Ma, whose cult was probably imported to Susa together with the Greek *apoikoi*.[74] Other inscriptions record manumissions of slaves.

---

[66] On Antioch, see Cohen 2006: 80–93; on Alexandria, see Fraser 1972.

[67] van de Mieroop 2007: 68–80; Harmanşah 2005.

[68] Sherwin-White and Kuhrt 1993: 172–8.   [69] *IEOG*, 416–24.   [70] van der Spek 2001.

[71] Sherwin-White and Kuhrt 1993: 155–9.   [72] *IG* XII.5, 715.   [73] le Rider 1965.

[74] *IEOG*, 180.

The public recording of manumissions is a typically Greek practice largely absent from non-Greek communities;[75] while most of the manumittors have Greek names, one female manumittor bears the Babylonian theophoric name Beltibanatis, showing the mixed composition of the citizen body.[76] The manumissions take the form of consecration of the slaves to various divinities. While some are dedicated to Greek deities like Artemis and Apollo, most are to the local deity Nanaia, showing the participation of Greek *apoikoi* in the worship of both Greek and non-Greek deities.[77] The interconnections between the Greek *apoikoi* and native cultural practices can also be seen in the case of writing practices.[78] On the one hand, the Greeks adopted the native medium of clay tablets for Greek inscriptions: a tablet from Babylon records the victors in typically Greek-style athletic games,[79] while a clay tablet from Susa records a payment in Greek.[80] In the opposite direction we encounter clay tablets on which the Greek alphabet is used to record texts in the Babylonian or Aramaic languages; it is unclear whether they were written by Greek trainees in a Babylonian scribal school or by Babylonians learning to use Greek to record their languages.[81]

This complexity is further demonstrated in the settlement of Aï Khanoum, founded in the late fourth century by the Seleucids in ancient Bactria (Afghanistan).[82] The public architecture of Aï Khanoum combines a variety of elements from different cultural traditions.[83] On the one hand, one finds a temple with indented niches which follows a Mesopotamian architectural tradition and a palatial building which follows the pattern of Persian and earlier Mesopotamian palaces; but the introduction of Corinthian columns in the Persian-style palace and the use of Greek as the administrative language for the bureaucratic transactions of the palace[84] show the intermingling of Greek and non-Greek traditions. On the other hand, traditional architectural elements of Greek culture are present: a gymnasion and a theatre represent the most characteristic examples. The heroon of Kineas the founder contained an inscription mentioning how a certain Clearchus had brought from Delphi the famous Delphic maxims, some of which were exhibited on the stele.[85] The excavators have also discovered Greek literary and philosophical texts, which testify to the maintenance of the networks which linked this faraway *apoikia* with the intellectual trends of the rest of the Greek world.[86]

---

[75] Vlassopoulos forthcoming b.   [76] *IEOG*, 195.   [77] *IEOG*, 189–200.
[78] Sherwin-White and Kuhrt 1993: 157–61.   [79] *IEOG*, 107.   [80] *IEOG*, 188.
[81] *IEOG*, 117–25.   [82] Rapin 1990.   [83] Bernard 1976; Mairs 2008, forthcoming.
[84] *IEOG*, 322–56.   [85] *IEOG*, 382–3.   [86] Rapin *et al.* 1987; Lerner 2003.

All these examples from Mesopotamia and central Asia show eloquently that the glocalisation of the polis model and of Greek culture took place in a complex and diversified context. It involved non-Greeks glocalising Greek culture, as well as Greeks adopting foreign cultural practices, such as the use of clay tablets. The glocalisation of Greek culture took place alongside local cultural forms: the Mesopotamian material culture of Failaka is accompanied by Greek inscriptions and Greek games. And finally, in many cases the different elements mix to create new hybrid forms: Greek manumission inscriptions record dedications to Elamite deities, while Corinthian columns appear in a Persian-style palace.

Glocalising the polis model did not necessarily make a non-Greek community Greek. But it meant that a non-Greek community could now participate in a process which modern scholars call peer–polity interaction.[87] This concept describes a process in which communities with similar features (peer polities) interact and influence each other not through a centre–periphery model, but through interconnections created and maintained by shared practices. By the Hellenistic period Greek poleis had created a vast repertoire of practices which maintained their peer–polity interaction.[88] This is impressively reflected in the inscriptions which record the efforts of Hellenistic cities to achieve international recognition of their newly established athletic and musical competitions, along with asylum status for themselves and their sanctuaries. In 208 the Asia Minor city of Magnesia on the Maeander sent at least twenty sacred delegations to achieve international recognition of her games in honour of Artemis Leucophryene as equal in importance to the Pythian Games of Delphi and recognition of the city's status as inviolable. More than two hundred cities, ranging from the archaic Greek *apoikiai* in Sicily to the new Hellenistic *apoikiai* in Iran, were approached by the envoys, and their responses inscribed on a single massive wall in the *agora* of Magnesia are a visual record of the extent of the Panhellenic community in the Hellenistic period.[89] Particularly noteworthy is the reply of Antioch in Persis, which stressed that its colonists originated from Magnesia.[90] By adopting the model of the polis, non-Greek communities could also opt to engage with the process of Greek-style peer–polity interaction; this involved not only their relationship to other poleis, but also the way they were constituted as communities and interacted with the novel world of Hellenistic rulers and their empires.[91] The adoption of the polis

[87] Renfrew and Cherry 1986.   [88] Ma 2003.   [89] *Rigsby*, 66–131.
[90] *OGIS*, 233; translated in *Austin*, 190.   [91] Ma 2000.

model by Sardis is an illuminating example. We have already examined the important role of Greek language, onomastics, cult and art in the city during the Persian era (pp. 251–2), but Sardis was nevertheless a satrapal capital and not a Greek polis. By the late third century this had changed completely: Sardis had a theatre, a gymnasion, a hippodrome and the typical political institutions of a Greek polis.[92] Its forms of interaction with Hellenistic rulers and other poleis are identical to those of the Greek cities; we even have a third-century decree of Delphi which renews the ancestral links with Sardis and approves the Sardian request for recognition of its musical and athletic competitions.[93]

7.2.2 The Panhellenic community

Without the globalisation and glocalisation of Greek culture by non-Greek communities it would have been impossible to talk about the other related, but distinct, process, that of Hellenisation. But the Hellenisation of non-Greek communities necessitated their incorporation within the Panhellenic community, in both its imaginary and organisational forms. We have seen how Greek myth was a potent means of intercultural communication through its location in space and time, and its incorporation of foreign heroes and foreign peoples (pp. 166–8). We have seen examples of how Greek heroes like Heracles could account for the origins of the Scythians or the Sicels (pp. 158, 181), how Perseus linked together Argives and Persians (p. 154) or how Danaus and his daughters linked Argos with Egypt (p. 196). During the archaic and classical periods we can observe only foreign kings (Xerxes, Amasis, Seuthes) or foreign individuals engaging in this interlinking process. Kinship diplomacy based on myth was a very common practice among Greek communities, and during the Hellenistic period it was significantly expanded and extensively deployed by non-Greek communities in order to create links with Greek communities and insert themselves within the Panhellenic community.[94]

The first evidence we have comes within a few years of Alexander's conquest: Argos recognised its kinship with the Pamphylian city of Aspendus and granted to the Aspendians the right to Argive citizenship among other privileges, a grant already extended to the Cilician city of Soloi.[95] But the most elaborate example, because it provides the mythical narratives through which kinship diplomacy was conducted, is an inscription

[92] Gauthier 1989: 151–70.   [93] *SIG*³, 578.
[94] *Curty*; Jones 1999; Lücke 2000; Patterson 2010.   [95] *SEG* XXXIV, 282; *Curty*, 3.

recording the application in 206/5 by the Dorian city of Kytenion in central Greece to the Lycian city of Xanthos for financial help in reconstructing its damaged walls.[96] We have seen how already in Homer the Lycian Glaucus narrates to Diomedes his descent from Bellerophon, who left Corinth and went to Lycia where he sired a progeny of kings (p. 174). The ambassadors from Kytenion now continued the story, telling how Glaucus was succeeded by his son Chrysaor, who sent his son Aor as leader of colonists back to Greece and was thus linked to the land of Doris, to which Kytenion belonged. The Xanthians could offer only a paltry sum; but their decision to inscribe the decree mentioning the embassy of the Kytenians along with the mythical stories narrated by the Kytenians that linked Xanthos to Greece demonstrates how important it was for them to be considered part of the Panhellenic community. Chrysaor was also the mythical founder of the Carian Chrysaoric League; and a myth similar to that narrated by the Kytenians underlies the contemporary decision of the Amphictyonic Council at Delphi to recognise the kinship between the Greeks and the Carian city of Alabanda, which was a member of the Chrysaoric League.[97]

This brings us to the second important facet of the Panhellenic community, participation in the Panhellenic festivals and games. An eloquent testimony of the incorporation of non-Greek communities within the Panhellenic community is the great third-century list of *theorodokoi*, individuals who hosted the Delphic sacred envoys announcing the games to their communities. This is a veritable geographic gazetteer of the Panhellenic world, whose focus is obviously mainland Greece and the Aegean, but which also ranges from the archaic Greek *apoikiai* in the west to the new Hellenised communities of Asia Minor and the Levant, from Aradus in Phoenicia to Mylasa in Caria and Sardis in Lydia.[98]

We have already seen how participation in these games was restricted to Greeks, and how Alexander I of Macedon had used myth in order to support his claim to be accepted as Greek (pp. 74–5). During the Hellenistic period many athletes from non-Greek communities of Asia started taking part in the games and thus bringing their countries within the Panhellenic community. An impressive illustration of this phenomenon is an inscription of around 200 in which the Phoenician city of Sidon honours its citizen Diotimus, son of Dionysius, who won the chariot race in the prestigious Panhellenic Games of Nemea. Diotimus' double allegiance is shown by his service in the traditional Phoenician office of *sufet*

---

[96] *SEG* XXXVIII, 1476; *Curty*, 75; translated in Ma 2003: 10–12.   [97] *FD* IV, 163; *Curty*, 13.
[98] Plassart 1921.

(judge) alongside his successful participation in Greek athletics. But most fascinating is the inscription's description of how Diotimus was 'the first of our citizens to bring back from Greece the glory of a victory in the chariot race to the house of the noble sons of Agenor', as well as the pride felt by Thebes in the victory of its Sidonian metropolis. For, as we have seen, according to Greek myth Thebes was founded by the Phoenician Cadmus, the son of Agenor (p. 195), and Diotimus belonged to the descendants of Agenor. The author of the honorary decree imagines Greece assembled at the Panhellenic Games and proclaiming: 'Not only do you excel in your ships, [Sidon], but also in your yoked [chariots which bring] victory.'[99] The Greek myth of Cadmus and Europa has opened the way to participation in Panhellenic Games for Hellenised Phoenicians, who have otherwise kept their native institutions.

The Hellenisation of non-Greek communities in Asia Minor and Syria was not complete or uncontested, nor did it efface the coexistence of multiple identities, some compatible and others not. It was not complete, because while it was only Greek that was used in public inscriptions, we do not know what language was spoken at home by those who did not have an opportunity to get a Greek education or those who lived in the country-side. We can hardly study the cultural and ethnic associations of those other groups, because we can only access forms of public communication in media which, although not restricted to the rich and powerful, were largely geared towards them. However, we do know that even in Roman times in some areas of Asia Minor non-Greek languages persisted in oral communication, even if they were no longer written down or, indeed, never had been.[100] Hellenisation was not uncontested, because it was always possible for outsiders to challenge the Hellenicity of the popula-tions of Asia Minor. The Athenians could dispute, when they wanted to, the Hellenicity of the Thebans or the Peloponnesians, because they were descended by the Phoenician Cadmus or the Lydian Pelops;[101] Greeks from mainland Greece, and later the Roman overlords, could dispute the Hellenicity of the new Greeks of Asia Minor out of prejudice or when it suited them to do so.[102]

Related to these issues was the coexistence of multiple identities. Because Greek myth had incorporated foreigners through heroic genealogies, and because the Barbarian repertoire of Greek culture had accorded such an

---

[99] *Moretti*, 41; translation from *Austin*, 140.

[100] See the case of Lycaonian, still spoken in Roman times, but never written down: *Acts of the Apostles*, 14.8–11; Brixhe 2010.

[101] See, e.g., Plato, *Menexenus*, 245c–d.   [102] Spawforth 2012: 11–18.

important place to non-Greeks, it was always possible for Hellenised non-Greeks to be both Greek and non-Greek at the same time or in different contexts. An illuminating example consists of the names given to the civic tribes of Sardis, when the Lydian city adopted the Greek polis model in the third century.[103] The location of Sardis and Lydia within Greek myth was an important factor in the choice of names; one tribe was called Dionysias, alluding to the birth of Dionysus on the Lydian mountain Tmolus, while another was called Pelopis, after Lydian Pelops, the ancestor of the Peloponnesians. But pride in the Lydian past was equally present; a third tribe was called Mermnas, after the legendary founder of the Lydian dynasty that ended with Croesus, a fourth Masdnis, after the first Lydian king, and a fifth Asias, after Asies, grandson of Masdnes and eponym of Asia, in a tradition that was already known to Herodotus in the fifth century.[104] Roman Sardis could call itself 'the mother of Asia and all Lydia and Greece', emphasising at the same time its Lydian identity, a Lydian myth about Asies and a Greek myth about Pelops.[105]

But what about the Barbarians? Did we not observe in Chapter 2 that one of the essential features of the Panhellenic community was its conception as a community under constant threat from and in constant state of enmity to the Barbarian enemy, and did we not observe also the various projects, usually in a hegemonic form, for providing leadership of the Panhellenic community against the Barbarians (pp. 61–76)? If so many non-Greek communities could now be incorporated within the Panhellenic community, were there any Barbarians left outside? We have continuously stressed the complex and contradictory aspects of Greek identity and the Panhellenic community, and these complexities and contradictions continued to be manifested in the Hellenistic period and later. There were, of course, non-Greeks who even in the Hellenistic period were not and would not be considered as part of the Panhellenic community. Notwithstanding the presence of Greek *apoikiai* in Babylonia or Iran, neither the Babylonians nor the Iranians were ever considered Greeks, even though the repertoire of alien wisdom meant that they had a very strong and respected presence within Hellenistic Greek culture, as we shall see.[106]

Furthermore, the Barbarian enemy was still a potent force that could be used to unite and/or justify the leadership of the Panhellenic community at various occasions during the Hellenistic period. The novel Barbarian enemy were the Gauls. The migration of Celtic groups eastwards, after their encounter with Rome in the fourth century, reached the southern Balkans

---

[103] Spawforth 2001: 385–6.   [104] 4.45.   [105] Herrmann 1993: 233–48.   [106] Momigliano 1975.

in 279, wreaking havoc among Greek and non-Greek communities. After defeating the Seleucid and Macedonian armies, the Gauls looted all the way to Delphi, where they were decisively defeated by the Aetolian League with the necessary divine help. After their defeat, some Celtic groups settled in Thrace, but a substantial number was invited to cross into Asia Minor and serve as mercenaries in the infighting among Hellenistic kings and cities. These Gauls settled in eastern Phrygia, which was renamed Galatia, and they used this area to campaign against and pillage extensive areas of Asia Minor. Fighting against the Gauls and defeating them became the equivalent of the Persian Wars for the Hellenistic Greeks.[107] The Aetolians' victory gave them great prestige and political power, and led to the establishment of the Eleutheria festival at Delphi to celebrate this Panhellenic victory.[108] The Seleucid and Attalid kings who defeated the Gauls in Asia Minor posed as saviours and defenders of Hellenism; and the famous sculptural group of the Battling Gauls from Attalid Pergamon demonstrates how Greek art continued to reflect on the Greek–Barbarian antithesis.[109]

7.3 Alternative globalisations

It would be misleading nevertheless to think that the Hellenistic period is merely the story of the twin processes of the globalisation of Greek culture and the Hellenisation of non-Greek people. We have seen how archaic and classical globalisation contained a variety of non-Greek currents alongside the Greek. Even though Greek-style globalisation became the dominant current in the Hellenistic period for reasons we have examined, again it was not the only current in this period. What follows is an exploration of these alternative currents, focusing in particular on the one that was perhaps the most influential: the Egyptian.

A significant factor in understanding these alternative globalising currents is the expansion and intensification of the world of networks. Our examination of the interactions of Greeks and non-Greeks in the world of networks during the archaic and classical periods focused primarily on areas outside the Aegean and the presence of Greek network actors in these areas. The existing evidence suggests that the presence of non-Greek network actors in the Aegean was limited during the archaic and classical periods; the networks crossing the Mediterranean and connecting Greek

---

[107] *SIG³*, 398; translated in *Austin*, 60. See also *Austin*, 63.   [108] Nachtergael 1977.
[109] Strobel 1996; Mitchell 1993, 2003.

communities to the wider world seem to have been maintained primarily by Greeks. Whether this is evidence of the peripheral position of the Greek world in relation to the older, wealthier and more powerful societies and states of the eastern Mediterranean, or whether it demonstrates Greek dominance of Mediterranean networks, is not something we can determine given the current state of modern scholarship.

But it is undoubtedly in the Hellenistic period that we start to have significant evidence for the large-scale presence of non-Greeks in the Greek cities of the Aegean.[110] The new port of Demetrias, established by Demetrius Poliorcetes at the beginning of the third century in Thessaly, is a characteristic example of the new circumstances. The epitaphs testify to the presence of an extensive international community. There are Phoenicians and other Levantines from Tyre, Sidon, Aradus, Ascalon, Gaza and Cition,[111] as well as Bithynians,[112] Thracians,[113] Carians from Memphis[114] and Illyrians.[115] Particularly fascinating is the presence of a Phoenician priest[116] and an Egyptian priest of Isis,[117] as well as the attestation of mixed marriages, such as the one between a Phoenician from Tyre and a Greek woman from Argos.[118]

The city of Rhodes is another case of a great Hellenistic port with an *emporion* of Mediterranean-wide importance, which hosted diasporas from many different areas.[119] Many foreigners came from neighbouring areas, such as the opposite coasts of Caria and Lycia, significant parts of which came under Rhodian control during the Hellenistic period, or from the more distant Asia Minor coasts of Pamphylia and Cilicia. There are multiple attestations of Phoenicians (from Aradus, Berytus, Sidon and Tyre), while particularly noteworthy is the presence of bilingual epitaphs and dedications;[120] but there are also immigrants from as far away as Bruttium, Lucania and Messapia in southern Italy. Many attested foreigners are of unclear status, and a significant number of them were probably slaves. In this case the range is even wider, and includes Gauls, Phrygians and Lydians from Asia Minor, Armenians, Medes and Persians from the east, Thracians, Maeotae and Sarmatians from the north, and Egyptians and Libyans from the south.[121]

But it is undoubtedly on Delos that we have the best evidence for what a Hellenistic international *emporion* looked like. Delos had been a religious

---

[110] Baslez 1985, 1987, 1988.   [111] Masson 1969; Lipiński 2004: 162–3.
[112] *Arvanitopoulos*, 41, 62.   [113] *Arvanitopoulos*, 48, 189.   [114] *Arvanitopoulos*, 89, 95.
[115] *Arvanitopoulos*, 86, 121, 170.   [116] *SEG* XXV, 681.   [117] *RICIS*, 112/0701.
[118] *Arvanitopoulos*, 107.   [119] Gabrielsen *et al.* 1999; see also Fraser 1977.   [120] Fraser 1970.
[121] Morelli 1955.

centre of Panhellenic importance already from the archaic period; but in the course of the Hellenistic period, and in particular after it was declared a free port without dues by the Romans in 166, it became an international entrepôt housing thousands of merchants from all over the Mediterranean. Delos was famous as a hub of the international slave trade; an inscription recording a collective epitaph for a large group of one individual's slaves, who probably died in some horrible accident, shows the international make-up of a slave household on Delos. It records seven slaves from the Black Sea (four Maeotae, two from Istria and one from Odessus), one from Mazaca in Cappadocia, one from Myndos in Caria, one from Side in Pamphylia, seven from Syria and Phoenicia (three from Apameia, two each from Rhosos and Marathus), two from Palestine (one each from Joppa and Marisa), one Nabataean Arab, and two from Cyrene in Libya.[122]

The presence of thousands of foreigners on Delos led to a double phenomenon; on the one hand, associations based on a common cult emerged in order to give to these foreign merchants a sense of communal life, as well as links and connections with other merchants, members of the local community and the ruling authorities.[123] Particularly interesting are the associations of Phoenician merchants and sailors; the association of worshippers of Heracles from Tyre identified the Tyrian god Melqart with Heracles, an identification already familiar to Herodotus,[124] and the association of the worshippers of Poseidon from Berytus identified Baal with Poseidon.[125] At the same time, the foreign merchants brought with them their cults and built sanctuaries and temples for their deities.[126] Excavations have revealed a large number of such sanctuaries: three different sanctuaries of the Egyptian god Sarapis and other Egyptian deities; another large sanctuary was built by residents from Hierapolis in northern Syria for their native cult of Atargatis and Hadad;[127] other sanctuaries were dedicated to the deities of the Palestinian cities of Ascalon and Iamneia. These sanctuaries of foreign deities looked very different from the standard Greek sanctuaries. There were no Greek-style columned temples, but instead open-court sanctuaries with small chapels, as well as installations such as the theatre in the Syrian sanctuary, used by the worshippers during sacred processions. Other inscriptions attest the worship of Arabian deities either addressed by their Arabian names (Oddos, Sin) or identified with Greek deities (Zeus-Dousares, Helius).[128]

[122] *EAD*, 30 418.   [123] Rauh 1993.   [124] Bonnet 1988.   [125] Bruneau 1970: 621–30.
[126] Baslez 1977.   [127] Lightfoot 2003: 44–50.   [128] Bruneau 1970: 457–80.

Let us now focus specifically on the Egyptian current of globalisation.[129] Until the end of the classical period this current was primarily maintained through the circulation of portable objects (pp. 241–2), but its intensity and media changed rapidly from the Hellenistic period onwards. This was the result of a complex set of factors. We need to take into account features that were long present before the Hellenistic period and in particular the role of the Barbarian repertoire in Greek culture. We have seen how Egypt played such an important role in this repertoire, from mythology all the way to utopia and alien wisdom (pp. 205–12). Equally important was the expansion of the world of networks; the establishment of cults to Egyptian and Egyptianising deities over the whole extent of the Mediterranean world and even further afield is predicated on this expansion. The creation of the Ptolemaic Empire was, finally, a crucial factor in putting into motion processes like the mass migration of Greeks and non-Greeks to Egypt, the creation of the great Mediterranean capital of Alexandria, the emergence of mixed Greco-Egyptian groups, and the elaboration of new prestigious forms of intercultural communication.

One major result of this bilingual and bicultural milieu is that for the first time we find a continuous series of non-Greek texts being translated into Greek. These translations are very diverse in form. While a second/third century CE stele recording a dedication of Moschion to Osiris for healing his foot takes the form of a truly bilingual poem, the translation of the Egyptian *Myth of the Sun's Eye* into Greek is very free, largely excising from the text Egyptian elements that the Greek audience would not be in a position to comprehend.[130] We have already seen how the *enkatochos* Apollonius was studying in the Sarapieion a Greek translation of the Demotic *Dream of Nectanebo*.

Alongside translations we have to situate a complex dialogue between Greek and Egyptian literary genres and ideas.[131] We have already seen how Greek authors like Plato could employ Egyptian themes within the alien wisdom mode (pp. 211–12); the employment of this mode in Greek culture was greatly expanded and intensified from the Hellenistic period onwards. At the one end of this spectrum one can find a variety of texts attributed to foreign sages, whose content is overwhelmingly Greek and whose non-Greek components do not range much beyond some exotic locale and an aura of alien wisdom. Perhaps the most characteristic example are the astrological, magical and theological texts attributed to the Persian prophet

---

[129] Versluys 2010.   [130] Thissen 1977; Fowden 1986: 45–74; Quack 2003: 330–2.
[131] Dieleman and Moyer 2010.

Zoroaster and other Persian magi, whose content is almost purely Greek and which seem divorced even from the information that other Greek authors had concerning Persian religion and philosophy.[132] Side by side, though, we can see other Greek texts which adopt or develop the format and motifs of Egyptian texts and develop a complex interpenetration of Greek and Egyptian ideas.[133] The most famous of these texts constitute the *Corpus Hermeticum*, a series of treatises in Greek attributed to Hermes Trismegistus, a composite of the Greek god Hermes and his Egyptian equivalent Thoth. These treatises usually take the form of teachings revealed by Hermes/Thoth or another Egyptian deity to a divine or mortal student; although the existing Hermetic treatises date from around the second century CE, they adapt the format of the earlier Egyptian *Book of Thoth* in order to present versions of Greek philosophical thinking which are interpenetrated with Egyptian religious ideas.[134]

Equally important was the participation of non-Greeks in Greek literary culture, achieved by presenting to a Greek audience the traditions and history of their own cultures. We have already noted the case of Xanthos of Lydia, but he appears to be a rather isolated example during the archaic and classical periods (pp. 185–6). From the Hellenistic period onwards this phenomenon becomes particularly prominent in Greek literary culture. The two most famous cases concern individuals in similar circumstances. The Egyptian priest Manetho and the Babylonian priest Berossus found themselves in positions of eminence as close collaborators of the first Ptolemaic and Seleucid kings, respectively, and both produced works which presented to a Greek audience the history and traditions of their native cultures.[135] Writing about the history of foreign societies like Egypt or Persia was one of the significant outcomes of the Greek textualisation of the encounters and interactions with non-Greeks in the four parallel worlds. These Greek accounts were not based on translations of non-Greek archives or written genres, but on the textualisation of an oral universe; accordingly, one of the most striking innovations of the works of Manetho and Berossus was the way in which they effectively translated their native literary genres for a Greek audience. At the same time, what is equally striking is that neither Manetho nor Berossus produced mere translations of non-Greek texts; their works engaged in a fascinating dialogue with the pre-existing Greek texts and discourses about their cultures.[136]

---

[132] Texts in Bidez and Cumont 1938; Beck 1991.   [133] Moyer 2011a: 208–73.
[134] Fowden 1986.   [135] Translated in Verbrugghe and Wickersham 1996.
[136] On Manetho, see Moyer 2011a: 80–141; on Berossus, see Haubold forthcoming b.

It is within this complex context that we have to situate the phenomenon of the remarkable globalisation of Egyptian cults across the whole extent of the Hellenistic Mediterranean and even further afield. An illuminating example is the case of Sarapis, an Egyptian deity whose cult, closely linked with that of Isis, expanded outside Egypt in a variously glocalised form from the early third century onwards.[137] Within a few years it is already attested in the farthest reaches of our parallel worlds, testifying to the intensity of the networks that carried these deities; from the Greek *apoikia* of Chersonesus in the Black Sea comes a dedication to Sarapis, Isis and Anubis,[138] while from the far east comes a Greek inscription from Hyrcania, around the Iranian Caspian Sea, recording the manumission of a slave through consecration to Sarapis.[139] These cults were often maintained by a diaspora of Egyptian priests. Already during the third century in Priene in Asia Minor the priest of Isis, Sarapis and the other Egyptian gods was required to be an Egyptian,[140] while on Delos, where there existed three different sanctuaries of Sarapis, a priest proudly described his origins in an Egyptian priestly family and how his grandfather brought the cult of Sarapis to Delos.[141]

In many sanctuaries of Isis across the Mediterranean world archaeologists have discovered texts which are known as Isis aretalogies. Aretalogies are texts which praise a divinity by listing their attributes, praising their powers and recording their miracles. What is remarkable about Isis aretalogies is that they represent the goddess not only as an all-powerful deity, but also as the creator of civilisation and human institutions, from marriage and laws to language and the avoidance of cannibalism. Even more remarkable is that these texts, although taking various forms in both poetry and prose, all ultimately descend from a common prose prototype in which the goddess speaks in the first person:

> I am Isis, ruler of every land
> I was taught by Hermes and with Hermes devised
> letters, both hieroglyphic and demotic, that all might not
> be written with the same.
> I gave laws to mankind and ordained
> what no one can change.[142]

[137] Fraser 1960, 1967; Merkelbach 1995; Borgeaud and Volokhine 2000.
[138] *RICIS*, 115/0302; Vinogradov and Zolotarev 1999.
[139] *RICIS*, 405/0101; Robert 1960: 85–91; for associated Egyptian objects, see Mairs 2007.
[140] *RICIS*, 304/0802.20–5.
[141] *RICIS*, 202/0101; translated in *Austin*, 151; Moyer 2011a: 142–207.   [142] *RICIS*, 302/0204.4–9.

The same text claims that this prototype is a translation into Greek of an Egyptian original that stood in the temple of Ptah at Memphis; although this is debatable, there is little doubt that the Greek text has been composed by someone who was fluent in Egyptian texts, as shown in particular by the deity's speaking in her own name, a feature wholly untypical of Greek texts.[143] We have already explored the Greco-Egyptian milieu where this Greek aretalogy was formulated. This text combines Greek with Egyptian ideas in a form that would be comprehensible to Greeks. But what is so illustrative of the processes of glocalisation is the variety of ways in which this text is adopted and adapted across the Mediterranean. Alongside faithful reproductions of the original Greek prose text with its Egyptian flavour,[144] we find, for example, a second-century text from Maroneia in Thrace reworking the prose prototype into a poem addressed to the deity. In it almost all Egyptian elements have been excised, and Isis is effectively subsumed by Demeter, with primacy of emphasis going to Athens and Eleusis, rather than to Egypt.[145] An alternative reworking took place in a first-century series of Greek texts inscribed on the gate posts of an Egyptian temple in the Fayum. These texts consist of three hymns to Isis composed by one Isidorus, who used Homeric diction, but also strengthened the Egyptian elements by mentioning Egyptian deities like the crocodile god Sokonopis. The author also appends a fourth hymn to the creator of the temple, the pharaoh Amenemhet III, with the explicit aim of translating his story and achievements for the 'men of mixed races' who live in the Fayum. But equally remarkable is the presentation of Isis as a universal goddess in terms clearly dependent on the long processes of interactions in the four parallel worlds:

> All mortals who live in the boundless earth,
> Thracians, Greeks and Barbarians
> Express your fair name, a name greatly honoured among all, (but)
> Each in his own language, in his own land.
> The Syrians call you Astarte, Artemis, Nanaia,
> The Lycian tribes call you Leto the Lady,
> The Thracians also name you as Mother of the Gods,
> And the Greeks Hera of the Great Throne, Aphrodite,
> Hestia the Goodly, Rhea and Demeter.
> But the Egyptians call you Thiouis (because they know) that You,
> being One, are all
> Other goddesses invoked by the races of men.[146]

[143] Quack 2003.   [144] *RICIS*, 113/0545, 202/1101.   [145] *RICIS*, 114/0202; Grandjean 1975.
[146] *SEG* VIII, 548.14–24; translation from Vanderlip 1972: 18.

All the above examples show how the glocalisation of Egyptian culture from the Hellenistic period onwards could take a variety of different forms, from an Egyptianising through a Hellenising to a universalising mode, often combining all three in complex ways. One of the most interesting examples dating after the Hellenistic period is Plutarch's *On Isis and Osiris*. This text combines a narration of impressive ethnographic accuracy of Egyptian tales about these deities, interspersed with Hellenising glosses, within an interpretative framework based on Greek philosophy and theology.[147]

There is no better final illustration of the interconnection of the processes we have been discussing than the case of Artemidorus of Perge. Born in a Pamphylian city in the initial stages of Hellenisation in the early third century, Artemidorus migrated to Egypt, where he served the Ptolemaic kings as an elephant hunter. We can see him making a dedication to Pan, a Greek interpretation of a local Egyptian deity, at el Kanais in the Eastern Desert, in a sanctuary going back to the second millennium.[148] But life subsequently brought Artemidorus to the Aegean island of Thera, where there existed a Ptolemaic garrison, and where he also managed to become a citizen. Among the multiple dedications that he erected there, we encounter not only Artemis of Perge, the *interpretatio graeca* of the chief deity of his Pamphylian home city,[149] but also a dedication to Sarapis, Isis and Anubis.[150] The world of networks, the world of the new empires, the Hellenisation of Pamphylian cities and Greek- and Egyptian-style globalisation are all brought together here in a single individual's life experience.[151]

7.4 Globalisation without Hellenisation

We have examined the relationship between Greek-style globalisation and Hellenisation, as well as the importance of alternative, non-Greek currents of globalisation. Globalisation can lead to the erosion of local cultures and identities, and this is partly what happened in Hellenistic Caria and Lydia; but globalisation is equally often accompanied by the glocalisation of the global *koine* by local cultures and communities in order to construct, defend or re-define their identities and traditions. It is time to look at how during the Hellenistic periods non-Greek communities glocalised Greek culture without entering the process of Hellenisation.

[147] Griffiths 1970; see also Richter 2011: 212–26.   [148] *OGIS* I, 70.   [149] *IG* XII.3, 1350.
[150] *IG* XII.3, 463/1388.   [151] *PP*, 15188.

We have mentioned above that the Hellenistic world included not only the successor empires and states ruled by Greco-Macedonian elites, but also new states created by descendants of the Persian aristocracy, or native grandees who took advantage of the dismemberment and division of Alexander's empire in order to carve out their own niches. This process was particularly strong in central, eastern and northern Asia Minor, which remained outside the path of Alexander's conquest; Bithynia, Cappadocia, Pontus, Armenia and Commagene were states that emerged out of this process. The rulers of these states adopted a range of policies that were vital for promoting the image of a Hellenistic king and for constructing Hellenistic kingdoms. These included the adoption of Greek as the means of public communication, the minting of Greek-style royal coins, the creation of royal courts in the Hellenistic manner and the recruitment of Greek professionals and soldiers to staff them, the use of the polis model for native communities and the creation of royal foundations, the making of benefactions and dedications to the great Panhellenic sanctuaries, as well as participation in Panhellenic festivals and games.[152]

It is worth focusing on the adoption of Greek as the language of communication and culture. The effective use of Greek as a means of communication in inscriptions and coins depended on the successful courting of Greek professionals and intellectuals by these non-Greek rulers. A characteristic example is the positive response of the Bithynian king Ziaelas to the request by the Aegean island of Cos for the recognition of its festival and the *asylia* of its sanctuary. If it is already telling that Cos should have sent envoys to Bithynia, the king's comments are even more illuminating: 'we do in fact exercise care for all Greeks who come to us, as we are convinced that this contributes in no small way to one's reputation'.[153] Plutarch narrates the famous story of how in 53 the severed head of the defeated Roman general Crassus was sent to the Parthian king who was in Armenia, and arrived while the actor Jason from Carian Tralleis was performing Euripides' *Bacchae*; the actor picked up Crassus' head in order to play the role of Agave, the slain Pentheus' mother.[154] This Armenian example of the performance of Greek theatre was not a one-off; from Armaouira in the mountains of Armenia come two early Hellenistic Greek inscriptions: one referring to the dispute between the poet Hesiod and his brother Perses in the *Works and Days*; and the other quoting and adapting verses from various plays of Euripides.[155]

---

[152] Michels 2009.   [153] *SIG*³, 456; translation from *Rigsby*, 11.11–17.
[154] *Life of Crassus*, 33.2–4.   [155] *IEOG*, 9–10.

Greek was also used as an official language of communication by the non-Greek states of the Far East. Already during the third century the emperor Ashoka the Great, who ruled over a substantial part of India, came to adopt Greek alongside Aramaic as a means of communicating his Buddhist philosophy.[156] Two inscriptions of Ashoka, one bilingual in Greek and Aramaic, the other in Greek, have been found at Alexandria in Arachosia, modern Kandahar in Afghanistan.[157] They are impressive translations of Indian texts exemplifying Ashoka's Buddhist philosophy; they are rendered in a form of Greek that rivalled the achievements of Greek chancelleries in Alexandria or Antioch.[158]

In the course of the second century the Parthians, a tribe originally from central Asia, came to conquer the Seleucid territories from India to northern Mesopotamia.[159] The Parthians adopted Greek as one of the official languages of their empire; the legends on Parthian coins remained in Greek till the first century CE.[160] But it is the use of Greek for two private contracts in Median Avroman, in northwestern Iran, which is telling; the second of these first-century contracts is clearly influenced by the tendency to employ the old Attic dialect instead of the standard *koine* dialect of the Hellenistic world.[161] The developments among Greek intellectuals that led to the formation of what is conventionally labelled the Second Sophistic were already present in far-away Media in the first century BCE![162] From third-century Kandahar to first-century Avroman these examples testify to the intensity of networks of communication that maintained Greek as a lingua franca.

The glocalisation of Greek culture by these non-Greek states in Asia Minor did not necessarily mean their Hellenisation. Many of these states were created by members of the Persian imperial diaspora and the Persian aristocracy that ruled these areas under the Persian Empire. Accordingly, Persian culture played an equally important role in these kingdoms. This is attested not only by the preponderance of Persian names like Mithridates and Ariarathes among these dynasties, but also by the extensive evidence for Iranian religious practices in Pontus, Cappadocia, Armenia and Commagene, which persisted even in Roman times.[163] But the most impressive case of hybridity between different currents of globalisation concerns the famous monument erected by Antiochus I of

---

[156] On Ashoka, see Thapar 1997.   [157] *IEOG*, 290–2.

[158] For the survival of Greek as a communicative medium in India until the second century CE, see Burstein 2010.

[159] Wiesehöfer 1996: 117–49.   [160] *IEOG*, 549–89.   [161] *IEOG*, 454–5.

[162] Cassio 1998: 1009–12.   [163] Boyce and Grenet 1991: 69–124, 254–352; S. Mitchell 2007.

Commagene on the summit of the Nemrud Dag Mountain in 62. The monument takes the form of a tumulus surrounded by three terraces. Two of the terraces sport rows of colossal enthroned statues, depicting Antiochus and four deities: Zeus-Oromasdes, Apollo-Mithras-Helios-Hermes, Artagnes-Heracles-Ares and the goddess Commagene. Two rows of stelae trace the ancestry of the king: on the paternal side they start with Dareius I and end with Antiochus' father, while on the maternal side they start with Alexander the Great and end with Laodice, Antiochus' mother and daughter of the Seleucid king Antiochus VII. While the statues of the deities represent a syncretism of Greek and Persian deities, the stelae emphasise Antiochus' ancestry from both the Persian kings as well as Alexander and his Hellenistic successors.[164] Both dynastic genealogy and religion emphasise the hybrid Greco-Persian glocalisation in the kingdom of Commagene.

The best documented case of Greek-style globalisation without Hellenisation concerns the Jews in the Hellenistic era.[165] After the conquest of the Persian Empire by Alexander, Judaea and Palestine became ultimately part of the Ptolemaic kingdom until 198, when they passed into the Seleucid realm.[166] The presence of Greek officials, soldiers and merchants in the area is well attested during the period of Ptolemaic rule;[167] this was accompanied by the adoption of the polis model by native communities around Judaea, a process that was particularly strong along the Palestinian coast and the east bank of the River Jordan, where the so-called Decapolis (Ten Cities) emerged.[168] Members of these communities became particularly prominent in the global *koine* of Greek culture; Gadara in the Decapolis was the birthplace of the philosopher Philodemus, the satirist Menippus, the poet Meleager and the orator Theodorus. Meleager, one of the major contributors to the *Greek Anthology* of epigrams, was proud both of his non-Greek origins and of his Greek culture: 'island Tyre was my nurse, and Gadara, which is Attic but lies in Syria, gave me birth ... if I am a Syrian, what wonder? Stranger, we live in one country, the world.'[169] Particularly noteworthy for the processes of glocalisation is Meleager's claim that Homer was Syrian, because he never presented his heroes eating fish, a religious taboo in certain areas of Syria.[170] Greek-style communities emerged also to the south of Judaea in Idumaea,

[164] Facella 2006, 2009.
[165] Tcherikover 1959; Hengel 1974; Schürer 1973, 1979, 1986, 1987; *CHJ*, 2.   [166] Hengel 1980.
[167] Durand 1997.   [168] Tcherikover 1959: 90–116; Cohen 2006: 225–303.
[169] *Anthologia Graeca*, 7.417.1–5.   [170] Athenaeus, *Deipnosophists*, 4.157b.

where the famous tomb paintings of Marisa featuring Greek mythological scenes testify to the glocalisation of Greek culture in the area.[171]

In 175 a Jewish initiative provides us with test case evidence for the glocalisation of Greek culture in the Hellenistic world. The Jewish High Priest Jason requested from the Seleucid king Antiochus IV permission to create a gymnasion in Jerusalem, introduce the institution of the *ephebeia* to the Jewish youth and reorganise the city as a polis named Antioch in Jerusalem. These proposals to adopt the polis model for Jerusalem met with little resistance, but in 167 infighting among the Jewish elite moved Antiochus to take the extraordinary measure of ordering the abolition of Jewish religious rituals, the introduction of pagan sacrifices and the persecution of offenders.[172] This led to the resistance movement of the Maccabees, which managed to force the Seleucids to terminate the persecution and restore Jewish practices; within a few decades the Hasmonaean dynasty that emerged out of the leadership of the resistance movement transformed the Jewish temple-state into a monarchy, originally as a Seleucid vassal and ultimately as an independent kingdom, conquering extensive territories in Palestine, Idumaea and Transjordan. The Hasmonaean state was a typical Hellenistic monarchy ruling over Jews and other non-Greeks, as well as the Greek-style poleis of the Palestinian coast and the Decapolis across the Jordan. The Hasmonaeans employed Greek-style architecture for their palaces, created Greek-style poleis like other Hellenistic rulers, adopted coinage with Greek and Hebrew legends and Jewish iconography, and used mercenaries.[173] Perhaps the most extravagant example of the extent to which Hellenistic Jews participated in the practices of Greek peer–polity interaction are the stories concerning the kinship between Jews and Spartans; mythology and fictive kinship were powerful elements in intercultural communication, as we have seen time and again.[174]

Alongside the relationship between Jews and the Hellenistic world of empires we have to situate the immense expansion of the Jewish diaspora. The archaic and classical world of empires had already made Jews migrate voluntarily or otherwise. Thousands of Jews were deported to Babylon between 586–538, and many of them chose to stay after the ending of their Babylonian captivity by Cyrus the Great;[175] Jewish mercenaries in the service of the Saite pharaohs remained in Egypt in Persian service, and established their own communities in the land as far south as

---

[171] Jacobson 2007.   [172] Millar 2006: 67–90.   [173] Gruen 1998: 1–40.
[174] Orrieux 1988; Gruen 1998: 253–68; Patterson 2010: 59–68.   [175] Bickerman 1984.

Elephantine.[176] Jewish migration to Egypt expanded massively in Hellenistic times, when Judaea and Palestine were under Ptolemaic rule.[177] Thousands of Jews migrated to Egypt as soldiers, merchants, artisans and farmers. In contrast to the earlier Jewish diaspora in Egypt and Babylonia that used Aramaic, the novel Hellenistic diaspora quickly adopted Greek to the extent of becoming monolingual. Yet, although Jewish immigrants adopted the Greek language, they retained their sense of identity; particularly fascinating are inscriptions in Greek on behalf of the Ptolemaic kings recording the setting-up of synagogues, religious buildings used for prayer and teaching by diaspora Jews, who could not participate in the cult at the Jerusalem Temple.[178]

The new Jewish diaspora was not restricted to Egypt, but spread out into Asia Minor, mainland Greece and the west.[179] Among the sanctuaries of the various foreign communities of merchants at Delos one also finds a Jewish synagogue.[180] But not all members of the Jewish diaspora had migrated willingly; we have in fact some tantalising evidence concerning Jewish slaves. In Oropus, on the border of Boeotia, somebody in the early third century manumitted a Jewish slave, who bore the Greek name Moschus, while his father bore the name Moschion. The inscription recording the manumission was set up in the healing sanctuary of Amphiaraus, because Moschus saw in his dream Amphiaraus and Hygieia ordering him to do so; Moschus saw the dream probably when taking part in an overnight incubation ceremony in the sanctuary.[181] The earliest attested Jew in Greek sources not only had a Greek name, but apparently also participated in non-Jewish religious practices. The opposite case is that of Antigona, a Jewish slave manumitted in 158/7 at Delphi together with her two daughters, Dorothea and Theodora. The two daughters carried Greek names (they both mean Gift of God), but names consistent with Jewish religious views, which were often borne by Diaspora Jews; their mother had kept her religion in captivity and had named, or convinced her master to name, her daughters in a manner consistent with these beliefs.[182]

What is most valuable in the case of Hellenistic Jews is the survival of their literature in a variety of languages.[183] Jews continued to compose works in Hebrew and Aramaic; but the glocalisation of Greek language not only among the Diaspora Jews, but also in Palestine, led to the creation

---

[176] Porten 1968.   [177] For the Jews in Egypt, see Mélèze Modrzejewski 1995.
[178] See, e.g., *OGIS* I, 96, 101; translated in *H-N*, 27–8.   [179] Barclay 1996.
[180] Bruneau 1970: 480–93.
[181] *SEG* XV, 293; translated in Noy *et al.* 2004: 177–80; Lewis 1997: 380–2.
[182] *SGDI*, 1722; translated in Noy *et al.* 2004: 171–3.   [183] Schürer 1986, 1987.

of a Jewish literature in Greek. This literature exhibits the full range of glocalising strategies we have examined in previous chapters (pp. 235–40). Given that Diaspora Jews quickly abandoned Aramaic and Hebrew and adopted Greek as the main language of communication, the translation of Jewish sacred literature, and in particular of the Pentateuch, the Torah, became essential for preserving Jewish identity and culture. According to the *Letter of Aristeas*, it was after an invitation from Ptolemy II that seventy-two Jewish elders translated the Bible into Greek, the famous Septuagint translation.[184] Whether the translation was a result of a Ptolemaic initiative from above or a Jewish initiative from below is still debated by scholars; what is important is that the Greek Bible was exclusively used by Diaspora Jews and made no impression on the wider Greek literary world until Roman times.[185] The participation of Hellenistic Jews in Greek literary culture did not come about through translations of Jewish texts into Greek; it necessitated instead adopting positions within the Barbarian repertoire of Greek culture. This is another illuminating example of the Janus face of Greek culture: its self-referential character which leaves little space for the employment of translated foreign genres and texts; and the diversity of the Barbarian repertoire, which leaves plenty of space for non-Greek cultures to exploit.

One such strategy was the incorporation of Jewish tradition within the time and space of Greek myth. Greek myths narrated how Heracles had defeated the Libyan giant Antaeus, civilised the country and sired, through Antaeus' wife, the ancestors of the Libyan tribes;[186] in Cleodemus Malchus' version, two sons of Abraham, Apher and Aphran, helped Heracles in subduing Antaeus, while Heracles married a daughter of Aphran, who gave birth to the ancestor of a Libyan tribe.[187] A related strategy was adopting the framework of alien wisdom in order to present Jewish wisdom and ideas in a Greek manner, and to argue in favour of the anteriority and superiority of Jewish culture in relation to Greek and other cultures. The historian Eupolemus narrated how Moses handed down the alphabet to the Phoenicians, who transmitted it to the Greeks,[188] while Artapanus described how Moses, known to the Greeks as Musaeus, became the teacher of Orpheus and taught mankind a number of important inventions, came to Egypt and re-organised Egyptian society, and became known to the Egyptians as Hermes because of his capacity to interpret sacred scriptures.

---

[184] Honigman 2003.   [185] Rajak 2009.   [186] Malkin 1994b: 181–7.

[187] *FGrH*, 727 F1; translated in Holladay 1983: 251–5; Gruen 1998: 151–3.

[188] *FGrH*, 723 F1; translated in Holladay 1983: 112–13.

Moses thus becomes the inventor of Greek wisdom as Musaeus and of Egyptian wisdom as Hermes Trismegistus.[189]

But it is the adoption of Greek literary genres by Hellenistic Jews developing Jewish culture which is most remarkable. The Jews possessed a rich historiographical tradition expressed in the chronicles incorporated within the Jewish Bible.[190] During the Persian and Hellenistic periods Jewish authors reworked and expanded their historiography in various genres and languages. Particularly prominent is the reworking of the historical memory of Jewish encounters with the Assyrian, Neo-Babylonian and Persian empires through the medium of 'historical fiction' in tales like those of the books of *Judith, Tobit, Esther* and *Daniel*. These tales explored the complexity of Jewish coexistence with and service under foreign empires, as well as the superiority of Jewish identity and culture in opposition to foreign enemies, in ways that parallel Greek texts relating to the Persian Empire that we examined in Chapter 5 (pp. 190–200). While these works were normally composed in Aramaic or Hebrew, they were quickly translated into Greek and there are even works like the *Third Book of Maccabees*, following the same Jewish tradition of 'historical fiction', which were composed in Greek.[191]

Another development was the adoption of the tradition of Greek-style historiography by Jewish authors.[192] Like Berossus and Manetho, Jewish authors presented their history and traditions to a wider audience in Greek. Demetrius' *On the Kings of Judaea* is a re-telling of Jewish history in Greek with strong interests in chronology and the harmonisation of Biblical traditions; his work is comparable to Hecataeus' approach to Greek traditions.[193] Perhaps the most ironic example of Jewish glocalisation of Greek culture is the historical narrative of the conflict between the Seleucids and the Maccabees written by Jason, a Diaspora Jew from Cyrene in Libya. Here Greek-style historiography is used to narrate in Greek the victory of Jewish rebels against a Greek empire.[194] But the most tantalising example of Jewish glocalisation concerns the adoption of Greek poetic genres for Jewish topics: particularly interesting are the works of two Jewish poets of the Hellenistic period who cannot be dated more closely.[195] Theodotus composed a hexameter epic on the rape of Jacob's daughter Dinah and the destruction of Shechem,[196] while Ezekiel's *Exagoge* is a Hellenistic Greek tragedy in iambic

---

[189] *FGrH*, 726 F3; translated in Holladay 1983: 208–17; Gruen 1998: 155–60.
[190] van Seters 1983.   [191] Johnson 2004.   [192] Holladay 1983.   [193] Gruen 1998: 112–18.
[194] Schürer 1986: 531–7.   [195] Holladay 1989.   [196] Gruen 1998: 120–5.

trimeters based on the Jewish Exodus from Egypt, with Moses as the protagonist![197]

Finally, the most important example of globalisation without Hellenisation is undoubtedly that of Rome. We have seen how already during the archaic period Greek art and myth were glocalised in Rome and elsewhere in Latium (pp. 26–7); various sources attest a variety of contacts and encounters with the Greek world during the classical period, but it was primarily in the course of the large-scale Roman expansion from the Hellenistic period onwards that the situation changed radically. During the third century Rome fought against and, finally, by 265 conquered the Greek *apoikiai* of southern Italy and Sicily; by 188 she had defeated both the Macedonian and the Seleucid kingdoms and declared the freedom and independence of the Greek poleis. By 146 Rome had conquered Macedonia and turned it into a province, defeated the rest of mainland Greece and destroyed Corinth; in the same year she conquered the Carthaginians and razed Carthage. In 133 the kingdom of Pergamum was bequeathed to Rome, and the Greek cities of Asia Minor became part of the Roman province of Asia. When in 29 Augustus annexed the Ptolemaic kingdom, the Greek world and the Mediterranean region as a whole had been fully conquered by Rome.[198]

Many aspects of Rome's glocalisation of Greek culture can be paralleled with those of earlier empires ruling over Greek communities, such as the Lydians and Persians. The Persians had looted Greek works of art from Athens, such as the Tyrannicides' statues, and the Romans expanded this practice on a grand scale, filling Roman temples, forums and villas with the spoils of Greek cities and sanctuaries, which provided a powerful stimulus to Roman art.[199] The Persians had been happy to deport and enslave conquered Greeks as well as employing Greek specialists and professionals, and the Romans expanded equally these practices. Greek deportees like the historian Polybius, Greek slaves as teachers, doctors and entertainers, as well as mobile professionals including philosophers, orators and scientists, were particularly common in Hellenistic Rome.[200] The Persians were adept at using Greek myth and fictive kinship to convince Argos to abstain from the Persian Wars (p. 154), or exploiting the Greek slogans of freedom and independence to intervene in Greek affairs from the King's Peace onwards (pp. 67–8); the Romans were equally adept at using Greek myth to create links with Greek communities, and manipulated splendidly the

---

[197] Jacobson 1983; Lafranchi 2006.   [198] Gruen 1986.   [199] Gruen 1992: 84–129; Miles 2008.
[200] Pliny, *Natural History*, 35.18; Rawson 1985.

Greek slogan of freedom to intervene and dominate the Panhellenic world.[201]

But there were also significant differences. The Roman imperial world was strongly linked with the world of networks. Thousands of Roman and Italian traders, sailors, artisans and financiers followed the path of Roman imperial expansion to the eastern Mediterranean and settled in Greek communities and international *emporia* like Delos.[202] The religious associations formed in these international *emporia* played a crucial role in the globalisation and glocalisation of cultural traditions across the Mediterranean;[203] it was in Delos that Italian and Roman merchants came across the glocalised Egyptian cults of Isis and Sarapis, and the networks linking them to Italy brought these cults to Campania, Rome and the rest of the western Mediterranean.[204]

Above all, it is the deeply referential nature of Roman culture which provides the strongest evidence for the glocalisation of Greek culture by the Romans. As late as the third century the Romans still had hardly anything worth calling literature, but in the wake of imperial expansion Latin literature emerged through the glocalisation of Greek models.[205] It is particularly remarkable that most of the creators of this new literature in Latin were not Romans. Livius Andronicus was a Greek slave whose translation of the *Odyssey* was the first work in literary Latin, and he composed tragedies and comedies in Latin after Greek models; another slave was the Carthaginian Terence who wrote comedies; while Ennius, who glocalised Greek epic to create Latin epic based on Roman themes, famously said that he had three hearts, since he spoke Greek, Oscan and Latin.[206] The ability of Romans to employ Greeks, Carthaginians and Oscans in order to create a Latin literature on the basis of Greek models is one of the most paradoxical examples of ancient glocalisation. We have seen how Egyptians, Babylonians and Jews glocalised Greek historiography or Greek poetry to define their identity and present their cultural tradition to a Mediterranean-wide audience; but while Egyptians or Jews glocalised Greek literature in Greek, the Romans were willing and able to glocalise Greek literature in Latin.[207] Equally important, though far less studied, are the complex ways in which Greeks glocalised Roman culture; particularly fascinating is the manner in which Greek elites responded to the Roman appropriation and reshaping of the Greek past.[208] Nevertheless, one thing is absolutely clear:

[201] Erskine 2001; Eilers 2009; Dmitriev 2001.   [202] Müller and Hasenohr 2002.
[203] Rauh 1993.   [204] Malaise 1972; Bricault 2001.   [205] Clauss 2010.
[206] Aulus Gellius, *Attic Nights*, 17.17.1.   [207] Momigliano 1975: 1–21.   [208] Spawforth 2012.

for all its extensiveness, the Roman glocalisation of Greek culture did not make the Romans Greeks.[209] It provided them rather with a set of cultural practices with which to define and reconstruct Roman identities, and with the manpower and techniques necessary for manning and ruling an empire. Instead of the Hellenisation of Rome, the Roman glocalisation of Greek culture allowed the Romans to live in a truly 'bilingual' fashion in a number of overlapping cultural identities: as Romans in certain activities and areas of life, and as Greeks in others.[210]

This final chapter has aimed to assess the continuities and changes from the picture drawn on the archaic and classical periods in the previous six chapters. There is no doubt that Alexander's conquest and the subsequent emergence of the Hellenistic empires were a significant novel feature of the interaction between Greeks and non-Greeks. For the first time a Greco-Macedonian elite was ruling over an immense number of non-Greek communities and cultures. Unsurprisingly, this led to important changes in the world of empires. Greek culture was now the culture of the ruling elite, and many individuals and groups chose to adopt this culture as a means of social advancement, or as a result of the intermarriages and other interactions put into motion by the Hellenistic empires. The prestige of these Hellenistic empires led to the glocalisation of Greek culture by states and communities from Pontus and Armenia to Parthia and India. The employment of Greek as a lingua franca in Mesopotamia, Iran or India was clearly the result of the new world of the Hellenistic empires.

But what is important to realise is that the Hellenistic globalisation of Greek culture was ultimately shaped by the developments that had taken place in the four parallel worlds during the archaic and classical periods. The glocalisation of the model of the polis by non-Greek communities could take place because such a canonical model had already developed in the world of *apoikiai* during the archaic and classical periods. Mausolus had already initiated this process during the fourth century, and the Hellenistic period saw its intensification. The Hellenisation of non-Greek communities in Asia Minor in particular was made possible by the peculiar form of the Panhellenic world; it was the inherently expandable nature of practices such as the Panhellenic Games and festivals that made possible the incorporation of the Macedonians within the Panhellenic community during the classical period, and the process expanded greatly in the Hellenistic period. Ultimately, it is hardly an accident that Hellenisation was deepest precisely

---

[209] For the complexity of Roman identities, see Dench 2005.   [210] Wallace-Hadrill 2008.

in those areas of Asia Minor (Caria, Lycia, Cilicia, Phoenicia) where the glocalisation of Greek culture had its most visible impact during the archaic and classical periods; this is particularly telling evidence for the argument in favour of continuity which has been presented in this book.

The glocalisation of Greek culture in the archaic and classical periods was not usually accompanied by Hellenisation, even where it was deepest: neither the Etruscans nor the Lycians became Hellenised, notwithstanding the strong employment of Greek culture in defining their identities and cultures. This disjunction between the glocalisation of Greek culture and Hellenisation *tout court* continued in the Hellenistic period and later: the examples of the Hellenistic Jews and Romans we have just examined are telling in this respect. Finally, we have stressed that while the globalisation of Greek culture was particularly important during the archaic and classical periods, the Greek current has to be situated alongside many other currents of globalisation and their diverse contents and means of transmission. Although the globalisation of Greek culture was even more important in the Hellenistic period, it was still accompanied by other currents of globalisation. In fact, one of the paradoxical consequences of the new Hellenistic empires was the transformation and intensification of the Egyptian current of globalisation.

The case for the continuity and constant diversity of the four parallel worlds for the whole of the first millennium BCE can thus be defended; the insufficiency of the traditional periodisation and its political explanations has hopefully been demonstrated. But this is not a call to ignore the importance of new factors and developments which were added to those inherited from the archaic and classical periods. The emergence during the Hellenistic period of the Roman Empire, an imperial world which was both non-Greek and deeply shaped by the glocalisation of Greek culture, is an important development which we have largely skipped in order not to explode the contents of this book and the competence of its author. As Xenophon put it, τὰ δὲ μετὰ ταῦτα ἴσως ἄλλῳ μελήσει.[211]

---

[211] 'The events after these will perhaps be the concern of somebody else': *Hellenica*, 7.5.27.

8 | Conclusions

One of the major arguments of this book is the necessity of dissociating the history of the relationship between Greeks and non-Greeks from the context of modern Orientalism and the modern confrontation between West and East. This implies challenging the identification of the modern Western scholar and reader with the ancient Greeks, seen as the originators of freedom and science in their confrontation with despotic and religious-minded Orientals; but it also challenges the identification of Greek attitudes towards Barbarians with the imperialist and colonialist attitudes of the modern West. There is no doubt that from the point of view of reception, both the inspiration from Greek democracy and freedom as well as the denigration of Oriental despotism and luxury are part of the history of the modern world; accordingly, scholars who work on the interaction between Greeks and non-Greeks cannot ignore these modern discourses and debates when conducting their research. But the mapping of the modern distinction between West and East onto the ancient interaction between Greeks and non-Greeks is deeply flawed, because it is deeply unhistorical. The Greeks did not confront the cultures of the Near East from the same standpoint as the Western imperialist societies confronting the modern Orient. When we remember that more Greeks fought on the Persian side in 480 or in 334, that Lydian and Thracian rulers received honours at Panhellenic sanctuaries such as Delphi, that Persian satraps received Athenian citizenship, that Carian rulers spread the institutions of the Greek polis, or the saga of the Greco-Persian family of Artabazus, it becomes obvious that the interactions between Greeks and non-Greeks took place in a world that was infinitely more complex than any simplistic distinction between West and East.

While there is no doubt that the discourse distinguishing Greek freedom from Oriental despotism was a Greek creation, this was only one among multiple coexisting ways of understanding the complex relations with non-Greeks. The Barbarian repertoire in Greek culture that we examined in Chapter 5 offered a variety of other discourses: myth as a means of exploring kinship between Greeks and Barbarians; the use of the Persian ruler Cyrus as a model for the relationship between education and power; the portrayal of Scythians or Ethiopians as utopian societies; or the attribution to non-Greek cultures of the most important elements of Greek culture, from religion to philosophy and mathematics.

During the archaic and classical periods, the Greek world constituted a small periphery next to a world that was older, richer and more powerful. Not only were the Greeks not in a position to dominate Near Eastern communities in the way that the modern West in the last two centuries has been, but large numbers of Greek mercenaries, artisans, artists and other professionals made a living by serving non-Greek rulers and communities. Greek *apoikiai* had little to do with modern Western colonialism: while on a few occasions they were able to rule over non-Greeks and even subjugate them, in the vast majority of cases they had to strike deals or recognise the suzerainty of non-Greek polities, while there were also many cases where they were conquered or destroyed by non-Greeks, or were transformed into complex Greco-Barbarian states. We have examined in detail why we need to dissociate the world of *apoikiai* from the modern concept of 'colonisation'; instead, we need to examine it within the wider processes of Mediterranean redistribution and as a perennial tug-of-war between the tendency to create frontier societies and the tendency to create model Greek communities participating in the Panhellenic world.

Nevertheless, dissociating the history of Greek–Barbarian interactions from a modern Eurocentric framework does not absolve the historian from the necessity of explaining the paradoxical importance of Greek culture in the Mediterranean world of the first millennium BCE. It is a historical fact, and not merely Eurocentric bias, that at the end of the first millennium a traveller across the Mediterranean would encounter various glocalised versions of Greek culture. We need to explain this historical phenomenon, instead of accepting a Eurocentric mode that takes it for granted, or a post-modern, politically correct mode that explains it away or refuses to recognise its existence: neither the Eurocentric belief in the inherent superiority of Greek culture, nor the misleading suggestion of political factors, such as the conquests of Alexander, can be accepted as explanations. The Eurocentric identification of the Greeks as the inventors of freedom, democracy and science, and the post-modernist identification of Greek culture with the imperialist and colonialist attitudes of the modern West, are two sides of the same coin: we need finally to set them aside in order to explore the peculiar nature of Greek culture and the peculiar historical context in which it interacted with non-Greek cultures.

I have tried to achieve this double aim by recourse to the concept of the four parallel worlds: the world of *apoikiai*; the world of networks; the world of empires; and the Panhellenic world. While the distinction between Greek and non-Greek must be retained, the ways in which this distinction was drawn in these four parallel worlds was very different, mattered in different ways and had different historical results. Greeks employed by the Persian Empire as administrators, vassals, doctors or artisans, alongside various other foreigners; non-Greek slaves in Greek communities and Barbarians accorded Greek citizenship; Greek merchants exchanging goods and making dedications in cosmopolitan *emporia* like Gravisca and Spina alongside merchants of various other cultures and ethnicities; Greeks inserted into Thracian structures of power through marriage and Thracian immigrants participating in an Athenian state cult for a Thracian deity; Greek *apoikiai* under the power of non-Greek rulers or ruling non-Greek communities; frontier societies with mixed populations and complex triangulations between Greek and non-Greek immigrants and native communities; Panhellenic warfare against the Barbarian enemy and dedications from and privileges to Barbarian rulers in Panhellenic sanctuaries. The list could be expanded *ad infinitum*, but it should have become obvious that no single and no simple dividing line between Greeks and non-Greeks ever existed or could exist.

But it is the historical results of this diversity which are particularly important. A first peculiar thing about the Greeks is precisely the coexistence and interaction between so many different parallel worlds. The Lydians participated in many ways in the world of empires, but they had nothing to do with the world of *apoikiai*; the Etruscans participated in the world of networks and had their own version of the world of *apoikiai*, but they had nothing to do with the world of empires. It is the location of Greek culture at the intersection of so many and so diverse parallel worlds of interaction that provides one explanation of its peculiar nature and its widespread globalisation.

The world of networks was crucial for the processes of globalisation we have been examining. Without the mobility of goods, people, ideas and technologies enabled by the networks of traders, artisans, religious specialists, entertainers and artists the specific form of globalisation that we encounter in the Mediterranean world of the first millennium would have been impossible. The world of networks provided a vector for the most diverse currents of globalisation: it carried Egyptian scarabs and Syrian amulets alongside Greek painted pottery and Etruscan amphoras, and the mixed cargoes of Mediterranean shipwrecks are a telling witness to this diversity (pp. 91–2). But the networks also provided an essential link between globalisation and glocalisation. It would be misleading to think in terms of a unilinear process in which globalisation spreads a global *koine*, which local communities merely glocalise. The world of networks provided a constant feedback loop in which globalisation affected local cultures, but in which the glocalised products were also fed back into the global *koine*. We have seen how artists working for Lycian elites glocalised the architectural form of the Greek temple in order to create elaborate funerary monuments for their Lycian employers; but the interconnectivity of networks meant that the Lycian glocalisation of Greek temple architecture was fed back into the system to become part of the global *koine*, and temple-form funerary monuments started to appear in Athens and the rest of the Mediterranean world (pp. 92–4).

The world of *apoikiai* created frontier societies and also provided Greek communities with control of vital resources, such as grain, which was then redistributed across the Mediterranean through the world of networks. But its most important contribution related to the emergence of a canonical model of the Greek polis and the canonical form of Greek culture (p. 277). The continuous experience of creating self-organised communities was effectively restricted to Greeks in the eastern Mediterranean (the western Mediterranean, as we have seen, is a different story). Year after year Greeks from the most diverse origins joined together in order to create organised communities. Out of the enormous diversity of Greek political, social and cultural institutions and practices, the process of creating *apoikiai* made the model of a Greek community become abstracted and canonical: a community with a citizen body divided into tribes, ruled by magistrates, council and assembly, equipped with a particular kind of public space, temples and buildings (agora, theatre, council house, gymnasion). This canonical form of Greek community and culture was already important in the archaic and classical periods, but it would play a crucial role from the Hellenistic period onwards.

The world of empires had a deep effect on Greek culture. Warfare played an important role, both in creating the discourse of the Panhellenic community in the aftermath of the Persian Wars (p. 61), and in providing employment for countless Greek mercenaries in Persian service (pp. 66–9). The Greeks were confronted with states and cultures that were profoundly older, richer and more powerful. We have seen various aspects of the Barbarian repertoire in Greek culture that would have been unthinkable without the interaction with the awe-inspiring world of empires: alien wisdom (pp. 206–14); the use of foreign rulers and communities as models and utopias (pp. 200–6); the depiction of historical events and personalities in Greek art (pp. 196–7); the impact of the Persian Empire in shaping new genres in Greek literature (pp. 218–22).

On the other hand, the Greeks were only one group alongside Jews, Carians or Babylonians among the diverse range of people that were mobilised and employed by the imperial powers. But it was the historical conjuncture of the particular form that the world of empires took in the late archaic and classical periods that played an important role in the globalisation of Greek culture. The Persian Empire did not spread or enforce a canonical set of Persian social and cultural practices on its diverse subject societies; nor can we find evidence of institutionalised practices which created an imperial Persian identity in parallel to the various local ones. The success of the Persian Empire was due to its ability to use local structures and practices in order to fulfil its imperial aims (p. 247). This peculiar Persian imperial world had two interlinked effects. On the one hand, it created an enormous space for globalisation through its mobilisation of a multiethnic and multilingual workforce of soldiers, administrators, artisans and entertainers (pp. 47–52); the creation of cosmopolitan palatial and satrapal centres (pp. 249–54); and the intensification of travel and communication. But the absence of an imperial cultural and social package meant that communities and rulers within the Persian Empire could choose from a wide range of currents in creating and redefining their cultures and identities (pp. 255–73). It is in this context that we have to situate the remarkable globalisation of Greek culture within the Persian Empire.

But there was also a peculiarity that was inherent in the fourth parallel world. Although the Panhellenic world represented the unity of Greek culture, it was at the same time an international world. Because the Panhellenic world lacked a centre and political, social or economic unity, it could be created and maintained only on the basis of some very peculiar practices. One of them was Greek myth and the art and literature that were based on it. We have seen how Greek myth was located in space and time in order to provide a connecting link among the diverse Greek communities. But its location in space and time meant that it was inherently expandable: accordingly, foreign space and foreign heroes were a constitutive feature of Greek myth. This meant that non-Greek cultures and communities were inherently present in Greek myth and the cultural, social and political practices that were based on it. Greek myth was a powerful medium of globalisation and glocalisation: it could encompass the whole world in its imaginary universe and it provided a desirable opportunity for local non-Greek cultures to see themselves within a wider whole in which they had been accorded a prominent position. Given the role of Lycia and Lycian heroes in Greek myth, it is not surprising that the Lycians were willing to represent Lycian heroes of Greek myth like Bellerophon in their funerary monuments (pp. 260–7).

On the other hand, the Panhellenic world had created institutions and practices that allowed the Greeks to define the borders of their community and to share an identity. The Panhellenic sanctuaries and games created a shared arena of display, competition and participation; the sacred envoys who travelled around the Mediterranean to announce the sacred truce for the games created a mental image of the borders of the Panhellenic community, while participating in the games provided a tangible means of testing who was part of that community and who was not (pp. 38–40). But these practices and institutions were inherently expandable, as was shown by the Macedonians in the classical period, and by an immense number of non-Greek communities from the Hellenistic period onwards. Participation in Panhellenic festivals and games provided a canonical and formalised way of becoming part of the Panhellenic community.

All these aspects were crucial for the transformations that took place in the course of the Hellenistic period. The emergence of the Hellenistic world of empires, in which Greco-Macedonian elites ruled over non-Greeks, was obviously an important development. The prestige and power of these empires brought the Greek current of globalisation to areas where it had never before existed; the states created by the descendants of the Persian imperial diaspora in Pontus or Armenia, or the new non-Greek dynasties of the Parthians or the Hasmonaeans, adopted important elements of Greek culture in forming their structures and identities. Many non-Greek subjects of these empires in Egypt, Syria or Mesopotamia chose to adopt Greek cultural practices as a means of social advancement. The Greek language became a lingua franca from the western Mediterranean all the way to Iran, central Asia and India.

But a political explanation of the globalisation of Greek culture in the Hellenistic world is insufficient. Not only had the phenomenon already started by the archaic period, but the Hellenistic developments were crucially shaped by the earlier developments in the four parallel worlds during the archaic and classical periods. The development of the canonical model of the Greek polis through the world of *apoikiai* provided a powerful medium for the glocalisation of Greek culture in the Hellenistic world. From Asia Minor and Syria to Mesopotamia, Iran and central Asia countless communities adopted and adapted the model of the polis and became part of the world of peer–polity interaction Greek-style (pp. 292–8). Panhellenic sanctuaries and games made possible the incorporation of non-Greek communities within the Panhellenic community and, accordingly, their Hellenisation (pp. 298–300). The world of Greek myth and the Barbarian repertoire in Greek culture enabled a massive expansion and intensification of the globalisation of Greek culture even in areas where the glocalisation of the model of the polis was non-existent or limited. We have seen how non-Greeks like the Egyptian Manetho, the Babylonian

Berossus, the Carthaginian Hasdrubal or the Jewish Ezekiel took part in the imaginary universe of Greek culture and literature by presenting their national traditions through the genre of Greek historiography, by participating in the Greek philosophical tradition or by writing tragedies in Greek about Moses (pp. 314–17). When Augustus brought to an end the world of the Hellenistic empires, he unified politically a Mediterranean world which consisted of various glocalised versions of Greek culture.

The diversity of the parallel worlds ensured the continuous diversity of Hellenistic globalisation and glocalisation. The existence of institutions and practices like the Panhellenic festivals and games made possible the incorporation into the Panhellenic community of those non-Greek communities that wished to take that step; but it was also possible to glocalise Greek culture without becoming part of the Panhellenic community. The universal landscape of Greek myth and the Barbarian repertoire of Greek culture allowed Jews, Romans or Carthaginians to glocalise Greek culture without necessarily becoming Hellenised (pp. 309–19). The creation of the Hellenistic world of empires in which Greco-Macedonian elites ruled over non-Greeks did not only intensify the globalisation of Greek culture; by creating a deeper interconnection between the world of empires and the Greek world it also intensified the spread of non-Greek currents of globalisation. We have examined the emergence of cosmopolitan *emporia* in various areas of mainland Greece, in Demetrias, Rhodes or Delos, and the communities of Phoenician, Syrian or Jewish merchants, artisans and sailors that became so prominent in them (pp. 302–4). We have also seen how the interconnection between developments in the Ptolemaic Empire in Egypt and the creation of mixed groups with hybrid practices, on the one hand, and the world of networks, on the other, led to the globalisation and glocalisation of Egyptian cults across the whole Mediterranean world (pp. 305–9).

We have seen how Droysen famously argued that the emergence of the universal religion of Christianity would have been impossible without the mixture between Greek and Near Eastern cultures in the aftermath of Alexander's conquests. Although in many ways Droysen's vision of the Hellenistic world was rather misleading, he had raised an important historical point. In the aftermath of the Second World War Karl Jaspers introduced the concept of the Axial Age in order to describe a series of fundamental transformations that took place simultaneously in China, India, Greece and other areas during the second half of the first millennium BCE.[1] According to Jaspers all these cultures experienced fundamental crises which challenged their order;

---

[1] Jaspers 1953.

in all Axial Age cultures there emerged a broadening of horizons, in which thinkers no longer took the particular social, political and moral order of their cultures for granted, but searched for transcendental solutions which were of potentially universal application. Greek philosophy, Buddhism and Jainism in India and the religion of post-exilic Judaism were results of this axial transformation, and their spread, development and interaction led to the emergence of the universalist monotheistic religions. Jaspers' arguments have been endlessly debated,[2] and it is doubtful whether the concept of an Axial Age is particularly helpful as an explanation for these transformations.[3] But the creation of intellectual systems of universal scope and their globalisation was something that undoubtedly took place in the Mediterranean and in other parts of the world, and which had very important ramifications for world history.[4]

We have followed the emergence and development of one such system in our discussion of the Barbarian repertoire in Greek culture. We have explored the various ways in which Greek thinkers created a cultural system which was deeply Hellenocentric and self-referential, but at the same time universalist in its extent and scope. Greek myth created an imaginary universe that could include the largest part of the known world; the textualisation of encounters and interactions created a variety of genres whose imaginary universe included the whole known world. The Greek discourses on the first inventors of things created a cosmopolitan universe of civilisation, art and science in which sages from very different cultures could make contributions. Manuals on politics, economics or warfare included examples and stratagems from all known cultures and communities. Political or moral philosophy could use Barbarian kings as models or present non-Greek communities as utopias. Ctesias' attempt to write the history of foreign empires and the emergence of universal history with Ephorus meant the creation of a historical universe in which all known cultures and communities could potentially be part. There is little doubt that this intellectual system was deeply Hellenocentric; but one of the major reasons for the widespread globalisation of Greek culture is that it provided a universalising system in which other cultures could find a place, and often a very prominent one.[5]

This peculiar cultural system is the most significant Greek legacy to the processes of globalisation that have continued since the first millennium BCE. But in contrast to traditional Eurocentric celebrations of the 'Greek miracle', it is not some innate feature of the Greeks, or their freedom and democracy, which is the explanation of this achievement. Rather, it is the

---

[2] See the latest discussion in Arnason *et al.* 2005.   [3] See, e.g., Assmann 2011: 263–7.
[4] Bentley 1993.   [5] Compare the argument of Bowersock 1990.

specific historical conjuncture of the Mediterranean and the Near East during the archaic and classical periods that explains why Greek culture developed its Barbarian repertoire in that particular way and why the globalisation of Greek culture was so widespread. It was the coexisting interaction of Greek culture with the four parallel worlds that created a Barbarian repertoire that was both Hellenocentric and universalist in its scope. It was also the peculiar form of imperial globalisation that characterised the Persian Empire in the archaic and classical periods that enabled the widespread glocalisation of Greek culture. Modern scholars have for far too long been accustomed to seeking some innate features of the West in its various incarnations as an explanation for the course of world history. This is no longer credible as an explanation of modern history,[6] and modern historians have developed approaches like that of 'connected history' in order to show that the emergence and development of the modern world is a global process.[7] It is hardly more credible to think in those traditional terms when it comes down to ancient history. It is the historical conjuncture of the four parallel worlds in the first millennium BCE that explains the particular forms of globalisation and glocalisation that we have encountered.

But at the same time the Barbarian repertoire shows that Greek culture is not just Greek: Greek culture as formed in the course of the archaic and classical periods is impossible to dissociate from its interactions with non-Greeks. Political theory, the quest to create an ideal community and universal historiography are undoubtedly great contributions of Greek culture to ongoing processes of globalisation which reach our present: but they are at the same time the result of the impact of the Persian imperial world on the communities of the archaic and classical Mediterranean, as filtered through the Greek–Barbarian repertoire. The Barbarian repertoire is both peculiarly Greek and constitutively non-Greek at the same time.

Understanding the nature of this peculiar cultural system and its long-term globalisation and glocalisation is a historical project with which scholars are only beginning to grapple. Future work could hopefully expand this in two directions. The very title of this book makes evident that it has approached the processes of ancient globalisation and glocalisation from one particular perspective: that of the relationship between Greeks and the various non-Greek cultures and communities. Although I have largely focused on Greek culture and its globalisation, I have continuously stressed that this was only one among various other currents of globalisation. I have continuously strived to show that the glocalisation of Greek cultures by non-Greek

---

[6] See, e.g., Bayly 2004.   [7] Subrahmanyam 1997.

communities was constantly accompanied by the glocalisation of other currents, although in different ways. I have also devoted much space to showing that Hellenistic globalisation was not tantamount to Hellenisation, by showing, for example, how the intensification of Greek globalisation was inseparable from the globalisation of Egyptian cults. But a full understanding of ancient globalisation and glocalisation will need to accord proper space to the Phoenician, Aramaic, Mesopotamian, Jewish and other currents of globalisation that have been only cursorily treated in this book.

In the course of this book I have tried to provide various comparative examinations in order to identify what was peculiar about Greek culture and its globalisation, but my examples have been largely limited to the first millennium and to the same area of the Mediterranean and the Near East. It would be highly illuminating to expand the comparison to other cultural systems that have been widely globalised and glocalised. Jaspers might have been wrong about the Axial Age, but his urge to expand our vision by taking into account globalised systems outside the Mediterranean is still salutary. The emergence of the Sanskrit cultural cosmopolis and its widespread globalisation in south and southeast Asia in the last 2,000 years have been brilliantly analysed by Sheldon Pollock.[8] As with Greek culture, the Indian world was not based around a dominant centre, and lacked political, social or economic unity; accordingly, Sanskrit culture was based on peculiar institutions and practices that allowed the creation and maintenance of cultural unity among Indian communities. As with Greek culture, the globalisation of Sanskrit culture was not the result of imperial imposition and cannot be accounted for through political explanations; it was rather the result of the interaction of a series of parallel worlds which included networks, empires and *apoikiai*, if of rather different forms. But it is the very different nature of the Sanskrit cosmopolis, when compared with the Barbarian repertoire of Greek culture, which can allow us to grasp deeper both the peculiarities of the Greek case as well as the similarities.

Equally important will be to study the transformations of Greek culture and its globalisation in the context of novel forms of imperial globalisation that emerged primarily in the first millennium CE. We have already mentioned how different Roman imperial globalisation was compared to that of earlier empires (pp. 243–6). The existence of a Roman social and cultural package (the city and its political organisation, fora, basilicas, baths) and the creation of institutionalised practices (the expansion of citizenship, provincial assemblies, imperial cult) which created a Roman imperial identity presented a novel form

---

[8] Pollock 2006.

of imperial globalisation. But this imperial globalisation was also deeply indebted to the glocalisation of Greek culture, although in peculiar ways: the ability of the Romans to glocalise Greek literature in their own Latin language, in contrast to all other Mediterranean cultures, and to spread this literature across their conquered territories, but in tandem with the spread of Greek literature, is a good expression of the paradox. What has been far less studied, and an important future desideratum, are the ways in which Roman imperial globalisation transformed Greek culture and its globalisation.

These are fascinating future prospects, but it is perhaps best to bring an already long account to an end. For the historian who attempts to write about the foreign country of the past and tackle an immense subject should always bear in mind his inherent similarity to the Barbarian prince whom Cavafy so memorably depicted:

> He was generally liked in Alexandria
> during the ten days he sojourned there,
> the potentate from Western Libya,
> Aristomenes, son of Menelaus.
> As with his name, his dress properly Greek.
> He gladly accepted the honours, but
> didn't solicit them; he was modest.
> He bought books in Greek,
> particularly on history and philosophy.
> But above all, he was a man of few words.
> He must be profound of thought, it was rumoured,
> and such people have it in their nature not to say much.
> He was neither profound of thought, nor anything.
> Just an ordinary, silly man.
> He assumed a Greek name, he dressed like a Greek,
> taught himself to behave-more or less-like a Greek;
> and trembled in his soul lest
> he mar the tolerable impression
> by speaking Greek with dreadful barbarisms,
> and have the Alexandrians poke fun at him,
> as is their habit ~ awful people.
> And for this reason, he confined himself to a few words,
> fearfully paying attention to the declensions and the accent;
> and he got bored no end, having
> so many things to say piled up inside him.[9]

---

[9] Cavafy 2007: 181.

Bibliography

Abdi, K. (2002) 'Notes on the Iranianization of Bes in the Achaemenid Empire', *Ars Orientalis* 32: 133–62.

Abu-Lughod, J. L. (1989) *Before European Hegemony: The World-System AD 1250–1350*. New York and Oxford.

Adams, C. and Roy, J. (eds) (2007) *Travel, Geography and Culture in Ancient Greece, Egypt and the Near East*. Oxford.

Adams, J. N. (2003) *Bilingualism and the Latin Language*. Cambridge.

Adiego, I. J. (2007) *The Carian Language*. Leiden and Boston, MA.

Akurgal, E. (1968) *The Birth of Greek Art: The Mediterranean and the Near East*, trans. W. Dynes. London.

Alam, M. (1998) 'The pursuit of Persian: language in Mughal politics', *MAS* 32(2): 317–49.

Albanese Procelli, R. M. (2003) *Sicani, Siculi, Elimi: Forme d'identità, modi di contatto e processi di trasformazione*. Milan.

Albertz, A. (2006) *Exemplarisches Heldentum: die Rezeptionsgeschichte der Schlacht an den Thermopylen von der Antike bis zur Gegenwart*. Munich.

Alonso-Nuñez, J. M. (1990) 'The emergence of universal history from the fourth to the second centuries BC', in *Purposes of History: Studies in Greek Historiography from the Fourth to the Second Centuries BC*, eds H. Verdin, G. Schepens and E. de Keyser. Louvain, 173–92.

Aly, W. (1921) *Volksmärchen, Sage und Novelle bei Herodot und seinen Zeitgenossen*. Göttingen.

Ampolo, C. (1976/7) 'Demarato: osservazioni sulla mobilità sociale arcaica', *DdA* 9/10: 333–45.

Ampolo, C. and Caruso, T. (1990/1) 'I Greci e gli altri nel Mediterraneo occidentale. Le iscrizioni greca ed etrusca di Pech-Maho: circolazione di beni, di uomini, d'istituti', *Opus* 9/10: 29–58.

Anderson, J. K. (1995) 'The Geometric Catalogue of Ships', in Carter and Morris (eds), *The Ages of Homer*, 181–91.

Anderson, M. J..(1997) *The Fall of Troy in Early Greek Poetry and Art*. Oxford.

Ando, C. (2000) *Imperial Ideology and Provincial Loyalty in the Roman Empire*. Berkeley, CA.

(2010) 'Imperial identities', in Whitmarsh (ed.), *Local Knowledge and Microidentities*, 17–45.

Andreae, B. and Schepkowski, N. S. (eds) (2007) *Malerei für die Ewigkeit: Die Gräber von Paestum*. Munich.

Appadurai, A. (ed.) (1986) *The Social Life of Things: Commodities in Cultural Perspective*. Cambridge.

(ed.) (2001) *Globalization*. Durham, NC and London.

Archibald, Z. H. (1998) *The Odrysian Kingdom of Thrace: Orpheus Unmasked*. Oxford.

Arnason, J. P., Eisenstadt, S. N. and Wittrock, B. (eds) (2005) *Axial Civilisations and World History*. Leiden and Boston, MA.

Asheri, D. (1983) *Fra ellenismo e iranismo: studi sulla società e cultura di Xanthos nella età achemenide*. Bologna.

(1988) 'Carthaginians and Greeks', *CAH*, IV², 739–80.

Asheri, D., Lloyd, A. and Corcella, A. (2007) *A Commentary on Herodotus Books I–IV*. Oxford.

Ashton, S-A. (2001) *Ptolemaic Royal Sculpture from Egypt: The Interaction between Greek and Egyptian Traditions*. Oxford.

Assmann, J. (2001) 'Sapienza e mistero: l'immagine greca della cultura egiziana', in Settis (ed.), *I Greci: I Greci oltre la Grecia*, 401–69.

(2002) *The Mind of Egypt: History and Meaning in the Time of Pharaohs*, trans. A. Jenkins. Cambridge, MA and London.

(2011) *Cultural Memory and Early Civilization: Writing, Remembrance and Political Imagination*, trans. D. H. Wilson. New York.

Ateşlier, S. (2001) 'Observations on an early classical building of the Satrapal period at Daskyleion', in Bakır (ed.), *Achaemenid Anatolia*, 147–68.

Aubet, M. E. (2001) *The Phoenicians and the West: Politics, Colonies and Trade*, trans. M. Turton, 2nd edn. Cambridge.

Austin, M. M. (1970) *Greece and Egypt in the Archaic Age*, PCPS Supplement No. 2. Cambridge.

(1990) 'Greek tyrants and the Persians', *CQ* 40: 289–306.

(2008) 'The Greeks in Libya', in Tsetskhladze (ed.), *Greek Colonisation*, vol. II, 187–217.

Bacon, H. (1961) *Barbarians in Greek Tragedy*. New Haven, CT.

Badian, E. (1982) 'Greeks and Macedonians', in *Macedonia and Greece in Late Classical and Early Hellenistic Times*, eds B. Barr-Sharrar and E. N. Borza. Washington, DC, 33–51.

Bäbler, B. (1998) *Fleißige Thrakerinnen und wehrhafte Skythen: Nichtgriechen im klassischen Athen und ihre archäologische Hinterlassenschaft*. Stuttgart.

(2005) 'Bobbies or boobies? The Scythian police force in classical Athens', in Braund (ed.), *Scythians and Greeks*, 114–22.

Bakır, T. (1997) 'Phryger in Daskyleion', in Gusmani *et al.* (eds), *Frigi e Frigio*, 229–38.

(ed.) (2001a) *Achaemenid Anatolia*. Leiden.

(2001b) 'Die Satrapie in Daskyleion', in Bakır (ed.), *Achaemenid Anatolia*, 169–80.

Bakır, T. and Gusmani, R. (1991) 'Eine neue phrygische Inschrift aus Daskyleion', *EA* 18: 157–64.

(1993) 'Graffiti aus Daskyleion', *Kadmos* 32: 135–44.

Bakker, E. J. (ed.) (2010) *A Companion to the Ancient Greek Language*. Malden, MA and Oxford.

Bakker, E. J., de Jong, I. J. F. and van Wees, H. (eds) (2002) *Brill's Companion to Herodotus*. Leiden, Boston, MA and Cologne.

Balcer, J. M. (1995) *The Persian Conquest of the Greeks 545–450 BC*. Konstanz.

Banari, V. (2003) 'Die Beziehungen von Griechen und Barbaren im nordwestlichen Pontos-Gebiet. Untersuchungen zu Handel- und Warenaustausch vom 7. bis. 3. Jh. v. Chr. auf Grundlage der archäologischen Funde und schriftlichen Quellen im Nordwesten des Schwarzen Meeres', PhD dissertation, University of Mannheim.

Barash, M. (1996) 'Visual syncretism: a case study', in Budick and Iser (eds), *The Translatability of Cultures*, 37–54.

Barclay, J. M. G. (1996) *Jews in the Mediterranean Diaspora: From Alexander to Trajan (323 BCE–117 CE)*. Edinburgh.

Barnett, R. D. (1974) 'A silver-head vase with Lycian inscriptions', in *Mansel' e Armagan/Mélanges Mansel*. Ankara, 893–901.

Barringer, J. M. (2008) *Art, Myth and Ritual in Classical Greece*. Cambridge and New York.

Baslez, M-F. (1977) *Recherches sur les conditions de pénétration et de diffusion des religions orientales à Délos*. Paris.

(1985) 'Présence et traditions iraniennes dans les cités de l'Egée', *REA* 87: 137–55.

(1987) 'Le rôle et la place des Phéniciens dans la vie économique des ports de l'Égée', in *Studia Phoenicia, vol. V: Phoenicia and the East Mediterranean in the First Millennium BC*, ed. E. Lipiński. Louvain, 267–85.

(1988) 'Les communautés d'Orientaux dans la cité grecque: formes de sociabilité et modèles associatifs', in Lonis (ed.), *L'étranger dans le monde grec*, 139–58.

Baurain, C., Bonnet, C. and Krings, V. (eds) (1991) *Phoinikeia grammata: lire et écrire en Méditerranée*. Namur.

Bayly, C. A. (2004) *The Birth of the Modern World 1780–1914: Global Connections and Comparisons*. Malden, MA and Oxford.

Beck, R. (1991) 'Excursus: Thus spake not Zarathushtra: Zoroastrian pseudepigrapha of the Greco-Roman world', in Boyce and Grenet with Beck, *A History of Zoroastrianism*, vol. III, 491–565.

Beckman, G. (2009) 'Hittite literature', in Ehrlich, *From an Antique Land*, 215–54.

Benoit, F. (1965) *Recherches sur l'hellénisation du Midi de la Gaule*. Aix-en-Provence.

Bentley, J. H. (1993) *Old World Encounters: Cross-Cultural Contacts and Exchanges in Pre-Modern Times*. New York and Oxford.

Bérard, C. (2000) 'The image of the Other and the foreign hero', in Cohen (ed.), *Not the Classical Ideal*, 390–412.

Berlinerblau, J. (1999) *Heresy in the University: The Black Athena Controversy and the Responsibilities of American Intellectuals.* New Brunswick, NJ.

Bernal, M. (1987) *Black Athena. The Afroasiatic Roots of Classical Civilization, vol. I: The Fabrication of Ancient Greece, 1785–1985.* London.

(1991) *Black Athena. The Afroasiatic Roots of Classical Civilization, vol. II: The Archaeological and Documentary Evidence.* London.

(2006) *Black Athena. The Afroasiatic Roots of Classical Civilization, vol. III: The Linguistic Evidence.* New Brunswick, NJ.

Bernard, A. and Masson, O. (1957) 'Les inscriptions grecques d'Abou Simbel', *REG* 70: 1–46.

Bernard, P. (1976) 'Les traditions orientales dans l'architecture gréco-bactrienne', *Journal Asiatique* 264: 245–75.

Berranger, D. (1983) 'Le relief inscrit en l'honneur des Nymphes dans les carrières de Paros', *REA* 85: 235–59.

Bertelli, L. (2001) 'Hecataeus: from genealogy to historiography', in Luraghi (ed.), *Historian's Craft in the Age of Herodotus,* 67–94.

Berti, F. and Guzzo, P. G. (eds) (1993) *Spina: storia di una città tra greci ed etruschi.* Ferrara.

Beschi, L. (1982) 'I donari tarantini a Delfi: alcune osservazioni', in *Aparchai. Nuove ricerche e studi sulla Magna Grecia e la Sicilia antica in onore di P. E. Arias,* eds M. L. Gualandi, L. Massei and S. Settis. Pisa, 227–38.

Best, J. G. P. (1969) *Thracian Peltasts and their Influence on Greek Warfare.* Groningen.

Beyer, I. (1976) *Die Tempel von Dreros und Prinias A und die Chronologie der kretischen Kunst der 8. und 7. Jhs. v. Chr.* Freiburg.

Bichler, R. (2000) *Herodots Welt: der Aufbau der Historie am Bild der fremden Länder und Völker, ihrer Zivilisation und ihrer Geschichte.* Berlin.

Bickerman, E. J. (1952) 'Origines gentium', *Classical Philology* 47(2): 65–81.

(1984) 'The Babylonian captivity', *CHJ* 1: 342–58.

Bidez, J. and Cumont, F. (1938) *Les mages hellénisés: Zoroastre, Ostanès et Hystaspe d'après la tradition grecque.* Paris.

Bietak, M. (ed.) (2001) *Archaische Griechische Tempel und Altägypten.* Vienna.

Bilde, P. *et al.* (eds) (1996) *Aspects of Hellenistic Kingship.* Aarhus.

Billows, R. A. (2010) *Marathon: How One Battle Changed Western Culture.* New York and London.

Bingen, J. (2007) *Hellenistic Egypt: Monarchy, Society, Economy, Culture.* Edinburgh.

Blakeway, A. (1935) '"Demaratus": a study in some aspects of the earliest Hellenisation of Latium and Etruria', *JRS* 25: 129–49.

Blümel, W. (1993) '*SGDI* 5727 (Halikarnassos): eine Revision', *Kadmos* 32: 1–18.

(1994) 'Über die chronologische und geographische Verteilung einheimischer Personennamen in griechischen Inschriften aus Karien', in Gianotta *et al.* (eds), *La decifrazione del cario,* 65–86.

Boardman, J. (1970) 'Pyramidal stamp seals in the Persian Empire', *Iran* 8: 19–45.

(1987) 'Amasis: the implications of his name', in *Papers on the Amasis Painter and His World*, ed. D. von Bothmer. Malibu, CA, 141–52.

(1994) *The Diffusion of Classical Art in Antiquity*. Princeton, NJ.

(1999) *The Greeks Overseas: Their Early Colonies and Trade*, 4th edn. London.

(2000) *Persia and the West: An Archaeological Investigation of the Genesis of Achaemenid Art*. London.

Boardman, J. et al. (eds) (1991) *The Assyrian and Babylonian Empires and Other States of the Near East, from the Eighth to the Sixth Centuries BC, CAH*, III.2². Cambridge.

Boedeker, D. and Sider, D. (eds) (2001) *The New Simonides: Contexts of Praise and Desire*. New York and Oxford.

Bollansée, J., Engels, J., Schepens, G. and Theys, E. (eds) (1998) *FrGrHist IV A: Biography, vol. I: The Pre-Hellenistic Period*. Leiden.

Bonnet, C. (1988) *Melqart: cultes et mythes de l'Héraclès tyrien en Méditerranée*. Louvain.

Borgeaud, P. (2004) *Mother of the Gods: From Cybele to Virgin Mary*, trans. L. Hochroth. Baltimore, MA and London.

Borgeaud, P. and Volokhine, Y. (2000) 'La formation de la légende de Sarapis: une approche transculturelle', *Archiv für Religionsgeschichte* 2: 37–76.

Bose, S. (2006) *A Hundred Horizons: The Indian Ocean in the Age of Global Empire*. Cambridge, MA and London.

Bosworth, A. B. (1980) 'Alexander and the Iranians', *JHS* 100: 1–21.

(1988) *Conquest and Empire: The Reign of Alexander the Great*. Cambridge.

(1996) *Alexander and the East: The Tragedy of Triumph*. Oxford.

Bovon, A. (1963) 'La représentation des guerriers perses et la notion de Barbare dans la première moitié du Ve siècle', *BCH* 87: 579–602.

Bowersock, G. W. (1990) *Hellenism in Late Antiquity*. Ann Arbor, MI.

Bowie, E. L. (2001) 'Ancestors of historiography in early Greek elegiac and iambic poetry', in Luraghi (ed.), *Historian's Craft in the Age of Herodotus*, 45–66.

Bowman, A. K. and Woolf, G. (eds) (1994) *Literacy and Power in the Ancient World*. Cambridge.

Bowra, C. M. (1956) 'A fragment of the Arimaspea', *CQ* 6: 1–10.

Boyce, M. and Grenet, F. with Beck, R. (1991) *A History of Zoroastrianism, vol. III: Zoroastrianism under Macedonian and Roman Rule*. Leiden.

Bradley, G. and Wilson, J-P. (eds) (2006) *Greek and Roman Colonization: Origins, Ideologies and Interactions*. Swansea.

Braun, M. (1938) *History and Romance in Graeco-Oriental Literature*. Oxford.

Braun, T. F. R. G. (1982a) 'The Greeks in the Near East', *CAH*, III.3², 1–31.

(1982b) 'The Greeks in Egypt', *CAH*, III.3², 32–56.

Braund, D. (ed.) (2005) *Scythians and Greeks: Cultural Interactions in Scythia, Athens and the Early Roman Empire (Sixth Century BC–First Century AD)*. Exeter.

(2007) 'Greater Olbia: ethnic, religious, economic and political interactions in the region of Olbia, *c.* 600–100 BC', in Braund and Kryzhitskiy (eds), *Classical Olbia and the Scythian World*, 37–77.

(2008) 'Scythian laughter: conversations in the northern Black Sea region in the fifth century BC', in Guldager Bilde and Petersen (eds), *Meetings of Cultures in the Black Sea Region*, 347–68.

Braund, D. and Kryzhitskiy, S. D. (eds) (2007) *Classical Olbia and the Scythian World: From the Sixth Century BC to the Second Century AD*. Oxford.

Bravo, B. (1968) *Philologie, histoire, philosophie de l'histoire: étude sur J. G. Droysen, historien de l'antiquité*. Breslau and Warsaw.

Bresson, A. (1980) 'Rhodes, l'Hellénion et le statut de Naucratis (VI–IVe siècle a.C.)', *DHA* 6: 291–349.

(1991) 'Le fils de Pythéas, Égyptien de Naucratis', in Fick and Carrière (eds), *Mélanges Étienne Bernand*, 37–42.

(2007a) 'La construction d'un espace d'approvisionnement: les cités égéennes et le grain de mer Noire', in Bresson *et al.* (eds), *Une koinè pontique*, 49–68.

(2007b) 'Les Cariens ou la mauvaise conscience du barbare', in Urso (ed.), *Tra oriente e occidente*, 209–28.

Bresson, A., Ivantchik, A. and Ferrary, J-L. (eds) (2007) *Une koinè pontique: Cités grecques, sociétés indigènes et empires mondiaux sur le littoral nord de la Mer Noire (VIIe siècle a.C.–IIIe siècle p.C.)*. Bordeaux.

Bresson, A. and Rouillard, P. (eds) (1993) *L'Emporion*. Paris.

Briant, P. (1988) 'Ethno-classe dominante et populations soumises dans l'Empire achéménide: le cas de l'Égypte', in *AchHist* 3, 137–73.

(1994) 'Sources gréco-hellénistiques, institutions perses et institutions macédoniens: continuités, changements et bricolages', in *AchHist* 8, 283–310.

(ed.) (1995) *Dans le pas des Dix-Mille. Peuples et pays du Proche-Orient vus par un grec*. Toulouse.

(1998a) 'Colonizzazione ellenistica e popolazioni del Vicino Oriente: dinamiche sociali e politiche di acculturazione', in Settis (ed.), *I Greci: Transformazioni*, 309–33.

(1998b) 'Cités et satrapes dans l'empire achéménide: Xanthos et Pixôdaros', *CRAI*: 305–40.

(1998c) 'Droaphernès et la statue de Sardes', in *AchHist* 11, 205–26.

(2002a) *From Cyrus to Alexander: A History of the Persian Empire*, 2nd edn, trans. P. T. Daniels. Winona Lake, IN.

(2002b) 'History and ideology: the Greeks and "Persian decadence"', in Harrison (ed.), *Greeks and Barbarians*, 193–210.

(2010) *Alexander the Great and his Empire: A Short Introduction*, trans. A. Kuhrt. Princeton, NJ.

Briant, P. and Boucharlat, R. (eds) (2005) *L'archéologie de l'empire achéménide: nouvelles recherches*. Paris.

Briant, P. and Chauveau, M. (eds) (2009) *Organisation des pouvoirs et contacts culturels dans les pays de l'empire achéménide*. Paris.

Briant, P. and Descat, R. (1998) 'Un registre douanier de la satrapie d'Egypte', in *Le commerce en Égypte ancienne*, eds N. Grimal and B. Menu. Cairo, 59–104.

Briant, P. and Joannès, F. (eds) (2006) *La transition entre l'empire achéménide et les royaumes hellénistiques: vers 350–300 av. J-C.* Paris.

Bricault, L. (2001) *Atlas de la diffusion des cultes isiaques: IVe s. av. J.-C.–IVe s. apr. J.-C.* Paris.

Bricault, L. and Versluys, M. J. (eds) (2010) *Isis on the Nile: Egyptian Gods in Hellenistic and Roman Egypt*. Leiden.

Bridges, E., Hall, E. and Rhodes, P. J. (eds) (2007) *Cultural Responses to the Persian Wars*. Oxford.

Briquel-Chatonnet, F. (ed.) (1996) *Mosaïque de langues, mosaïque culturelle: le bilinguisme dans le Proche-Orient ancien*. Paris.

Brisson, L. (2000) 'L'incantation de Zalmoxis dans le *Charmide* (156d–157c)', in Robinson and Brisson (eds), *Plato*, 278–86.

Brixhe, C. (ed.) (1993a) *La Koinè grecque antique, vol. I: Une langue introuvable?* Nancy.

(1993b) 'Le grec en Carie et en Lycie au IVe siècle: des situations contrastées', in Brixhe (ed.), *La Koinè grecque antique*, vol. I, 59–82.

(2010) 'Linguistic diversity in Asia Minor during the Empire: *Koine* and non-Greek languages', in Bakker (ed.), *A Companion to the Ancient Greek Language*, 228–52.

Bruneau, P. (1970) *Recherches sur les cultes de Délos à l'époque hellénistique et à l'époque impériale*. Paris.

Bruns-Özgan, C. (1987) *Lykische Grabreliefs des 5. und 4. Jahrhunderts v. Chr.* Tübingen.

Bryce, T. R. (1986) *The Lycians in Literary and Epigraphic Sources*. Copenhagen.

(1990/1) 'Lycian Apollo and the authorship of the "Rhesus"', *CJ* 86: 144–9.

(2003) *Letters of the Great Kings of the Ancient Near East: The Royal Correspondence of the Late Bronze Age*. London and New York.

Budick, S. and Iser, W. (eds) (1996) *The Translatability of Cultures: Figurations of the Space Between*. Stanford, CA.

Burbank, J. and Cooper, F. (2010) *Empires in World History: Power and the Politics of Difference*. Princeton, NJ and Oxford.

Burkert, W. (1985) *Greek Religion: Archaic and Classical*, trans. J. Raffan. Oxford.

(1987) *Ancient Mystery Cults*. Cambridge, MA and London.

(1992) *The Orientalising Revolution: Near Eastern Influence on Greek Culture in the Early Archaic Age*, trans. W. Burkert and M. E. Pinder. Cambridge, MA.

(2003) *Kleine Schriften, vol. II: Orientalia*. Göttingen.

(2004) *Babylon, Memphis, Persepolis: Eastern Contexts of Greek Culture*. Cambridge, MA.

(2009) 'Sardanapal zwischen Mythos und Realität: Das Grab in Kilikien', in Dill and Walde (eds), *Antike Mythen*, 502–15.

Burn, A. R. (2002) *The Persian Wars: The Greeks and the Defence of the West, c. 546–478 BC*. London.

Burstein, S. M. (2008) 'Greek identity in the Hellenistic period', in Zacharia (ed.), *Hellenisms*, 59–77.

(2009) 'Hecataeus of Miletus and the Greek encounter with Egypt', *AWE* 8: 133–46.

(2010) 'New light on the fate of Greek in ancient Central and South Asia', *AWE* 9: 181–92.

Butcher, K. (1988) *Roman Provincial Coins: An Introduction to the 'Greek Imperials'*. London.

Buttrey, T. V. (1982) 'Pharaonic imitations of Athenian tetradrachms', in *Proceedings of the Ninth International Congress of Numismatics I*, eds T. Hackens and R. Weiller. Luxembourg, 137–41.

Buxton, A. H. (2002) 'Lydian Royal Dedications in Greek Sanctuaries', PhD dissertation, University of California, Berkeley.

Buxton, R. (1994) *Imaginary Greece: The Contexts of Mythology*. Cambridge.

(ed.) (1999) *From Myth to Reason: Studies in the Development of Greek Thought*. Oxford.

Cahill, N. D. (ed.) (2010) *The Lydians and their World*. Istanbul.

Cahn, H. A. and Gerin, D. (1988) 'Themistocles at Magnesia', *NC* 148: 13–20.

Cahn, H. A. and Mannsperger, D. (1991) 'Themistocles again', *NC* 151: 199–202.

Campbell, D. A. (1983) *The Golden Lyre: The Themes of the Greek Lyric Poets*. London.

Campbell, G. L. (2006) *Strange Creatures: Anthropology in Antiquity*. London.

Camporeale, G. (2000) *Die Etrusker: Geschichte und Kultur*, trans. H. Scharelka. Düsseldorf and Zurich.

Canciani, F. (1978) 'Lydos, ein Sklave?', *Antike Kunst* 21: 17–22.

Canfora, L. (1987) *Ellenismo*. Rome and Bari.

Capecchi, G. (1991) 'Grecità linguistica e grecità figurativa nella più antica monetazione di Cilicia', *Quaderni storici* 76: 67–103.

Carr, D. M. (2005) *Writing on the Tablet of the Heart: Origins of Scripture and Literature*. Oxford and New York.

Carr, D. M. and Conway, C. M. (2010) *An Introduction to the Bible: Sacred Texts and Imperial Contexts*. Malden, MA and Oxford.

Carradice, I. (ed.) (1987a) *Coinage and Administration in the Athenian and Persian Empires*. Oxford.

(1987b) 'The "regal coinage" of the Persian Empire', in Carradice (ed.), *Coinage and Administration*, 73–95.

Carstens, A. M. (2010) 'The Labraunda sphinxes', in Nieling and Rehm (eds), *Achaemenid Impact in the Black Sea*, 41–6.

Carter, J. B. and Morris, S. P. (eds) (1995) *The Ages of Homer: A Tribute to Emily Townsend Vermeule*. Austin, TX.

Carter, J. B. and Steinberg, L. J. (2010) 'Kouroi and statistics', *AJA* 114: 103–28.

Cartledge, P. (1987) *Agesilaos and the Crisis of Sparta*. London.

(1990) 'Fowl play: a curious lawsuit in classical Athens (Antiphon XVI, frr. 57–9 Thalheim)', in *Nomos: Essays in Athenian Law, Politics and Society*, eds P. Cartledge, P. Millett and S. Todd. Cambridge, 41–61.

(2002) *The Greeks: A Portrait of Self and Others*, 2nd edn. Oxford.

(2006) *Thermopylae: The Battle that Changed the World*. London.

Cartledge, P. and Greenland, F. R. (eds) (2010) *Responses to Oliver Stone's Alexander: Film, History, and Cultural Studies*. Madison, WI.

Casabonne, O. (ed.) (2000) *Mécanismes et innovations monétaires dans l'Anatolie achéménide: numismatique et histoire*. Istanbul.

(2004) *La Cilicie à l'époque achéménide*. Paris.

Cassio, A. C. (1998) 'La lingua greca come lingua universale', in Settis (ed.), *I Greci: Transformazioni*, 991–1013.

Castriota, D. (1992) *Myth, Ethos and Actuality: Official Art in Fifth-Century* BC *Athens*. Madison, WI.

Cavafy, C. P. (2007) *The Collected Poems*, trans. E. Sachperoglou. Oxford.

Cawkwell, G. (2005) *The Greek Wars: The Failure of Persia*. Oxford.

Cerchiai, L. (1995) *I Campani*. Milan.

Chadwick, J. (1990) 'The Pech-Maho lead', *ZPE* 82: 161–6.

Chaniotis, A. (1997) 'Theatricality beyond the theatre: staging public life in the Hellenistic world', *Pallas* 47: 219–59.

Chapot, V. *et al.* (1914) *L'Hellénisation du monde antique*. Paris.

Childs, W. A. P. (1978) *The City-Reliefs of Lycia*. Princeton, NJ.

Christ, M. (1994) 'Herodotean kings and historical inquiry', *CA* 13: 167–202.

Christian, D. (2004) *Maps of Time: An Introduction to Big History*. Berkeley, CA and London.

Clarysse, W. (1985) 'Greeks and Egyptians in the Ptolemaic army and administration', *Aegyptus* 65: 57–66.

(1992) 'Some Greeks in Egypt', in Johnson (ed.), *Life in a Multi-Cultural Society*, 51–6.

(2010) 'Bilingual papyrological archives', in *The Multilingual Experience in Egypt, from the Ptolemies to the Abbasids*, ed. A. Papaconstantinou. Farnham, 47–72.

Clarysse, W. and Thompson, D. J. (2006) *Counting the People in Hellenistic Egypt, vol. II: Historical Studies*. Cambridge.

Classen, C. J. (1959) 'The Libyan god Ammon in Greece before 331 BC', *Historia* 8: 349–55.

Clauss, J. J. (2010) 'From the head of Zeus: the beginnings of Roman literature', in Clauss and Cuypers (eds), *A Companion to Hellenistic Literature*, 463–78.

Clauss, J. J. and Cuypers, M. (eds) (2010) *A Companion to Hellenistic Literature*. Chichester.

Clayton, P. A. and Price, M. J. (1988) *The Seven Wonders of the Ancient World*. London.

Cohen, B. (ed.) (2000) *Not the Classical Ideal: Athens and the Construction of the Other in Greek Art*. Leiden.

Cohen, G. M. (1995) *The Hellenistic Settlements in Europe, the Islands, and Asia Minor*. Berkeley, CA.

(2006) *The Hellenistic Settlements in Syria, the Red Sea Basin, and North Africa*. Berkeley, CA and London.

Coldstream, J. N. (1969) 'The Phoenicians of Ialysos', *BICS* 16: 1–8.

Colonna, G. (1993) 'Doni di Etruschi e di altri barbari occidentali nei santuari panellenici', in Mastrocinque (ed.), *I grandi santuari della Grecia e l'Occidente*, 43–67.

Colvin, S. (2004) 'Names in Hellenistic and Roman Lycia', *YCS* 31: 44–84.

(2010) 'Greek dialects in the archaic and classical ages', in Bakker (ed.), *A Companion to the Ancient Greek Language*, 200–12.

Cook, E. (2004) 'Near Eastern sources for the palace of Alkinoos', *AJA* 108: 43–77.

Corcella, A. (1996) '"Ecateo di Mileto così dice"', *QdS* 43: 295–301.

Corrigan, E. H. (1979) 'Lucanian Tomb Paintings Excavated at Paestum 1969–1972: An Iconographic Study', PhD dissertation, Columbia University, New York.

Cribiore, R. (2001) *Gymnastics of the Mind: Greek Education in Hellenistic and Roman Egypt*. Princeton, NJ.

Cristofani, M. (1983) *Gli Etruschi del mare*. Milan.

(1996) *Etruschi e altre genti nell'Italia preromana: mobilità in età arcaica*. Rome.

Curtin, P. D. (1984) *Cross-Cultural Trade in World History*. Cambridge.

d'Agostino, B. (2006) 'The first Greeks in Italy', in Tsetskhladze (ed.), *Greek Colonisation*, vol. I, 201–37.

d'Agostino, B. and Ridgway, D. (eds) (1994) *Apoikia: scritti in onore di Giorgio Buchner*. Naples.

Dalley, S. (2001) 'Assyrian court narratives in Aramaic and Egyptian: historical fiction', in *Historiography in the Cuneiform World*, eds T. Abusch *et al.* Bethesda, MD, 149–61.

Dana, M. (2007) 'Lettres grecques dialectales nord-pontiques (sauf IGDOP 23–26)', *REA* 109: 67–97.

(2011a) 'Les relations des cités du Pont-Euxin ouest et nord avec les centres cultuels du monde grec', *ACSS* 17: 47–70.

(2011b) *Culture et mobilité dans le Pont-Euxin. Approche régionale de la vie culturelle des cités grecques*. Paris.

Danzig, G. (2007) 'Xenophon's wicked Persian, or what's wrong with Tissaphernes? Xenophon's views on lying and breaking oaths', in Tuplin (ed.), *Persian Responses*, 27–50.

Darbandi, S. M. R. and Zournatzi, A. (eds) (2008) *Ancient Greece and Ancient Iran: Cross-Cultural Encounters*. Athens.

Daumas, M. (2009) *L'or et le pouvoir: armement scythe et mythes grecs*. Paris.

Daviau, M., Wevers, J. W. and Wigl, M. (eds) (2001) *The World of the Aramaeans*, vols I–III. Sheffield.

Davis, W. M. (1979) 'Plato on Egyptian art', *JEA* 65: 121–7.

(1981) 'Egypt, Samos, and the archaic style in Greek sculpture', *JEA* 67: 61–81.

Dawson, D. (1992) *Cities of the Gods: Communist Utopias in Greek Thought*. New York.

de Angelis, F. (1998) 'Ancient past, imperial present: the British Empire in T. J. Dunbabin's *The Western Greeks*', *Antiquity* 72: 539–49.

(2000) 'Estimating the agricultural base of Greek Sicily', *Papers of the British School at Rome* 68: 111–48.

(2002) 'Trade and agriculture at Megara Hyblaia', *OJA* 21: 299–310.

(2003) *Megara Hyblaia and Selinous: The Development of Two Greek City-States in Archaic Sicily*. Oxford.

de Grummond, N. T. (2006) *Etruscan Myth, Sacred History and Legend*. Philadelphia, PA.

de Hoz, P. (2010) 'Les écritures', in Étienne (ed.), *La Méditerranée au VIIe siècle av. J.-C.*, 59–90.

de Juliis, E. (1996) *Magna Grecia: L'Italia meridionale dalle origini leggendarie alla conquista romana*. Bari.

de la Genière, J. (1978) 'Ségeste et l'hellénisme', *MEFRA* 90: 33–49.

de Simone, C. (1972) 'Per la storia degli imprestiti greci in etrusco', in *Aufstieg und Niedergang der Römischen Welt I.2*, ed. H. Temporini. Berlin, 491–521.

Debord, P. (1999) *L'Asie mineure au IVe siècle (412–323 a.C.): pouvoirs et jeux politiques*. Bordeaux.

Delemen, I. (ed.) (2007) *The Achaemenid Impact on Local Populations and Cultures in Anatolia (Sixth–Fourth Centuries BC)*. Istanbul.

Delneri, F. (2006) *I culti misterici stranieri nei frammenti della commedia attica antica*. Bologna.

Deltour-Levie, C. (1982) *Les piliers funéraires de Lycie*. Louvain.

Demargne, P. (1958) *Fouilles de Xanthos, vol. I: Les piliers funéraires*. Paris.

Demargne, P. and Childs, W. A. P. (1989) *Fouilles de Xanthos, vol. VIII: le monument des Néréides*, 1–2. Paris.

Demetriou, D. A. (2011) 'What is an emporion? A reassessment', *Historia* 60: 255–72.

(2012) *Negotiating Identity in the Ancient Mediterranean: The Archaic and Classical Greek Multiethnic Emporia*. Cambridge.

Dench, E. (1995) *From Barbarians to New Men: Greek, Roman and Modern Perceptions of Peoples from the Central Apennines*. Oxford.

(2005) *Romulus' Asylum: Roman Identities from Alexander to the Age of Hadrian*. Oxford.

Dentzer, J. M. (1982) *Le motif du banquet couché dans le Proche-Orient et le monde grec du VIIe au IVe siècle avant J.-C.* Rome.

Descœudres, J. P. (ed.) (1990) *Greek Colonists and Native Populations*. Canberra and Oxford.

Devambez, P. (1981) 'Amazones', *LIMC* I: 586–653.

Dewald, C. and Marincola, J. (eds) (2006) *The Cambridge Companion to Herodotus*. Cambridge.

Dickie, H. (1996) *Talking Trojan: Speech and Community in the Iliad*. Oxford.

Dieleman, J. and Moyer, I. S. (2010) 'Egyptian literature', in Clauss and Cuypers (eds), *A Companion to Hellenistic Literature*, 429–47.

Dietler, M. (1999) 'Consumption, cultural frontiers, and identity: anthropological approaches to Greek colonial encounters', in *Confini e frontiera*, 475–501.

(2007) 'The Iron Age in the western Mediterranean', in Scheidel *et al.* (eds), *Cambridge Economic History of the Greco-Roman World*, 242–76.

(2010) *Archaeologies of Colonialism: Consumption, Entanglement, and Violence in Ancient Mediterranean France*. Berkeley, CA and London.

Dietler, M. and López-Ruiz, C. (eds) (2009) *Colonial Encounters in Ancient Iberia: Phoenician, Greek, and Indigenous Relations*. Chicago, IL and London.

Dihle, A. (1994) *Die Griechen und die Fremden*. Munich.

Dilke, O. A. W. (1985) *Greek and Roman Maps*. Ithaca, NY.

Dill, U. and Walde, C. (eds) (2009) *Antike Mythen: Medien, Transformationen und Konstruktionen*. Berlin and New York.

Dmitriev, S. (2001) *The Greek Slogan of Freedom and Early Roman Politics in Greece*. Oxford.

Domaradzki, M., Domaradzka, L., Bouzek, J. and Rostropowicz, J. (eds) (2000) *Pistiros et Thasos: structures économiques dans la péninsule balkanique aux VIIe–IIes siècles avant J.-C.* Opole.

Domínguez, A. J. (1999) 'Hellenisation in Iberia? The reception of Greek products and influences by the Iberians', in Tsetskhladze (ed.), *Ancient Greeks West and East*, 301–29.

Dorati, M. (2000) *Le Storie di Erodoto: etnografia e racconto*. Pisa.

Dougherty, C. (1993) *The Poetics of Colonisation: From City to Text in Archaic Greece*. New York and Oxford.

(2001) *The Raft of Odysseus: The Ethnographic Imagination of Homer's Odyssey*. New York.

Dougherty, C. and Kurke, L. (eds) (2003) *The Cultures within Ancient Greek Culture: Contact, Conflict, Collaboration*. Cambridge.

Dover, K. J. (1978) *Greek Homosexuality*. Cambridge, MA.

Dowden, K. (1997) 'The Amazons: development and functions', *Rheinisches Museum* 140: 97–128.

Drews, R. (1973) *The Greek Accounts of Eastern History*. Washington, DC.

Droysen, J. G. [1836–43] (1877/8) *Geschichte des Hellenismus*, 2nd edn. Gotha.

Dubois, L. (1989) *Inscriptions grecques dialectales de Sicile*. Rome.

(1995) *Inscriptions grecques dialectales de Grande Grèce, vol. I: Colonies eubéennes, colonies ioniennes, emporia*. Geneva.

(1996) *Inscriptions grecques dialectales d'Olbia du Pont*. Geneva.

(2002) *Inscriptions grecques dialectales de Grande Grèce, vol. II: Colonies achéennes*. Geneva.

Due, B. (1989) *The Cyropaedia: Xenophon's Aims and Methods*. Aarhus.

Dunbabin, T. J. (1948) *The Western Greeks*. Oxford.

Durand, X. (1997) *Des Grecs en Palestine au IIIe siècle avant Jésus-Christ: le dossier syrien des archives de Zènon de Caunos, 261–252*. Paris.

Dusinberre, E. R. M. (2003) *Aspects of Empire in Achaemenid Sardis*. Cambridge.

Eddy, S. K. (1961) *The King is Dead: Studies in the Near Eastern Resistance to Hellenism 334–31 BC*. Lincoln, NE.

Edwards, R. B. (1979) *Kadmos the Phoenician: A Study in Greek Legends and the Mycenaean Age*. Amsterdam.

Ehrlich, C. S. (ed.) (2009) *From an Antique Land: An Introduction to Ancient Near Eastern Literature*. Lanham, MD.

Eichner, H. (1993) 'Probleme von Vers und Metrum in epichorischer Dichtung Altkleinasiens', in *Die epigraphische und altertumskundliche Erforschung Kleinasiens*, eds G. Dobesch and G. Rehrenböck. Vienna, 97–169.

Eilers, C. (ed.) (2009) *Diplomats and Diplomacy in the Roman World*. Leiden and Boston, MA.

Elayi, J. (1987) *Recherches sur les cites phéniciennes à l'époque perse*. Naples.

(1988a) *Pénétration grecque en Phénicie sous l'Empire perse*. Nancy.

(1988b) 'Les sarcophages phéniciens d'époque perse', *IA* 23: 275–322.

(2005) *'Abd'aštart Ier, Straton de Sidon: un roi phénicien entre orient et occident*. Paris.

Elsner, J. (2006) 'Classicism in Roman art', in Porter (ed.), *Classical Pasts*, 276–300.

Erskine, A. (2001) *Troy between Greece and Rome: Local Tradition and Imperial Power*. Oxford.

(ed.) (2003) *A Companion to the Hellenistic World*. Malden, MA and Oxford.

(2005) 'Unity and identity: shaping the past in the Greek Mediterranean', in Gruen (ed.), *Cultural Borrowings*, 121–36.

Étienne, R. (ed.) (2010) *La Méditerranée au VIIe siècle av. J.-C. (essais d'analyses archéologiques)*. Paris.

Fabbrini, F. (1983) *Translatio imperii: l'impero universale da Ciro ad Augusto*. Rome.

Facella, M. (2006) *La dinastia degli Orontidi nella Commagene ellenistico-romana*. Pisa.

(2009) 'Dareius and the Achaemenids in Commagene', in Briant and Chaveau (eds), *Organisation des pouvoirs et contacts culturels*, 379–414.

Fales, F. M. (1982) 'The enemy in the Assyrian royal inscriptions: the "moral judgement"', in Nissen and Renger (eds), *Mesopotamien und seine Nachbarn*, 425–35.

(1993) 'Storia di Ahiqar tra Oriente e Grecia: la prospettiva dall'antico Oriente', *QdS* 38: 143–66.

Fantasia, U. (1993) 'Grano siciliano in Grecia nel V e IV secolo', *ASNP* 23: 9–31.

Fehr, B. (1971) *Orientalische und griechische Gelage*. Bonn.

(1997) 'Society, consanguinity and the fertility of women: the community of deities on the Great Frieze of the Pergamum altar as a paradigm of cross-cultural ideas', in *Conventional Values of the Hellenistic Greeks*, eds P. Bilde *et al.* Aarhus, 48–65.

Feldman, M. H. (2005) *Diplomacy by Design: Luxury Arts and an 'International Style' in the Ancient Near East, 1400–1200* BCE. Chicago, IL.

Ferris, I. M. (2000) *Enemies of Romans: Barbarians through Roman Eyes*. Stroud.

Ferron, J. (1993) *Sarcophages de Phénicie: sarcophages à scènes en relief*. Paris.

Fick, N. and Carrière, J-C. (eds) (1991) *Mélanges Étienne Bernand*. Paris.

Finkelberg, M. (2005) *Greeks and Pre-Greeks: Aegean Prehistory and Greek Heroic Tradition*. Cambridge.

Fischer-Hansen, T. (2002) 'Reflections on native settlements in the dominions of Gela and Akragas: as seen from the perspective of the Copenhagen Polis Centre', in *Even More Studies in the Ancient Greek Polis*, Papers from the Copenhagen Polis Centre No. 6, ed. T. H. Nielsen. Stuttgart, 125–86.

Fisher, N. and van Wees, H. (eds) (1998) *Archaic Greece: New Approaches and New Evidence*. London.

Fleischer, R. (1983) *Der Klagefrauensarkophag aus Sidon*. Tübingen.

Fless, F. and Lorenz, A. (2005) 'Die Nekropolen Pantikapaions im 4. Jh. v. Chr.', in Fless and Treister (eds), *Bilder und Objekte als Träger kultureller Identität*, 17–25.

Fless, F. and Treister, M. (eds) (2005) *Bilder und Objekte als Träger kultureller Identität und interkultureller Kommunikation im Schwarzmeergebiet*. Rahden.

Flower, M. A. (2012) *Xenophon's Anabasis or The Expedition of Cyrus*. New York.

Fol, A. and Hammond, N. G. L. (1988) 'Persia in Europe, apart from Greece', *CAH*, IV², 234–53.

Fornasier, J. (2001) *Jagddarstellungen des 6.–4. Jhs. v. Chr.: eine ikonographische und ikonologische Analyse*. Münster.

Fornasier, J. and Böttiger, B. (eds) (2002) *Das bosporanische Reich*. Mainz.

Fortenbaugh, W. W. and Pender, E. (eds) (2009) *Heraclides of Pontus: Discussion*. New Brunswick, NJ.

Foster, B. R. (2005) *Before the Muses: An Anthology of Akkadian Literature*, 3rd edn. Bethesda, MD.

Foucart, P-F. (1890) 'Inscriptions de la Carie', *BCH* 14: 363–76.

Fowden, G. (1986) *The Egyptian Hermes: A Historical Approach to the Late Pagan Mind*. Cambridge.

Fowler, R. L. (1996) 'Herodotos and his contemporaries', *JHS* 116: 62–87.

(2000) *Early Greek Mythography, vol. I: Text and Introduction*. Oxford.

(2006) 'Herodotus and his prose predecessors', in Dewald and Marincola (eds), *Cambridge Companion to Herodotus*, 29–45.

Foxhall, L. (1998) 'Cargoes of the heart's desire: the character of trade in the archaic Mediterranean world', in Fisher and van Wees (eds), *Archaic Greece*, 295–309.

(2005) 'Village to city: staples and luxuries? Exchange networks and urbanisation', in *Mediterranean Urbanisation, 800–600* BC, eds R. Osborne and B. Cunliffe. Oxford, 233–48.

Foxhall, L., Gehrke, H-J. and Luraghi, N. (eds) (2010) *Intentional History: Spinning Time in Ancient Greece*. Stuttgart.

Francis, E. D. and Vickers, M. (1984) 'Green goddess: a gift to Lindos from Amasis of Egypt', *AJA* 88: 68–9.

Franks, H. M. (2009) 'Hunting the eschata: an imagined Persian empire on the lekythos of Xenophantos', *Hesperia* 78: 455–80.

Fraser, P. M. (1960) 'Two studies on the cult of Sarapis in the Hellenistic world', *OpAth* 3: 1–54.

(1967) 'Current problems concerning the early history of the cult of Sarapis', *OpAth* 7: 23–45.

(1970) 'Greek–Phoenician bilingual inscriptions from Rhodes', *BSA* 65: 31–6.

(1972) *Ptolemaic Alexandria*, vols I–III. Oxford.

(1977) *Rhodian Funerary Monuments*. Oxford.

Frederiksen, M. (1984) *Campania*. Oxford.

Froidefond, C. (1971) *Le mirage égyptien dans la littérature grecque d'Homère à Aristote*. Aix-en-Provence.

Gabelmann, H. (1984) *Antike Audienz- und Tribunalszenen*. Darmstadt.

Gabrielsen, V. (2008) 'Provincial challenges to the imperial centre in Achaemenid and Seleucid Asia Minor', in *The Province Strikes Back: Imperial Dynamics in the Eastern Mediterranean*, eds B. Forsén and G. Salmieri. Helsinki, 15–44.

et al. (eds) (1999) *Hellenistic Rhodes: Politics, Culture, and Society*. Aarhus.

Gajdukevič, V. F. (1971) *Das bosporanische Reich*. Berlin.

Gale, N. H. and Stos-Gale, Z. A. (1986) 'Oxhide copper ingots in Crete and Cyprus and the Bronze Age metals trade', *BSA* 81: 81–100.

Gallo, P. and Masson, O. (1993) 'Une stèle "hellénomemphite" de l'ex-collection Nahman', *BIFAO* 93: 265–76.

Garlan, Y. (1974) *Recherches de poliorcétique grecque*. Paris.

(ed.) (1999) *Production et commerce des amphores anciennes en Mer Noire*. Aix-en-Provence.

Garland, R. (2001) *The Piraeus: From the Fifth to the First Century* BC, new edn. London.

Garvie, A. F. (2009) *Persae: Aeschylus*. Oxford.

Gauthier, P. (1989) *Nouvelles inscriptions de Sardes*, vol. II. Geneva.

Gavriljuk, N. A. (2006) 'The Graeco-Scythian slave trade in the sixth and fifth centuries BC', in *The Cauldron of Ariantas: Studies Presented to A. N. Ščeglov on the Occasion of his 70th Birthday*, eds P. Guldager Bilde, J. M. Højte and V. F. Stolba. Aarhus, 75–85.

Gehrke, H-J. (2005) 'Heroen als Grenzgänger zwischen Griechen und Barbaren', in Gruen (ed.), *Cultural Borrowings*, 50–67.

George, A. R. (2003) *The Babylonian Gilgamesh Epic*. Oxford.

Georges, P. (1987) 'Darius in Scythia: the formation of Herodotus' sources and the nature of Darius' campaign', *AJAH* 11: 97–147.

(1994) *Barbarian Asia and the Greek Experience: From the Archaic Period to the Age of Xenophon*. Baltimore, MA and London.

(2000) 'Persian Ionia under Darius: the Revolt reconsidered', *Historia* 49: 1–39.

Gera, D. L. (1993) *Xenophon's Cyropaedia: Style, Genre and Literary Technique*. Oxford.

Giangiulio, M. (1996) 'Avventurieri, mercanti, coloni, mercenari. Mobilità umana e circolazione di risorse nel Mediterraneo arcaico', in Settis (ed.), *I Greci: Formazione*, 497–525.

Gianotta, M. E. *et al.* (eds) (1994) *La decifrazione del cario*. Rome.

Gillis, D. (1979) *Collaboration with the Persians*. Wiesbaden.

Gilula, D. (2000a) 'Hermippus and his catalogue of goods (fr. 63)', in *The Rivals of Aristophanes*, eds D. Harvey and J. Wilkins. London, 75–90.

(2000b) 'Stratonicus, the witty harpist', in *Athenaeus and his World: Reading Greek Culture in the Roman Empire*, eds D. Braund and J. Wilkins. Exeter, 423–33.

Giovannini, A. (2007) *Les relations entre États dans la Grèce antique: du temps d'Homère à l'intervention romaine (ca. 700–200 av. J.-C.)*. Stuttgart.

Giuliani, L. (2003) *Bild und Mythos: Geschichte der Bilderzählung in der griechischen Kunst*. Munich.

Gočeva, Z. and Popov, D. (1986) 'Bendis', *LIMC* II: 95–7.

Gorre, G. (2009) *Les relations du clergé égyptien et des Lagides d'après des sources privées*. Louvain.

Gottschalk, H. B. (1980) *Heraclides of Pontus*. Oxford.

Goudriaan, K. (1988) *Ethnicity in Ptolemaic Egypt*. Amsterdam.

Graf, F. (2011) 'Myth and Hellenic identities', in *A Companion to Greek Mythology*, eds K. Dowden and N. Livingstone. Malden, MA and Oxford, 211–26.

Graham, A. J. (1982) 'The colonial expansion of Greece', *CAH*, III.3², 83–162.

Grallert, S. (2001) 'Akkulturation im ägyptischen Sepulkralwesen: der Fall eines Griechen in Ägypten zur Zeit der 26. Dynastie', in Höckmann and Kreikenbom (eds), *Naukratis*, 183–95.

Grandjean, Y. (1975) *Une nouvelle arétalogie d'Isis à Maroneia*. Leiden.

Gras, M. (1995) *La Méditerranée archaïque*. Paris.

(1997) 'L'Occidente e i suoi conflitti', in Settis (ed.), *I Greci: Definizione*, 61–85.

Gras, M., Rouillard, P. and Teixidor, J. (1989) *L'univers phénicien*. Paris.

Gray, V. J. (1998) *The Framing of Socrates: The Literary Interpretation of Xenophon's Memorabilia*. Stuttgart.

(ed.) (2010) *Xenophon*. Oxford.

(2011) *Xenophon's Mirror of Princes: Reading the Reflections*. Oxford.

Greaves, A. M. (2010) *The Land of Ionia: Society and Economy in the Archaic Period*. Malden, MA and Oxford.

Greco, E. (1992) *Archeologia della Magna Grecia*. Rome and Bari.

Greco, E. and Lombardo, M. (eds) (2007) *Atene e l'Occidente*. Athens.

Greenfield, J. C. (1985) 'Aramaic in the Achaemenid Empire', *CHI* 2: 698–713.

Griffiths, A. (1987) 'Democedes of Croton: a Greek doctor at the court of Darius', in *AchHist* 2, 37–51.

Griffiths, J. G. (1965) 'A translation from the Egyptian by Eudoxus', *CQ* 15: 75–8.

(1970) *Plutarch's De Iside et Osiride*. Cardiff.

(1985) 'Atlantis and Egypt', *Historia* 34: 3–28.

Gruen, E. S. (1986) *The Hellenistic World and the Coming of Rome*. Berkeley, CA.

(1990) *Studies in Greek Culture and Roman Policy*. Leiden.

(1992) *Culture and National Identity in Republican Rome*. Ithaca, NY.

(1993) 'The polis in the Hellenistic world', in *Nomodeiktes: Greek Studies in Honour of Martin Ostwald*, eds R. M. Rosen and J. Farrell. Ann Arbor, MI, 339–54.

(1998) *Heritage and Hellenism: The Re-Invention of Jewish Tradition*. Berkeley, CA.

(2002) *Diaspora: Jews amidst Greeks and Romans*. Cambridge, MA and London.

(ed.) (2005) *Cultural Borrowings and Ethnic Appropriations in Antiquity*. Stuttgart.

(ed.) (2010) *Cultural Identity in the Ancient Mediterranean*. Los Angeles, CA.

(2011) *Rethinking the Other in Antiquity*. Princeton, NJ and Oxford.

Gürtekin-Demir, G-R. (2002) 'Lydian painted pottery at Daskyleion', *AS* 52: 111–43.

Gufler, B. (2002) 'Orientalische Wurzeln griechischer Gorgo-Darstellungen', in Schuol *et al.* (eds), *Grenzüberschreitungen*, 61–81.

Guldager Bilde, P. and Petersen, J. H. (eds) (2008) *Meetings of Cultures in the Black Sea Region: Between Conflict and Co-Existence*. Aarhus.

Gulletta, M. I. (1994) 'Eco di voci greche da Spina, l'etrusca "*civitas in Umbris*"', in Ἱστορία: *studi offerti dagli allievi a Giuseppe Nenci*, ed. S. Alessandrì. Galatina, 245–60.

Gunn, B. (1943) 'Notes on the Naukratis stela', *JEA* 29: 55–9.

Gunn, G. C. (2011) *History without Borders: The Making of an Asian World Region, 1000–1800*. Hong Kong.

Gunter, A. C. (2009) *Greek Art and the Orient*. Cambridge.

Guralnick, E. (1978) 'The proportions of kouroi', *AJA* 82: 461–72.

(1985) 'Profiles of kouroi', *AJA* 89: 399–409.

(1996) 'The monumental new kouros from Samos: measurements, proportions and profiles', *Archäologischer Anzeiger* 4: 505–26.

Gusmani, R. and Polat, G. (1999) 'Manes im Daskyleion', *Kadmos* 38: 137–62.

Gusmani, R., Salvini, M. and Vannicelli, P. (eds) (1997) *Frigi e Frigio*. Rome.

Habicht, C. (2006) *Hellenistic Monarchies: Selected Papers*. Ann Arbor, MI.

Haft, A. (1984) 'Odysseus, Idomeneus, and Meriones: the Cretan lies of Odyssey 13–19', *CJ* 79: 289–306.

Hagemajer Allen, K. (2003a) 'Becoming the "Other": attitudes and practices at the Attic cemeteries', in Dougherty and Kurke (eds), *Cultures within Ancient Greek Culture*, 207–36.

(2003b) 'Intercultural exchanges in fourth-century Attic decrees', *CA* 22: 199–246.

Haider, P. W. (1996) 'Griechen im Vorderen Orient und in Ägypten bis ca. 590 v. Chr.', in Ulf (ed.), *Wege zur Genese griechischer Identität*, 59–115.

(2001) '"Das Buch vom Fayum" und seine Historisierung bei Herodot', in *Althistorische Studien im Spannungsfeld zwischen Universal- und*

Wissenschaftsgeschichte: Festschrift für Franz Hampl, eds P. W. Haider and R. Rollinger. Stuttgart, 127–56.

(2004) 'Kontakte zwischen Griechen und Ägypten und ihre Auswirkungen auf die archaisch-griechische Welt', in Rollinger and Ulf (eds), *Griechische Archaik*, 447–91.

Hall, E. (1989) *Inventing the Barbarian: Greek Self-Definition through Tragedy*. Oxford.

(2006) *The Theatrical Cast of Athens: Interactions between Ancient Greek Drama and Society*. Oxford.

Hall, J. M. (1997) *Ethnic Identity in Greek Antiquity*. Cambridge.

(2002) *Hellenicity: Between Ethnicity and Culture*. Chicago, IL.

(2004) 'How "Greek" were the early western Greeks?', in Lomas (ed.), *Greek Identity in the Western Mediterranean*, 35–54.

Hallo, W. W. (1996) *Origins: The Ancient Near Eastern Background of Some Modern Western Institutions*. Leiden, New York and Cologne.

Hammond, N. G. L. (1998) 'The Branchidae at Didyma and in Sogdiana', *CQ* 48: 339–44.

Hansen, M. H. (ed.) (2002) *A Comparative Study of Six City-State Cultures*. Copenhagen.

(ed.) (2005) *The Imaginary Polis*. Copenhagen.

Hansen, M. H. and Nielsen, T. H. (eds) (2004) *An Inventory of Archaic and Classical Poleis*. Oxford and New York.

Hansen, W. (2002) *Ariadne's Thread: A Guide to International Tales Found in Classical Literature*. Ithaca, NY and London.

Harmanşah, Ö. (2005) 'Spatial Narratives, Commemorative Practices and the Building Project: New Urban Foundations in Upper Syro-Mesopotamia during the Early Iron Age', PhD dissertation, University of Pennsylvania.

Harris, E. M. (1989) 'Iphicrates at the court of Cotys', *AJP* 110: 264–71.

Harrison, T. (2000) *The Emptiness of Asia: Aeschylus' Persians and the History of the Fifth Century*. London.

(ed.) (2002) *Greeks and Barbarians*. Edinburgh.

Hartog, F. (1988) *The Mirror of Herodotus: The Representation of the Other in the Writing of History*, trans. J. Lloyd. Berkeley, CA.

Haubold, J. (2007) 'Xerxes' Homer', in Bridges *et al.* (eds), *Cultural Responses to the Persian Wars*, 47–63.

(forthcoming a) 'Ethnography in the *Iliad*', in *Epic Space*, eds M. Skempsis and I. Ziogas. Leiden.

(forthcoming b) 'Berossos', in *Romance between Greece and the East*, ed. T. Whitmarsh. Cambridge.

Hawkins, S. (2010) 'Greek and the languages of Asia Minor to the classical period', in Bakker (ed.), *A Companion to the Ancient Greek Language*, 213–27.

Haynes, S. (2000) *Etruscan Civilization: A Cultural History*. London.

Heckel, W. (2006a) *Who's Who in the Age of Alexander the Great: Prosopography of Alexander's Empire*. Malden, MA and Oxford.

(2006b) 'Mazaeus, Callisthenes and the Alexander Sarcophagus', *Historia* 55: 385–96.

Heidel, W. A. (1935) 'Hecataeus and the Egyptian priests in Herodotus, Book II', *Memoirs of the American Academy of Arts and Sciences* 18: 53–134.

(1943) 'Hecataeus and Xenophanes', *AJP* 64: 257–77.

Hemelrijk, J. M. (1984) *Caeretan Hydriai*. Mainz.

Hengel, M. (1974) *Judaism and Hellenism: Studies in their Encounter in Palestine during the Early Hellenistic Period*, vols I–II, trans. J. Bowden. London.

(1980) *Jews, Greeks and Barbarians: Aspects of the Hellenisation of Judaism in the Pre-Christian Period*, trans. J. Bowden. London.

Henkelman, W. (2006) 'The birth of Gilgameš (Ael. NA XII.21): a case-study in literary receptivity', in Rollinger and Truschnegg (eds), *Altertum und Mittelmeerraum*, 807–56.

Herman, G. (1987) *Ritualised Friendship and the Greek City*. Cambridge.

(1990) 'Patterns of name diffusion within the Greek world and beyond', *CQ* 40: 349–63.

Herrmann, P. (1993) 'Inschriften von Sardeis', *Chiron* 23: 223–63.

Heurgon, J. (1966) 'The inscriptions of Pyrgi', *JRS* 56: 1–15.

Hicks, R. I. (1962) 'Egyptian elements in Greek mythology', *TAPA* 93: 90–108.

Hind, J. (1994) 'The Bosporan kingdom', *CAH*, VI², 472–511.

Hingley, R. (2005) *Globalizing Roman Culture: Unity, Diversity and Empire*. London.

Hirsch, S. W. (1985) *The Friendship of the Barbarians: Xenophon and the Persian Empire*. Hanover, CT and London.

Hodos, T. (2006) *Local Responses to Colonization in the Iron Age Mediterranean*. London.

Höckmann, U. (2001) '"Bilinguen": Zu Ikonographie und Stil der karisch-ägyptischen Grabstelen des 6. Jhs. Methodische Überlegungen zur griechischen Kunst der archaischen Zeit in Ägypten', in Höckmann and Kreikenbom (eds), *Naukratis*, 217–32.

(ed.) (2007) *Archäologische Studien zu Naukratis*. Worms.

Höckmann, U. and Kreikenbom, D. (eds) (2001) *Naukratis: Die Beziehungen zu Ostgriechenland, Ägypten und Zypern in archaischer Zeit*. Möhnesee.

Hölbl, G. (1979) *Beziehungen der ägyptischen Kultur zu Altitalien*, vols I–II. Leiden.

(1986) *Ägyptisches Kulturgut im phönikischen und punischen Sardinien*, vols I–II. Leiden.

Hölscher, T. (1973) *Griechische Historienbilder des 5. und 4. Jahrhunderts v. Chr.* Würzburg.

(2000) 'Feindwelten – Glückswelten: Perser, Kentauren und Amazonen', in *Gegenwelten zu den Kulturen Griechenlands und Roms in der Antike*, ed. T. Hölscher. Leipzig, 287–320.

(2004) *The Language of Images in Roman Art*, trans. A. Snodgrass and A. Künzl-Snodgrass. Cambridge.

Hölscher, U. (1988) *Die Odyssee: Epos zwischen Märchen und Roman*. Munich.

Hoffman, G. L. (1997) *Imports and Immigrants: Near Eastern Contacts with Iron-Age Crete*. Ann Arbor, MI.

Hoffner, H. A., Jr. (1998) *Hittite Myths*, 2nd edn. Atlanta, GA.

Hofstetter, J. (1978) *Die Griechen in Persien: Prosopographie der Griechen im persischen Reich vor Alexander*. Berlin.

Holladay, C. R. (1983) *Fragments from Hellenistic Jewish Authors, vol. I: Historians*. Chico, CA.

(1989) *Fragments from Hellenistic Jewish Authors, vol. II: Poets*. Atlanta, GA.

Holt, F. L. (1999) *Thundering Zeus: The Making of Hellenistic Bactria*. Berkeley, CA.

Honigman, S. (2003) *The Septuagint and Homeric Scholarship in Alexandria: A Study in the Narrative of the Letter of Aristeas*. London and New York.

Hopfner, T. (1925) *Orient und griechische Philosophie*. Leipzig.

Hopkins, A. G. (ed.) (2002) *Globalization in World History*. New York and London.

Horden, P. and Purcell, N. (2000) *The Corrupting Sea: A Study of Mediterranean History*. Oxford.

Hordern, J. H. (2002) *The Fragments of Timotheus of Miletus*. Oxford.

Horky, P. S. (2009) 'Persian cosmos and Greek philosophy: Plato's associates and the Zoroastrian *Magoi*', *Oxford Studies in Ancient Philosophy* 37: 47–103.

Hornblower, S. (1982) *Mausolus*. Oxford.

(1994) 'Persia', *CAH*, VI², 45–96.

Hornblower, S. and Morgan, C. (eds) (2007) *Pindar's Poetry, Patrons and Festivals, from Archaic Greece to the Roman Empire*. Oxford.

Hose, M. (2002) *Aristoteles: Die historischen Fragmente*. Berlin.

Hülden, O. (2001) 'Überlegungen zur Bedeutung der Amazonomachie am Maussolleion von Halikarnassos', in Klinkott (ed.), *Anatolien im Lichte kultureller Wechselwirkungen*, 83–105.

Hunter, R. (ed.) (2005) *The Hesiodic Catalogue of Women: Constructions and Reconstructions*. Cambridge.

Hurst, H. and Owen, S. (eds) (2005) *Ancient Colonizations: Analogy, Similarity and Difference*. London.

Huß, W. (1994) *Der Makedonische König und die Ägyptischen Priester*. Stuttgart.

Isaac, B. (1986) *The Greek Settlements in Thrace until the Macedonian Conquest*. Leiden.

(2004) *The Invention of Racism in Classical Antiquity*. Princeton, NJ.

Ivantchik, A. (1999) 'Une légende sur l'origine des Scythes (Hdt. IV, 5–7) et le problème des sources du Scythikos logos d'Hérodote', *REG* 112: 141–92.

(2006) '"Scythian" archers on archaic Attic vases: problems of interpretation', *ACSS* 12: 197–271.

Ivantchik, A. and Licheli, V. (eds) (2007) *Achaemenid Culture and Local Traditions in Anatolia, Southern Caucasus and Iran: New Discoveries*. Leiden and Boston, MA.

Jackman, T. (2006) 'Ducetius and fifth-century Sicilian tyranny', in Lewis (ed.), *Ancient Tyranny*, 33–48.

Jacobs, B. (1987) *Griechische und persische Elemente in der Grabkunst Lykiens zur Zeit der Achämenidenherrschaft*. Jonsered.

Jacobson, D. M. (2007) *The Hellenistic Paintings of Marisa*. Leeds.

Jacobson, E. (1995) *The Art of the Scythians: The Interpenetration of Cultures at the Edge of the Hellenic World*. Leiden, New York and Cologne.

Jacobson, H. (1983) *The Exagoge of Ezekiel*. Cambridge.

Jaspers, K. (1953) *The Origin and Goal of History*, trans. M. Bullock. London.

Jeffery, L. and Morpurgo Davies, A. (1970) 'Poinikastas and poinikazen: BM 1969.4–2.1, a new archaic inscription from Crete', *Kadmos* 9: 118–54.

Jenkins, I. (2006) *Greek Architecture and its Sculpture in the British Museum*. London.

Jennings, J. (2011) *Globalizations and the Ancient World*. Cambridge.

Jigoulov, V. S. (2010) *The Social History of Achaemenid Phoenicia: Being a Phoenician, Negotiating Empires*. London and Oakville, CT.

Johnson, J. H. (ed.) (1992) *Life in a Multi-Cultural Society: Egypt from Cambyses to Constantine and Beyond*. Chicago, IL.

Johnson, S. R. (2004) *Historical Fictions and Hellenistic Jewish Identity: Third Maccabees in its Cultural Context*. Berkeley, CA and London.

Johnston, A. (1972) 'The rehabilitation of Sostratos', *PdP* 27: 416–23.

    (1979) 'An Athenian rho in the Adriatic?', *ZPE* 34: 277–80.

Johnston, A. and Pandolfini, M. (2000) *Gravisca: Le iscrizioni*. Bari.

Jones, C. P. (1999) *Kinship Diplomacy in the Ancient World*. Cambridge, MA and London.

Jouguet, P. (1928) *Alexander the Great and the Hellenistic World: Macedonian Imperialism and the Hellenization of the East*, trans. M. R. Dobie. London.

Jüthner, J. (1923) *Hellenen und Barbaren: aus der Geschichte des Nationalbewußtseins*. Leipzig.

Kah, D. and Scholz, P. (eds) (2007) *Das hellenistische Gymnasion*, 2nd edn. Berlin.

Kammerzell, F. (1993) *Studien zu Sprache und Geschichte der Karer in Ägypten*. Wiesbaden.

Kaplan, P. (2003) 'Cross-cultural contacts among mercenary communities in Saite and Persian Egypt', *MHR* 18: 1–31.

    (2006) 'Dedications to Greek sanctuaries by foreign kings in the eighth through sixth centuries BCE', *Historia* 55(2): 129–52.

Keen, A. G. (1998) *Dynastic Lycia: A Political History of the Lycians and their Relations with Foreign Powers c. 545–362 BC*. Leiden, Boston, MA and Cologne.

Kemp, B. J. (1989) *Ancient Egypt: Anatomy of a Civilisation*. London and New York.

Kienast, D. (1973) *Philipp II. von Makedonien und das Reich der Achaimeniden*. Munich.

Kim, H. J. (2009) *Ethnicity and Foreigners in Ancient Greece and China*. London.

Kindstrand, J. F. (1981) *Anacharsis: The Legend and the Apophthegmata*. Uppsala.

Kingsley, P. (1994) 'From Pythagoras to the Turba philosophorum: Egypt and Pythagorean tradition', *Journal of the Warburg and Courtauld Institutes* 57: 1–13.

(1995) 'Meetings with Magi: Iranian themes among the Greeks, from Xanthus of Lydia to Plato's Academy', *Journal of the Royal Asiatic Society* 5(2): 173–209.

Kirk, G. S. (1970) *Myth: Its Meaning and Functions in Ancient and Other Cultures.* Cambridge.

(1974) *The Nature of Greek Myths.* Harmondsworth.

Kirk, G. S., Raven, J. E. and Schofield, M. (1983) *The Presocratic Philosophers: A Critical History with a Selection of Texts,* 2nd edn. Cambridge.

Kleemann, I. (1958) *Der Satrapen-Sarkophag aus Sidon.* Berlin.

Kleingünther, A. (1934) Πρῶτος εὑρετής: *Untersuchungen zur Geschichte einer Fragestellung.* Leipzig.

Klinkott, H. (ed.) (2001) *Anatolien im Lichte kultureller Wechselwirkungen: Akkulturationsphänomene in Kleinasien und seiner Nachbarregionen während des 2. und 1. Jahrtausends v. Chr.* Tübingen.

Konstan, D. (1991) 'What is Greek about Greek mythology?', *Kernos* 4: 11–30.

Kopcke, G. and Tokumaru, I. (eds) (1992) *Greece between East and West: 10th–8th Centuries BC.* Mainz.

Kottsieper, I. (2009) 'Aramaic literature', in Ehrlich (ed.), *From an Antique Land,* 393–444.

Kouremenos, A., Chandrasekaran, S. and Rossi, R. (eds) (2011) *From Pella to Gandhara: Hybridisation and Identity in the Art and Architecture of the Hellenistic East.* Oxford.

Kraay, C. M. (1976) *Archaic and Classical Greek Coins.* New York.

Krentz, P. (2010) *The Battle of Marathon.* New Haven, CT and London.

Kryzhitskiy, S. D. (2007) 'Criteria for the presence of Barbarians in the population of early Olbia', in Braund and Kryzhitskiy (eds), *Classical Olbia and the Scythian World,* 17–22.

Kuhrt, A. (1995) *The Ancient Near East, c. 3000–330 BC,* vol. II. London.

(1996) 'The Seleucid Kings and Babylonia: new perspectives on the Seleucid realm in the East', in Bilde *et al.* (eds), *Aspects of Hellenistic Kingship,* 41–54.

(1998) 'The Old Assyrian merchants', in *Trade, Traders and the Ancient City,* eds H. Parkins and C. Smith. London and New York, 15–29.

(2002) 'Babylon', in Bakker *et al., Brill's Companion to Herodotus,* 475–96.

(2007) *The Persian Empire: A Corpus of Sources from the Achaemenid Period.* New York.

Kuhrt, A. and Sherwin-White, S. (eds) (1987) *Hellenism in the East: The Interaction of Greek and Non-Greek Civilisations from Syria to Central Asia after Alexander.* London.

Kurke, L. (1991) *The Traffic in Praise: Pindar and the Poetics of Social Economy.* Ithaca, NY.

(1992) 'The politics of ἀβροσύνη in archaic Greece', *CA* 11: 91–120.

La'da, C. A. (2002) *Foreign Ethnics in Hellenistic Egypt.* Louvain.

(2003) 'Encounters with ancient Egypt: the Hellenistic Greek experience', in Matthews and Roemer (eds), *Ancient Perspectives on Egypt,* 157–69.

Labudek, J. (2010) 'Late Period Stelae from Saqqara: A Socio-Cultural and Religious Investigation', MPhil dissertation, University of Birmingham.

Lafranchi, P. (2006) *L'Exagoge d'Ezéchiel le Tragique*. Leiden and Boston, MA.

Lancellotti, M. G. (2002) *Attis. Between Myth and History: King, Priest and God.* Leiden, Boston, MA and Cologne.

Lane Fox, R. (1973) *Alexander the Great*. London.

(ed.) (2004a) *The Long March: Xenophon and the Ten Thousand*. New Haven, CT and London.

(2004b) 'Sex, gender and the other in Xenophon's Anabasis', in Lane Fox (ed.), *The Long March*, 184–214.

(2007) 'Alexander the Great: "Last of the Achaemenids"?', in Tuplin (ed.), *Persian Responses*, 267–311.

(2008) *Travelling Heroes: Greeks and their Myths in the Epic Age of Homer*. London.

Langer-Karrenbrock, M-T. (2000) *Der Lykische Sarkophag aus der Königsnekropole von Sidon*. Münster.

Laronde, A. (1990) 'Greeks and Libyans in Cyrenaica', in Descœudres (ed.), *Greek Colonists and Native Populations*, 169–80.

Lasserre, F. (1966) *Die Fragmente des Eudoxos von Knidos*. Berlin.

Lauffer, S. (1955/6) *Die Bergwerkssklaven von Laureion*, vols I–II. Wiesbaden.

Launey, M. (1950) *Recherches sur les armées hellénistiques*, vols I–II. Paris.

Laurence, R., Esmonde Cleary, S. and Sears, G. (2011) *The City in the Roman West c. 250 bc–c. ad 250*. Cambridge.

Lavelle, B. M. (1992) 'The Pisistratids and the mines of Thrace', *GRBS* 33: 5–23.

Lazenby, J. F. (1993) *The Defence of Greece, 490–479 bc*. Warminster.

le Guen, B. (2003) 'Théâtre, cités et royaumes en Anatolie et au Proche-Orient de la mort d'Alexandre le Grand aux conquêtes de Pompée', *Pallas* 62: 329–55.

le Rider, G. (1965) *Suse sous les Séleucides et les Parthes: les trouvailles monétaires et l'histoire de la ville*. Paris.

(2001) *La naissance de la monnaie: pratiques monétaires de l'Orient ancien*. Paris.

le Roy, C. (1982/3) 'Aspects du plurilinguisme dans la Lycie antique', *Anadolu* 22: 217–26.

Lee, J. W. I. (2007) *A Greek Army on the March: Soldiers and Survival in Xenophon's Anabasis*. Cambridge.

Lefkowitz, M. R. (1996) *Not Out of Africa: How Afrocentrism Became an Excuse to Teach Myth as History*. New York.

Lefkowitz, M. R. and Rogers, G. M. (eds) (1996) *Black Athena Revisited*. Chapel Hill, NC.

Legras, B. (2002) 'Les experts égyptiens à la cour des Ptolémées', *Revue historique* 624: 963–91.

(2011) *Les reclus grecs du Sarapieion de Memphis: une enquête sur l'hellénisme égyptien*. Louvain.

Lejeune, M. (1983) 'Rencontres de l'alphabet grec avec les langues barbares au cours du Ier millénaire av. J.-C.', in *Modes*, 731–53.

Lejeune, M., Pouilloux, J. and Solier, Y. (1988) 'Étrusque et ionien archaïques sur un plomb de Pech Maho (Aude)', *Revue archéologique de Narbonnaise* 21: 19–59.

Lemaire, A. (2000) 'Remarques sur certaines légendes monétaires ciliciennes (Ve–IVe s. av. J.-C.)', in Casabonne (ed.), *Mécanismes et innovations monétaires*, 129–41.

(2001) 'Les inscriptions araméennes de Daskyleion', in Bakır (ed.), *Achaemenid Anatolia*, 21–35.

Lemaire, A. and Lozachmeur, H. (1996) 'Remarques sur le plurilinguisme en Asie Mineure à l'époque perse', in Briquel-Chatonnet (ed.), *Mosaïque de langues, mosaïque culturelle*, 91–123.

Lembke, K. (2001) *Phönizische anthropoide Sarkophage*. Mainz am Rhein.

(2004) *Die Skulpturen aus dem Quellenheiligtum von Amrit: Studien zur Akkulturation in Phönizien*. Mainz am Rhein.

Lendle, O. (1995) *Kommentar zu Xenophons Anabasis (Bücher 1–7)*. Darmstadt.

Lenfant, D. (2004) *Ctésias de Cnide. La Perse. L'Inde: autres fragments*. Paris.

(2009) *Les Histoires perses de Dinon et d'Héraclide*. Paris.

Lepore, E. (1968) 'Per una fenomenologia storica del rapporto citta-territorio in Magna Grecia', in *La città e il suo territorio: atti del settimo convegno di studi sulla Magna Grecia*, ed. P. Romanelli. Naples, 29–66.

Lerner, J. D. (2003) 'The Aï Khanoum philosophical papyrus', *ZPE* 142: 45–51.

Lévy, E. (1984) 'Naissance du concept de barbare', *Ktèma* 9: 5–14.

Lewis, D. (2011) 'Near Eastern slaves in classical Attica and the slave trade with Persian territories', *CQ* 61: 91–113.

Lewis, D. M. (1977) *Sparta and Persia*. Leiden.

(1992) 'The Thirty Years' Peace', *CAH*, V^2, 121–46.

(1994) 'The Persepolis Tablets: speech, seal and script', in Bowman and Woolf (eds), *Literacy and Power in the Ancient World*, 17–32.

(1997) *Selected Papers in Greek and Near Eastern History*. Cambridge.

Lewis, N. (1986) *Greeks in Ptolemaic Egypt: Case Studies in the Social History of the Hellenistic World*. Oxford.

Lewis, S. (ed.) (2006) *Ancient Tyranny*. Edinburgh.

Lightfoot, J. L. (2003) *Lucian: On the Syrian Goddess*. Oxford.

Lipiński, E. (1995) *Dieux et déesses de l'univers phénicien et punique*. Louvain.

(2000) *The Aramaeans: Their Ancient History, Culture, Religion*. Louvain.

(2004) *Itineraria Phoenicia*. Louvain, Paris and Dudley, MA.

Lissarrague, F. (1990) *L'autre guerrier. Archers, peltastes, cavaliers dans l'imagerie attique*. Paris and Rome.

Liverani, M. (2001) *International Relations in the Ancient Near East, 1600–1100 BC*. Basingstoke and New York.

Livingstone, N. (2001) *A Commentary on Isocrates' Busiris*. Leiden, Boston, MA and Cologne.

Llewellyn-Jones, L. and Robson, J. (2010) *Ctesias' History of Persia: Tales of the Orient*. London.

Lloyd, A. B. (1975) *Herodotus Book II, vol. I: Introduction*. Leiden.

(1976) *Herodotus Book II, vol. II: Commentary, 1–98*. Leiden.

(1988) *Herodotus Book II, vol. III: Commentary, 99–182*. Leiden.

(2007) 'Egyptians abroad in the late period', in Adams and Roy (eds), *Travel, Geography and Culture in Ancient Greece*, 31–43.

Lloyd, G. E. R. (1966) *Polarity and Analogy: Two Types of Argumentation in Early Greek Thought*. Cambridge.

Lomas, K. (ed.) (2004) *Greek Identity in the Western Mediterranean*. Leiden and Boston, MA.

Long, T. (1986) *Barbarians in Greek Comedy*. Carbondale and Edwardsville, IL.

Lonis, R. (ed.) (1988) *L'étranger dans le monde grec*. Nancy.

López-Ruiz, C. (2010) *When the Gods Were Born: Greek Cosmogonies and the Near East*. Cambridge, MA and London.

Loprieno, A. (1988) *Topos und Mimesis: zum Ausländer in der ägyptischen Literatur*. Wiesbaden.

Louden, B. (2011) *Homer's Odyssey and the Near East*. Cambridge.

Loukopoulou, L. D. (1989) *Contribution à l'histoire de la Thrace Propontique durant la période archaïque*. Athens.

Lücke, S. (2000) *Syngeneia: epigraphisch-historische Studien zu einem Phänomen der antiken griechischen Diplomatie*. Frankfurt am Main.

Luraghi, N. (ed.) (2001) *The Historian's Craft in the Age of Herodotus*. Oxford.

(2006) 'Traders, pirates, warriors: the proto-history of Greek mercenary soldiers in the Eastern Mediterranean', *Phoenix* 60: 21–47.

Luukko, M., Svärd, S. and Mattila, R. (eds) (2009) *Of God(s), Trees, Kings and Scholars: Neo-Assyrian and Related Studies in Honour of Simo Parpola*. Helsinki.

Lyons, C. L. and Papadopoulos, J. K. (eds) (2002) *The Archaeology of Colonialism*. Los Angeles, CA.

Ma, J. (2000) *Antiochos III and the Cities of Western Asia Minor*. Oxford.

(2003) 'Peer polity interaction in the Hellenistic age', *Past & Present* 180: 9–39.

(2004) 'You can't go home again: displacement and identity in Xenophon's *Anabasis*', in Lane Fox (ed.), *The Long March*, 330–45.

Ma, J., Papazarkadas, N. and Parker, R. (eds) (2009) *Interpreting the Athenian Empire*. London.

MacDonald, B. R. (1981) 'The emigration of potters from Athens in the late fifth century BC and its effect on the Attic pottery industry', *AJA* 85: 159–68.

Magee, G. B. and Thompson, A. S. (2010) *Empire and Globalisation: Networks of People, Goods and Capital in the British World, c. 1850–1914*. Cambridge.

Mairs, R. R. (2007) 'Egyptian artefacts from Central and South Asia', in *Current Research in Egyptology 2005*, eds R. Mairs and A. Stevenson. Oxford, 74–89.

(2008) 'Greek identity and the settler community in Hellenistic Bactria and Arachosia', *Migrations & Identities* 1: 19–43.

(2011a) 'The places in between: model and metaphor in the archaeology of Hellenistic Arachosia', in Kouremenos *et al.*, *From Pella to Gandhara*, 177–89.

(2011b) *The Archaeology of the Hellenistic Far East: A Survey. Bactria, Central Asia and the Indo-Iranian Borderlands, c. 300 BC–AD 100*. Oxford.

(forthcoming) 'The "Temple with Indented Niches" at Ai Khanoum: ethnic and civic identity in Hellenistic Bactria', in *Cults, Creeds and Competitions in the Post-Classical Greek City*, eds O. van Nijf and R. Alston. Louvain.

Malaise, M. (1972) *Les conditions de pénétration et de diffusion des cultes égyptiens en Italie*. Leiden.

Malkin, I. (1994a) 'Inside and outside: colonisation and the formation of the mother city', in d'Agostino and Ridgway (eds), *Apoikia*, 1–9.

(1994b) *Myth and Territory in the Spartan Mediterranean*. Cambridge.

(1998) *The Returns of Odysseus: Colonization and Ethnicity*. Berkeley, CA and London.

(ed.) (2001) *Ancient Perceptions of Greek Ethnicity*. Washington DC.

(2002a) 'Exploring the concept of "foundation": a visit to Megara Hyblaia', in *Oikistes: Studies in Constitutions, Colonies and Military Power in the Ancient World Offered in Honour of A. J. Graham*, eds V. B. Gorman and E. W. Robinson. Leiden, 195–225.

(2002b) 'A colonial middle ground: Greek, Etruscan and local elites in the bay of Naples', in Lyons and Papadopoulos (eds), *Archaeology of Colonialism*, 151–81.

(2004) 'Postcolonial concepts and ancient Greek colonisation', *Modern Language Quarterly* 65: 341–64.

(2011) *A Small Greek World: Networks in the Ancient Mediterranean*. New York.

Malkin, I., Constantakopoulou, C. and Panagopoulou, K. (eds) (2009) *Greek and Roman Networks in the Mediterranean*. London and New York.

Mari, M. (2002) *Al di là dell'Olimpo: Macedoni e grandi santuari della Grecia dall'età arcaica al primo ellenismo*. Athens.

Marinatos, N. (2000) *The Goddess and the Warrior: The Naked Goddess and Mistress of Animals in Early Greek Religion*. London and New York.

Marincola, J. (ed.) (2007a) *A Companion to Greek and Roman Historiography*, vols I–II. Malden, MA and Oxford.

(2007b) 'Universal history from Ephorus to Diodorus', in Marincola (ed.), *Companion to Greek and Roman Historiography*, 171–9.

Markoe, G. (1985) *Phoenician Bronze and Silver Bowls from Cyprus and the Mediterranean*. Berkeley, CA and London.

(2000) *Phoenicians*. London.

Marksteiner, T. (2002) 'Städtische Stukturen im vorhellenistischen Lykien', in Hansen (ed.), *A Comparative Study of Six City-State Cultures*, 57–72.

Masson, O. (1969) 'Recherches sur les Phéniciens dans le monde hellénistique', *BCH* 93: 679–700.

(1972) 'La grande imprécation de Sélinonte (*SEG* XVI, 573)', *BCH* 96: 377–88.

(1978) *Carian Inscriptions from North Saqqara and Buhen*. London.

(1987) 'L'inscription d'Éphèse relative aux condamnés à mort des Sardes (*I. Ephesos* 2)', *REG* 100: 224–39.

Masson, O. and Yoyotte, J. (1988) 'Une inscription ionienne mentionnant Psammétique Ier', *EA* 11: 171–9.

Mastrocinque, A. (ed.) (1993) *I grandi santuari della Grecia e l'Occidente*. Trento.

Mathieson, I. *et al.* (1995) 'A stela from the Persian period from Saqqara', *JEA* 82: 23–41.

Matthaei, A. and Zimmermann, M. (eds) (2009) *Stadtbilder im Hellenismus*. Berlin.

Matthews, R. and Roemer, C. (eds) (2003) *Ancient Perspectives on Egypt*. London.

Mattingly, D. J. (2011) *Imperialism, Power and Identity: Experiencing the Roman Empire*. Princeton, NJ.

Mattison, K. M. (2009) 'Recasting Troy in Fifth-Century Attic Tragedy', PhD dissertation, University of Toronto.

McKechnie, P. (1989) *Outsiders in the Greek Cities in the Fourth Century* BC. London and New York.

Mehl, A. (2003) 'Gedanken zur "herrschenden Gesellschaft" und zu den Untertanen im Seleukidenreich', *Historia* 52: 147–60.

Meier, C. (2011) *A Culture of Freedom: Ancient Greece and the Origins of Freedom*, trans. J. Chase. Oxford and New York.

Meier, M., Patzek, B., Walter, U. and Wiesehöfer, J. (2004) *Deiokes, König der Meder: Ein Herodot-Episode in ihren Kontexten*. Stuttgart.

Meiggs, R. (1972) *The Athenian Empire*. Oxford.

Melchert, C. G. (ed.) (2003) *The Luwians*. Leiden and Boston, MA.

Mele, A. (2011) 'Italía terra di vitelli: considerazioni storiche sull'origine del geonimo *Italía*', *Incidenza dell'antico* 9: 33–63.

Mélèze-Modrzejewski, J. (1995) *The Jews of Egypt: From Ramesses II to Emperor Hadrian*, trans. R. Cornman. Edinburgh.

Mellink, M. (1991) 'The native kingdoms of Anatolia', *CAH*, III.2^2, 619–65.

(1998) *Kızılbel: An Archaic Painted Tomb Chamber in Northern Lycia*. Philadelphia, PA.

Merkelbach, R. (1970) 'Grabepigramm auf eine Hellenomemphitin', *ZPE* 6: 174.

(1995) *Isis regina – Zeus Sarapis: die griechisch–ägyptische Religion nach den Quellen dargestellt*. Stuttgart.

Mertens, D. (1984) *Der Tempel von Segesta und die dorische Tempelbaukunst des griechischen Western in klassischer Zeit*. Mainz.

Michalowski, P. (2010) 'Masters of the four corners of the heavens: views of the universe in early Mesopotamian writings', in Raaflaub and Talbert (eds), *Geography and Ethnography*, 147–68.

Michels, C. (2009) *Kulturtransfer und monarchischer 'Philhellenismus': Bithynien, Pontos und Kappadokien in hellenistischer Zeit*. Göttingen.

Mildenberg, L. (1998) *Vestigia Leonis: Studien zur antiken Numismatik Israels, Palästinas und der östlichen Mittelmeerwelt*. Freiburg.

(2000) 'On the so-called satrapal coinage', in Casabonne (ed.), *Mécanismes et innovations monétaires*, 9–20.

Miles, M. M. (2008) *Art as Plunder: The Ancient Origins of Debate about Cultural Property*. Cambridge.

Mileta, C. (2009) 'Überlegungen zum Charakter und zur Entwicklung der neuen Poleis im hellenistischen Kleinasien', in Matthaei and Zimmermann (eds), *Stadtbilder im Hellenismus*, 70–89.

Mill, J. S. [1846] (1978) 'Grote's History of Greece, I', reprinted in *Collected Works, vol. XI: Essays on Philosophy and the Classics*. Toronto, 271–305.

Millar, F. (2006) *Rome, the Greek World, and the East, vol. III: The Greek World, the Jews and the East*. Chapel Hill, NC.

Millard, A. R. (1983) 'Assyrians and Arameans', *Iraq* 45: 101–8.

Millender, E. G. (1996) '"The Teacher of Hellas": Athenian Democratic Ideology and the "Barbarization" of Sparta in Fifth-Century Greek Thought', PhD dissertation, University of Pennsylvania.

Miller, M. C. (1995) 'Priam, king of Troy', in Carter and Morris (eds), *The Ages of Homer*, 449–65.

(1997) *Athens and Persia in the Fifth Century* BC: *A Study in Cultural Receptivity*. Cambridge.

(2000) 'The myth of Bousiris: ethnicity and art', in Cohen (ed.), *Not the Classical Ideal*, 413–42.

(2003) 'Art, myth, and reality: Xenophantos' lekythos re-examined', in *Poetry, Theory, Praxis: The Social Life of Myth, Word and Image in Ancient Greece*, eds E. Csapo and M. C. Miller. Oxford, 19–47.

(2005) 'Barbarian lineage in classical Greek mythology and art: Pelops, Danaos and Kadmos', in Gruen (ed.), *Cultural Borrowings*, 68–89.

Millett, M. (1990) *The Romanisation of Britain: An Essay in Archaeological Interpretation*. Cambridge.

Mitchell, L. G. (1997) *Greeks Bearing Gifts: The Public Use of Private Relationships in the Greek World, 435–323* BC. Cambridge.

(2001) 'Euboean Io', *CQ* 51: 339–52.

(2006) 'Greeks, barbarians and Aeschylus' *Suppliants*', *G&R* 53: 205–23.

(2007) *Panhellenism and the Barbarian in Archaic and Classical Greece*. Swansea.

Mitchell, S. (1993) *Anatolia: Land, Men and Gods, vol. I: The Celts in Anatolia and the Impact of Roman Rule*. Oxford.

(2003) 'The Galatians: representation and reality', in Erskine (ed.), *A Companion to the Hellenistic World*, 280–93.

(2007) 'Iranian names and the presence of Persians in the religious sanctuaries of Asia Minor', in *Old and New Worlds in Greek Onomastics*, ed. E. Matthews. Oxford, 151–71.

Möller, A. (2000) *Naukratis: Trade in Archaic Greece*. Oxford and New York.

(2001) 'The beginning of chronography: Hellanicus' *Hiereiai*', in Luraghi (ed.), *Historian's Craft in the Age of Herodotus*, 241–62.

Moers, G. (2010) 'The world and the geography of otherness in pharaonic Egypt', in Raaflaub and Talbert (eds), *Geography and Ethnography*, 169–81.

Momigliano, A. (1971) *The Development of Greek Biography*. Cambridge, MA.

(1975) *Alien Wisdom: The Limits of Hellenisation*. Cambridge.

Moran, W. L. (1992) *The Amarna Letters*. Baltimore, MD and London.

Morelli, D. (1955) 'Gli stranieri in Rodi', *Studi classici e orientali* 5: 126–90.

Moreno, A. (2007) *Feeding the Democracy: The Athenian Grain Supply in the Fifth and Fourth Centuries BC*. Oxford.

Morgan, C. (1990) *Athletes and Oracles*. Cambridge.

Morgan, T. (1998) *Literate Education in the Hellenistic and Roman Worlds*. Cambridge.

Morpurgo Davies, A. (2002) 'The Greek notion of dialect', in Harrison (ed.), *Greeks and Barbarians*, 153–71.

Morris, I. (1986) 'The use and abuse of Homer', *CA* 5.1: 81–138.

Morris, S. P. (1992) *Daidalos and the Origins of Greek Art*. Princeton, NJ.

(2006) 'The view from East Greece: Miletus, Samos and Ephesus', in Riva and Vella (eds), *Debating Orientalization*, 66–84.

Moscati, S. (ed.) (2001) *The Phoenicians*. London and New York.

Most, G. W. (2003) 'Violets in crucibles: translating, traducing, transmuting', *TAPA* 133: 381–90.

Moyer, I. S. (2011a) *Egypt and the Limits of Hellenism*. Cambridge.

(2011b) 'Court, *chora* and culture in late Ptolemaic Egypt', *AJP* 132: 15–44.

Müller, C. (2010) *D'Olbia à Tanaïs. Territoires et réseaux d'échanges dans la mer Noire septentrionale aux époques classique et hellénistique*. Bordeaux.

Müller, C. and Hasenohr, C. (eds) (2002) *Les Italiens dans le monde grec (IIe siècle av. J.-C –Ier siècle ap. J.-C.): circulation, activités, intégration*. Athens.

Müller, C. W. (ed.) (1992) *Zum Umgang mit fremden Sprachen in der griechisch-römischen Antike*. Stuttgart.

(2006) *Legende, Novelle, Roman: dreizehn Kapitel zur erzählenden Prosaliteratur der Antike*. Göttingen.

Müller, K. E. (1972) *Geschichte der antiken Ethnographie und ethnologischen Theoriebildung: von den Anfängen bis auf die Byzantinischen Historiographen*, vol. I. Wiesbaden.

Munson, R. V. (2001) *Telling Wonders: Ethnographic and Political Discourse in the Work of Herodotus*. Ann Arbor, MI.

Murphy, D. J. (2000) 'Doctors of Zalmoxis and immortality in the *Charmides*', in Robinson and Brisson (eds), *Plato*, 287–95.

Murray, O. (ed.) (1990) *Sympotica: A Symposium on the Symposion*. Oxford.

Murray, O. and Price, S. (eds) (1990) *The Greek City-State from Homer to Alexander*. Oxford.

Muth, S. (2008) *Gewalt im Bild: das Phänomen der medialen Gewalt im Athen des 6. und 5. Jahrhunderts v. Chr*. Berlin.

Nachtergael, G. (1977) *Les Galates en Grèce et les Sôtéria de Delphes*. Brussels.

Nagy, G. (1990) *Pindar's Homer: The Lyric Possession of an Epic Past*. Baltimore, MD.

Naso, A. (ed.) (2006) *Stranieri e non cittadini nei santuari greci*. Florence.

Nesselrath, H-G. (1996) 'Herodot und der griechische Mythos', *Poetica* 28: 275–96.

Nichols, A. G. (2011) *Ctesias, On India: Translation and Commentary*. London.

Nieling, J. and Rehm, E. (eds) (2010) *Achaemenid Impact in the Black Sea: Communication of Powers*. Aarhus.

Nielsen, T. H. (2007) *Olympia and the Classical Hellenic City-State Culture*. Copenhagen.

Niemeier, W-D. (2001) 'Archaic Greeks in the Orient: textual and archaeological evidence', *BASOR* 322: 11–32.

Niemeyer, H. G. (2006) 'The Phoenicians in the Mediterranean. Between expansion and colonisation: a non-Greek model of overseas settlement and presence', in Tsetskhladze (ed.), *Greek Colonisation*, vol. I, 143–68.

Nissen, H-J. and Renger, J. (eds) (1982) *Mesopotamien und seine Nachbarn: Politische und kulturelle Wechselbeziehungen im Alten Vorderasien vom 4. bis 1. Jahrtausend v. Chr.* Berlin.

Nollé, M. (1992) *Denkmäler vom Satrapenbesitz Daskyleion: Studien zur graeco-persischen Kunst*. Berlin.

Noy, D., Panayotov, A. and Bloedhorn, H. (2004) *Inscriptiones Judaicae Orientis, vol. I: Eastern Europe*. Tübingen.

Nylander, C. (1968) 'ΑΣΣΥΡΙΑ ΓΡΑΜΜΑΤΑ: remarks on the 21st "Letter of Themistocles"', *OpAth* 8: 119–36.

(1971) *Ionians in Pasargadae: Studies in Old Persian Architecture*. Uppsala.

Oberleitner, W. (1994) *Das Heroon von Trysa: ein lykisches Fürstengrab des 4. Jahrhunderts v. Chr.* Mainz am Rhein.

Oded, B. (1979) *Mass Deportations and Deportees in the Neo-Assyrian Empire*. Wiesbaden.

Olmstead, C. M. (1950) 'A Greek lady from Persepolis', *AJA* 54: 10–18.

Olson, S. D. (2002) *Aristophanes: Acharnians*. Oxford.

(2007) *Broken Laughter: Select Fragments of Greek Comedy*. Oxford.

Orrieux, C. (1988) 'La "parenté" entre Juifs et Spartiates', in Lonis (ed.), *L'étranger dans le monde grec*, 169–91.

Osanna, M. (1992) *Chorai coloniali da Taranto a Locri: documentazione archeologica e ricostruzione storica*. Rome.

Osborne, M. J. (1981–3) *Naturalization in Athens*, vols I–III. Brussels.

Osborne, M. J. and Byrne, S. G. (1996) *The Foreign Residents of Athens. An Annex to the Lexicon of Greek Personal Names: Attica*. Louvain.

Osborne, R. (1993) 'À la grecque', *JMA* 6: 231–7.

(1996a) 'Pots, trade and the archaic Greek economy', *Antiquity* 70: 31–44.

(1996b) *Greece in the Making, 1200–479 BC*. London.

(1998) 'Early Greek colonisation? The nature of Greek settlement in the West', in Fisher and van Wees (eds), *Archaic Greece*, 251–70.

(2001) 'Why did Athenian pots appeal to the Etruscans?', *World Archaeology* 33: 277–95.

(2008) 'Reciprocal strategies: imperialism, barbarism and trade in archaic and classical Olbia', in Guldager Bilde and Petersen (eds), *Meetings of Cultures in the Black Sea Region*, 333–46.

(2009) 'What travelled with Greek pottery?', in Malkin *et al.* (eds), *Greek and Roman Networks in the Mediterranean*, 83–93.

(2011) *The History Written on the Classical Greek Body*. Cambridge.

Ostwald, M. and Lynch, J. P. (1994) 'The growth of schools and the advance of knowledge', *CAH*, VI², 592–633.

Owen, S. (2005) 'Analogy, archaeology and archaic Greek colonization', in Hurst and Owen (eds), *Ancient Colonizations*, 5–22.

Pagden, A. (2008) *Worlds at War: The 2,500-Year Struggle between East and West*. Oxford.

Palagia, O. (2005) 'Interpretations of two Athenian friezes: the temple on the Ilissos and the temple of Athena Nike', in *Periklean Athens and its Legacy: Problems and Perspectives*, eds J. M. Barringer and J. M. Hurwit. Austin, TX, 177–92.

(2008) 'The marble of Penelope from Persepolis and its historical implications', in Darbandi and Zournatzi (eds), *Ancient Greece and Ancient Iran*, 223–37.

Papadodima, E. (2010) 'The Greek/Barbarian interaction in Euripides' *Andromache, Orestes, Heracleidae*: a reassessment of Greek attitudes to foreigners', *Digressus* 10: 1–42.

Parker, A. J. (1992) *Ancient Shipwrecks of the Mediterranean and the Roman Provinces*. Oxford.

Parker, C. H. (2010) *Global Interactions in the Early Modern Age, 1400–1800*. Cambridge.

Parker, G. (2008) *The Making of Roman India*. Cambridge.

Parker, R. (1996) *Athenian Religion: A History*. Oxford.

Paspalas, S. (2006) 'The Achaemenid Empire and the northwestern Aegean', *AWE* 5: 90–120.

Patterson, L. E. (2010) *Kinship Myth in Ancient Greece*. Austin, TX.

Payen, P. (1997) *Les îles nomades: conquérir et résister dans l'Enquête d'Hérodote*. Paris.

Pearson, L. (1939) *Early Ionian Historians*. Oxford.

Pedley, J. G. (1974) 'Carians in Sardis', *JHS* 94: 96–9.

(1990) *Paestum: Greeks and Romans in Southern Italy*. London.

Pelling, C. (1997) 'East is East and West is West – or are they? National stereotypes in Herodotus', *Histos* 1: 51–66.

(2002) 'Speech and action: Herodotus' Debate on the Constitutions', *PCPS* 48: 123–58.

Pernigotti, S. (1999) *I Greci nell'Egitto della XXVI dinastia*. Imola.

Petersen, J. H. (2010) *Cultural Interactions and Social Strategies in the Pontic Shores: Burial Customs in the Northern Black Sea Area, c. 550–270 BC*. Aarhus.

Picard, C. (1931) 'Les influences étrangères au tombeau de Petosiris: Grèce ou Perse?', *BIFAO* 30: 201–27.

Picard, O. (2000) 'Monnayages en Thrace à l'époque achéménide', in Casabonne (ed.), *Mécanismes et innovations monétaires*, 239–53.

Planeaux, C. (2000/1) 'The date of Bendis' entry into Attica', *CJ* 96.2: 165–92.

Plaoutine, N. (1937) 'An Etruscan imitation of an Attic cup', *JHS* 57: 22–7.

Plassart, A. (1921) 'Inscriptions de Delphes, la liste des Théorodoques', *BCH* 45: 1–85.

Pollock, S. (2006) *The Language of Gods in the World of Men: Sanskrit, Culture and Power in Premodern India*. Berkeley, CA and London.

Pontrandolfo, A. (1982) *I Lucani: etnografia e archeologia di una regione antica*. Milan.

 (1987) 'Un'iscrizione posidoniate in una tomba di Fratte di Salerno', *AION (arch)* 9: 55–63.

Pontrandolfo, A. and Rouveret, A. (1983) 'La rappresentazione del barbaro in ambiente magno-greco', in *Modes*, 1051–66.

 (1992) *Le tombe dipinte di Paestum*. Modena.

Poo, M. (2005) *Enemies of Civilization: Attitudes toward Foreigners in Ancient Mesopotamia, Egypt, and China*. Albany, NY.

Porten, B. (1968) *Archives from Elephantine: The Life of an Ancient Jewish Military Colony*. Berkeley, CA.

Porten, B. and Gee, J. (2001) 'Aramaic funerary practices in Egypt', in Daviau *et al.* (eds), *The World of the Aramaeans*, vol. II, 270–307.

Porter, J. (ed.) (2006) *Classical Pasts*. Princeton, NJ.

Pouilloux, J. (1954) *Recherches sur l'histoire et les cultes de Thasos*. Paris.

Poulsen, F. (1912) *Der Orient und die frühgriechische Kunst*. Leipzig.

Powell, B. B. (1991) *Homer and the Origin of the Greek Alphabet*. Cambridge.

Préaux, C. (1978) *Le monde hellénistique: la Grèce et l'Orient (323–146 av. J.-C.)*, vols I–II. Paris.

Price, S. (1984) *Rituals and Power: The Roman Imperial Cult in Asia Minor*. Cambridge.

Pugliese Carratelli, G. (ed.) (1987) *Magna Grecia: lo sviluppo politico, sociale ed economico*. Milan.

 (ed.) (1988) *Magna Grecia: via religiosa e cultura letteraria, filosofica e scientifica*. Milan.

Purcell, N. (1990) 'Mobility and the polis', in Murray and Price (eds), *The Greek City-State*, 29–58.

 (1994) 'South Italy in the fourth century BC', *CAH*, VI², 381–403.

 (2005) 'Colonisation and Mediterranean history', in Hurst and Owen (eds), *Ancient Colonizations*, 115–39.

Quack, J. F. (2003) '"Ich bin Isis, die Herrin der beiden Länder": Versuch zum demotischen Hintergrund der memphitischen Isisaretalogie', in *Egypt – Temple of the Whole World: Studies in Honour of Jan Assmann*, ed. S. Meyer. Leiden, 319–65.

Quaegebeur, J. (1990) 'Les rois saïtes amateurs de vin', *Ancient Society* 21: 241–71.

Raaflaub, K. A. (2004) *The Discovery of Freedom in Ancient Greece*, trans. R. Franciscono. Chicago, IL and London.

(2009) 'Learning from the enemy: Athenian and Persian "instruments of empire"', in Ma *et al.* (eds), *Interpreting the Athenian Empire*, 89–124.

Raaflaub, K. A. and Talbert, R. J. A. (eds) (2010) *Geography and Ethnography: Perceptions of the World in Pre-Modern Societies*. Malden, MA and Oxford.

Radner, K. (2009) 'The Assyrian king and his scholars: the Syro-Anatolian and the Egyptian schools', in Luukko *et al.* (eds), *Of God(s), Trees, Kings and Scholars*, 221–38.

Raeck, W. (1981) *Zum Barbarenbild in der Kunst Athens im 6. und 5. Jahrhundert v. Chr.* Bonn.

Rajak, T. (2009) *Translation and Survival: The Greek Bible of the Ancient Jewish Diaspora*. Oxford.

Rapin, C. (1990) 'Greeks in Afghanistan: Aï Khanum', in Descœudres (ed.), *Greek Colonists and Native Populations*, 329–42.

Rapin, C., Hadot, P. and Cavallo, G. (1987) 'Les textes littéraires grecs de la Trésorerie d'Aï Khanoum', *BCH* 111: 225–66.

Rauh, N. K. (1993) *The Sacred Bonds of Commerce: Religion, Economy and Trade Society at Hellenistic Roman Delos, 166–87 BC*. Amsterdam.

Rawson, E. (1985) *Intellectual Life in the Late Roman Republic*. London.

Ray, J. D. (1988) 'Egypt 525–404 BC', *CAH*, IV², 254–86.

Reichel, M. (2010) 'Xenophon's *Cyropaedia* and the Hellenistic novel', in Gray (ed.), *Xenophon*, 418–38.

Reinhardt, K. (1965) 'Herodots Persergeschichten', in *Herodot: eine Auswahl aus der neueren Forschung*, ed. W. Marg. Darmstadt, 320–69.

Renfrew, A. C. and Cherry, J. F. (eds) (1986) *Peer Polity Interaction and Socio-Political Change*. Cambridge.

Rhodes, P. J. (1992) 'The Delian League to 449 BC', *CAH*, V², 34–61.

Rhodes, P. J. and Lewis, D. M. (1997) *The Decrees of the Greek States*. Oxford.

Richardson, N. J. (1992) 'Panhellenic cults and Panhellenic festivals', *CAH*, V², 223–44.

Richter, D. S. (2011) *Cosmopolis: Imagining Community in Early Classical Athens and the Early Roman Empire*. New York.

Richter, G. M. A. (1946) 'Greeks in Persia', *AJA* 50: 15–30.

(1948) 'An Etruscan scarab', *Metropolitan Museum of Art Bulletin* 6(8): 222–3.

Ridgway, D. (1992) *The First Western Greeks*. Cambridge.

(2006) 'Early Greek imports in Sardinia', in Tsetskhladze (ed.), *Greek Colonisation*, vol. I, 239–52.

Ritner, R. K. (1992) 'Implicit models of cross-cultural interaction: a question of noses, soap, and prejudice', in Johnson (ed.), *Life in a Multi-Cultural Society*, 283–90.

Riva, C. and Vella, N. C. (eds) (2006) *Debating Orientalization: Multidisciplinary Approaches to Processes of Change in the Ancient Mediterranean*. London and Oakville, CT.

Roaf, M. and Boardman, J. (1980) 'A Greek painting at Persepolis', *JHS* 100: 204–6.

Robert, L. (1960) *Hellenica XI–XII*. Paris.

(1962) *Villes d'Asie Mineure: études de géographie ancienne*, 2nd edn. Paris.

(1963) *Noms indigènes dans l'Asie Mineure gréco-romaine*. Paris.

Robertson, R. (1992) *Globalization: Social Theory and Global Culture*. London.

Robinson, T. M. and Brisson, L. (eds) (2000) *Plato: Euthydemus, Lysis, Charmides. Proceedings of the V Symposium Platonicum: Selected Papers*. Sankt Augustin.

Rodríguez Somolinos, H. (1996) 'The commercial transaction of the Pech Maho lead: a new interpretation', *ZPE* 111: 74–8.

Röllig, W. (1992) 'Asia Minor as a bridge between East and West: the role of the Phoenicians and Aramaeans in the transfer of culture', in Kopcke and Tokumaru (eds), *Greece between East and West*, 93–102.

Rolle, R. (1989) *The World of the Scythians*, trans. G. Walls. London.

Roller, L. E. (1994) 'Attis on Greek votive monuments: Greek god or Phrygian?', *Hesperia* 63: 245–62.

(1999) *In Search of God the Mother: The Cult of Anatolian Cybele*. Berkeley, CA and London.

Rollinger, R. (1993) *Herodots babylonischer Logos: eine kritische Untersuchung der Glaubwürdigkeitsdiskussion an Hand ausgewählter Beispiele*. Innsbruck.

Rollinger, R., Luther, A. and Wiesehöfer, J. (eds) (2007) *Getrennte Wege? Kommunikation, Raum und Wahrnehmung in der Alten Welt*. Frankfurt am Main.

Rollinger, R. and Truschnegg, B. (eds) (2006) *Altertum und Mittelmeerraum: Die antike Welt diesseits und jenseits der Levante. Festschrift für Peter W. Haider zum 60. Geburtstag*. Stuttgart.

Rollinger, R. and Ulf, C. (eds) (2004) *Griechische Archaik: interne Entwicklungen – externe Impulse*. Berlin.

Romm, J. S. (1992) *The Edges of the Earth in Ancient Thought: Geography, Exploration and Fiction*. Princeton, NJ.

Roosevelt, C. H. (2009) *The Archaeology of Lydia, from Gyges to Alexander*. Cambridge.

Root, M. C. (1979) *The King and Kingship in Achaemenid Art: Essays on the Creation of an Iconography of Empire*. Leiden.

(1985) 'The Parthenon frieze and the Apadana reliefs at Persepolis: reassessing a programmatic relationship', *AJA* 89: 103–20.

(1991) 'From the heart: powerful Persianisms in the art of the western Empire', in *AchHist* 6, 1–29.

(1998) 'Pyramidal stamp seals: the Persepolis connection', in *AchHist* 11, 257–89.

Rosivach, V. J. (2000) 'The Thracians of *IG* II² 1956', *Klio* 82: 379–81.

Rostovtzeff, M. I. (1922) *Iranians and Greeks in South Russia*. Oxford.

Roy, J. (1967) 'The mercenaries of Cyrus', *Historia* 16: 287–323.

(2007) 'Xenophon's *Anabasis* as a traveller's memoir', in Adams and Roy (eds), *Travel, Geography and Culture in Ancient Greece*, 66–77.

Rusyayeva, A. S. (2007) 'Religious interactions between Olbia and Scythia', in Braund and Kryzhitskiy (eds), *Classical Olbia and the Scythian World*, 93–102.

Rutherford, I. (2009) 'Hesiod and the literary traditions of the Near East', in *Brill's Companion to Hesiod*, eds F. Montanari, A. Rengakos and C. Tsagalis. Leiden, 9–35.

Rutter, K. N. (1979) *Campanian Coinages, 475–380 BC*. Edinburgh.

(1997) *The Greek Coinages of Southern Italy and Sicily*. London.

Ruzicka, S. (1992) *Politics of a Persian Dynasty: The Hecatomnids in the Fourth Century BC*. Norman, OK.

(2010) 'The "Pixodarus Affair" reconsidered again', in *Philip II and Alexander the Great: Father and Son, Lives and Afterlives*, eds E. Carney and D. Ogden. Oxford, 3–11.

(2012) *Trouble in the West: Egypt and the Persian Empire, 525–332 BCE*. New York.

Said, E. (1978) *Orientalism*. New York and London.

Saïd, S. (2002) 'Greeks and Barbarians in Euripides' tragedies: the end of differences?', in Harrison (ed.), *Greeks and Barbarians*, 62–100.

Salmeri, G. (2004) 'Hellenism on the periphery: the case of Cilicia and an etymology of *soloikismos*', *YCS* 31: 181–206.

Salviat, F. (1986) 'Le vin de Thasos. Amphores, vin et sources écrites', in *Recherches sur les amphores grecques*, eds J-Y. Empereur and Y. Garlan. Paris, 145–95.

Sánchez, P. (2001) *L'Amphictionie des Pyles et des Delphes: recherches sur son rôle historique, des origines au IIe siècle de notre ère*. Stuttgart.

Sanders, S. L. (2009) *The Invention of Hebrew*. Urbana and Chicago, IL.

Savalli, I. (1988) 'L'idéologie dynastique des poèmes grecs de Xanthos', *AC* 57: 103–23.

Savalli-Lestrade, I. (1998) *Les philoi royaux dans l'Asie hellénistique*. Geneva.

Schauenburg, K. (1975) 'Eurymedon eimi', *Mitteilungen des Deutschen Archäologischen Instituts (Athens)* 90: 97–121.

Scheer, T. S. (1993) *Mythische Vorväter: zur Bedeutung griechischer Heroenmythen im Selbstverständnis kleinasiatischer Städte*. Munich.

Scheidel, W., Morris, I. and Saller, R. (eds) (2007) *The Cambridge Economic History of the Greco-Roman World*. Cambridge.

Schepens, G. (1998) 'Skylax of Karyanda, no. 1000', in Bollansée *et al.* (eds), *FrGrHist IV A*, 2–27.

Schepens, G. and Theys, E. (1998) '1001 (= 765). Xanthos of Lydia', in Bollansée *et al.* (eds), *FrGrHist IV A*, 28–39.

Schmaltz, B. (1983) *Griechische Grabreliefs*. Darmstadt.

Schmitt, R. (1992) 'Assyria grammata und ähnliche: was wussten die Griechen von Keilschrift und Keilinschriften?', in Müller (ed.), *Zum Umgang mit fremden Sprachen in der griechisch-römischen Antike*, 21–35.

(2007) 'Volksetymologische Umdeutung iranischer Namen in griechischen Überlieferung', in Rollinger *et al.* (eds), *Getrennte Wege?*, 363–80.

Schneider-Herrmann, G. (1996) *The Samnites of the Fourth Century BC as Depicted on Campanian Vases and in Other Sources.* London.

Schürer, E. (1973) *The History of the Jewish People in the Age of Jesus Christ (175 BC–AD 135),* vol. I, revised edn. Edinburgh.

(1979) *The History of the Jewish People in the Age of Jesus Christ (175 BC–AD 135),* vol. II, revised edn. Edinburgh.

(1986) *The History of the Jewish People in the Age of Jesus Christ (175 BC–AD 135),* vol. III.1, revised edn. Edinburgh.

(1987) *The History of the Jewish People in the Age of Jesus Christ (175 BC–AD 135),* vol. III.2, revised edn. Edinburgh.

Schütrumpf, E. (ed.) (2008) *Heraclides of Pontus: Texts and Translations.* Piscataway, NJ and London.

Schuol, M., Hartmann, U. and Luther, A. (eds) (2002) *Grenzüberschreitungen: Formen des Kontakts zwischen Orient und Okzident im Altertum.* Stuttgart.

Schweyer, A-V. (2002) *Les Lyciens et la mort: une étude d'histoire sociale.* Istanbul.

Scott, M. (2010) *Delphi and Olympia: The Spatial Politics of Panhellenism in the Archaic and Classical Periods.* Cambridge.

Seager, R. (1994) 'The Corinthian War', *CAH*, VI², 97–119.

Seibt, G. F. (1977) *Griechische Söldner im Achaimenidenreich.* Bonn.

Sekunda, N. (1988) 'Persian settlement in Hellespontine Phrygia', in *AchHist* 3, 175–96.

Serra Ridgway, F. R. (1990) 'Etruscans, Greeks, Carthaginians: the sanctuary at Pyrgi', in Descœudres (ed.), *Greek Colonists and Native Populations*, 511–30.

Settis, S. (ed.) (1996) *I Greci. Storia, cultura, arte, società, vol. II: Una storia greca. I. Formazione.* Turin.

(ed.) (1997) *I Greci. Storia, cultura, arte, società, vol. II: Una storia greca. II. Definizione.* Turin.

(ed.) (1998) *I Greci. Storia, cultura, arte, società, vol. II: Una storia greca. III. Transformazioni.* Turin.

(ed.) (2001) *I Greci. Storia, cultura, arte, società, vol. III: I Greci oltre la Grecia.* Turin.

Seyer, M. (2007) *Der Herrscher als Jäger: Untersuchungen zur königlichen Jagd im persischen und makedonischen Reich vom 6.–4. Jahrhundert v. Chr. sowie unter den Diadochen Alexanders des Großen.* Vienna.

Sgouropoulou, C. (2004) 'Ο κόσμος της Ανατολής στην ελληνική εικονογραφία της ύστερης κλασικής εποχής', *Εγνατία* 8: 203–37.

Shapiro, H. A. (1983) 'Amazons, Thracians, and Scythians', *GRBS* 24: 105–14.

(2000) 'Modest athletes and liberated women: Etruscans on Attic black-figure vases', in Cohen (ed.), *Not the Classical Ideal*, 315–37.

Shaw, J. W. (1989) 'Phoenicians in southern Crete', *AJA* 93: 164–83.

Shepherd, G. (2005) 'The advance of the Greeks: Greece, Great Britain and archaeological empires', in Hurst and Owen (eds), *Ancient Colonizations*, 23–44.

Sherwin-White, S. and Kuhrt, A. (1993) *From Samarkhand to Sardis: A New Approach to the Seleucid Empire*. London.

Shipley, G. (2000) *The Greek World after Alexander, 323–30 BC*. London.

Simms, R. (1988) 'The cult of the Thracian goddess Bendis in Athens and Attica', *Ancient World* 18: 59–76.

(1989) 'Isis in Classical Athens', *CJ* 84: 216–21.

Simpson, W. K. (ed.) (2003) *The Literature of Ancient Egypt*. New Haven, CT and London.

Skinner, J. (2010) 'Fish heads and mussel-shells: visualising Greek identity', in Foxhall *et al.* (eds), *Intentional History*, 137–60.

(2012) *The Invention of Greek Ethnography: Ethnography and History from Homer to Herodotus*. New York.

Skon-Jedele, N. J. (1994) 'Aigyptiaka: A Catalogue of Egyptian and Egyptianizing Objects from Greek Archaeological Sites, ca. 1100–525 BC, with Historical Commentary', PhD dissertation, University of Pennsylvania.

Small, A. (2004) 'Some Greek inscriptions on native vases from south east Italy', in Lomas (ed.), *Greek Identity in the Western Mediterranean*, 267–85.

Smith, R. R. R. (2007) 'Pindar, athletes and the statue habit', in Hornblower and Morgan (eds), *Pindar's Poetry, Patrons and Festivals*, 83–139.

Smoláriková, K. (2000) 'The Greek cemetery at Abusir', *Archiv Orientalni Supplement* 9: 67–72.

Snodgrass, A. M. (1998) *Homer and the Artists*. Cambridge.

(2005) '"Lesser breeds": the history of a false analogy', in Hurst and Owen (eds), *Ancient Colonizations*, 45–58.

Solovyov, S. L. (1999) *Ancient Berezan: The Architecture, History and Culture of the First Greek Colony in the Northern Black Sea*. Leiden.

Sourvinou-Inwood, C. (1990) 'What is *polis* religion?', in Murray and Price (eds), *The Greek City-State*, 295–322.

(2005) *Hylas, the Nymphs, Dionysos and Others: Myth, Ritual, Ethnicity*. Stockholm.

Spawforth, A. (2001) 'Shades of Greekness: a Lydian case study', in Malkin (ed.), *Ancient Perceptions of Greek Ethnicity*, 375–400.

(2012) *Greece and the Augustan Cultural Revolution*. Cambridge.

Spivey, N. (1991) 'Greek vases in Etruria', in *Looking at Greek Vases*, eds T. Rasmussen and N. Spivey. Cambridge, 131–50.

Spivey, N. and Stoddart, S. (1990) *Etruscan Italy: An Archaeological History*. London.

Starr, C. G. (1975) 'Greeks and Persians in the fourth century BC: a study in cultural contacts before Alexander', *IA* 11: 39–99.

(1977) 'Greeks and Persians in the fourth century BC: a study in cultural contacts before Alexander, II', *IA* 12: 49–116.

Stazio, A. (1987) 'Monetazione delle "poleis" greche e monetazione degli "ethne" indigeni', in Pugliese Carratelli (ed.), *Magna Grecia*, 151–72.

Steingräber, S. (2006) *Abundance of Life: Etruscan Wall Painting*, trans. R. Stockman. Los Angeles, CA.

Stephens, S. A. (2003) *Seeing Double: Intercultural Poetics in Ptolemaic Alexandria*. Berkeley, CA.

Stevenson, R. B. (1997) *Persica: Greek Writing about Persia in the Fourth Century BC*. Edinburgh.

Stolper, M. and Tavernier, J. (2007) 'From the Persepolis Fortification Archive Project, 1: an Old Persian administrative tablet from the Persepolis Fortification', *Arta* 2007.001: 1–28.

Strauss, B. S. (2004) *Salamis: The Greatest Battle of the Ancient World, 480 BC*. London.

Strobel, K. (1996) *Die Galater: Geschichte und Eigenart der keltischen Staatenbildung auf dem Boden des hellenistischen Kleinasiens, vol. I: Untersuchungen zur Geschichte und historischen Geographie des hellenistischen und römischen Kleinasiens*. Berlin.

Stronk, J. P. (1995) *The Ten Thousand in Thrace: An Archaeological and Historical Commentary on Xenophon's Anabasis VI iii– VII*. Amsterdam.

(2010) *Ctesias' Persian History, Part I: Introduction, Text and Translation*. Düsseldorf.

Stucky, R. A. (1984) *Tribune d'Echmoun: ein griechischer Reliefzyklus des 4. Jahrhdt. in Sidon*. Basel.

(1993) *Die Skulpturen aus dem Eschmun-Heiligtum bei Sidon: Griechische, römische, kyprische und phönizische Statuen und Reliefs vom 6. Jahrhundert vor Chr. bis zum 3. Jahrhundert nach Chr*. Basel.

(2005) *Das Eschmun-Heiligtum von Sidon: Architektur und Inschriften*. Basel.

Subrahmanyam, S. (1997) 'Connected histories: notes towards a reconfiguration of early modern Eurasia', *MAS* 31: 735–62.

(2006) 'A tale of three empires: Mughals, Ottomans and Habsburgs in a comparative perspective', *Common Knowledge* 12: 66–92.

Summerer, L. and von Kienlin, A. (2010) 'Achaemenid impact in Paphlagonia: rupestral tombs in the Amnias valley', in Nieling and Rehm (eds), *Achaemenid Impact in the Black Sea*, 195–221.

Tagliamonte, G. (1994) *I figli di Marte: mobilità, mercenari e mercenariato italici in Magna Grecia e Sicilia*. Rome.

Tanner, J. (2003) 'Finding the Egyptian in early Greek art', in Matthews and Roemer (eds), *Ancient Perspectives on Egypt*, 115–43.

Tatum, J. (1989) *Xenophon's Imperial Fiction: On the Education of Cyrus*. Princeton, NJ.

Tavernier, J. (2007) *Iranica in the Achaemenid Period (ca 550–330 BC). Lexicon of Old Iranian Proper Names and Loanwords, Attested in Non-Iranian Texts*. Louvain.

Tcherikover, V. (1959) *Hellenistic Civilisation and the Jews*, trans. S. Applebaum. Jerusalem.

Terrenato, N. (2005) 'The deceptive archetype: Roman colonialism in Italy and postcolonial thought', in Hurst and Owen (eds), *Ancient Colonizations*, 59–72.

Thapar, R. (1997) *Aśoka and the Decline of the Mauryas*, 2nd edn. Delhi.

Thissen, H. J. (1977) 'Graeco-ägyptischer Literatur', *LdÄ* II: 873–8.

Thomas, R. (1989) *Oral Tradition and Written Record in Classical Athens*. Cambridge.

(2000) *Herodotus in Context: Ethnography, Science and the Art of Persuasion*. Cambridge.

Thompson, D. J. (1988) *Memphis under the Ptolemies*. Princeton, NJ.

(2001) 'Hellenistic Hellenes: the case of Ptolemaic Egypt', in Malkin (ed.), *Ancient Perceptions of Greek Ethnicity*, 301–22.

Thonemann, P. (2009) 'Lycia, Athens and Amorges', in Ma *et al.* (eds), *Interpreting the Athenian Empire*, 167–94.

Tigay, J. H. (1982) *The Evolution of the Gilgamesh Epic*. Wauconda, IL.

Too, Y. L. (1995) *The Rhetoric of Identity in Isocrates: Text, Power, Pedagogy*. Cambridge.

Torelli, M. (1977) 'Il santuario Greco di Gravisca', *PdP* 32: 398–458.

Tosto, V. (1999) *The Black-Figure Pottery Signed NIKOSTHENESEPOIESEN*. Amsterdam.

Treister, M. Y. (1996) *The Role of Metals in Ancient Greek History*. Leiden and New York.

Trendall, A. D. (1989) *Red-Figure Vases of South Italy and Sicily*. London.

Trenkner, S. (1958) *The Greek Novella in the Classical Period*. Cambridge.

Trevett, J. (1992) *Apollodoros, the Son of Pasion*. Oxford.

Tribulato, O. (2010) 'Literary dialects', in Bakker (ed.), *A Companion to the Ancient Greek Language*, 388–400.

Tsetskhladze, G. R. (1998a) 'Who built the Scythian and Thracian royal and elite tombs?', *OJA* 17: 55–92.

(ed.) (1998b) *The Greek Colonisation of the Black Sea Area: Historical Interpretation of Archaeology*. Stuttgart.

(ed.) (1999) *Ancient Greeks West and East*. Leiden, Boston, MA and Cologne.

(2000) 'Pistiros in the system of Pontic emporia', in Domaradzki *et al.* (eds), *Pistiros et Thasos*, 233–46.

(2004) 'On the earliest Greek colonial architecture in the Pontus', in Tuplin (ed.), *Pontus and the Outside World*, 225–78.

(ed.) (2006a) *Greek Colonisation: An Account of Greek Colonies and Other Settlements Overseas*, vol. I. Leiden and Boston, MA.

(2006b) 'Revisiting ancient Greek colonisation', in Tsetskhladze (ed.), *Greek Colonisation*, vol. I, xxiii–lxxxiii.

(ed.) (2008) *Greek Colonisation: An Account of Greek Colonies and Other Settlements Overseas*, vol. II. Leiden and Boston, MA.

Tsiafakis, D. (2000) 'The allure and repulsion of Thracians in the art of classical Athens', in Cohen (ed.), *Not the Classical Ideal*, 364–89.

Tuna-Nörling, Y. (2001) 'Attic pottery from Dascylium', in Bakır (ed.), *Achaemenid Anatolia*, 109–22.

Tuplin, C. (1987) 'The administration of the Achaemenid Empire', in Carradice (ed.), *Coinage and Administration*, 109–67.

  (1996a) *Achaemenid Studies*. Stuttgart.

  (1996b) 'Xenophon's *Cyropaedia*: education and fiction', in *Education in Greek Fiction*, eds A. H. Sommerstein and C. Atherton. Bari, 65–162.

  (1999) 'Greek racism? Observations on the character and limits of Greek ethnic prejudice', in Tsetskhladze (ed.), *Ancient Greeks West and East*, 47–75.

  (ed.) (2004) *Pontus and the Outside World: Studies in Black Sea History, Historiography and Archaeology*. Leiden and Boston, MA.

  (2007a) 'Continuous histories (*Hellenica*)', in Marincola (ed.), *Companion to Greek and Roman Historiography*, 159–70.

  (ed.) (2007b) *Persian Responses: Political and Cultural Interaction with(in) the Achaemenid Empire*. Swansea.

  (2008) 'The Seleucids and their Achaemenid predecessors: a Persian inheritance?', in Darbandi and Zournatzi (eds), *Ancient Greece and Ancient Iran*, 109–36.

  (2010) 'The limits of Persianization: some reflections on cultural links in the Persian Empire', in Gruen (ed.), *Cultural Identity in the Ancient Mediterranean*, 150–82.

Uehlinger, C. (ed.) (2000) *Images as Media: Sources for the Cultural History of the Near East and the Eastern Mediterranean (1st Millennium BCE)*. Göttingen.

Ulf, C. (ed.) (1996) *Wege zur Genese griechischer Identität: die Bedeutung der früharchaischen Zeit*. Berlin.

Urso, G. (ed.) (2007) *Tra oriente e occidente: indigeni, greci e romani in Asia Minore*. Pisa.

Ustinova, Y. (1999) *The Supreme Gods of the Bosporan Kingdom: Celestial Aphrodite and the Most High God*. Leiden and Boston, MA.

van de Mieroop, M. (2007) *The Eastern Mediterranean in the Age of Ramesses II*. Malden, MA and Oxford.

van der Meer, L. B. (1995) *Interpretatio Etrusca: Greek Myths on Etruscan Mirrors*. Amsterdam.

van der Spek, R. J. (2001) 'The theatre of Babylon in cuneiform', in *Veenhof Anniversary Volume*, ed. W. H. van Soldt. Leiden, 445–56.

van Groningen, B. A. (1933) *Aristote: le second livre de l'Économique*. Leiden.

van Seters, J. (1983) *In Search of History: Historiography in the Ancient World and the Origins of Biblical History*. New Haven, CT and London.

Vanderlip, V. F. (1972) *The Four Greek Hymns of Isidorus and the Cult of Isis*. Toronto.

Vanschoonwinkel, J. (2006a) 'Mycenaean expansion', in Tsetskhladze (ed.), *Greek Colonisation*, vol. I, 41–113.

  (2006b) 'Greek migrations to Aegean Anatolia in the early Dark Age', in Tsetskhladze (ed.), *Greek Colonisation*, vol. I, 115–41.

Vasunia, P. (2001) *The Gift of the Nile: Hellenizing Egypt from Aeschylus to Alexander*. Berkeley, CA and London.

Veligianni-Terzi, C. (2004) *Οι ελληνίδες πόλεις και το βασίλειο των Οδρυσών από Αβδήρων πόλεως μέχρι Ίστρου ποταμού*. Salonica.

Verbrugghe, G. P. and Wickersham, J. M. (1996) *Berossos and Manetho, Introduced and Translated*. Ann Arbor, MI.

Versluys, M. J. (2010) 'Understanding Egypt in Egypt and beyond', in Bricault and Versluys (eds), *Isis on the Nile*, 8–36.

Versnel, H. S. (1990) *Ter Unus. Isis, Dionysos, Hermes: Three Studies in Henotheism*. Leiden, New York and Cologne.

Vinogradov, J. G. [1980] (1997) 'Die historische Entwicklung der Poleis des nördlichen Schwarzmeersgebietes im 5. Jahrhundert v. Chr.', in Vinogradov, *Pontische Studien*, 100–32.

   [1987] (1997) 'Der Pontos Euxeinos als politische, ökonomische und kulturelle Einheit und die Epigraphik', in Vinogradov, *Pontische Studien*, 1–73.

   (1997) *Pontische Studien: kleine Schriften zur Geschichte und Epigraphik des Schwarzmeerraumes*, trans. B. Böttger. Mainz.

Vinogradov, J. G. and Kryžickij, S. D. (1995) *Olbia: Eine altgriechische Stadt im Nordwestlichen Schwarzmeerraum*. Leiden, New York and Cologne.

Vinogradov, Y. G. and Zolotarev, M. I. (1999) 'Worship of the sacred Egyptian triad in Chersonesus (Crimea)', *ACSS* 5: 357–81.

Vittmann, G. (2003) *Ägypten und die Fremden im ersten vorchristlichen Jahrtausend*. Mainz am Rhein.

Vlassopoulos, K. (2007) *Unthinking the Greek Polis: Ancient Greek History beyond Eurocentrism*. Cambridge.

   (2010a) *Politics: Antiquity and its Legacy*. London.

   (2010b) 'Athenian slave names and Athenian social history', *ZPE* 175: 113–44.

   (2011) 'Two images of ancient slavery: the "living tool" and the "*koinônia*"', in *Sklaverei und Zwangsarbeit zwischen Akzeptanz und Widerstand*, ed. E. Herrmann-Otto. Hildesheim, 467–77.

   (forthcoming a) 'The Stories of the Others: storytelling and intercultural communication in the Herodotean Mediterranean', in *Ancient Ethnography: New Approaches*, eds E. Almagor and J. Skinner. London.

   (forthcoming b) 'The end of enslavement, Greek style', in *The Oxford Handbook of Greek and Roman Slaveries*, eds S. Hodkinson, M. Kleijwegt and K. Vlassopoulos. Oxford.

von Gall, H. (1966) *Die paphlagonischen Felsgräber: Eine Studie zur kleinasiatischen Kunstgeschichte*. Tübingen.

von Graeve, V. (1970) *Der Alexandersarkophag und seine Werkstatt*. Tübingen.

Waldbaum, J. C. (1997) 'Greeks in the East or Greeks and the East? Problems in the definition and recognition of presence', *BASOR* 305: 1–17.

Wallace-Hadrill, A. (2008) *Rome's Cultural Revolution*. Cambridge.

Wallinga, H. T. (2005) *Xerxes' Greek Adventure: The Naval Perspective*. Leiden and Boston, MA.

Watkins, C. (1995) 'Greece in Italy outside Rome', *Harvard Studies in Classical Philology* 97: 35–50.

Waywell, G. B. (1993) 'The Ada, Zeus and Idrieus relief from Tegea in the British Museum', in *Sculpture from Arcadia and Laconia*, ed. O. Palagia. Oxford, 79–86.

Webb, V. (1978) *Archaic Greek Faience: Miniature Scent Bottles and Related Objects from East Greece, 650–500 BC*. Warminster.

Welskopf, M. (1989) *The So-Called 'Great Satraps' Revolt', 366–360 BC*. Stuttgart.

Wentker, H. (1956) *Sizilien und Athen: die Begegnung der attischen Macht mit den Westgriechen*. Heidelberg.

West, M. L. (1966) *Theogony: Hesiod*. Oxford.

(1971) *Early Greek Philosophy and the Orient*. Oxford.

(1978) *Hesiod: Works and Days*. Oxford.

(1985) *The Hesiodic Catalogue of Women*. Oxford.

(1993) *Greek Lyric Poetry: The Poems and Fragments of the Greek Iambic, Elegiac, and Melic Poets (Excluding Pindar and Bacchylides) Down to 450 BC*. Oxford.

(1997) *The East Face of Helicon: West Asiatic Elements in Early Poetry and Myth*. Oxford.

(2010) *The Hymns of Zoroaster: A New Translation of the Most Ancient Sacred Texts of Iran*. London and New York.

West, S. (1984) 'Io and the dark stranger (Sophocles, Inachus F 269a)', *CQ* 34: 292–302.

(1991) 'Herodotus' portrait of Hecataeus', *JHS* 111: 144–60.

(2003) 'Croesus' second reprieve and other tales of the Persian court', *CQ* 53: 416–37.

White, D. (1967) 'The post-classical cult of Malophoros at Selinus', *AJA* 71: 335–52.

White, R. (1991) *The Middle Ground: Indians, Empires, and Republics in the Great Lakes Region, 1650–1815*. New York.

Whitehead, D. (1990) *Aineias the Tactician: How to Survive Under Siege*. Oxford.

Whitehouse, R. and Wilkins, J. (1989) 'Greeks and natives in south-east Italy: approaches to the archaeological evidence', in *Centre and Periphery: Comparative Studies in Archaeology*, ed. T. Champion. London, 102–26.

Whitley, J. (2001) *The Archaeology of Ancient Greece*. Cambridge.

Whitmarsh, T. (ed.) (2010) *Local Knowledge and Microidentities in the Imperial Greek World*. Cambridge.

Wickersham, J. M. (1991) 'Myth and identity in the archaic polis', in *Myth and the Polis*, eds D. C. Pozzi and J. M. Wickersham. Ithaca, NY, 16–31.

Wiesehöfer, J. (1996) *Ancient Persia from 550 BC to 650 AD*, trans. A. Azodi. London and New York.

Wiesehöfer, J., Rollinger, R. and Lafranchi, G. B. (eds) (2011) *Ktesias' Welt/Ctesias' World*. Wiesbaden.

Willi, A. (2003) *The Languages of Aristophanes: Aspects of Linguistic Variation in Classical Attic Greek*. Oxford.

Wills, L. M. (1990) *The Jew in the Court of the Foreign King: Ancient Jewish Court Legends*. Minneapolis, MN.

Wilson, J-P. (2006) '"Ideologies" of Greek colonization', in Bradley and Wilson (eds), *Greek and Roman Colonization*, 25–57.

Winnicki, J. K. (2009) *Late Egypt and her Neighbours: Foreign Population in Egypt in the First Millennium* BC. Warsaw.

Winter, I. J. (1995) 'Homer's Phoenicians: history, ethnography, or literary trope? [A perspective on early Orientalism]', in Carter and Morris (eds), *The Ages of Homer*, 247–71.

Wirbelauer, E. (2005) 'Eine Frage von Telekommunikation? Die Griechen und ihre Schrift im 9.–7. Jahrhundert v. Chr.', in Rollinger and Ulf (eds), *Griechische Archaik*, 187–206.

Wiseman, T. P. (2004) *The Myths of Rome*. Exeter.

Wörrle, M. (1996/7) 'Die Inschriften am Grab des Apollonios am Asartas von Yazir in Ostlykien', *Lykia* 3: 224–38.

Wolf, E. R. (1982) *Europe and the People without History*. Berkeley, CA.

Wonder, J. W. (2002) 'What happened to the Greeks in Lucanian-occupied Paestum? Multiculturalism in southern Italy', *Phoenix* 56: 40–55.

Woodard, R. D. (2010) 'Phoinikēia Grammata: an alphabet for the Greek language', in Bakker (ed.), *A Companion to the Ancient Greek Language*, 25–46.

Woolf, G. (1996) 'Becoming Roman, staying Greek: culture, identity and the civilising process in the Roman East', *PCPS* 40: 116–43.

　(1998) *Becoming Roman: The Origins of Provincial Civilisation in Gaul*. Cambridge.

　(2011) *Tales of the Barbarians: Ethnography and Empire in the Roman West*. Oxford.

　(2012) *Rome: An Empire's Story*. New York.

Yntema, D. (2000) 'Mental landscapes of colonization: the ancient written sources and the archaeology of early colonial Greek south-eastern Italy', *Bulletin Antieke Beschaving* 75: 1–49.

Yoyotte, J. (1969) 'Bakhthis: religion égyptienne et culture grecque à Edfu', in *Religions en Égypte hellénistique et romaine*. Paris, 127–41.

Zaccagnini, C. (1982) 'The enemy in the Neo-Assyrian royal inscriptions: the "ethnographic" description', in Nissen and Renger (eds), *Mesopotamien und seine Nachbarn*, 409–24.

Zacharia, K. (ed.) (2008) *Hellenisms: Culture, Identity, and Ethnicity from Antiquity to Modernity*. Aldershot.

Zaghloul, E-H. O. M. (1985) *Frühdemotische Urkunden aus Hermupolis*. Cairo.

Zhmud, L. (2006) *The Origin of the History of Science in Classical Antiquity*. Berlin and New York.

Zimmermann, K. (1980) 'Tätowierte Thrakerinnen auf griechischen Vasenbildern', *Jahrbuch des Deutschen Archäologischen Instituts* 95: 163–96.

Zoeppfel, R. (2006) *Aristoteles Oikonomika: Schriften zu Hauswirtschaft und Finanzwesen*. Berlin.

Zournatzi, A. (2000) 'Inscribed silver vessels of the Odrysian kings: gifts, tribute, and the diffusion of the forms of "Achaemenid" metalware in Thrace', *AJA* 104: 683–706.

Index locorum

Literary sources

Note: reference numbers for the relevant corpora of fragments of ancient authors appear within brackets next to the name of the author; for the abbreviations of the various corpora, see the List of Abbreviations. The capital letters F and B stand for fragment, the capital letter T for testimony.

Abaris (*BNJ* 34)
    F1–2: 208
Aelian
    Various History
        12.1: 90
Aeneas the Tactician
    15.9–10: 201
    16.14: 201
    24.3–14: 201
    31.25–7: 201
    31.35: 201
    37.6–7: 201
    40.4: 201
Aeschylus
    The Persians
        181–99: 195
    Suppliant Women
        277–90: 196
Alcaeus of Mytilene (*L-P*)
    F45: 177
    F69: 177
    F350: 177
Alcman of Sparta (*Page*)
    F16: 177
Anacreon of Teos (*Page*)
    F347: 177
    F356b: 178
    F417: 177
Anaxandrides (*K-A*, II)
    F40: 191
    F42: 124
Anthologia Graeca
    7.417: 312
Antiphon of Athens
    On the Murder
        of Herodes
        20: 125

Antiphon the Sophist (*D-K* 87)
    B44: 194
Archilochus of Paros (*West*)
    F2: 120, 177
    F5: 120, 177
    F19: 176
    F22: 120
    F42: 178
    F93: 177
    F102: 120
    F216: 177
Aristeas of Proconnesus
    (*BNJ* 35)
    F2: 175
    F7: 175
Aristophanes
    Acharnians
        141–50: 137
        153–72: 125, 191
    Birds
        1615–82: 191
    Thesmophoriazusae
        1001–231: 191
    Wasps
        828: 89
Aristotle (*Rose*)
    Barbarian Customs
        F604–11: 202
    Constitution of the Athenians
        15: 123
    Metaphysics
        981b20–5: 210
    Politics
        1272b24–1273b26: 204
        1315b26: 134
        1324a5–b25: 202
        1329b: 202

Epigraphical and papyrological sources

Index

(The numbers in square brackets indicate the map in which the place name appears.)

Made in the USA
Columbia, SC
24 August 2021